Brain-Based Therapy
with Children
and Adolescents

Brain-Based Therapy with Children and Adolescents

Evidence-Based Treatment for
Everyday Practice

By
John B. Arden
Lloyd Linford

WILEY

John Wiley & Sons, Inc.

Copyright © 2009 by John Wiley & Sons, Inc. All rights reserved.

Published by John Wiley & Sons, Inc., Hoboken, New Jersey.
Published simultaneously in Canada.

For general information on our other products and services please contact our Customer Care Department within the U.S. at (800) 762-2974, outside the United States at (317) 572-3993 or fax (317) 572-4002.

Wiley also publishes its books in a variety of electronic formats. Some content that appears in print may not be available in electronic books. For more information about Wiley products, visit our website at www.wiley.com.

Library of Congress Cataloging-in-Publication Data:

Arden, John Boghosian.
  Brain-based therapy with children and adolescents : evidence-based treatment for everyday practice / by John Arden, Lloyd Linford.
      p. ; cm.
  Includes bibliographical references and index.
  ISBN 978-0-470-13891-5 (pbk. : alk. paper)
  1. Developmental psychobiology. 2. Child psychiatry. I. Linford, Lloyd. II. Title.
  [DNLM: 1. Mental Disorders–therapy. 2. Psychotherapy–methods. 3. Adolescent.
  4. Child. 5. Evidence-Based Medicine–methods. 6. Psychophysiology.   WS 350.2 A676b 2009]
  RJ131.A73 2009
  618.92'89–dc22   2008022834

Printed in the United States of America

10 9 8 7 6 5 4 3 2 1

For our sons
Paul and Gabe Arden
and
Zack and Scott Linford
and
those who will share their future

Contents

Acknowledgments

Brain-Based Therapy would not have come into existence without the support and contributions of many people. First and foremost, we are indebted to our wives, Vicki Arden and Pam Valois, for their encouragement, scalding editorial comments, and good-hearted willingness to sacrifice countless evenings and weekends to this project. The inspiration for this book emerged from conversations with clinical experts and scientists presenting at Kaiser's Annual Northern California Psychiatry and Chemical Dependency Conference. We would like to thank the other members of the Conference's planning group—Marion Lim-Yankowitz, Marilyn McPherson, Caryl Polk, and John Peters—who, over the last 16 years, have helped create these memorable gatherings in San Francisco. We would particularly like to thank Debbie Mendlowitz and Steve Miller for insuring that child work has had a place at the conference. Among the many outstanding academics and clinicians who contributed ideas they articulated on the conference podium, we especially thank Jim Grigsby, who helped formulate the idea for this book and edit the appendix, and Lou Cozolino, who has set a high standard for integrating neuroscience and psychotherapy in his own writing and clinical work. Conversations with Dr. Cozolino led to the idea for the BASE, a mnemonic that condenses our ideas about brain-based treatment into a practical and teachable form. Helen Mayberg's work on depression from a neuroanatomical and neurodynamic perspective has shaped our thinking about depression.

   Like a tripod, this book is supported by three legs, each in its own way indispensable to our model of brain-based therapy: neuroscience, attachment studies, and research into evidenced-based treatments for specific psychological disorders. Regarding the latter, we received ongoing support and stimulation from the members of Kaiser's Best Practices Steering Committee, to whom we express our thanks. In particular we must acknowledge Elke Zuercher-White's generous sharing of her scholarship and insight into the origins and treatment of OCD, panic disorder, and social anxiety disorder. Dr. Anna Wong, the leader of Kaiser's ADHD Best

Practices Workgroup and the coauthor of its clinical recommendations, changed our minds about ADD in two or three brilliant conversations about brain-based attentional disorders. Drs. Zuercher-White and Wong read and commented on chapters in the book that resulted in critical changes and improvements. Child psychologist and psychoanalyst Tom Cohen also read and made invaluable improvements to the chapter on ADHD. Dr. Daniel Pickar made editorial comments on the entire text. Without the ongoing dedication of our organization and its leader, Dr. Robin Dea, to child and family services, this book would not have been possible. One of us (LL) came to Kaiser in the 1970s because of its excellent training program in child treatment; another of us (JA) is now responsible for insuring that these high standards are carried forward for another generation of therapists. We would like to thank the Medical Center Training Directors, supervisors, interns, post-docs, and most of all the patients who have helped educate us about the psychology of the child.

Finally, we would like to thank the great team at Wiley whose professionalism and commitment to clinically relevant books is exemplary. Peggy Alexander, Marquita Flemming, Kim Nir, and Katie DeChants at Wiley have been generous and helpful throughout this project.

Although many excellent brains were involved in the creation of this book, only two are responsible for its errors and omissions.

—John Arden, Sebastopol, California
—Lloyd Linford, Piedmont, California

Preface

Helping children in trouble is an aspiration that is for the most part built into the brains and hearts of adults, and predates our origins as *Homo sapiens*. But as an actual *vocation* in the western sense, it is quite recent. The child-helping professions originated in 19th-century Europe and America. Urbanization and factory-based work left parents with less time for their families, and children were exposed to many new challenges and stressors. Cut loose from their religious and agrarian moorings, social values began to drift. Widespread literacy and compulsory education fueled the process of change. Not coincidentally, child psychiatry, psychology, and social work all originated in this period. Social work was born in the slums of London and New York, and child psychology's roots go back to 19th-century Austria and France. Siegfried Bernfeld (1922), August Aichorn (1926/1955), and Anna Freud (Burlington & Freud, 1940; Freud, 1946) blended their devotion to children with fealty to Sigmund Freud.

The approaches used by Anna Freud and others had, of necessity, to take stock of the unique challenges of working with children. While doing psychotherapy with adult patients may allow us to forget how embedded each individual is in a social system, children never let us forget this fact. The psychological assessment of a child must include an evaluation of the psychological strengths and weaknesses of parents and siblings, of actual sources of anxiety, and of actual experiences of trauma and loss.

The works of these early social workers, marriage and family counselors, and child psychologists continue to constitute the core curriculum for all students of our art, yet they all leave something out. They all underplay the actual basis for child psychology: the developing brain. As we suggested in Volume 1 of this series, *Brain-Based Therapy with Adults*, the two greatest minds in nineteenth-century psychology, Sigmund Freud and William James, were talented and expert neurophysiologists. Yet both abandoned the biological study of the brain in favor of more theoretical pursuits about how the mind works. Freud's "Project for a Scientific Psychology" (1895/1958) sets out the aspirations shared by many psychotherapists today: to construct a theory of the mind (and therapy) that rests on solid biological evidence. Strangely, Freud never published the "Project" in his lifetime, whether because he had reservations about abandoning his work as a neurologist or for other reasons we will never know.

Understanding the neurobiology of attachment and relationships—how the brain insures the continuity of early patterns of relating *and at the same time has the capacity for changing them*—is basic to the new curriculum for child psychotherapists and pediatric residents. It is one thing to talk about this issue with adults, where therapists are preoccupied with brain changes that, in the developmental scheme of things, are more in the nature of a tune-up than a complete overhaul. It is another thing to look at the unfolding of the brain in children, where the changes are dramatic and ongoing. Children are exquisitely sensitive to the environment and change in relationship to it even before birth—and it is the brain that makes this apparent paradox of innate structure and almost infinite plasticity possible.

In our view, the most important development in psychology in the last decade is the emergence of attempts to synthesize developmental psychology, neuroscience, and psychotherapy. In the work of Schore (1994), Segal (1999), and Cozolino (2006), links have been made between the brain and the mind in psychodynamic therapy. Developmental pathology breaks new ground in taking a fundamentally integrative approach to the attachment literature of psychological theory (Cicchetti, et al, 2006; Sroufe et al., 2005). The biological approaches of Jerome Kagan and Mary Rothbart synthesize perspectives from the temperament literature and evolutionary biology (Kagan, 2004). Some long-standing theory-based observations—for example, Melanie Klein's idea that parents have the capacity to project unconscious anger into their child, unconsciously identify with the anger, and then punish the child for aggressive behavior—suddenly makes sense on the biological as well as the clinical level (Klein, 1975/1921–1945). So far no one has attempted to apply these lessons specifically to working therapeutically with children in a broader psychological frame of reference. That is a goal of this book.

For most therapists, however, the big question is still "So what?" What difference will understanding how the brain develops and functions make in doing the actual work of child psychotherapy? How does this new knowledge relate to the ideas and clinical methods of such giants of child psychology as Anna Freud (Sandler & Freud, 1985), Piaget (1951), Winnicott (1941/1975; 1975), and Bowlby (1969)? What difference is it going to make when I next close the door and begin an hour with an active and oppositional child? In this volume, we hope to answer these questions, and the answers we propose are encouraging in terms of how much of the traditional theory and technique are not just salvageable in the new neurobiological frame of reference, but actually clarified and put on firmer ground.

For child psychotherapists, developmental neuroscience currently has an importance comparable to the role of the frontier in 19th-century America. Horace Greeley, a newspaperman of that period, advised a reader to "Go west, young man!" because Greeley saw that was where opportunity and the future were to be found. We feel similarly about the new frontier that is opening up as a result of developmental neuroscience: it is a domain of knowledge that is rich and attainable, and it will become vital territory in the career of psychotherapists. To produce lasting change in developing children, we must understand how young brains (as well as young minds) work. The approach offered in this book attempts to synthesize what is known about developing brains and the therapeutic approaches that have been supported by research. By combining the findings of developmental neuroscience with evidence-based practice, we offer a brain-based therapy for children.

CHAPTER 1

Changing and Staying the Same

No matter where you go, life moves forward like a heavy wheel and it never stops regardless of any circumstance. It just moves forward regardless, and I find that extremely humbling.

—Lisa Kristine, Photographer

CHILD THERAPISTS WORK in the space between the stable and changeable aspects of personality and character, using the therapeutic relationship to promote a healthy adaptation to living in a complex social world. The discovery that such a relationship could change the mind ignited the psychotherapeutic revolution in psychiatry. It does not seem widely remembered that the discovery was made by pioneers who at the time were immersed in the study of the brain and nervous system. Between 1877 and 1900 (when *The Interpretation of Dreams* was published), Freud authored more than 100 works on neuroscience. (For an interesting discussion, see Solms & Saling, 1990.) As a neurologist, Freud revised the prevailing view of his scientific contemporaries that the brain did its work piecemeal, with specific parts performing particular tasks in a straightforward way. In a short article on aphasia, for example, Freud rejected the localization hypothesis in favor of the concept of a "speech field" in the brain (1888/1990), a view more in accord with that of modern neuroscience.

Like Freud, William James was also a neurophysiologist. While his work is ultimately less useful to clinicians than Freud's, James nonetheless laid the basis for much of current cognitive science, and in that sense was a precursor to behaviorism and cognitive behavioral therapy. In his 1890 *Principles of Psychology*, James discusses some ideas that came to have

1

enduring importance in psychological studies, including associative learn-ing, chains of operant learning, and fear conditioning. His theory of emotion was based on the idea that feelings arise not from thoughts or fantasies but rather from visceral and muscular responses to outside stimuli. *The Principles of Psychology* includes detailed diagrams of the brain and a review of Broca and Wernicke's areas (two areas of the brain that are key to our ability to express and understand language). Regarding the seat of consciousness, James concluded:

> For practical purposes, nevertheless, and limiting the meaning of the word consciousness to the personal self of the individual, we can pretty confident-ly answer the question prefixed to this paragraph by saying that *the cortex is the sole organ of consciousness in man.* If there be any consciousness pertaining to the lower centres, it is a consciousness of which the self knows nothing. (James, 1890, p. 67)

Subsequent clinically-oriented psychologists followed Aristotle, Descartes, and James in largely disregarding the brain, and followed Freud in focusing on case studies and on developmental cognitive and behavioral norms. Abandoning brain science in favor of pure psychology allowed psychotherapists to employ methods considered "unscientific" by biolog-ical scientists. These included the use of insight and empathy as ways of understanding the mind. The separation from neurology allowed thera-pists to grasp a truth about neuroscience that for many years eluded scientists in laboratory: the brain is exquisitely sensitive to the inter-personal environment of relationships. Particularly in childhood, relation-ships are as important as food and warmth.

Psychotherapy's discoveries about human nature and development outstripped what could be demonstrated in the neuroscience labs of the same period. But in pursuing the purely psychological strategy of Freud and James, those of us who have grown up in the psychodynamic and behavioral traditions postponed an important reality check on intuitive hypothesizing and speculation.

The way in which contemporary neuroscience causes us to revise the common psychodynamic understanding of unconscious phenomena exemplifies the value of an integrated neurodevelopmental model. Classical psychoanalytic theorists tended to portray the unconscious as the Puritans portrayed hell—a cauldron of aggressive and libidinal impulses threatening to spill over and destroy both the social order and the individual's cohesive sense of goodness. Later psychodynamic ther-apists viewed it in less vivid terms, as the repository for socially and personally unacceptable impulses. In contemporary neuroscience, if the Freudian unconscious exists at all, it is seen as a small subset of a much larger area of mental life that functions outside of awareness. Much of what the brain does never achieves consciousness, nor would there be a purpose in its doing so. Neuroscientists are careful to use the term "nonconscious" as an adjective, not (as the Freudians tend to do) as a noun. The mind, in the new neuroscience, is a process rather than a thing or a place. Neurodynamic therapists are less impressed with insight than with integrating brain functions and the psychological domains of thought, emotion, and behavior.

Neuroscientific research has demonstrated that nonconscious functioning has a developmental history that is often clinically relevant, one that clinicians should be generally aware of. A brain module that plays a key role in certain types of memories is the *hippocampus* (or little "seahorse") located near the center of the brain at the heart of the so-called limbic system. The hippocampus is critical in forming memories about events that can be brought to consciousness. It organizes and coordinates input not only from many other parts of the brain but from the whole nervous system in a way that permits these inputs to be stored as explicit memories. Adults who have the misfortune of losing all or part of this small brain module (such as the famous patient H.M., about whom we wrote in *Brain-Based Therapy with Adults*) stop coding long-term explicit memories, as was the case with H.M. immediately after the surgery that removed his left and right hippocampi.

Hippocampal functioning changes over time, by parallel developmental processes in many other brain modules. The sequence in which the underlying biology of memory emerges is clinically important: *the specific loops between the hippocampus and the cortex that allow us to explicitly recall events from the past do not become functional until about age 2.* We do not have the capacity to organize explicit memories before that age. No matter how much we analyze the defenses of a child or adult patient, these memories cannot be "uncovered." Infantile amnesia is not psychogenic, as Freud proposed, but an artifact of this developmental sequence. This fact about the development of the explicit autobiographical memory system has a significant impact on the child's personality and sense of personal continuity and identity.

Other memory systems come on line earlier in life. The *implicit memory system* (including procedural and emotional memory), is powerfully influenced by a module located quite close to the hippocampus, called the *amygdala* (or "almond," so-named because of its shape). The amygdala, like the hippocampus, is *bilateral*; that is, it is made up of two relatively small pieces of real estate, one in each hemisphere of the brain. The amygdala is a powerful mediator of somatic reactions to stress and a potent influence in the laying down of nonconscious emotional memories. These memory systems can be sensed only through the hints and feints of behavior. Thus when we as therapists explicitly interpret a behavior that is linked to (for example) an implicit memory of repeated infantile abandonments in an 8-year-old patient, we are constructing a new narrative with the patient, and not "uncovering" it.

NEURODYNAMICS: SELF-ORGANIZATION AND CHILD DEVELOPMENT

The mind is an example of an "emergent process," a phenomena found only in complex systems, such as a child's brain. Emergent processes are the surprising effects produced by the interaction of elements in a complex system, such as the interaction between the hippocampus and the cerebral cortex. Complex systems such as the mind/brain process transform the roles of the component subsystems themselves—very much a case of the whole being greater than the sum of the parts (Arden, 1996; Grigsby & Stevens, 2000).

COMPLEXITY

Complex systems have several important qualities in common, one being that although typically they are made up of many parts, *the relationship between the parts is more important than the function of any one component.* For air-breathing mammals, for example, the lungs are a vital organ of the circulatory system, but lung functions are affected by larger somatic systems, especially the brain. Conversely, the lungs are much impacted by the vigor of the tiny processes in the cells that make up the lungs themselves. Children's brains are also made up of many different highly interrelated parts, or modules, which are modified by developmental phases and by experience. When a single cell reproduces itself, creating identical twin offspring, a long process of differentiating begins. One of these cellular offspring will become the great-grandparent of cells that make up the gut; the other the neurons in the visual cortex at the back of the brain. Given that the two offspring are initially identical to the parent cell, what is built-in is the capacity to respond to, among other things, the cell's location in the environment of the womb and later its location in the fetus.

When a normal baby emerges into the world a scant 9 months or so after the first mitosis, this system of intense gene-environment interaction continues the work of differentiation. Still in a premature state compared to all other newborn mammals, but with many highly differentiated systems, human babies are especially designed to attach to caregivers. *In this sense, the child is a subsystem in an interactive social system of other individuals and groups.* Like other living systems, the newborn's brain balances between stability and disequilibrium; and also like other living systems (von Bertalanffy, 1968), it has the capacity to organize itself (Arden, 1996). As we describe in Chapter 2, infants have emerged from the evolutionary process custom-made to attract just the kind of attention they need to survive and prosper. Whatever neurological structure they bring into the world immediately begins interacting with, and is changed by, the environment.

How do complex systems organize and maintain themselves and deal with new inputs into their system? The capacity to maintain a degree of stability in a changing environment is one shared by all complex systems, whether alive or not.

An example of this self-organizing property in a nonliving system is the "behavior" of the planet Saturn and its rings. Through the telescopes of Earth-bound stargazers, Saturn's rings look like solid flat bands of color attached around the waist to the orb of the planet. Closer observation, however, shows the rings to be made up of billions of rocks hurtling around the planet at tremendous velocity. Moreover, the rings are actually discrete modules in a large, complex system, with empty space separating them.

This pattern is what students of dynamics call an *attractor*, a pattern of activity or structure the system can assume at minimal expense in energy. The whole system can be said to be self-organizing in the sense that a rock that happens into one of the no-fly zones between the rings will be pulled into an adjoining ring by the force of gravity. A rock that tries to go its own way must tap into some source of energy to stay out of the attractor pattern. All complex systems, including children's brains, share common elements, and this is one of them: *change often requires additional energy*. Resistance is not necessarily a willful act of rebellion so much as the tendency of systems (but far more complex) to remain in inertia and conserve energy (Grigsby & Stevens, 2000).

The child's brain shares some of the dynamic complexity of Saturn's ring system, including the capacity to organize and maintain itself in certain patterns of activity. Students of dynamics call these patterns "attractors" whether they are the way boulders and bits of debris orbit Saturn or are "traits" we see in a child. But the complexity of a neonate's brain dwarfs that of the giant planet's ring system. The fertilized egg and every subsequent cell in the body of the fetus retains all the information in its DNA that is required to make *any* of the specialized cells in the body. Every cell seems to be responsive to and changed by environmental factors. Between 10 and 26 weeks, fetuses generate on average 250,000 new neurons *per minute*. By birth each of these cells will be virtually exactly in the right spot, ready to sprout a precise network of *dendrites*, or extensions from the neuron used to communicate with colleagues. The dendrites grow in the direction of neurons that will become part of networks required to launch the brain functions that come on line at birth or in the months and years afterward.

How do these cells strike exactly the right equilibrium between stability and the capacity to change? As the internal microelectrical storms within the neuron result in the cell "firing" and discharging a cascade of neurotransmitters in the direction of colleague cells, the recipient of the transmitter reacts. The transmission electrifies or calms down the weather inside the neighboring cell, and mental life begins. There are a staggering number of cells involved in the whole system. Newborn babies have twice as many neurons as their mothers, and the pace at which they start to wire in reaction to outside stimulation is astonishing. Within an hour after birth, the infant starts to imitate the facial expressions of those around him or her (Meltzoff & Moore, 1977), and very soon prefers the configuration of human features to anything else in the visual environment (Bebee & Lachman, 2002). We do not really understand how neurons seem to "know" their proper destinations, nor how they also seem to know which other cells, sometimes far away, they should connect with. What we do understand is that the whole system is exquisitely attuned to sensing the environment; and that the environment immediately begins to play a major role in reorganizing the newborn brain. This is one of the enduring self-organizing properties of the human nervous system.

COMPLEXITY AND ENVIRONMENTAL SENSITIVITY

Helping children requires an appreciation of how susceptible each child is to the relationships surrounding him and some understanding of how he views the world at any particular time in his development. Relationships drive human development, and the child's relationship with her therapist is just one in a constellation of attachments to adult caregivers and peers. Helping facilitate change in a child's adaptation to the specifics of his family and the outside world is always balanced with where the child is starting from. In this context, the therapeutic process is a dialogue between the child's existing ways of interpreting feelings and events and the therapist's more developmentally advanced capacity to understand and interpret these phenomena. More than that, child therapy is a bond between two people that produces change in the brains of both participants.

The extent to which children are embedded in an interpersonal environment is illustrated by research on the effects of environments that are either deprived or particularly stimulating. Rene Spitz (1983), a psychiatrist and close associate of Anna Freud, was a pioneer in the area of exploring the interactive role of brain development and relationship-dependent learning in infancy. He originated a method of studying infants and children in relationally impoverished environments, a technique as important in our understanding of the delicate interplay of love and brain tissue in children as the study of the effects of head trauma has been in the evolving model of adult brain functioning. The principle here is that to understand how things usually work, look at what happens when they go disastrously wrong. Spitz studied medically hospitalized infants and formulated the concepts of hospitalism and anaclitic depression. Left alone for long periods of time, the infants in Spitz's studies typically actively protested and then, if no one responded, withdrew and became passive. Infantile withdrawal could become complete and lead to an ultimately fatal shutting down. Babies, Spitz proposed, can die from not being touched, spoken to, looked in the eye, smiled at, and bounced.

Romanian orphanages have been an important field site for researchers interested in infant maternal and social deprivation. After the overthrow of the Ceausescu government in 1989, more than 150,000 children were found languishing in orphanages. Many were malnourished, neglected, and dying of infectious diseases in disproportionate numbers. In these settings, one person typically cared for approximately 30 children. Babies were fed and kept clean but their psychological needs ignored. Many had resorted to methods of self-stimulation, such as head banging, rocking incessantly, and hand flapping. A major cause of their multiple developmental delays was the lack of consistent human contact during critical periods (Kuhn & Schanberg, 1998).

Infants of less than a year who had been placed in Romanian orphanages for more than 8 months were shown to have higher cortisol blood levels (an indicator of significant stress) than orphans adopted within the first 4 months of their lives—and cortisol levels continued to increase for those left in the institutions for more than 8 months (Gunmar, 2001). Cortisol is an important part of the brain's arousal system, which works well over relatively short-term periods. Long-term stress dysregulates the system by negatively affecting the functioning of the hippocampus (and even its size) and by throwing the amygdala into overdrive.

British child psychiatrist and neuroscientist Sir Michael Rutter compared 156 Romanian orphans who were adopted by age 3.5 to 50 nondeprived children who were adopted before 6 months of age (Rutter et al., 2001). All the children were followed longitudinally and were examined for a variety of behavioral problems including attachment and emotional problems, attention deficit hyperactivity disorder (ADHD), autism, cognitive impairment, peer relationship problems, and conduct problems. The Romanian children were more likely to exhibit behavior problems in four of the seven domains: attachment problems, ADHD, autistic-like problems, and cognitive impairment. These difficulties were more likely to occur among children who left Romania after their second birthday. Those children adopted prior to 6 months of age resembled a sample of nondeprived children adopted in the United Kingdom. The risk of developing behavioral problems increased linearly if adopted after 6 months of age from a Romanian orphanage and the risk was greatest for children adopted after age 2. Interestingly, even in the sample adopted after age 2, 20% to 25% of the adopted children did not develop behavior problems by age 6.

In Canada, Fisher and colleagues documented the breadth of some of the results of trauma in Romanian children adopted by parents in British Columbia (Fisher, Ames, Chisholm, & Savoie, 1995). They found that children who had spent at least 8 months in a Romanian orphanage had significant developmental problems; those who spent under 4 months in orphanages did not. Romanian orphans adopted by American families have shown many symptoms of early social deprivation. These children often appear stoic, uninterested in play, tend to hoard food, and rarely cry or express pain. Imaging studies show abnormalities in the brains of orphans consistent with these behavioral deficits. Areas vital for conducting relationships and self-regulation, such as the *orbtial frontal cortex* (OFC), are underactivated relative to those of normal children (Chugani et al., 2001).

Maternal deprivation apparently also causes significant neurochemical abnormalities. Research on adult animals separated at birth from their mothers has revealed persistent irregularities in the production and normal functioning of neurotransmitters (the chemicals that communicate across the synapses that separate neurons). *Dopamine*, a transmitter important in the experience of pleasure and reward, is one of the neurochemicals affected by attachment experiences. Early deprivation alters the expression of the genes that regulate dopamine manufacture and the role dopamine plays in mediating stress. The negative effects of early maternal separation identified in other animal studies include: the expression of serotonin receptors in RNA, the expression of benzodiazepine receptors, and the infant's sensitivity to morphine and to glucocortocoid receptors related to the stress response. (See Wexler, 2006, for a review.) The work of developmentalists such as Spitz and of contemporary neuroscientists on the devastating effects of early interpersonal deprivation have changed social policy around the world. As studies have accumulated confirming that stable relationships are a basic nutrient of development, the research has helped transform protocols in orphanages, pediatric wards, and daycare centers. Institutions with the resources to do so have moved to provide higher levels of interaction and consistent caretakers for infants. Unfortunately, where the resources to make these changes are lacking, the toll on infants continues unabated.

Neuroplasticity and Neurogenesis

Studies of children in so-called enriched environments take a different slant on the issue of the impact of environmental factors on brain development but produce results consistent with research on extreme deprivation. Animal subjects are often used as stand-ins for humans in these studies because these studies use post-intervention autopsies; and rats are particularly popular because they breed readily in captivity and mature relatively quickly. Over 40 years of exposing rats to enriched environments has shown a wide variety of structural changes in their brains. These include overall increases in brain weight and density, more growth in the *dendrites*, increased density of dendritic spines (which facilitates interneuronal communication), more synapses per neuron (ditto), more multiple synaptic buttons (ditto again), and more granular cells in the dentate gyrus of the hippocampus. (See Cicchetti & Curtis, 2006, for a review.)

The last finding—that the brain actually makes *new* neurons in response to environmental stimulation—is an important one. Researchers from the Salk Institute for Biological Studies in San Diego put adult mice in cages equipped with tunnels, wheels, and other environmental attractions. They found that the mice placed in the enriched cages developed 15% more neural cells than mice put in standard cages. As expected, they performed better on various cognitive and memory tests and were found to have enlarged hippocampi (Kemperman et al., 1998). The so-called neuronal proliferation appeared to involve the precursor to neurons called neuroblasts, which develop out of stem cells. Normally, stem cells and neuroblasts develop throughout adulthood but do not generally survive to become new neurons. The Salk group, however, demonstrated that cognitive stimulation in enriched environments increases the neuroblasts' odds of becoming actual neurons.

These findings contradicted a belief long held by most neuroscientists that we are born with all the neurons we will ever have. Studies such as the Salk Institute's have changed the field's collective mind. The discovery that new neurons are created in specific areas of the brain, such as the dentate gyrus of the hippocampus, has deepened recognition of the brain's responsiveness to new learning. Taking psychotherapy as an example of an enriched interpersonal environment, it is probable that neurogenesis comes into play in our offices as well as in the laboratory. It has been estimated that as much as 85% of the dentate gyrus neurons are generated postnatally. These granule cells are excitatory and use glutamate as their primary neurotransmitter. Kemperman and colleagues (1998) also found new neurons in the dentate gyrus of mice placed in enriched environments. Gould and colleagues (1999) have demonstrated the same phenomenon in the brains of adult monkeys.

With some intuitive sense of the power of the environment to affect biological changes in the brain, the educational system has tried to harness enrichment as an intervention. Head Start is a sterling example of such a program. Imaging or other direct evidence of structural change in the brains of Head Start children is not available, but changes in the behavior of children who participate provides strong clues as to what is going on in their heads. An increase in average IQ scores and positive impacts on school and social competence are among the program's benefits (Lazar, Darlington, Murray, Royce, & Snipper, 1982). Another program, the Abecedarian Project, has also shown positive effects on the cognitive development of high-risk young children (Gottlieb & Blair, 2004; Ramey et al., 2000). Children who attended the program achieved a 5-point IQ advantage over controls. The enrollees showed a 50% reduction in failing grades in elementary school compared to controls, and between the ages of 12 and 15, they scored well on a variety of achievement tests. Those children who were at the greatest risk—for example, those with mothers who had IQs lower than 70—benefited most from participation in the program.

Genetics and Environmental Effects

Studies of adoption generally (but not always) support the importance of the environmental contributions to individual development. In one study, children whose biological families had a history of violence were adopted into families with no such history. Only 13% of the adopted cohort expressed antisocial traits as they grew up, in contrast to 45% of children from nonviolent biological origins adopted into families with aggressive histories (Cadoret, 1995).

Twin studies produce perhaps the most compelling examples of the relative importance of environmental versus genetic influences on the development of particular psychological traits. In one such study, identical twins described as "secure" in their initial assessment were placed in settings with an anxious adoptive parent. Outcomes suggested that anxiety is catching, insofar as the twins typically developed the anxious trait of the adoptive parent (Bokhorst et al., 2003).

A child's environment may include a mixture of risk and protective factors. For example, a longitudinal study conducted on the Hawaiian island of Kauai followed 700 children born in 1955. Half of the children lived in poverty and half in relative affluence. One-third of the study population developed behavioral problems. Those particularly susceptible were exposed to risk factors such as prenatal illness, chronic poverty, parental psychopathology, and family instability. But interestingly, some 70 children (10% of the population) who had been exposed to multiple risk factors nevertheless grew into caring and competent adults. The protective factors for these children were identified as including the following:

- The mother's caregiving competence
- The child's own social maturity, autonomy, sense of self-efficacy, and scholastic competence
- Emotional support from the extended family and friends

The interplay between the expression of genetic endowment and the stimulating effects of the environment come together in a complex, mutually reinforcing pattern we called *nurtured nature* in the adult volume of this series. We use the term to capture the reciprocal impacts of interpersonal environment and the brain of a developing person, regardless of their age. Overall, the relationship between risk and resilience within the nurtured nature paradigm draws on many factors. In Rutter's study of severely deprived Romanian orphans adopted by British families, 20% to 25% of the children were able to rebound and assume a normal developmental course within a loving family. The factors involved in the success stories are a blend of the personal and the systemic, just as they were in the Hawaiian children.

In terms of the mixture of protective and risk factors that characterize the genetics and environments of the children we see, the therapist's job is complex. Development is not based on nature or nurture alone. Every child comes into the world with a unique genetic history. Maximizing their potential for resilience in the face of risk is the task of brain-based therapy. We seek to recruit and foster the protective factors by positively impacting the parenting children get and by offering a relatively brief exposure to a cognitively and emotionally enriched environment. In Chapter 2 we examine attachment as an aspect of "nurture" and the child's temperament as a force of "nature."

DEVELOPING BRAIN

What makes us so susceptible to environmental influence? How is it possible to change in the course of a therapeutic relationship? The answer to these questions lies in the anatomical structure, dynamic functioning, and developmental history of the brain. Three types of brain development have been identified: *gene driven, experience expectant,* and *experience dependent* (Black, Jones, Nelson, & Greenough, 1998; Greenough, Black, & Wallace, 1987).

GENE-DRIVEN DEVELOPMENT

Gene-driven brain development is relatively insensitive to experience. Much of this development occurs prenatally (e.g., in the migration of neurons to their appropriate anatomical positions). Prenatally, the brain begins as a hollow cylinder, called a neural tube. Neurons are generalized along the inner walls of the neural tube and migrate to their proper locations (Kolb, 1989). The most prolific period of embryonic neuron formation (neurogenesis), as we've noted, is between 10 and 26 weeks. The brain overproduces neurons and will sacrifice about half of them in a process known as *apoptosis,* or neural pruning. Apoptosis (a phenomena of programmed cell death) is characterized by cell shrinkage and fragmentation of the nucleus, followed by the removal of the dead cell by phagocytes.

Cell migration essentially involves neurons positioning themselves in areas of the brain with semispecialized functions. For example, in the cortex, neurons migrate to six cortical layers, each having distinct functions. The neurons within each layer project to specific targets or receive afferents from specific sources. For example, layer 2 neurons participate in short inter-cortical connections. Layer 3 neurons participate in longer range cortico-cortical connections as well as interhemispheric communication across the *corpus callosum,* the central bridge linking the two hemispheres of the brain. Layer 4 targets nerve fibers coming from the thalamus (the central switchboard of the brain). Layer 5 is the origin of projections from the cortex to subcortical structures, such as the amygdala and cerebellum (at the back of the brain, near the brain stem). Layer 6 neurons project *to* the thalamus (in contrast to layer 4). About the connectivity of the neurons in layer 1, as yet we know very little.

Cell migration is complete by 7 months gestational age (Huttenlocher, 1990). However, genetic defects or exposure to teratogens may produce disruptions in the migration of neurons to their expected destination (Gressens, 2000). These events can occur as a result of the mother's exposure to neurotoxins, including alcohol and drugs.

After neurons have migrated to their home territory in the nervous system, cell elaboration marks the next phase in brain development. In this phase, axons and dendrites form synapses with other cells. Just as the developing brain produces more neurons than it will need, it also produces more synapses than will survive. The brain of an infant or toddler has far more synapses than an adult's brain. At peak times, as many as 100,000 synaptic connections will be pruned (Kolb, 1995). Neurons and synapses that survive are the winners in a process called *neural Darwinism*, with "fitness" determined by the frequency of contact from other neurons (Edelman, 1993). Those that are relatively isolated die off.

Hemispheric Specialization

A general overview of brain processes and modules appears in the appendix of this book; but for the present, we must note one of the best-known anatomical features: the brain, like the face, is *bilateral*. The left side and right sides look slightly different if you examine them closely; and they are somewhat specialized in function (although just how much, and in whom, is a matter of lively debate, with Nobel Prizes awarded to the winners). There is evidence that hemispheric specialization begins prenatally and that, at birth and for some time afterward, the right hemisphere is more dominant in infant functioning. Areas of specialization that are generally agreed on in the literature are shown in Table 1.1. A caveat is that females typically demonstrate less hemispheric specialization than do males, and males may be overrepresented in the specialization data.

In general, the right hemisphere is linked to novelty and the left hemisphere to routine (Goldberg, 2001). The way in which the brain processes music is an example. An overgeneralized and now-discredited belief is that music appreciation is a right-hemisphere task. It now appears that musically *naive* people process music with their right hemisphere because of the novelty. Trained musicians, however, process music mostly

Table 1.1

Hemispheric Specialization of the Cortex

Major Area	Subsection	Functions/Characteristics
Cerebral cortex	Right hemisphere	Deals with novelty, the "whole picture," consciousness of spatial arrangements, negative emotions. Develops faster than the left hemisphere over the course of the first two years. In most individuals, the right hemisphere "cannot talk"; later it is associated with withdrawal, passivity, and "moving inward"
	Left hemisphere	Deals with repetitive stimuli and detail; it learns language; proccesses positive emotion and explicit memories; and generates active engagement with the world.

on the left (Bever & Chiarello, 1974). Consistent with this finding, Alex Martin and colleagues from the National Institute of Mental Health used positron emission tomography (PET) scans to measure blood flow patterns and demonstrated that as individuals learn tasks, novel information initially is processed by their right hemisphere. When the information becomes familiar and routine, it is lateralized to the left hemisphere (Martin, Wiggs, & Weisberg, 1997). This appears to be the case with both verbal and nonverbal information. Individuals demonstrate fascinating and heartening capacities to deal with adverse brain events in regard to these standard hemispheric arrangements; for example, a child who suffers right-hemisphere damage is likely to recover some capacity to process novel stimuli. The earlier in life the damage is sustained, the more likely the person will recover significant functioning.

Postnatal Development: Also a part of gene-driven development is the pace at which the normal brain in an average environment develops. At birth, babies' brains have achieved only 25% of their adult weight—but their bodies, by comparison, weigh just 5% (on average) of what they will weigh as an adult. At 6 years of age, the child's brain has attained 90% of its adult weight (Kolb & Wishaw, 2003). This accelerated brain growth in childhood is one of the developmental landmarks that differentiate us from other species. The fastest developing part of the child's brain is the cerebral cortex, including the *prefrontal cortex* (PFC), at the forefront of the frontal lobes. It facilitates cognitive, emotional, and social functioning at a uniquely human level. But this high-powered "wetware" inside the child's skull requires high maintenance. Honed by evolution to nurture and protect this most unique evolutionary advantage of our species, the human brain predisposes us to want to live in families, form long-term relationships, and sublimate sexual and aggressive wishes to maintain durable bonds. Brizendine (2007) documents the significant changes in neuroanatomy and physiology that are characteristic of pregnancy. She goes so far as to call the cumulative alterations in neuroanatomical structure, hormone levels, and conditioned response patterns that are typical of pregnant women and mothers of newborns "the mommy brain." Although poets may tell us more about love than the average psychotherapy book, from the brain's point of view, love is simply the brain's way of nurturing another brain.

Experience-Expectant Development: Experience-expectant development occurs during critical periods. Most developmental theorists have moved to the term *sensitive periods* to describe these epochs and define them in terms of three factors:

1. Physiological readiness
2. The developing child's need for certain favorable environmental inputs attuned to maturational progress
3. The child's ability to adapt to less than perfect environments

Sensitive periods link our capacity to do something new with the brain's need for certain experiences to feed its development. For example, most children take their first steps at approximately 12 months of age, give or take a few months. By this age, the brain is much better able to synthesize auditory, visual, and kinesthetic neuronal processing in a way that allows babies to orient visually to the sound of the mother's voice. Using PET technology, Chugani (1998) has shown that during the first year of life, the brain develops in "phylogenic order"; in other words, more primitive areas develop first, followed by more advanced ones, such as the cortex. The senses of seeing, hearing, tasting, touching, and smelling develop before the modules that connect these senses and foster children's capacity to experience the world in a more integrated way. What could be more exciting than propelling oneself through this newly assembled sensate world while keeping in good contact with the secure base of the attachment figure?

Language acquisition is another example of the interplay of sensitive periods and learning. By age 2, an average child has a working vocabulary of about 50 words. By age 3, vocabulary has typically exploded to 1,000 words or more (Dunbar, 1996). It is possible to learn a language after the sensitive period of childhood passes, but adults do not learn as quickly. We rarely learn to speak a second language without an accent if we do not learn by age 12.

Overall, sensitive periods represent optimum times when developing children can learn new skills and their brains maintain and strengthen the networks that support newly learned "attractors." The neurons and synapses that are not activated are eliminated. If children endure deprivation or experience abuse during these sensitive periods, there will be deleterious—but not necessarily permanent—effects on their brains and subsequent behaviors (Black, Jones, Nelson, & Greenough, 1998). A summary of the basic psychobiological changes in development during the first 8 years of life can be found in Table 1.2.

The timing of sensitive periods is determined by many different factors. One is the occurrence of apoptosis (pruning), which, as discussed, follows the prenatal overproduction of neurons. As many as one-half of the neurons that were produced in utero die off after birth. Huge numbers of synapses between neurons are also pruned.

As we noted earlier, *glial cells* provide insulation for the axons and promote more efficient firing. Glial (from the Greek for "glue") cells provide support and nutrition, maintain homeostasis, and participate in signal transmission through the nervous system. Glia outnumber neurons in the human brain by a ratio of about 10 to 1 (Society for Neuroscience, 2000). Once regarded as the drones of the brain, glial cells have more recently attracted considerable attention because they appear to be doing more in the way of complex dynamic functions than just tending neurons (Vernadakis, 1996). The insulation glials add to neural networks significantly increases the speed and efficiency of neural networks, and this in turn plays a part in the emergence of sensitive periods in the nervous system. Sensitive periods also may be associated with an increased presence of *neurotrophic factors*, such as brain-derived neurotrophic factor (BDNF), substances that promote growth and development of neurons. And finally, pronounced developmental advances are associated with the appearance of new or more robust synaptic connections between neurons and with growth of dendrites and dendritic spines (which reach out and receive input from other neurons).

A large and fascinating body of research has shown that early attachment from birth to 12 months constitutes a sensitive period that has profound effects on the individual's mental health throughout life. (See Wallin, 2007 and Beebe & Lachmann, 2002 for summaries.) Earlier we noted that research on maternal deprivation demonstrates a strong relationship between duration and resilience. That is, the child's capacity to

Table 1.2

Major Brain and Functional Changes through Middle Childhood

Age	Brain Changes	Psychological Changes
8–12 weeks	Synaptic contact between supplementary motor area, cingulate cortex	Inhibition of brain stem reflexes; decrease in crying and endogenous smiling
	Myelination of the pyramidal tracts	Enhanced recognition memory
	Growth of hippocampus	Established circadian rhythm
	Increase in melatonin synthesis	
7–12 months	Enhanced growth of the frontal lobes	Enhanced working memory
	Development in the hippocampus	Stranger and separation fears
	Myelination of connections between amygdala and cortex	Schematic concepts
	Refinement of sleep	
12–24 months	Growth in layer 3 of prefrontal cortex	Language
	Enhanced linking of the two hemispheres	Inference
	Elongation of dendrites in Wernicke's (speech) area	Moral sense
	Increased GABA and acetylcholine activity in layer 3	Self-awareness
2–8 years	Brain attains 90% of its weight	Integration of past and present
	Peak synaptic density in prefrontal cortex	Increased reliance on semantic categories
	Peak glucose uptake	Ability to detect relations between different categories
	Pruning	Increased goal-directed behavior
	Peak density of GABA and glutamate receptors	
	Peak dopamine and norepinephrine receptors	
	Myelination of long cortical tract	
	Shift in blood flow from right to left hemisphere	
	Maximum differentiation in hippocampus	

Source: Modified from Kagan & Herschkowitz, 2005.

recover from the longer the deprivation goes on during attachment's most sensitive period—the first 2 years of life—the more likely the individual is to show profound effects in later development. This early bonding period is one of the most important in human development.

Experience-Dependent Learning: The long and profound dependency of the human infant, combined with the plasticity of the infant's brain, fosters experience-dependent learning. Other species, with their genetically programmed behavioral tropes, are skewed toward the nature (genetic) side of things, but human infants are uniquely sensitive to and dependent on nurture. This hunger for experience-dependent interpersonal contact dynamically interacts with the more fixed aspects of human nature (in the form of sensitive periods, temperament, and genetic expression). Genes provide a starting point and define potentials. With development, experience increasingly takes on a major role in shaping the child's brain.

The development and maturation of various areas of the brain is facilitated by the process known as *myelination*. Formed by the glial cells, myelin is a thick, fatty substance that coats axons and facilitates the efficiency and potency of their transmissions. Myelination is analogous to coating electrical wires with plastic to achieve greater conduction. Myelination increases the speed of axonal conduction by a factor of 20. This "white" matter forms a significant part of the brain. Myelination occurs in regions of the brain that are developing new skills and is one of the key processes involved in the explosive growth of new skills in sensitive periods. It prepares the brain for increasing responsiveness to the environment and increasing reliance on experience-dependent learning.

The development of the child's cerebral cortex follows an asymmetrical course. During the first 3 years of life, as measured by blood flow to the cerebral cortex, the right hemisphere (which is more closely linked to emotional and other nonverbal internal experience) develops more quickly (Chiron et al., 1997) than the left. The pace of hemispheric development starts to shift at around age 2 and provides the neuronal foundation for the spurt in language development in toddlers. Beginning around age 3, the development of the left hemisphere kicks into high gear. The major functional areas of the cerebral cortex and subcortical areas are shown in Tables 1.3 and 1.4.

The period of time required for the human prefrontal cortex (the part of the brain that has most to do with planning, considered judgment, and decision making) to reach maturity—is lengthy. Long-term parenting relationships are required to maximally nurture this process not only in

Table 1.3

Principal Areas of the Cerebral Cortex and Their Functions

Major Module	Location	Functions
Frontal lobes		
Prefrontal cortex (PFC)	At the front of the frontal lobes, in front of motor and premotor sections of frontal lobes	Involved in almost every problem therapists work with: relationships, depression, anxiety, OCD, schizophrenia, ADD. The probable seat of personality.
		Home of executive functions that plan complex actions, orchestrate thoughts and actions in accordance with internal goals, differentiate among conflicting thoughts, make qualitative and moral judgments, predict outcomes and future consequences of current activities, and exercise social "control" (ability to suppress urges that could otherwise lead to unacceptable outcomes).
Orbitofrontal cortex (OFC)	Part of the PFC in frontal lobes behind eyes	Required for emotional decision-making and affect regulation; its influence on personality and behavior is virtually ubiquitous. Coordinates input of anterior cingulate cortex, amygdala, and hippocampus. Seems to mediate "high-road" solutions to emotional problems and down-regulate "low-road" ones. Believed to be critical in coding explicit a "theory of mind" (i.e., a cognitive-emotional model of what is in the mind of another person).
Dorsolateral cortex (DLPFC)	Part of the PFC at top and on sides of frontal lobes	Working memory and attention, temporal sequencing
Temporal lobe		Includes auditory cortex and medial temporal lobe, which includes the *amygdala* (important in facial recognition, coding of implicit emotional memory, and activation of the hypothalamic-pituitary-adrenal axis) and the *hippocampus* (critical in coding explicit memory, contextualizing experience, and emotion regulation).
Parietal lobe		Visuospatial cognition, synesthesia, mathematical thought, and imagery of movement strongly depend on this region. Einstein's was especially large.
Occipital lobe		Contains the primary visual cortex

19

Table 1.4

Principal Noncortical Areas of the Brain and Their Associated Functions

Major Module	Location	Functions and characteristics
Limbic areas		
Amygdala	Bilateral, limbic area	Works at least from birth on. Vital in facial recognition; encoding of implicit emotional memories; activation of startle and fear responses; activation of hypothalamic-pituitary-adrenal (HPA) axis and sympathetic nervous system.
Hippocampus	Bilateral, limbic area	Not very functional until about 18 months of age. Critical to encoding of explicit emotional memory, contextualization of experience, and emotion regulation; when functioning well, helps down-regulate the HPA.
Anterior cingulate cortex (ACC)	Between limbic areas and cortex, just above corpus callosum connecting left and right hemispheres	Error recognition, emotion formation and regulation, anticipating rewards, decision making and empathy. Contains *spindle neurons*, specialized cells that play a part in making snap judgments.
Thalamus		"Relay station" to the cerebral cortex.
Pituitary gland		Secretes hormones regulating homeostasis.
Hypothalamus		Regulates autonomic nervous system via hormone production and release; helps regulate blood pressure, heart rate, hunger, thirst, sexual arousal, and sleep/wake cycle.
Cerebellum	Bottom of brain, between brain stem and limbic areas	Regulates and coordinates motion and balance and sequencing of complex cognitive tasks.

children, but in adolescents and young adults as well. Some research estimates that the prefrontal cortex does not become fully myelinated until the second decade of life.

NEUROPLASTICITY

Experience-dependent brain development relies on the brain's astonishing capacity to create itself in concert with environmental inputs, such as appropriate emotional nurturing. Experience-dependent brain development is a process that is not contingent on any one sensitive period but occurs across the lifetime. The plasticity of the child's brain allows us to wire-in fundamentally important skills and processes, such as language and countless implicit cultural rules. But studies demonstrate that placticity is one of the basic self-organizing properties of the human brain in all its developmental epochs (Kendall & Squire, 2000). Canadian psychologist Donald Hebb described the basic biological process that underlies this neuroplasticity in his landmark book, *The Organization of Behavior*, published over a half century ago (Hebb, 1949/1998). A now-famous paraphrase of Hebb's landmark central idea is "Cells that fire together wire together." As Hebb put it:

> The assumption can be precisely stated as follows: when an axon of cell A is near enough to excite a cell B and repeatedly or persistently takes part in firing it, some growth process or metabolic change takes place in one or both cells such that A's efficiency, as one of the cells firing B, is increased. (1949/1980, p. 62)

Once two neurons communicate with each other it becomes easier for them to do so again, and it takes less energy to do so. Hebbian learning is based on the way that dendrites from one neuron reach out toward colleagues with which they are in frequent contact, thus making connections between them more efficient. On the macro level of our experience and behavior, the simple but crucial principle here is that *the more often we do something, the more likely we are to do it again*. Use creates structure; and structure is the basis for memory, moods, habitual cognitive patterns, and behavior. Hebb's principle—that we are prone to repeat what we have repeated—is key to answering a question that inevitably crosses the minds of therapists at some point: why does a bright and sophisticated adult of 20—or 30 or 60—continue to chose partners so remarkably like the false, selfish, or envious parent who was a cause of so much pain in childhood?

The answer to is locked up in our implicit emotional memory patterns, and is ruled by Hebb's law.

Dante Cicchetti and John Curtis (2006) describe the importance of neural plasticity to the study of the developing brain:

> The study of neural plasticity in modern neuroscience and associated disciplines has brought to bear a wide range of empirical methodologies to describe all aspects of the observed dynamic processes at the synaptic and cellular levels that appear to underlie neural plasticity. Neural plasticity is increasingly viewed as a dynamic nervous system process that orchestrates nearly constant neurochemical, functional, and structural CNS [central nervous system] alterations in response to experience. (p. 26)

Neuroplasticity is supported by Hebbian modifications in the synapses and by the pruning of neurons in apoptosis. Other microprocesses constantly occurring in the neurons also contribute to it, down to the level of a single ion channel (Kolb & Gibb, 2002; Segal, 2003).

Neuroplasticity and Hebbian learning underlie other forms of learning and memory. Musicians who use specific fingers to play their instruments have enlarged somatosensory strips associated with those fingers (Elbert, Pantev, Wienbruch, Rockstroh, & Taub, 1995; Pantev, Engelien, Candia, & Elbert, 2001). Blind Braille readers have enlarged areas in the parts of their cortex associated with their reading finger compared to blind non-Braille readers and to sighted people (Pascual-Leone & Torres, 1993). Consistent with this growing body of literature, researchers in London scanned brains of cab drivers and compared them to the brains of normal subjects. Investigators hypothesized that cab drivers develop a visuospatial map of London in their heads, and would require brains capable of supporting this feat. The drivers did indeed have larger right posterior hippocampi. The longer drivers had been on the job, the more pronounced the enlargement (Maguire et al., 2000). Adults who have practiced juggling three balls over a 3-month period show an increase in gray matter in the midtemporal area and left posterior intraparietal sulcus. After 3 months of little or no juggling, the volume of gray matter decreased and approached baseline values (Draganski et al., 2003).

These studies were conducted with adults; the potential for neuroplasticity with children is much greater. Although the Hebbian principle has conservative consequences (as, e.g., early attachment experiences become "wired in"), some characteristics of neurons and the relationships between them favor the capacity to respond to novelty. Neural metabolism supports neuroplasticity as well as stability. Neuroplasticity is very much affected by contextual change. Early childhood is a period of prolific synaptic formation. The brain of the child enables certain kinds of experience that exercise the existing neurodynamics in a way that ends up producing further neurodynamnic development and more behavioral capacity as development proceeds.

CHAPTER 2

Temperament and Neurodynamics

S TUDENTS OF HUMAN evolution assume that if a particular characteristic—such as having five fingers or an unusually well-developed ability to communicate—is shared by all members of the primate order, that trait has been passed down to us from the progenitors of us all. Being "social animals" is one of the most important of these common primate traits. Primates rely on each other for survival, and develop elaborate social systems and social signals to bond together. Chimps, gorillas, and orangutans make vocalizations that sound very like laughter when they wrestle, play-chase, and tickle each other. Monkeys, apes, and man share an intense interest in one or more of their kind, whether they are baboons, which tend to live in troops of many animals, or gibbons, which live only with their mates.

We see the effects of the evolutionary importance of bonding and its intimate connection to the human brain in the birth process itself. The neonate's physical and neurological prematurity is an accommodation to two major evolutionary trends: our upright posture (which limits the architecture of the pelvis and the maximum width of the birth canal) and the human infant's relatively huge head. The evolutionary compromise to these conflicting trends is that infants are born soft-headed and not able to do much for themselves. Their brains are primed for explosive growth in the first two years of life, and as convincing as the infant's helplessness appears, healthy babies are in fact not only competent but expert at activating their parents' caregiving schemata. Unable to perambulate on their own or even to cling, neonates are cared for—under optimum conditions—24 hours a day for many weeks, as their super-abundance of neurons compete to see which will survive and become part of a mature brain. Not until infants are 18 months old will they attain the competence with which many other young animals are born.

Evolution has tuned the chemistry of the brain to produce changes in both mother and infant that set the stage for postpartum bonding. Proges-terone jumps up 10 to 100 times its normal level during the first trimester in the pregnant woman. Estrogen increases too—to counteract high levels of cortisol and other stress hormones in the fetus and placenta. The mother's brain changes slightly during gestation and then begins to change again shortly before birth, in preparation for the expanded psychological functions she needs for postpartum attachment. The mother's brain is activated by a spike in the powerful hormone oxytocin, which both starts uterine contrac-tions and precipitates the formation of new neuronal connections. Breast-feeding has its own neurochemical reinforcements, including spikes of oxytocin, dopamine, and prolactin. In other mammals, this hormonal surge seems to launch attachment-specific capacities; in sheep, for example, it appears to endow ewes with a heightened olfactory sense and allows them to identify their baby lambs by smell. Louann Brizendine (2007) has written about the combined effects of oxytocin, estrogen, and dopamine increases on the brain, behavior, and the subjective world of new mothers:

> [The] human mother . . . will be able to pick out her own baby's smell above all others with about 90% accuracy. This goes for her baby's cry and body movements too. The touch of her baby's skin, the look of its little fingers and toes, its short cries and gasps—all are now tattooed on her brain. Within hours to days, overwhelming protectiveness may seize her. Maternal ag-gression sets in. Her strength and resolve to care for and protect this little being completely grab the brain circuits. She feels as if she could stop a moving truck with her own body to protect her baby. Her brain has been changed and along with it her reality. It is perhaps the biggest reality change of a woman's life. (pp. 102)

On the other side of the equation, the human newborn comes with stan-dard equipment that includes more than 20 involuntary reflexes. Con-trolled by the brain stem, most of these simple behavioral responses will be suppressed and replaced at some point in childhood as the cortex grows and expands the sphere of voluntary behavior; but for the neonate many of these reflexes strengthen the infants' capacity to connect with the mother. Rooting and sucking reflexes help neonates find the nipple and automatic hand-grasping and automatic reaching-out-of-the-arms-when-dropped help babies maintain physical contact with the mother. Closely allied to the reflexes are universal infant preferences for looking at the human face and listening to the sound of the mother's voice.

All the interpersonal behaviors so important in the mother–infant relationship—holding, touching and nursing; separating and coming back together—have neurological causes and consequences. The neurochemicals of pleasure and connection—oxytocin, prolactin, endorphins, and dopamine—both sponsor and are stimulated by interactions between mother and baby. As we discussed in Chapter 1, infants begin life genetically equipped to be responsive to the environment, and prepared to start changing in relationship to it. While we see interactions between more fixed characteristics ("nature") and more flexibly and environmentally influenced ones ("nurture") at every level, the relative mix of these two factors varies considerably. In this chapter we will look at temperament, a major factor on the "nature," end of the nature–nurture spectrum in childhood.

CLASSICAL VIEWS

Before the behaviorists made their environmentalist claim that we are only who we have been taught to be, the philosophical basis for this view was established by a seventeenth-century Englishman, John Locke. Locke held that the mind is a tabula rasa, or blank slate. Years of dialog (if not diatribe) between differing schools of philosophy and psychology about this principle have produced agreement on at least one point: Locke was wrong in claiming that children are born without unique predispositions. Although genes do not determine behavior, they increase the probability of certain behaviors developing. Genes interact with the environment and can be turned on or turned off by exposure to environmental factors, and by "epigenetic" factors we are just beginning to understand. Temperament is a constellation of these biologically influenced traits that are fundamental determinants of young personalities.

Locke was dissenting from the concept of innate character that dates back at least to the Greco-Roman world. This classical theory envisioned four major personality types: the sanguine person who was positive and outgoing as a result of a predominance of blood; the melancholic person who was prone to fear and sadness because of a predominance of black bile; the choleric person who was prone to depression and irritability owing to a predominance of yellow bile; and the phlegmatic person who was slow to excitation because of a superabundance of phlegm.

The four humors were thought to interact with the two universal polarities: warm versus cool and dry versus moist (Siegel, 1968). Children who were impulsive and irrational were assumed to have been born with an excess of the moist element (Kagan, 1998). The polarities, in turn, were associated with the fundamental substances in the world: earth, water, fire, and air. The Greeks assumed that the balance of these four substances created the inner states responsible for the outwardly visible variations in the emotional, cognitive, and behavioral makeup of individuals. This theory influenced medical practice through the Middle Ages and the Renaissance. It is actually quite close to the one maintained by modern biological psychiatry for the last 40 years or so, if one substitutes the names of the major neurotransmitters that allow neurons to communicate with each other for the elements of the Greeks.

TEMPERAMENT IN CONTEMPORARY PSYCHOLOGY

In the twentieth century, Carl Jung (1921/1971) introduced the temperament-based concepts of introversion and extroversion, terms that rapidly became part of the language of psychology and filtered into popular culture. Hans Eysenck (1952) went beyond a clinical and theoretical level and attempted to develop a typology based on a factor-analytic approach. The contemporary formulation of temperament grew out of the observations of Alexander Thomas and Stella Chess (1977) and their pioneering work in the New York Longitudinal Study (Chess & Thomas, 1990).

Thomas and Chess identified nine dimensions of temperament based on parental interviews. Although these dimensions are not independent of one another, they serve as general categories of constitutional reactivity and self-regulation. They include:

1. **Activity level.** Refers to how physically active the infant is, the relative proportions of active and inactive periods, including activity observed when the infant is sleeping.
2. **Rhythmicity.** Involves the predictability of sleeping, eating, and elimination. Some infants eat every few hours; others eat only sporadically. Some infants may sleep through the night not long after birth; others take months to do so.
3. **Adaptability.** Involves the ease of dealing with new situations. Does the infant modify her responses to changes and novelty or resist them? Some infants adjust cooperatively to new situations, such as to having their clothes changed, but others do not.
4. **Intensity.** Involves the energy level of reaction to a stimulus.

5. **Dominant mood.** Is the child's behavior usually friendly, pleasant, and happy, and the mood positive, or is it unpleasant, unfriendly, and the mood negative?
6. **Distractibility.** Refers to the effect of environmental stimuli on the child's behavior. One child may be engrossed in a particular toy and ignore the introduction of another one; a second child may drop the first toy and immediately shift to the new one.
7. **Attention span/persistence.** Refers to the length of time an infant pursues an activity and the continuation of attention. After an interruption, some infants may not return to a toy and seem to have forgotten about it; other children eagerly come back to it.
8. **Threshold.** Refers to the intensity level of a stimulus that is needed before an infant responds. For example, some infants can sleep through very loud sounds; others may startle at the sound of a gently closing door.
9. **Approach/withdrawal.** Refers to the way an infant initially responds to a stimulus, such as a toy, food, or a person. Some react enthusiastically to the introduction of a toy by smiling and gesticulating, while others push it away or ignore it.

Based on these dimensions, Thomas and Chess (1977) created three temperamental categories.

1. **Easy.** These infants approach objects with an engaging mood, are regular in rhythmicity, respond well to new situations, and are typically cheerful. They comprise 40% of the population.
2. **Slow to warm up.** Generally shy and inhibited, these infants initially react to the unfamiliar by withdrawal and occasionally show mild distress in reaction to it. They are hesitant to accept change. They comprise about 15% of the population.
3. **Difficult.** These children are generally irritable, withdraw from unfamiliarity, and adapt poorly. They are irregular in feeding, elimination, and sleep. They comprise about 10% of the population.

These three categories described about two-thirds of Thomas and Chess's sample. The remaining third of the population was difficult to classify. Research suggests that there is a genetic basis for these predispositions. For example, from as early as 3 months of age and through the first year of life, identical twins are more similar than fraternal twins on measures such as activity level, ability to pay attention, and shyness (Cherny, Fuler, Corley, Plomin, & DeFries, 1994; Emde et al., 1992; Manke, Saudino, & Grant, 2001).

Longitudinal studies that have examined temperament have shown various levels of continuity between the temperament of young children and the adults they go on to become. For example, 3-year-olds in New Zealand who were observed as shy described themselves at age 18 as cautious when facing new challenges or dangerous situations (Caspi & Silva, 1995). In Iceland, shy and overcontrolled children were more likely than their classmates to remain shy as adolescents (Hart, Hoffman, Edelstein, & Keller, 1997). And in Holland, Dutch mothers who described their 2-year-olds as shy and dysphoric continued to see them in these terms five years later (Stams, Juffer, & van IJzendoorn, 2002).

TEMPERAMENT–ENVIRONMENTAL INTERACTIONS

How caretakers respond to the child's temperament is the most powerful modifier of innate characteristics. When researchers interviewed subjects ages 18 to 22 and gave them questionnaires to assess their current level of adjustment, they found little continuity between an early classification as "easy" or "difficult" and the subject's current life adjustment. However, when the temperament traits had been noted at 3 or 4 years of age, those described as "difficult" were less able to adjust to adult life than those who as children had been categorized as "easy." The assessment of the continuity of the subject's activity level shows similar results. When measured before 1 year of age, the correlation with later activity level is not as strong as it is when measured later in childhood. A more stable activity level is established after 12 months of age with accrued interactions between innate factors and the attachment relationship (see Rothbart & Bates, 1998, for a review).

This line of research suggests that, à la Hebb, if traits endure throughout critical periods, they are more likely to persist into later life. The issue of duration and timing is not just a function of nature (temperament); it is a function of nurture (caregiving) as well. As noted in Chapter 1 in our discussion of research on Romanian orphans, parenting can repair the neurodynamic damage inflicted by influence of neglect or abuse. Those orphans who were adopted before age 2 and had spent less than 6 months in an orphanage were more responsive to the later effect of nurturing adoptive parents. Those adopted *after* age 2 and who had a relatively longer tenure in an orphanage were less resilient. Temperamental factors, while not necessarily hard-wired, may start to appear the longer they are unmodified by environmental influences in early childhood. This is especially true of factors that persist into adolescence.

Even after the pioneering contributions of Thomas and Chess, defining temperament is controversial and challenging. For example, Rothbart and Posner (2006) cite several reasons why the construct of "difficult" is problematic; foremost among these is the lack of precision and reliability in the term itself. Among its other uses, however, Chess and Thomas's list of temperamental variations suggests the challenges to attunement faced by both parents in attempting to shape innate characteristics through a relationship, especially in families with multiple children. If a child's activity or intensity level, for example, conflicts with the parents', the child may not receive the optimum support needed to develop.

Chess and Thomas (1990) used the phrase *goodness of fit* to describe how the temperament dynamics of a child do or do not fit the expectations of the parent or the demands of a family system. A poor fit theoretically results in behavioral problems; a good one should predict healthy development. Children benefit most not from perfect fits but from "good enough" ones. Conflict, stress, and dissatisfaction can fuel development as well as frustrate it. In Chess and Thomas's study (1990), relatively successful development depended more than anything on this one factor—the goodness of fit between children and their parents.

An influential model of how genes interact with the environment was proposed by Irving Gottesman (1974), who suggested that genes set a "reaction range" of upper and lower limits to our development. The gene-environment interactions can be passive, evocative, or active (Scarr, 1992, 1993). For example, children with active temperaments may attend their fathers' soccer league games, become vicariously involved, and get interested in the sport. Later they may play soccer with others and elicit praise from their parents. These children's genetic predisposition toward an active temperament helped create a situation where their temperament is supported and rewarded. As they grow older, they may independently seek out other ways to express their active temperament, such as going dancing. They engage in what Scarr has called niche-picking, where they find slots that fit their genetic predisposition for an active temperament.

What do temperament studies teach us? Overall, there is a dynamic bidirectional interaction between children's experience in the world and their physiology. For example, a study of Masai infants in Kenya found that infants who were temperamentally difficult seemed to do better over time than temperamentally easy infants (DeVries, 1989). The researchers speculated that since the region has scarce resources, the fussier infants were more likely to get their needs met. In this case, difficult temperaments could be seen as advantageous from a Darwinian point of view. Some researchers have found that variations in the tone of the nervous system influence a child's adaptability. For example, the vagus nerve ("vagus" means wanderer) is one of twelve cranial nerves. It is the only one that extends out of the brainstem, down through the neck and chest and into the gut, where it contributes to the innervation of the viscera. The outgoing motor fibers of the vagus nerve represent most of the cranial component of the parasympathetic part of the autonomic nervous system. Fox and Field (1989) found that 3-year-olds with higher vagal nerve tone made a more rapid adjustment to preschool than those with lower tone. Similarly, Katz and Gottman (1995) reported that children with low vagal tone at age 5 adapted poorly to marital hostility and had more problem behaviors at age 8 than those with higher vagal tone.

In examining the relationship between children's temperament and their environment, Jerome Kagan described an extremely inhibited 2-year-old boy who by adolescence was much less sensitive. The reactive sympathetic nervous system that he had as a toddler was less obvious in the 13-year-old. Even inherited physiology that may bias children toward a particular behavior or trait can change over time through encouragement and training. Kagan (1998) describes the change in the conceptualization of temperament and development:

> The old view that the relation between brain and behavior was unidirectional is being replaced with a more dynamic perspective that accepts the fact that psychological states can influence not only brain physiology but also . . . the degree of activity of particular genes, and their products. Glucocorticoids and other chemicals produced by psychological states can turn off or on genes that control the density of receptors on neurons and, as a consequence, alter the reactivity of the central nervous system. (p. 190)

"Kagan Babies:"   The bidirectional interaction between biology and behavior contributes to self-reinforcing neurodynamic syndromes (or "attractors"). Children who were observed to have specific temperamental traits after age 2 continued to have the same traits and the underlying neurodynamics associated with those traits later in childhood. In a large-scale study of children's temperament employing an international sample, Jerome Kagan demonstrated that some temperamental factors are remarkably persistent over time. Babies assessed as inhibited typically are seen as shy and averse to novelty when they reach grade school. These children become hyperaroused by startling or novel events. They often carry these timid and shy traits into maturity (Kagan & Snidman, 2004). Some of these inhibited "Kagan babies" were examined with functional magnetic resonance imaging technology at age 22. According to the scans, when these

subjects were exposed to novelty, their amygdalas, important in the circuitry of anxiety and fear, were overactive relative to those of controls (Schwartz et al., 2003). On the other hand, Kagan reported that despite what the brain scans would predict about adult character, only one-third of the "inhibited" babies showed timidity as they entered early adulthood. Many of the children in his sample learned to resist the impulse to withdraw and pushed themselves to engage. No doubt important relationships assisted them in overcoming their default temperaments. Temperament may have constrained them but did not determine what they became as adults.

Hemispheric Specialization: A series of studies have indicated that shy children exhibit more activity in the right frontal cerebral cortex than in the corresponding area of the left hemisphere. The growing evidence basis that particular affects are biased to one hemisphere or the other has, as we will see in later chapters, important clinical implications. The left frontal lobe has been associated with processing positive feelings and approach behaviors; the right hemisphere with negative feelings and withdrawal behaviors (Davidson et al., 2000). This appears to be the case both for transient affective responses and for moods of considerable duration. For example, upbeat and "happy" musical excerpts activate the left frontal cortex; excerpts that generate sadness activate the corresponding module on the right side (Schmidt, Trainor, & Santesso, 2003).

Based on electroencephalogram (EEG) measurements, shy children show more right-frontal than left-frontal activation (Finman et al., 1989; Fox, Calkins, & Bell, 1994). Using a thermography scanner to measure the temperature of the right and left foreheads, researchers found that shy children show a reverse in the usual pattern. Whereas the left foreheads of uninhibited children and adults are on average 10 degrees cooler than their right foreheads, inhibited children are more likely to have warmer right foreheads than uninhibited children (Kagan, 1994), suggesting heightened right-side activity.

Another study showed similar asymmetry with fingertips. At 21 months and 4.5 years of age, the fingertips and forehead temperatures matched the asymmetry of EEG activation in inhibited and uninhibited children. Other results also showed greater right-hemisphere activation for the inhibited group (see Kagan, 1998, for a review). In yet another study, 2-year-old boys and girls who had cooler left- compared to right-side foreheads smiled more frequently and had lower heart rates during the laboratory battery of tests (Kagan, Arcus, Snidman, & Rimm, 1995).

   Children with shy temperaments tend to react intensely to new situations and to withdraw when confronted with novelty. They tend to respond to emotional expressivneness in others with bilateral frontal activation (Dawson, 1994). The degree of arousal of the amygdala-driven fear circuits determines whether, in the face of such stimulation, a person suspends other thoughts and feelings or not. If the level of fear engendered in these experimental situations is beyond the child's learned or temperamental tolerance, higher-level cortical processes for overcoming or modulating anxiety are suspended, and the focus is likely to be on developing a fight-or-flight strategy for dealing with the situation at hand.

Amygdala and Anterior Cingulate Cortex: Constitutional differences in temperament also involve the amygdala and a part of the cortex known as the anterior cingulate (ACC) (Kagan & Snidman, 1991). Increased desynchronization of the alpha frequencies in the right frontal lobe seems to follow activation of the amygdala (Kapp, Supple, & Whalen, 1994). The amygdalar transmissions stimulate the neurodynamic equivalent of the emotion of fear in the cortex, and the person sees the situation as frightening.
   The ACC has been associated with monitoring conflict, pain perception, attention to error, and emotional regulation. As 4-year-olds build denser connections between their amygdala and ACCs, they become better able to master fears, such as phobias about the toilet, hidden monsters in nightmares, and social anxiety in nursery school. Another factor in emotion management is hemispheric dominance. The right hemisphere of the brain, associated with negative affects and with behavioral withdrawal, has been shown to be dominant in infants who later are assessed as having shy temperaments (Davidson, 1992).
   Rothbart and Bates (1998) have proposed that a range of processes directly or indirectly affects links between temperament and adjustment. In more extreme cases, temperament can have a direct effect on either psychopathology or healthy adaptation. For example, extreme shyness may contribute to the vulnerability of developing anxiety disorders, such as social phobia. Negativity may increase vulnerability to later depression. Adaptability, by contrast, may directly contribute to greater adjustment later in life. Modifying shy or negative tendencies demands consistent expectations, structure, and support. Child therapists are in a special position to appreciate how difficult a task it is for parents to supply these elements on a consistent basis to a problematic child, or where the match between the child's temperament and the parent's is less than optimal.

CHANGING THE GIVENS

The genes that support temperaments are not static or fixed. A child's brain is sensitive to enriched or deprived environments, and children are highly motivated to adapt to attachment figures. In enriched environments, novel stimulation in particular excites the neuroplastic capacities of the child's brain. Jerome Kagan (1998) writes:

> These discoveries imply that a child's experiences might be able to mute or enhance an initial temperamental disposition. Specifically, an infant born with a physiology that contributed to high reactivity and fearfulness, but who experiences subsequently a supportive environment without major uncertainties, might undergo physiological changes in those brain circuits that mediate emotional reactivity and become minimally distressed. The initial genetic endowment is not deterministic and the phenotype is subject to modification by experience. (p. 218)

Kagan (1992) has shown that the combination of supporting shy children's emotional experience and also their "pushing the envelope" to overcome uncertainty can help children develop more confidence. When a shy child is parented (or treated in psychotherapy) with a combination of emotional attunement, encouragement, and reassurance to explore novel situations, change usually occurs. That child's capacity to tolerate new experiences is enhanced by modeling and gentle encouragement (Kagan, 1994).

Some parenting styles and strategies are more effective than others depending on the child's temperament. For example, Kochanska (1994) reported that a maternal discipline style that deemphasizes power works much better than power-based approaches with fearful and anxious children, but not with nonfearful and nonanxious children. A warm and responsive relationship between parent and child compensates for deficits associated with fearfulness. In general, child therapists should coach parents to encourage their children to challenge maladaptive temperamental traits. Unconditional support without the encouragement to change problematic defenses and behaviors nurtures the neurodynamics that underlie the maladaptive behaviors. For example, rationalizing children's shyness and facilitating avoidance or withdrawal perpetuates an asymmetric right-frontal activation pattern. As Kagan and Snidman (2004) write:

> Parents should not overprotect high-reactive infants from all novelty or changes, even though some loving parents are tempted to do so. Parents who gradually expose their high-reactive infants to feared targets can help them overcome their initial tendency to avoid the unfamiliar. (p. 27)

Too much reluctance to make a child unhappy results in bad parenting. If a child is hesitant to meet new children, the parent should be both comforting and challenging, encouraging the child to learn to regulate distress while engaging the new children. Therapists can support parents in providing this kind of encouragement to modify avoidant, shy, or irritable behavior. Encouraging parents to balance encouragement with exposure to feared situations—by arranging play dates; participation in group activities such as sports, scouting or school clubs; and sharing stories about how much is to be gained by going out in the world to meet the unfamiliar all potentially alter the biological basis of temperamental factors. Parents of low-reactive children, by contrast, may most need therapeutic support in being consistent disciplinarians. Low-reactive children, especially if they are male, may tend to have trouble "being good" (i.e., resisting various impulses that, if not actually antisocial, are at least ill-advised actions). They need parenting that clarifies the right course of action and incentivizes it. These children require consistent, fair, and firm parenting, especially in response to tantrums and pushing the limits.

A parent-child group format was developed within the Kaiser Permanente Medical Center system to address potential mismatches between children's temperament and parents' attunement to it. Called the Temperament-Based Behavioral Group Therapy for Parents and Preschoolers Program (and nicknamed the TOTS Program), it teaches parents how to be flexible and present despite the pushes and pulls of the child's temperament (Becking, Wilson, & Reiser, 1999). The net effect is to bolster those elements in the parent-child relationship that really do match.

COMMUNICATING EMOTIONS

The capacity to understand and model the emotional state of the parents during the first few years of life is hard-wired into the child's brain. Infants are neurologically primed for bonding. Touch is a critical aspect of early communication and bonding (Sapolsky, 1998). Even physical proximity is important; it has been shown to directly shape the electrical activity in each individual's brain (McCraty et al., 1998). From birth, children's emotions function as a means of communication with caregivers. Their infantile emotional expressions can be understood as a combination of reactions to their bodily state, as proto-thoughts, and as responses to environmental stimuli ranging from the emotional climate in the room at the moment to the status of the attachment relationship.

Emotional attunement is one way parents can understand how their baby is doing; watching the unfolding of developmental landmarks is another. At about 4 months of age, *spindle cells* make their appearance and start their migration to the orbitofrontal cortex and ACC. Much larger than ordinary neurons, spindle cells facilitate the development of intelligent behavior and the capacity to respond to changing conditions and cognitive dissonance. They eventually become widely connected to diverse parts of the brain and are essential to the human ability to focus on difficult problems. How richly and where spindle cells connect with other cells depends on the baby's experience of the interpersonal environment. A warm and loving family atmosphere promotes strong and healthy connections; family stress and poor bonding promotes the opposite (Allman, 2001). Early nurturance also can stimulate the growth of glucocorticoid receptors in various parts of the body and the brain, allowing children to down-regulate sensitivity to stress (Levine, 2001).

AMYGDALA AND ATTACHMENT

The amygdala plays a major role in mediating early attachment relationships. Located in the so-called limbic areas, the amygdala is perhaps the most important part of the "fearful brain." Highly connected with both the cortex and with other areas regulating autonomic responses, the amygdala stamps incoming stimuli with emotional value in a quick-and-dirty, black-white, good-bad manner. The amygdala may be stimulated by internal stimuli (e.g., from the gut) as well as external stimuli (e.g., from the ears). Along with the right hemisphere, the amygdala is involved in appraising the meaning of facial expressions and other emotional communications from caregivers. These communications are an important source of basic data used in formulating everything from attachment schemata to first impressions in social encounters.

FACIAL EXPRESSION

The eminent psychologist Paul Ekman (1993; Ekman & Frieson, 1972) identified facial expression as the royal road to emotional communication and empathy. Infants in all cultures appear to be hard-wired to prefer looking at human faces over anything else. Within a few hours postpartum, newborns can open their mouths and stick out their tongues in imitation of adults. Infants are primed to look at and track faces within hours after birth (Goren, Sarty, & Wu, 1975). By two weeks of age, they prefer looking at their mother's face rather than a woman who is a stranger (Carpenter, 1974). As an illustration of the inherent capacity of social relatedness, smiling is so deeply wired into the brain that infants born with only a brain stem show the endogenous smiling reaction characteristic of normal babies (Herschowitz, Kegan, & Zilles, 1997). Very young infants smile when their stomachs are full, during rapid-eye-movement sleep, and in response to the touch or voice of parents.

Endogenous smiling normally disappears at about 2 to 3 months of age. By 10 to 20 weeks, infants start responding to the human voice or face with a broad grin referred to as a social smile (Haviland & Lelwica, 1987). Around the same time, there is a reduction in crying, an increase in face-to-face communication between mother and infant, and more frequent social smiling (de Weerth & van Geert, 2002). Social smiling is based on the brain's growing capacity to respond to environmental cues, and an extension of infantile capacities to regulate the behavior of caretakers. The development of social smiling is seen across cultures. Navajo parents, for example, look for social smiling around 2 to 3 months. The "first smile ceremony" is a feast hosted by the person who received the gift of the child's first voluntary social smile (Chisholm, 1996).

Normal young infants widen their lips when looking at a happy face and pout when looking at a sad one. In humans, the facial muscles are connected directly to the skin, which gives us an unparalleled ability to capture and transmit expressive signals.

Ekman (1993) has demonstrated that the facial expressions used to communicate core emotions—anger, fear, and approval—are the same in every culture and every human being. From early on, we know how to use this universal vocabulary. Congenitally blind babies smile at their mothers, and all caregiving adults believe they know what is being communicated when a screaming baby's face contracts like a fist. No one—whether they hail from Brooklyn or Papua New Guinea—makes the corners of the mouth to go up to express disgust. The language of emotions expressed on our faces spans cultures, and the developmental chasm between parent and infant as well. The face provides a common language at a time when the baby's emotionally connected right hemisphere dominates psychological life, well before the left hemisphere's symbolic system of speech makes it the "dominant" hemisphere.

Watching the face with the eyes, listening to the emotional timbre of vocalizations, and using subtle olfactory cues, mother and infant together begin building attunement and shared emotional regulation. This "affective attunement" is contingent on the parent's capacity to provide a secure base and a holding environment so that the infant feels connected and also responded to as a separate subjective being (Siegel, 1999; Siegel & Hartzell, 2004; Trevarthen, 1993). The therapeutic relationship—a relationship analogous to, but distinct from, the child's relationships with other caregivers—is possible because of this early social neurobiological experience.

Emotions prepare us to act in situations that have high personal relevance (Saarni, Mumme, & Campos, 1998). According to the functionalist approach to the study of emotion, emotions highlight goals and intentions in the context of particular interactions with others (Barrett & Campos, 1987). In the child–parent interaction, each party to the transaction must recognize and respond to the other's emotions. A child's ability to recognize facial expressions of emotion appears to develop in stages (Baldwin & Moses, 1996; Walker-Andrews, 1997). During the first 6 weeks of life, infants are not good at scanning faces. As a consequence, they do not recognize facial expressions (Field & Walden, 1982). After 6 weeks of age, babies increasingly discriminate one individual from another when viewing their faces and use both facial expression and voice cues to identify the emotional state of others (Caron, Caron, & MacLean, 1988).

The facial expressiveness of infants keeps pace with their growing skills in interpreting these expressions in others. By 3 to 4 months of age, facial expressions of sadness and anger can be induced experimentally in infants by taking away a teething toy or restraining the infant's arm (Lewis, Alessandri, & Sullivan, 1990). Research suggests that by 5 to 6 months of age, babies pass another developmental landmark in exercising a capacity to mirror the facial expression (happy or sad) of others and in demonstrating a preference for some expressions over others (Balabon, 1995; Izard et al., 1995).

Infants master the capacity to use the facial expression of fear between 7 and 8 months—at the same time they develop stranger anxiety (Harwood, Miller, & Vasta, 2008). Although not all babies show stranger anxiety or show it to the same degree, there is evidence that infants exhibit less anxiety the more strangers they are exposed to (Gullon & King, 1997). The development of working memory contributes to the development of fearful reactions in general and separation anxiety in particular. The growth of the infant's prefrontal cortex and the strengthening of connections between this higher cognitive module and temporal lobe structures such as the amygdala, give babies the ability to retrieve schemata from the immediate past and hold them in the present-consciousness of working memory (Christoff, Ream, Geddes, & Gabrieli, 2003). While basic to the appraisal of social information and the assimilation of emotionally encoded social memories, this capacity can also produce distress reactions (Kagan & Herschkowitz, 2005).

EMOTION-REGULATING RELATIONSHIPS

By the end of the first year of life, babies begin to use the emotional expressions of others to regulate their own emotions (Feinman, Roberts,

Hsieh, Sawyer, & Swanson, 1992). They develop expectancies about how important caregivers are going to react to their own expressions and look to their mothers and fathers for guidance when they are uncertain about what to do next (Beebe & Lachmann, 2002).

Referred to as *social referencing*, babies rely on a trusted adult to provide them with the emotional information they will use to interpret and respond to ambiguous situations. Babies respond to ambiguous perceptual situations, such as the "visual cliff" experiment (where the mother encourages the baby to crawl out onto a transparent panel covering a sharp drop-off, requiring the infant to override the amygdalar signals that it is dangerous to do so) based on social referencing. The willingness of babies to approach and interact with a stranger depends on the parents' voice and facial expression (Baldwin & Moses, 1996). Parents often use social referencing to the advantage of the family system. The more complex self-conscious emotions—guilt, pride, shame, and embarrassment—typically do not arise until after about 24 months of age (Tangey & Fischer, 1995). These complex social emotions typically are interpersonal at the outset and arise in situations that involve injury or enhancement of the child's sense of self. Toilet training is perhaps the most famous occasion for the development of these feelings, but there are likely to be many smaller opportunities for the experience of shame, pride, and guilt in the course of a toddler's day. A frequent outcome of successful child and family treatment is helping parents move from a reliance on punitive and humiliating methods for shaping and disciplining the child's character to practices that promote more positive feelings in the child and rely on negative reinforcement to extinguish aversive behavior.

Culture shapes the way the emotions are expressed, managed, and interpreted (Harword et al., 2008); it begins to assert an influence very early on. For example, among the Kaluli people in Papua, New Guinea, babies are seen as helpless creatures who have "no understanding." Based on of this belief, adults do not engage infants in communication. Although mothers are attentive to their children's needs and use an infant's name, they frequently do not look into the child's eyes when doing so. Looking into someone's eyes is associated with witchcraft. Thus mothers hold their babies facing outward (Ochs & Schieffelin, 1984).

Among the Gussi in Kenya, mothers prefer to dampen their infants' intense emotional displays, whether positive or negative (Dixon, Tronick, Keeler, & Brazelton, 1981). Similarly, among the Utku in northern Canada, displays of anger are discouraged once a child is weaned (Briggs, 1970). In Japan, too, negative emotion is discouraged. Parents model emotional restraint, even when they oppose their children. They express their displeasure indirectly with silence or withdrawal of attention (Azuma, 1996; Miyake, Campos, Bradshaw, & Kagan, 1986). In all cultures, infants express emotions but gradually learn the *emotional display rules* that govern appropriate emotional expressions (Underwood, Coie, & Herbsman, 1992). Knowing the rules about emotional communication and being able to appraise the emotional communications of others accurately is but one of the myriad gifts bestowed by the attachment relationship between parent and child.

CHAPTER 3

Attachment and Subjectivity

You can observe a lot just by watching.

—Yogi Berra

P LATO, IN HIS *Republic*, put forth a provocative idea about improving the character of children. The philosopher proposed that in the best of all possible worlds, select children would be placed in the care of the state, where they could be shielded from the character flaws of their parents and tutored in philosophy and politics. Plato suggested the outraged parents be made to draw lots with nothing but short straws, so that "they will accuse their own ill-luck and not the rulers." No doubt Plato was thinking of the benefits to society of a citizenry raised free of early vice and cruelty and of the evils that were visited on the young by their guardians in Athenian society. But well over two millennia later, when the first serious research was undertaken about how children raised in institutional settings actually fared, disturbing trends became obvious. The clinical and research observations of institutionalized children initiated in the 1930s became a cornerstone of modern child psychotherapy. These inquiries suggested that depriving children of "good enough" experiences with caretakers has profound negative effects on their later development.

FREUD, KLEIN, AND WINNICOTT

Politics and war altered the growth of the child mental health professions in the 1930s. In Europe, the National Socialists labeled psychoanalysis a "Jewish science," in effect banishing it from mainstream practice and crippling psychoanalytic training programs. Before the outbreak of World

War II, among other refugees fleeing Nazi Germany were child psycho-analysts. Many sought sanctuary in Great Britain and the Americas. Sigmund Freud himself arrived in London in 1938 accompanied by his daughter, Anna, in what would become a permanent exile for them both. Their arrival had far-reaching consequences for child psychotherapists. As one of the founders of the profession, Anna Freud was a traditionalist with well-defined views about the mental capacities of the infant and the development of the child. Although psychoanalysis was already well established in England, a substantial number of British child analysts adhered to a version of it that departed in some significant ways from the classical view. The arrival of the Freuds destabilized the comfortable controversies within the British Psychoanalytical Society and eventually resulted in a three-way schism in British child training institutes, one dominated by Anna Freud, a second by Melanie Klein, and the third by the so-called Independents. A major issue in this controversy was the nature of infant mentality in the first year of life.

Melanie Klein emigrated to London from Berlin in the 1920s, well before the ascendance of Hitler and institutionalized anti-Semitism in Europe. Along with Anna Freud, she was one of the first psychological therapists to use play as the "conversation" in child therapy. By the time the Freuds arrived, Klein was confidently asserting that infants, virtually from birth, have the mental capacity to differentiate between themselves and their "primary objects" (i.e., their mothers). This capacity, according to Klein and the expanding circle of her disciples, was the basis for infantile fantasies of ecstatic union, envious destruction, and even cannibalism. Vulnerable to vividly hallucinogenic experiences of "good" and "bad," depending on their internal physiological state of arousal and frustration, infants struggled to develop a more stable sense of reality. In Klein's psychology, this battle between loving preservation and hateful destructiveness largely supplanted the classical Oedipus complex as the centerpiece of psycholog-ical life. She forced analysts and other psychologists to start taking infancy seriously.

Melanie Klein never converted Miss Freud to her position, but to her credit, Freud had better things to do than dispute the Kleinians. She soon became engaged with the British children orphaned by the war and trau-matized by bombing raids in the London Blitz of 1940. Miss Freud became expert about the importance of early trauma and object loss by observing the effects of it daily over the course of several years. With Dorothy Burlington, Freud created the Hampstead Nursery, which served as both a child psychological treatment clinic and a shelter for homeless children. Also with Burlington, Freud published books such as *Young Children in Wartime*

(Burlington & Freud, 1943a), *War and Children* (Burlington & Freud, 1943b), and *Infants without Families* (Freud & Burlington, 1944). Her Hampstead clinic went on to become one of the most important child therapy training centers in the world.

Melanie Klein was less interested in institutionalized infants than in the fantasies of the children who were brought to her for analysis (1975/1921– 1945). She treated and supervised a number of analytic candidates who would later become seminal figures in their own right. One of these was an experienced pediatrician named Donald Winnicott (1941/1975a). Winnicott maintained a busy pediatric practice where he indulged his passionate interest in the child's psychological emergence out of infancy. Like Klein, Winnicott believed that even very young infants can differentiate themselves from their mothers in a shadowy, psychotic sort of way. But unlike her, and more like the classical Freudians, Winnicott was interested in observing what actually happened in the mother–infant relationship. Infants, as far as Winnicott could see, discovered the world only after being forced to acknowledge that their malevolent fantasies had failed to destroy it. Coming from the position that "there is no such thing as a baby" (i.e., babies cannot survive prolonged separation from their caregivers), Winnicott (1965/1990) traced the baby's emergence into childhood in distinct mental stages.

Winnicott's concepts of *good-enough mothering*, the *holding environment*, and the *transitional object* are of enduring value for child therapists. His good-enough mother robustly weathers the demands of the external world, the physical demands of pregnancy and childbirth, the exhausting demands of nursing a new baby, and, in the midst of exhaustion, *enjoys* it all. Winnicott recognized that mothering involves juggling multiple demands and managing powerful stressors, both internal and external.

Especially important, in Winnicott's view, is the mother's emotional *attunement* to the baby, her intuitive sense of what the baby needs to be happy and thrive while she juggles the many demands of living (Winnicott, 1965; see also Stern, 1985). Winnicott had a balanced and historically precocious sense—inherited from Melanie Klein—that, along with consuming needs for protection and love, even very young infants have competencies and a drive to exercise them. This view is consistent with the understanding of later developmental psychologists, and temperament researchers such as Chess and Thomas (1990). The dialectical balance between nurturing and caregiving on one hand and frustrating and building autonomy on the other is the essential task of parenting. Good-enough mothers are generally right about the intuitive guesses they make about this balance.

Perfect is not "good enough." *Impingements* (imperfections in mothering) occur when a mother fails to help her child adapt to the world. Most impingements are minor disruptions that result in the child experiencing a moderate degree of stress repeatedly. In Winnicott's view of the developmental process, these impingements normally do not lead to delays or barriers in the developmental process. On the contrary, they are essential to building the infant's capacity to function independently—to feel like a subject rather than an object—and to satisfy him- or herself. The countless little impingements that occur over the course of growing up provide both parents and children with practice in what may be the sine qua non of developmental success: the ability to repair ruptures in relationships.

Suckling infants, according to Winnicott, take in psychological nutrients as well as protein from their mother's milk. Their mothers give babies the makings of a good relationship, and babies' brains wire these nutrients in to implicit memories of being held and fed.

> [T]he baby has instinctual urges and predatory ideas. The mother has a breast and the power to produce milk, and the idea that she would like to be attacked by a hungry infant. These two phenomena do not come into contact with each other till the mother and child live an experience together. (Winnicott, 1975, p. 152; quoted in Phillips, 1993)

Winnicott uses the term *mirroring* to describe the process by which mothers attune to the child's needs and feelings (1967/1971). The disorganized and extreme experiences of an immature brain are networked through the mother's fully mature one and then reflected back to the baby in ways that are more cohesive and emotionally nuanced. Stern (1985) stresses the importance of the good-enough parent mirroring the child's affects in such a way that it is clear that these affects are being *imitated*; that is, in a way that says "This is my impression of *you* filtered through *me*" rather than "I feel just as you do." Like Winnicott, Stern came to see the importance of the holding relationship in therapy as curative in itself, even if nothing is "interpreted" by the therapist (Stern, 1985).

Good-enough parenting mirrors the infant's needs and accurately predicts how the child will react to an intervention. When good-enough parents deliver just what the child wants at the moment he wants it, the parents promote secure attachment. When good-enough parents do not deliver the goods on time or deliberately deny the child what he is seeking, the child does not just wait. When a parent interacts with the child to calm the distress, the wiring necessary for self-calming—or to continue to yell when dissatisfied—is activated and reinforced in the child. Frustration and conflict provide opportunities to model repair of ruptures in a relationship. The trick in good-enough parenting is not meeting the child's every need but rather in understanding when enough is enough: enough waiting, enough gratification, enough togetherness, enough separation. Minor impingements help developing children prepare for the world. Research supports the conclusion that mild to moderate stress promotes neuro-plasticity and positive coping responses to stress (Heuther, 1998); just as brief and moderate stress enhances brain development (DiPietro, 2004).

Major impingements in the infant's expectations of care are another matter. They occur when parents are unable to provide adequate support and attunement because of their own psychological or situational prob-lems, or when for any other reason they are unable to shield the child from overwhelming stress. Major impingements occur in situations of physical, sexual, and emotional abuse, experiences that so overtax children's capac-ities to manage internal stresses that they can result in direct physical deterioration in developing brains and the acquisition of traumatic implicit memories—topics we discuss in Chapter 4.

Parents may be unprepared for parenthood and unable to place their own needs aside and respond to the needs of their child. Under these conditions, children have more difficulty organizing a coherent sense of self and a consistent model of self-in-relation-to-others. Optimally, how-ever, children adapt to changing conditions in relationships with different family members, friends at school, and so on. How successfully they are able to construct the world as a place that is at once familiar and fresh, as an environment that requires an open stance toward new events, helps define their mental health over time. Privileging stability inevitably means heightened psychological stress. Too much flexibility may leave the child with too few internalized reference points to provide a good, solid sense of subjectivity. Winnicott masterfully captures the infant-as-constructivist balancing stability and plasticity in interacting with an experimental object in his paper "The Observation of Infants in a Set Situation" (1941/1975a).

In the "set situation," Winnicott asks the mother to sit opposite him with the angle of a table coming between him and her, and the baby sitting securely on her knee. Putting mother and baby at ease, Winnicott at some point places the experimental object—a shiny spatula, or tongue depressor—at the edge of the table, "and I invite the mother to place the child in such a way that, if the child should wish to handle the spatula, it is possible." Winnicott identifies two stages in how various infants he assessed in this situation reacted. His narrative is worth quoting at length:

Stage 1. The baby puts his hand to the spatula, but at this moment discovers unexpectedly that the situation must be given thought. He is in a fix. Either with his hand resting on the spatula and his body quite still he looks at me and his mother with big eyes, and watches and waits, or, in certain cases, he withdraws interest completely and buries his face in the front of his mother's blouse. It is usually possible to manage the situation so that active reassurance is not given, and it is very interesting to watch the gradual and spontaneous return of the child's interest in the spatula.

Stage 2. All the time, in the "period of hesitation" (as I call it), the baby holds his body still (but not rigid). *Gradually he becomes brave enough to let his feelings develop,* and then the picture changes quite quickly. The moment at which this first phase changes into the second is evident, for the child's acceptance of the reality of the desire for the spatula is heralded by a change in the inside of the mouth, which becomes flabby, while the tongue looks thick and soft, and saliva flows copiously. Before long he puts the spatula into his mouth and is chewing it with his gums, or seems to be copying father smoking a pipe. The change in the baby's behavior is a striking feature. Instead of expectancy and stillness there now develops self-confidence, and there is free bodily movement, the latter related to manipulation of the spatula.

I have frequently made the experiment of trying to get the spatula to the infant's mouth during the stage of hesitation. Whether the situation corresponds to my normal or differs from it in degree or quality, I find that it is impossible during this stage to get the spatula to the child's mouth apart from the exercise of brutal strength. In certain cases where the inhibition is acute any effort on my part that results in the spatula being moved towards the child produces screaming, mental distress, or actual colic.

The baby now seems to feel that the spatula is in his possession, perhaps in his power, certainly available for the purposes of self-expression. (1941/1975a, pp. 53–54; emphasis added)

What is required of the mother in this experiment is not that she *just* be good enough but that she *only* be good enough. In other words, since life is imperfect, a good-enough mother prepares her child for the imperfections in life by being imperfect herself. There is wide latitude in parenting, but good-enough parenting does not include too much distance or a smothering closeness. Winnicott observed some mothers who, seemingly because of their anxiety or perfectionism, could not prevent themselves from getting involved in the experiment themselves. In effect, maternal intervention deprived infants of the chance to get lost in their own subjectivity, bring the little bit of the world that is the doctor's spatula under their power, and make it "available for the purposes of self-expression." What is required of infants here? As Winnicott puts it, being "brave enough to let his feelings develop" and go on constructing the world with a sense of subjective pleasure and confidence in self-initiated experience.

In the observations where mothers became overinvolved—and this seemed to represent more a stable feature of their mothering styles than a transient impingement—their babies tended to overaccommodate, developing what Winnicott called "a false self." Parents who strive to make the world a totally safe place and to insulate their children from any experience of disappointment or pain fail in a particular way therapists often encounter in more privileged families. Like parents, as therapists we are required to help children and their developing brains balance safety and novelty, satisfaction and fantasizing about the unattainable. Sometimes we must shelve our many ideas about what children *should* do in favor of a felt sense that the most important thing going on in the therapy is the children's creation of their subjective world.

ATTACHMENT

For all his non-Kleinian fascination with the symbiotic interactions between mothers and their babies and his skepticism about interpretation as the curative element in psychotherapy, Winnicott nevertheless was reportedly distressed by the antics of a younger analyst, John Bowlby (1969, 1973). Much of the psychoanalytic establishment shared his reaction to Bowlby's apparent abandonment of the canon of psychoanalytic theory in favor of direct observation of mothers and infants in their homes and other nonclinical settings. Bowlby, like Yogi Berra, happily inferred things about the state of mind of mothers and children just from watching their behavior. In the process, he revolutionized our understanding of attachment, separation, and loss (Bowlby, 1969, 1973, 1980).

Bowlby (who, like Winnicott, was supervised for a time by Melanie Klein) took exception to Klein's sole focus on children's fantasies about their parents. Like Anna Freud, some of Bowlby's experiences impressed him with the power of external events to shape the child's development. After World War II, the World Health Organization commissioned Bowlby to conduct observations of war orphans. He described the devastating psychological problems incurred by toddlers who were hospitalized or institutionalized and separated from their parents (Bowlby, 1951).

Working in the 1950s and 1960s at Tavistock in the Bloomsbury area of London, Bowlby developed the concepts of *safe haven, attachment figures,* and *proximity seeking,* based on the observation that infants try to stay physically close to their caretakers for nurturance and safety. Bowlby also laid the conceptual groundwork for two brilliant young researchers, Mary Ainsworth and her student, Mary Main (Ainsworth, Blehar, Waters, & Wall, 1978; Main, 1995).

THE INFANT STRANGE SITUATION

Originally a psychologist at the University of Toronto, Ainsworth developed a reputation as a diagnostician in her pre-attachment studies, coauthoring a book with the Rorschach expert Bruno Klopfer. After moving to London with her husband in 1950, Ainsworth took a job with Bowlby as a researcher, exploring the effects of childhood separation from the mother. She explored the "patterns of communication" between mother and infant and how the infant used the mother as a *secure base* for her explorations of the world.

Ainsworth came to see that the attachment relationship develops in stages. She validated her stage theory cross-culturally after she and her husband moved from London to Uganda. Yet another move found her in Baltimore, Maryland, in the early 1960s, where she created the classic method for studying infant–parent relationships and generating data about them. In Ainsworth's "Infant Strange Situation" (ISS), she and her colleagues looked at how young children respond to the presence of a stranger and how they deal with the momentary absence of the mother. The ISS has now been used in hundreds of studies throughout the world. The first step in the procedure involves observation of a mother and baby at home. When the infant reaches 1 year of age, the infant and mother are brought in to the observation laboratory, and the baby's reaction to five situations is carefully noted:

1. Mother and infant are alone together.
2. A stranger is introduced into the setting with the mother and infant.
3. The mother leaves the room for 3 minutes and the stranger stays with the baby.
4. Both mother and stranger are absent and the baby is alone.
5. The mother returns.

Infants display a range of behaviors to all five situations but particularly in regard to the mother's absence and return. Most babies show some distress when the mother leaves, but readily use her return in the way described by Bowlby, seeking proximity to calm themselves. Between half and two-thirds of infants in nonclinical populations appear to behave in this way (van IJzendoorn & Bakerman-Kranenburg, 1997). After the 3-minute separation, most infants are quite easily calmed in the reunion, but some less so, and some babies behave as if they could care less that the mother has come back. Based on this "reunion behavior," Ainsworth identified particular infantile attachment styles. These patterns of attachment play an important role in the developing child's characteristic ways of regulating emotion and communicating with others (Main, Hesse, & Kaplan, 1985).

Ainsworth and her colleagues identified three attachment types: secure, avoidant, and resistant/ambivalent patterns (Ainsworth et al., 1978). Mary Main and Judith Solomon identified a fourth type, the insecure disorganized/disoriented attachment pattern (Main & Solomon, 1990). *Secure* infants play with the toys in the experimental setting and explore the room with zest. When their moms leave the room, they show signs of missing her and may cry at the second separation. When she returns, they become excited and seek out physical contact with her—but do not cling. They settle down and get back to play. Their mothers tend to be encouraging and helpful. Secure attachments are the product of good-enough parenting and the parent's sensitivity to the infant's nonverbal signals and needs (Ainsworth et al., 1978; deWolff & van IJzendoorn, 1997).

Secure attachment limits elevations in the hormone cortisol, a common neurochemical measure of the level of stress. In a securely attached dyad, the parent perceives and responds to the child's inner state (Fonagy & Target, 2006). This attuned relationship allows the child to create a sense of cohesion and interpersonal connection, and results in improved self-regulation down to the physiological level of stress. Daniel Siegel notes that "repeated experiences that become encoded in implicit memory as expectations and then as mental models or schemata of attachment . . . help the child feel an internal sense of . . . a secure base in the world" (Siegel, 1999, p. 67). Strengthening the attachment skills of mothers appears to enhance infantile stress hardiness, especially if the child is inclined to be inhibited behaviorally (Cicchetti & Curtis, 2006).

Infants with ambivalent and avoidant attachment styles do not fare so well. Insecurely attached toddlers who tend to withdraw in the ISS show elevated cortisol levels (Nachmias, Gunnar, Mangelsdorf, Parritz, & Buss, 1996). Anxious-ambivalently attached babies seek out their mothers but are not easily soothed. Often their mothers are inconsistently available to them, and the babies' stress worsens with the mothers' stress (and probably vice versa). Infants classified as anxious-resistant make it harder for their caregivers to settle them down after reunions. They tend to be angry, squirming, push away after seeking to be held, or simply fuss. Mothers of infants with this attachment style have been described as the least aware of mothers, and their infants lag behind others. For example, at 9 months of age, anxious-resistant babies score lower on the Baley Motor Indices than their peers with secure or avoidant styles.

Avoidant infants do not cry when their mothers leave; when their mothers come back, the babies tend to avoid or ignore them. That is, these infants behave in the same apparently stoic way whether the mother is there or not. If picked up, these babies will lean away and try to squirm loose. Throughout the ISS, the primary focus of such babies is on the toys in the observation room. Avoidantly attached children tend to give the mother a glance as she reenters the room or shun her altogether. These children do not seem to expect comfort, and indeed the mothers often appear to be challenged in providing it. Avoidantly attached children must rely on their own internal capacities for self-regulation because their mothers are not available. These babies would seem to be good candidates for developing narcissistic or schizoid personality traits at a later date.

In Ainsworth's research on avoidantly attached infants, their parents were characterized by emotional distance and neglectful and rejecting behavior (Ainsworth et al., 1978). Subsequent studies have found that these parents have less emotional attunement with their babies and tend to display facial expressions that are inconsistent with their emotional reactions (Beebe & Lachmann, 1994). Avoidantly attached children are more often seen as controlling and are disliked by their peers (Ogawa et al., 1997). Twenty to 30% of nonclinical (low-risk) infants observed are avoidantly attached to their mothers (Main, 1995).

Infants classified as *resistant* or *ambivalent* tend to have parents who are inconsistently available, responsive, and perceptive of their needs. At times, their parents intrude their own states of mind onto these infants, who are at risk of developing what Winnicott called a "false self." As babies, they react to inconsistency by being hard to soothe and they seem anxious. Resistant or ambivalent infants show little interest in exploring or playing with the toys, seem preoccupied with their mothers and may be distressed even prior to the physical separation. When the mothers return, these infants do not seem to take comfort and fail to settle down. During the ISS, they typically seek proximity to the mother when she returns to the room but apparently do not feel secure enough to return to play. Five to 15% of infants observed have resistant or ambivalent attachments to their mothers (Ainsworth et al., 1978).

Insecure attachment, especially the *disorganized* pattern, occurs with maltreated infants (Rogosch, Cicchetti, Shields, & Toth, 1995). Infants classified as disorganized/disoriented tend to have parents who communicate to them in a frightened, frightening, or disorienting manner (Main & Solomon, 1990). In the ISS, during the reunion with their mothers these infants exhibit such behaviors as "freezing" in a trancelike state or turning in circles (Main & Hesse, 1990; Main & Soloman, 1990). Approximately 80% of disorganized attachments are associated with parental maltreatment. Not surprisingly this attachment style is also associated with more social, cognitive, and emotional problems later in life (Ogawa et al., 1997).

The first response of children in need of help is a cry for help. But if no help arrives, children hyperaroused with anxiety turn inward for a sense of safety, essentially going away from the traumatic situation. If the situation goes on too long, the baby is likely to shift into a pattern (or *attractor*) of dissociation (Perry et al., 1995). Disorganized/disoriented infants appear disconnected, and their responses seem inappropriate to the conditions in the room. For children who begin the developmental journey with a disorganized attachment to caregivers, both internal and external help is experienced as unreliable and they are forced to rely instead on their own infantile self-regulatory schematas.

Other research approaches, such as monitoring blood for cortisol levels and frame-by-frame analyses of videotaped interactions between moms and babies, give us a model for understanding how experiences such as those modeled in the ISS can have such lasting consequences. In studies using a technique called "still face," for example, the mother suddenly adopts a fixed neutral expression, resisting the infant's robust attempts to get her to interact with her normal repertoire of facial and verbal communications. When the babies get tired of trying to get a response, they typically cry, fuss, or break off visual contact and appear withdrawn. Even after the mother resumes her normally expressive communications, the infant is likely to persist in his negative mood. Tronic (1989) interprets this as evidence that even very young infants must have the capacity to "recall" previous experiences. Three-month old infants "are not simply under the control of the immediate stimulus [and these] events have lasting effects, that is, they are internally represented" (Tronik, 1989, p. 114). Such representations are nonconscious and embedded in the brain's implicit memory systems. They will never attain consciousness. The attachment literature teaches us that babies use these early representations to construct what become in effect, "rules." These are schemata that guide the child's choices and predispose him to feel certain emotions through subsequent interpersonal encounters of even the most intimate kind. As Beebe and Lachmann (2002) summarize the conclusions of many infant studies, "the infant forms prototypes, that is, generalized categories or models of patterns and interactions, which become represented as 'rules' of the relationship. A self-regulatory style is represented within these prototypes of patterns of interaction" (p. 175). From the point of view of child therapy, this is to say that from the beginning, the child's sense of self is *embedded in interactions* with caregivers and others, such as the therapist, to whom the child has the opportunity to become attached.

CROSS-CULTURAL VARIATIONS

Some cultures seem to promote one attachment type over another. In northern Germany, for example, a preponderance of avoidant patterns of attachment have been reported (Grossman et al., 1981). In Japan, there is apparently a preponderance of ambivalent and hard-to-soothe infants (Miyake et al., 1986; Takahashi, 1990). Among kibbutzim in Israel, studies indicate that infants become unusually upset when the stranger enters the attachment testing situations (see Saarni et al., 1998, for a review). Security measures adopted to protect the community from terrorist attacks create a generalized distrust of strangers. It is hypothesized that because infants are very sensitive to the emotional communication of others, they internalize this reaction (Saarni et al., 1998). How does this occur? Beebe and Lachmann (2002) document the importance of "cross-modal matching" in the infant's brain. For example, within an hour of birth most infants demonstrate the capacity to link the visual cortex with the part of the premotor cortex that controls facial expression, giving infants the capacity to imitate the facial expressions of those around them. In the ensuing weeks and months, the brain develops powerful linkages between the infant's internal emotional state and perceived cues of the emotional state of others. As Beebe and Lachmann (2002) report:

> Davidson and Fox [1982] showed that, by 10 months, the brain is . . . lateralized for positive and negative affect. As an infant watched a video of a laughing actress, his brain showed the pattern of positive affects (EEG activation of the left frontal lobe). As an infant watched a video of a crying actress, his brain showed a pattern of negative affect (EEG activation of the right frontal lobe). Thus, the mere perception of emotion in the partner creates a resonant emotional state in the perceiver. (p. 37)

Infants within a particular culture adapt to specific parenting styles that are more common in that culture and develop particular types of patterns of attachment. For example, in northern Germany, it is not uncommon for mothers to leave infants briefly unattended at home or even outside of supermarkets. Infants adapt to these exposures to separateness by learning to be less reliant on their attachments. When the mothers return, these infants often show muted or no reaction. Not surprisingly, 49% of the infants tested using the ISS employed these essentially avoidant strategies to cope with the structured separations.

In Japan, by contrast, mothers and infants are rarely separated. Babysitting is uncommon and when it does occur, it generally involves the grandparents. During the ISS, unusual numbers of Japanese infants get very upset and are hard to console after reunion. Interestingly, the attachment exerts a stronger influence than does temperament variables. For example, Japanese infants have been reported to be significantly less irritable than European-American infants; they also have a lower frequency of an allele for the serotonin-transporter genes associated with irritability (Kumakira et al., 1991). Yet in the ISS, Japanese infants show greater anxiety. This suggests the degree to which infants develop expectancies and make predictions based on experiences that are consistent and repeatable. These expectancies are an early cognitive strategy with important uses in affective self-regulation. Babies do not appreciate it when these expectations are not met and will try to countercondition their parents into complying.

Ideally, whatever the cultural demands, children learn to maintain flexibly organized behavior in the face of a highly aroused state or tension. Variations in the capacity to adapt forms the core of individual personality differences (Sroufe, 1996). In essence, attachment theory shows us the extent to which we learn *how* to feel in early relationships, and that what we learn to do with these feelings is affected by the culture we live in as it is mediated through the attachment relationship.

ATTACHMENT, EMOTION REGULATION, AND PSYCHOPATHOLOGY

Securely attached children are empowered to look outward toward the world because they are in possession of what Erik Erikson (1963) called "basic trust." These children have implicit mental models of a secure base that are as nonconscious and enduring as the motor schema for upright locomotion. Stored in implicit memory, these models later cause us to be attracted to other people or find them aversive. Ambivalently attached children endure inconsistently available parents. The distress of these children becomes a dominant affect in their relationships later in life.

They look to others for help in regulating their emotional lives yet are likely to feel they are venturing out onto thin ice every time they rely on others for support and understanding. They put up with people who are unreliable, though familiar, *because* these strangers are inconsistent. Cozolino (2006) suggests that attachment schemata "contain a prediction of the likelihood that being with others will result in a positive or negative emotional state" (p. 183). Siegel (1999) points out that these schemata allow us from childhood onward to create generalizations and summaries of past experiences.

Attachment research indicates that babies with a secure attachment are likely to experience more positive relationships and life satisfaction. Good-enough parenting is optimal because a good dose of frustration helps drive development. The great cognitive-developmental psychologist Jean Piaget referred to the mind's capacity to resolve discrepancies between existing developmental structures and novel stimuli as "accommodation" (Piaget, 1951, 1952). Discrepancies between existing neurodynamic systems and environmental input provoke activation of networks in the left prefrontal cortex—the seat of conscious planning and a part of the brain associated with positive emotional experience. In the process, this left activation helps suppress the stormy moods and social withdrawal that are characteristic of right-hemisphere processing. (Recall that right-hemispheric dominance is a characteristic of mood disorders both in early childhood and later on.)

The quality of early attachments affects the unfolding development of social competence in childhood. Securely attached infants and preschoolers have been shown to be more confident, more empathic, more popular with peers, and are more cooperative (Thompson, 1999; Weinfield, Stroufe, Egeland, & Carlson, 1999). They also are better at regulating their emotions (Conteras, Kerns, Weiner, Gentzler, & Tomich, 2000). In contrast, insecurely attached children are likely to be negatively biased when interpreting the behavior of other people (Conteras et al., 2000). Insecure children interpret being bumped by another child as motivated by ill will, while the securely attached child tends to interpret it as an accident.

Based on a meta-analytic analysis of the literature, a significant but modest association was found between attachment types in the ISS and emotional clusters correlated with temperament (Fox, Kimmerly, & Schafer, 1991). Irritable babies create more stress for parents. If the parents also struggle with economic, social, or other environmental stressors, they may well respond to their infant with less sensitivity. Over time, this combination of infant irritability and parental strains contributes to the development of an insecure attachment relationship (Vaughn & Bost, 1999).

Sroufe and colleagues (Sroufe, Egeland, Carlson, & Collins, 2005) conducted a 30-year longitudinal study of 180 children born into poverty, taking multiple assessments beginning before birth and throughout the 30 years. The investigators paid careful attention to attachment relationships, temperament styles, and other factors that influence development. With respect to attachment, Sroufe et al. (2005) found resistant and avoidant attachment styles were associated with the development of later depression. These researchers proposed that avoidant attachments lead to depression based on a sense of alienation, whereas adults with anxious attachments get depressed because of an internalized sense of helplessness and doubt. Disorganized attachment is linked with adult dissociative disorders.

In contrast to their findings about attachment style, Sroufe and colleagues (2005) found that the more innate factor of temperament was not strongly associated with later psychiatric problems. In cases where temperament did have predictive value, it was as one of a set of interactive variables, which were predominantly experiential. Some relationship in these studies was found between temperament and anxious attachment. When the infants scored low on irritability, the sensitivity of maternal care became a more important factor, whereas high infant irritability muted this effect. Sroufe and colleagues (2005) summed up these interactions between temperament and parenting by noting that:

> Irritability predicts crying in the Strange Situation, especially during separations, but not settling and returning to play during reunions. Thus, maternal sensitivity distinguished secure and insecure infants, and temperament predicted type of insecurity and a sub-category placement. (p. 112)

It appears that the interaction between temperament and variations in maternal behavior is more important for infants who are vulnerable to distress than for those who are less fretful or irritable (Mangelsdorf, Gunnar, Vestenbaum, Lang, & Adresas, 1990).

These findings strongly support the idea that vulnerability to psychological problems later in life is a product of early childhood experience. The more prolonged the exposure to the pathogenic situation (e.g. parenting that is not attuned to infantile needs), the more difficult it is to change the long-term consequences. There is strong research support for the universally held view of child therapists that the earlier a problem is recognized and treated, the better the outcome is likely to be and that early intervention can head off later problems.

Sroufe and colleagues (2005) advocate for early intervention with parents as soon as the child's vulnerability becomes obvious, especially if risk factors, such as extreme environmental stressors and disturbed attachment relationships, are present. In another longitudinal study, Caspi and colleagues (2003) compared data from assessments of one hundred 3-year-old children to the self-assesments of these subjects at age 26. The investigators captured follow-up data from 96% of the original sample and found remarkable continuity between the observations made by others at age 3 and the subjects' self-reported assessments of their adult personalities. Subjects who were notably undercontrolled at age 3 tended, at age 26, to describe themselves as more labile, more alienated, and experiencing higher stress. Those who were inhibited and high on avoidance at age 3 were low on positive emotionality, social potency, and achievement as young adults.

Early attachment occurs before two vitally important developmental landmarks: the development of language, and the shift from right- to left-hemisphere dominance. While the right hemisphere appraises situations, contextualizes them, and establishes their meaning, the left hemisphere brings into play language and social skills that modify the right hemisphere's bias toward introversion and negativity. The brain's development unfolds partly on the basis of genetic instructions and in part as a product of early attachment relationships.

ADULT ATTACHMENT

Mary Main and her colleagues at the University of California, Berkeley, have shown that the attachment history of parents is a powerful predictor of how they behave toward their child and how they respond to their baby's inborn temperament (Main, 1995). Using an interview instrument called the Adult Attachment Inventory (AAI), Main and others have examined the relationship between early childhood experience and adult adjustment and the relationship between the attachment style of the parents and that of their infants. The AAI is essentially a structured developmental autobiography that yields a reliable estimation of parental attachment style.

Parents of infants with a secure attachment style are statistically likely to have detailed episodic memories of their own childhoods and to view their own parents and childhoods in an emotionally nuanced and realistic way. However, what matters most in terms of the predictive power of these autobiographical stories is their narrative *coherence*. Coherence—a product of integration between left and right prefrontol cortical faculties—matters even more than the incidence of actual trauma or loss in the histories of these subjects.

Philip Shaver (1999) found that 55% of adults fall into the "secure" category of adult attachment. With reasonable ease these adults get close to others and feel comfortable in relationships. They expect their partners to be emotionally available and to support them during hardship. They feel worthy of affection and care. Their relationships tend to be trusting and intimate. Approximately 20% of adult subjects demonstrate anxious attachment styles. This group worries that their partners do not really love them. They feel unworthy, tend to be clingy, and are prone to obsessive preoccupations with love and security. They worry about abandonment and are prone to jealousy. Avoidant attachment styles are about as common as the anxious type. People with the avoidant schemata are uncomfortable in intimate relationships. They have a hard time trusting their partners and generally do not verbalize or otherwise directly express their feelings. Their emotional reactions tend to be consciously unavailable and they expect their partners to be untrustworthy.

Generations of attachment researchers have demonstrated robust and persistent correlations between the parent's attachment schema and that of the child (Main et al., 1985). Main started her explorations of the mother–infant relationship with Bowlby's concept that the product of the child's primary attachment experiences is the gradual construction of an "internal working model." The model functions as a portable secure base, allowing the child to balance relatedness and free exploration of the environment (Bowlby, 1969). Main went on to demonstrate that only individuals with a secure attachment could be said to have a *singular* attachment schema; everyone else suffers from inconsistency and unpredictability. Singularity confers abundant advantages emotionally, cognitively, and relationally throughout life. Everyone else, according to Main, builds "multiple models" of how to feel and what's supposed to happen in relationships. Unlike the secure model that fosters relational ease and flexible exploratory behavior, multiple models are made to accommodate the inconsistencies of a caregiver's foibles. A parent with narcissistic tendencies who is by turns available and unavailable to the child—or a depressed parent who is loving but frequently preoccupied—requires the child to develop a "false self" in order to compensate for the ups and downs.

Secure attachment is probably a distributed variable; some people have attained it, others not, and many are somewhere in between. The latter two groups share, to one degree or another, the problematic cognitive and emotional qualities Main attributed to insecure individuals. Moreover, parents who in other circumstances pass for secure will not do so under the prolonged duress of parenting a difficult child. Stress reveals that they are actually endowed with multiple models and widely different capacities for parenting. Although attachment researchers habitually look at the impact of parents on the formation of the child's attachment schema, working with troubled children teaches us to look at the child's effects on the parents as well.

METACOGNITION AND SELF-REGULATION

Main's ideas about the multiple models of attachment that are the legacy of an insecure or inconsistent primary relationship led her to formulate the theory-bridging concept of *metacognition* (Main, 1991). Operating like Piaget's formal operations—a way of thinking that allows us to think *about* thinking and to conduct increasingly sophisticated thought experiments in our minds—metacognition puts relationships and emotion regulation on a different plane. It allows secure individuals to think about mental life in general and question its particulars. Metacognition gives us the capacity to appreciate the "merely representational nature" of our own (or others') thoughts and feelings. It allows us to notice that we are "in a mood" right now and speculate about why. Lacking this cognitive tool, we are more likely to feel we are *in* the mood than that the mood is in *us*; without this faculty, states of mind subsume identity (see Wallin, 2007, for a review).

In our opinion, Main's greatest contribution has been this, her understanding of how security leaves the infant with a single, integrated model that fosters the later construction of a particular kind of cognitive structure. The baby represents viscerally and neurodynamically the mother's emotional expressions and her reactions to his communications, developing expectancies about what follows what in an encounter, what is likely to work, and what is not permitted. Infants develop a sense of self in the context of other selves, imitating their mothers and seeing themselves imitated in return. The baby learns, rhythmically, to anticipate the response to an action (such as crying or seeking contact) and in this way begins to put together myriad bodily and emotional events into an experience of an actor, a self. The mutual interactions of the mother and infant stimulates cross-modal regulation between the limbic areas and the right hemisphere of the cortex, such that an implicit set of "rules" regarding the self and others is eventually arrived at. When fully developed, metacognition liberates the child from the grasp of innate factors such as temperament, giving him the power to think about feelings and anticipate the consequences of reacting. It is a way of thinking that exploits the full neurodynamic potential for psychological self-regulation.

CHAPTER 4

Rupture and Repair in Caregiving Relationships

As human beings, our greatness lies not so much in being able to remake the world—that is the myth of the atomic age—as in being able to remake ourselves.

—Mahatma Gandhi

ATTUNEMENT BETWEEN A baby and her mother confers a wealth of benefits on the very young child. An attuned relationship leads to the capacity to identify and regulate emotions later in life and the lack of one is associated with emotional dysregulation and alexithymia (from the Greek "without words for emotions"). As discussed in Chapter 3, attunement does not require perfectly consistent matches between mothers and infants. In fact the "good enough" standard includes the idea that some mismatching is optimal. It gives the baby opportunities for developing more robust self-regulatory schemata and builds the infantile brain. From the caretaker's side of things, mismatching provides the opportunity to work on repairing ruptures in the relationship, an essential skill in maintaining the security of the parent-child relationship. In repair as in mirroring, however, a shared capacity for accurately reading emotions in the other party is a basic requirement of secure parent-child relationships. Poor attunement interferes with the child's ability to read emotional cues from facial expressions and tone of voice. It stunts children's development of the "theory of mind" required to accurately model what significant others are thinking and feeling.

Studies of the brain systems that down-regulate levels of the major hormones of stress—the glucocorticoids (GCs)—suggest that early positive maternal care protects the hippocampus from the destructive physiological effects of stress (Meaney et al., 2001). The hippocampus is the "mapper" that translates the ongoing flow of experience into explicit memory (and thus is fundamental to children's subjective experience of themselves). It is the gatekeeper that determines what will enter the stream of explicit memories that are stored elsewhere in the brain. Traumatic stress or poor maternal care exposes the hippocampus to the impact of GCs (in humans, cortisol) without the protective negative feedback system that shuts down GC production. Prolonged exposure of the hippocampus to high levels of GCs results in its actual physical shrinkage (Bremner et al., 1997). This fact on its own suggests the degree to which the quality of maternal care affects the developing child's brain, but there are many other neurodynamic consequences of maternal care as well.

ATTACHMENT RUPTURES AND THE BRAIN

Abused children are hypervigilant for signs that abuse may occur again. They show increased startle responses; they tend to perceive anger in neutral or even sad faces; and their brains show stronger resting-state activation than the brains of nonabused children (Pollack, 2001). They also tend to take more time to scan faces for potentially angry expressions (Pollack & Tolley-Schell, 2003).

The quality of attachment in all relationships at any age varies on a moment-by-moment basis. The parties involved sometimes are completely lost in their own subjectivity and at other times are keenly aware of what the other person is feeling or they are acutely aware of what *they* are feeling toward the other party in the interaction. An acute breakdown in attunement—or, more likely, a significant number of such incidents— negatively impacts the construction of the neural circuitry of emotion regulation in children (Schore, 1994). If the parent "repairs" these ruptures, however, a child's neural system benefits not only from the restoration of parental "mindsight" but from the example of how to restore a problematic relationship. Ruptures in the child's sense of parental attunement inevitably occur when the parent makes the child wait for gratification or denies it. These experiences promote independence and the internalization of self-discipline. It is part of the therapist's job to help parents and children articulate what these experiences feel like and to try to understand what they feel like to the other party. Ultimately, we are helping children to integrate connections between their prefrontal cortex and subcortical areas to learn to regulate affect. In the process, parents may learn about parenting and their own child and about their own attachment and emotion-regulation schemata as well. We could say that enhancing what Mary Main (1991) called metacognition is the goal of all child therapies.

Regulating affect is a main function of the orbitofrontal area of the frontal lobes—the part of the brain right behind the eyes. Damage to the orbitofrontal cortex (OFC) results in diminished capacity to inhibit urges, impulses, and emotional expressions. People with OFC damage are impulsive and emotionally uninhibited. As adults, they can be reckless drivers on the road. While walking through stores, they may shoplift on impulse and, if caught, overreact, perhaps resisting arrest. Interpersonally, they can be rude, sexually inappropriate, boastful, selfish, and antisocial. Not surprisingly, individuals with damaged OFCs have more frequent run-ins with the police and the legal system. Over 100 years ago, neurologists in Europe called the constellation of problems arising from OFC damage pseudopsychopathic syndrome. Atypical development of the OFC is no doubt a contributing factor in some of the oppositional conduct disorders we see in our offices.

Infants and their parents develop an interactional synchrony that allows both parties to be "on" or "off" at the same time (Kaye, 1982). This synchrony between infants and parents may involve turn taking, as when the mother smiles or makes a cooing sound to her baby, and the baby orients and responds in kind. For the infant, turn taking represents the first dialog between self and another person (Mayer & Tronik, 1985). Reciprocity is disrupted when the mother displays no facial expression at all or gives nonverbal signals that are incongruent with her tone of voice or the affect appropriate to the interaction. In the "still face" studies we discussed in Chapter 3, mothers deliberately presented a blank and expressionless face to their babies, and the babies reactions were closely documented (Ellworth, Muir, & Hains, 1993; Segal et al., 1995). Initially, the babies in these studies attempted to engage their mothers by vocalizing, pointing, and looking inquisitively at them. When the mothers failed to respond, the babies showed growing signs of distress and protested. Eventually, their babies looked away and withdrew. How often such experiences are repeated in the baby's normal setting are likely to become as deeply structured neurodynamically as innate temperament factors.

MATERNAL DEPRESSION

People born with a genetic predisposition to depression may not actually develop it. Whether they do so or not is likely to be a matter of exposure to complex environmental triggers, and one of the most powerful of these is the presence of a mood disorder in the mother's history. Maternal depression affects children pre- and postnatally. In a sample of depressed pregnant women, the fetuses showed higher baseline heart rate and heightened sensitivity to vibroacoustic stimulation (Allister, Lester, Carr, & Liu, 2001; Monk et al., 2004). These indications of a fetal brain in a dysregulated state are consistent with a pattern that is a precursor to mature depressive states.

Postpartum, common results of the mother's depressive disorder include disruptions in the attunement between mother and infant. One of the tenets of attachment theory is that children must, for Darwinian reasons of survival, adapt to their parents. Thus, children of depressed parents do their utmost to accommodate to the emotional climate set by their parents. When their baby cries, needs comforting, or nurturance, depressed mothers may be too overwhelmed to respond (Meaney, 2001). If mothers are asked in an experimental situation to feign depression, their babies became transiently distressed as well. When mothers decrease the quality of their facial displays, minimize body movements, limit physical contact, and talk in a slow monotone, their babies cry more and arch their backs (Cohen & Tronick, 1982). Depressed mothers tend to look away from their babies and get angrier than mothers who are not depressed. They also tend to be more intrusive and less warm. More often than do nondepressed mothers, they have problems synchronizing the timing of interactions with their infants. When their babies cry, depressed mothers have difficulty soothing them. They lack the energy to smile and talk in the lilting tones of "motherese" that nondepressed mothers use for intimate proto-conversations with their babies.

Infants tend to generalize their reactions to the moods of their mothers, developing attachment schemata for managing interpersonal affects. Thus, children of depressed mothers show depressed behavior even in the presence of nondepressed adults (Field et al., 1995). Reporting an exception to this widely supported finding, one study found that children of depressed mothers exhibited no more sadness, withdrawal, or passivity than other children in a common preschool environment (Pelaez-Nogueras, Field, Cigales, Gonzalez, & Clasky, 1994). Although resilience in relation to depressive mothering is a function of many factors, maternal depression, on average, bequeaths multiple deficits and developmental problems to infants, deficits that are expressed neurobiologically and behaviorally (Field, 2005). Infants of depressed mothers show more aversion and helplessness, and they vocalize less. They have higher heart rates, decreased vagal tone, and exhibit delays in development at 12 months of age. Using the Infant Strange Situation, Gunnar and Vazquez (2006) report that cortisol levels predict the security of the infant's attachment style with depressed mothers. By the end of the first year of life, secure attachment optimally provides a stress buffer for an infant or toddler in the presence of the attachment figure. In contrast, unresponsive, insensitive, or intrusive maternal care does not. Depressed mothers often are sufficiently withdrawn from reality that the attentional capacities of "good enough" attunement are simply beyond them.

What we see in the behavioral and attachment studies of the effects of maternal deprivation is consistent with research on depression's neurodynamic and neurochemical effects on babies. The hormone cortisol is used as a neurodynamic marker of stress. Elevated cortisol levels are implicated in both anxiety disorders and depression. Cortisol activates many parts of the brain, has a normal daily cycle, and—through the power of the threat-sensitive amygdala to control its release—is an effective agent for jump-starting our reactions to short-term stressors. The cortisol cycle is *supposed* to peak and subside in a relatively brief period of time. Under the impact of chronic stress, however, cortisol levels peak, stay elevated, and do not return to baseline. Stable elevated levels of cortisol shrink the hippocampus (impacting its encoding of new explicit memories) and activate the amygdala (perpetuating the elevated-cortisol dysregulation). The normal cortisol cycle begins with a spurt in the morning to get us out of bed and tapers off in the evening before bedtime. Dysregulated cortisol cycles can be a cause of insomnia.

The specific impacts of maternal depression on the cortisol cycle may be to some extent a matter of the particular infants involved, but the general pattern shows strong relationship between maternal depression and dysregulated cycles in the infant. Although the general finding is heightened cortisol (Dawson & Ashman, 2000), in one study, *low* morning cortisol levels in 3-year-olds were associated with how clinically depressed the mother was during the child's first year of life. Ashman and colleagues also found that the presence of maternal depression during the first 2 years of a child's life was the best predictor of the child's cortisol production at 7 years of age (Ashman, Dawson, Panagiotgides, Yamada, & Wilkinson, 2002). The dysregulation of the cycle sometimes defies the usual pattern in other ways as well. Adolescents whose mothers were depressed during their first year were found to have one or more days of *elevated* cortisol in the morning (Halligan, Herbert, Goodyer, & Murray, 2004).

Depressed mothering apparently induces other features of the neurochemistry of depression in their infants. In one study, infants with depressed mothers showed both higher levels of stress hormones and reduced levels of dopamine and serotonin (Field et al., 1998). Children with low levels of these neurotransmitters are likely to have more difficulty regulating their emotions and exhibit delays in developing a capacity to engage others with synchrony (Tronick & Weinberg, 1997).

The abnormalities one sees in the neurodynamics of infants with depressed mothers are typical of what one sees in the brains of depressed older children and adults. People with more activity in the right prefrontal cortex (PFC), that part of the right frontal lobe at the very front of the brain, experience more negative affect and react more to sad events or stories. By contrast, the higher the level of *left* PFC activation, the happier and more optimistic the subject is likely to feel (Hugdahl & Davidson, 2003). These same neurodynamic and emotion-regulation tendencies are seen in infants. Children of depressed mothers show an overactivation of the right frontal lobe and underactivation of the left frontal lobe. Infants who are crying or sad show greater right-frontal electroencephalogram (EEG) activity; infants displaying what has been called "approach emotions," such as action-oriented behaviors and happiness, show more left-frontal EEG activity (Bell & Fox, 1994). Infants of depressed mothers show a disruption in the integration of right- and left-hemispheric processing (Dawson et al., 1997). Right-frontal asymmetry (i.e., more right PFC activity) is associated both with feeling more negative emotions more often and with heightened difficulty in modulating negative mood. Increased right PFC activity is also linked with heightened responsiveness to negative stimuli and a predisposition to withdrawal behaviors.

Theoretically, infants of depressed mothers are at some risk for underdevelopment of their left hemispheres. Recall the Hebbian principle that the nervous system is predisposed to do what it has done before. We are inclined to keep doing whatever we are *already* doing or know how to do. The left PFC in the infant's brain, which processes joy, is less likely to be activated by interactions with a depressed mother who rarely, if ever, feels joyful herself. The left hemispheres of these infants are likely to remain unengaged while their right hemispheres are disproportionately stimulated by the mother's depressive affects and behavior. EEG studies of infants of depressed mothers illustrate this pattern—dampened left-hemisphere functioning and increased activation of the right hemisphere (Field et al., 1995). If maternal depression has gone on for more than a year, infants show prolonged impairment in left-hemisphere activation (Dawson, 1994).

A shy child, too, may bias right frontal over left frontal lobe activity, whereas an active and bold child may show the reverse tendency. Developmental studies suggest that attachment experiences and temperament tendencies may influence these asymmetrical types of frontal activation (Dawson, 1994; Field, Fox, Pickens, & Nawrocki, 1995). When mothers are depressed and the number of shared positive emotional states is decreased, both mother and infant typically are seen as withdrawn, and both tend to exhibit decreased left frontal activity. If depression continues, this pattern of cerebral activation may continue beyond the first year of life (Dawson, 1994). For example, preschool children of depressed mothers show right-frontal EEG asymmetry and lack of empathy (Jones et al., 2000). They have also been shown to have EEG abnormalities while processing facial expressions (Diego et al., 2004).

Zahn-Waxler and colleagues (Zahn-Waxler & Radke-Yarrow, 1990; Zahn-Waxler, Cole, & Baraett, 1991) noted that children whose mothers were chronically depressed appeared overwhelmed and overly responsible in their interactions with their mothers. Some of the children developed a repertoire of precocious strategies to "repair" their mothers' unhappiness. Neurodynamically predisposed and socialized to be attuned to relationships and to feel responsible for the well-being of others (Brizendine, 2007), girls may be particularly vulnerable to investing inordinate emotional energy in repairing their depressed mothers.

Dealing with the sequelae of maternal depression is a major challenge for child therapists. Whereas fathers often find ways to absent themselves, mothers typically do not leave, but they do get depressed. As part of the mood disorder, they have problems controlling their emotions, are quicker to show anger, and engage less with their children. And their children respond to maternal deprivation by missing the exploration, play, and engagement with other children that drives the development of the brain in childhood. In a summing up of the large body of literature on infants of depressed mothers, Cicchetti and Curtis (2006) write:

> [The] inability of mothers with depressive disorder to provide their children with adequate positive emulsion and to facilitate their children's self regulation of emotion not only affects their children's behavioral regulation capacities but also exerts an impact on neurobiological systems that underlie those capacities. (p. 38)

There is much in the literature on the effects of maternal depression for clinicians to ponder. On its face, the research points out the importance of screening for the possibility of a mood disorder in mothers (in fact, in both parents) at the outset of treatment. Treating maternal depression is every bit as important as treating the child's. Early identification of maternal depression could result in a more organized and upstream approach to the problems of child mental health. In one study, mothers were taught a simple technique of massaging their infants that positively affected bonding and altered the course of attachment (Field, 1997). In another successful program, parents were coached in how to express positive emotions and communicate affection and care for their children (Cumberland-Li, 2003). Ultimately, a thoughtful consideration of maternal depression and the burden of suffering it involves must lead child therapists to advocate for a more integrated and accessible behavioral healthcare system.

STRESS, DEVELOPMENT, AND PARENTAL ABUSE

Stress, no less than maternal depression, impacts the child's developing brain and influences subsequent psychological development. Prenatal stress has been associated with multiple medical problems. Hyperactivity, irritability, language deficits, and lower IQ scores have all been identified as consequences of maternal stress (Hansen et al., 2000). Severe stress during pregnancy changes fetal neurotransmitter levels and prematurely activates the hypothalamic-pituitary-adrenal (HPA) axis, which is an important stress-response regulation system in the body (Gunnar and Vazquez, 2006).

Stress is prenatally contagious. Elevated cortisol levels in the fetuses of chronically stressed pregnant mothers produce corrosive effects on the developing brain (Essex, Klein, Eunsuk, & Kalin, 2002). Prolonged prenatal cortisol elevation inhibits fetal neurogenesis (the production of new neurons, including stem cells), promotes the dysregulation of neuronal migration patterns, and even appears to result in an irreversible loss of brain weight (Edwards & Burnham, 2001). Prolonged high concentrations of cortisol can prenatally suppress the immune system and produce hypertension (Maccari et al., 2003). Postpartum, these prenatal events are likely to result in a child who is more difficult and challenging to take care of, ratcheting up the chances of yet more environmental stress in the mother's life. In one study, Halligan and colleagues reported that adolescents with elevated cortisol levels had more trouble regulating their stress than did normal teens (Halligan et al., 2004).

Stress affects the ability of the brain to grow and thrive. Brain-derived neurotropic factor (BDNF) is a neuropeptide that acts as a kind of fertility drug for neurons, at least in the hippocampus and probably in other areas of the brain as well. The production of new hippocampal neurons is particularly important in the development of healthy memory functions. As noted above, the hippocampus is adversely affected by elevated cortisol; in some depressed subjects, the hippocampus appears to have lost 20% of its volume, presumably as an effect of chronic cortisol exposure. One theory holds that BDNF, in addition to nurturing neurons to reinforce crucial hippocampal functions, also erects a sort of chemical shield to protect the hippocampus from cortisol's corrosive effects. Stress takes its toll even on this protective system, however, reducing overall BDNF and messenger-RNA levels.

Early stressors generate neurodynamic effects in fetuses and young infants that can result in a cascade of negative effects in subsequent developmental periods. Children under stress may become less flexible in new situations and fall back on old behavioral responses rather than inventing new ones. Their responses to environmental change are limited by the imperative of the Hebbian legacy of pathological sensitivity and heightened physiological reactivity (Cicchetti & Curtis, 2006). As a result of the lack of fit between these defensive strategies and the environmental problems they are designed to solve, children under stress are likely to experience much more failure and negative feedback than children who are more fortunate. This forecast is especially probable for children coping with the internalized effects of physical, emotional, and sexual abuse. Childhood abuse has been identified as a factor in diminished left-hemisphere activation and left-hippocampal volume and development (Bremner et al., 1997). Some brain-imaging studies report a similar finding of problems in the integration of the left- and right-hemisphere functions, probably as the result of diminished corpus callosum size, especially in boys (Teicher, 2003). Adults physically or sexually abused as children have been found to have incomplete left-hippocampal development (see Howe, Toth, & Cicchetti, 2006 for review).

The cingulate cortex—the area of the brain right next to the corpus colosum—has many cortisol receptors and is correspondingly sensitized to the impact of this stress hormone. The cingulate cortex (and the most forward, or *anterior*, part, the *anterior cingulate cortex* [ACC]) participates with the frontal lobes in mediating goal-directed behavior. The cingulate directs efficient attention and inhibits irrelevant or impulsive actions; it helps generate what psychodynamic therapists refer to as "aim-inhibited activity" (Markowitsch, Vanderkerckhove, Lanfermann, & Russ, 2003; Stuss et al., 2002). Research reports that increased levels of cortisol affect the self-control of preschool aged children when they are engaged in challenging tasks, probably as an artifact of cortisol-ACC interaction (Gunnar, Tout, deHaan, Pierce, & Stansburg, 1997).

Cortisol is implicated in a range of problems, from simply being "stressed out" to depression and generalized anxiety. These problems actually arise from a dysregulation in the normal self-limiting cycle of the HPA and the subsequent release of cortisol. After a spike in cortisol induced by sustained stress, cortisol receptors at various sites in the brain (including the hippocampus) are supposed to signal the amygdala that there is no cause for alarm. As long as the amygdala remains activated, however, this is not what is likely to occur. Cortisol levels stay high. Abused children have significantly elevated morning cortisol levels relative to other maltreated and nonmaltreated children (Cicchetti & Rogosch, 2001a). Different patterns of initial cortisol levels and daily fluctuation are linked with basic psychological defense constellations, such as internalizing and externalizing styles. These differences, in turn, are associated with whether the child has been abused or not.

Childhood adversity has been associated with the diminished potential for adult neurogenesis (Mirescu, Peters, & Gould, 2004). The ACC seems to play an important role in the expression of posttraumatic stress disorder (PTSD). Perhaps because of the effects of cortisol and other stress hormones, in people with PTSD, the ACC is abnormally inhibited in response to emotionally charged stimuli (Bremner et al., 2004).

Based on their 30-year longitudinal study, Sroufe and colleagues (2005) found that some form of abuse was the strongest predictor of childhood depression. Next was maternal depression, with an impact dramatically greater for girls. By adolescence, maternal depression was significant *only* for girls (Sroufe et al., 2005). Although a child's language development—as measured by sentence complexity and the size and lexical richness of the vocabulary—is known to be tightly coupled with socioeconomic status (Hoff, 2003), Cicchetti and colleagues have found similarly powerful links between language development and child abuse (Eigsti & Cicchetti, 2004). Abused children are deprived of the emotional security and neurochemical serenity the brain requires to become all that it can become.

In a review of research on trauma, memory, and developmental neuroscience, Howe and colleagues (2006) note that both explicit and implicit memories are subject to significant modifications as a result of exposure to traumatic events. Among other things, victims of abuse are subject to misleading and false memories. Memories associated with childhood trauma, either physical or sexual, are not easily forgotten or suppressed when the perpetrator was a parent.

> [A]lthough the studies that exist regarding the effects of trauma on memory have some intriguing ideas and speculation, existent empirical studies do not substantiate the theoretical claims that traumatized individuals utilize fundamentally different memory process than non-traumatized persons (p. 638).

In other words, moving a child from so-called "repressed" memories of abuse to a definitive story about what happened through interpretation of vague but emotionally charged memory fragments is both dangerous and probably antitherapeutic. It is likely that any abused child we see in our offices will be in a high degree of conflict about discussing their victimization with us, but not because the events are repressed or not remembered. Play therapy is often an ideal medium for allowing the child to "reconstruct" what happened in a safe and expressive way, and for the therapist to empathize with the conflicts of loyalty, fears of retribution, and overwhelming sense of responsibility many children feel after abusive experiences.

The capacity of children to accurately recognize emotion in other people is much affected by their exposure to situations that require accommodation to too much aggression or too much (or too little) engagement with an adult. Some parents lack the attentional and emotion-regulation skills needed for good-enough parenting. Others cannot reliably self-regulate in a manner that makes child sexual, physical, or mental abuse an absolute taboo. Another group of parents, in which fathers are over-represented, err by absenting themselves from the care and nurture of children. Some experts feel that neglect is the most grievous of these parenting sins. Neglected children who have experienced a lack of care and responsiveness have great difficulty recognizing different emotional states in themselves and in others (Pollack & Sinha, 2002). They more often misunderstand the social dynamics in a situation and are more easily emotionally hurt than children who have no history of neglect. Neglected children are less able to engage in supportive and successful relationships (Lynch & Cicchetti, 1998). By contrast, physically abused children may be as sensitive as controls are in differentiating emotional states in themselves and others. Physically abused children tend more often to see anger in neutral facial expressions than do other children. Neglected children are more likely to have a response bias to see sadness.

Once the therapist has some sense of whether their history includes having to accommodate to a depressed, abusive, or neglectful parent, some basic interventions suggest themselves. For all three groups, psychotherapy can provide a good-enough holding environment that can be both a healing and a learning experience. Talking about feelings and about the various kinds of things that can rupture a relationship—too much sadness, anger, or loss—helps activate the left PFC and shift the balance from an overactive right hemisphere to an appropriate bilateral balance. Even if children have been traumatized and biased to read threat where there is no threat, they can learn to read social skills accurately. As with many other things in the world of children, however, the success and scope of treatment ultimately depends on the goodwill of their parents.

COCONSTRUCTING NARRATIVES

It is an almost universal experience of childhood that the child listens to the parents' stories about family history that include a collection of long-departed or little-known relatives, and convey implicit meanings about values and roles. These stories provide the context for children to see themselves as participants and full members of the family. These narratives play a fundamental role in the interactions between parent and child. Following the development of the explicit memory system, which depends on the maturation of the hippocampus, children and parent(s) coconstruct other narratives, often starring the child himself. Parents help children construct personal histories by telling stories about their infancies, who they were when they were little, and how all the other family members fit into the children's lives. By hearing these narratives in their various versions often enough, children learn how to narrate to *themselves*. As autobiographical and episodic vignettes, these narratives constitute an important part of the content of the explicit memory system and therefore of the child's psychological infrastructure.

Narratives weave a linguistic fabric of personal identity. They provide a kind of map to where children have been and where they are going. As children move toward the future with the continuity of their past, narratives provide a way to organize their own emotional experience.

Language and the left hemisphere's organizational tendencies permit the therapist and child to talk about the child's existing narrative and reconstruct it. Therapists can help children challenge maladaptive narratives and construct new and more adaptive ones. For example, if a child's existing narrative is set in a hostile and rejecting world, and she considers herself in the story as one worthy of being rejected, the inevitable slights, bullying, and social failures of the school day serve to justify the old narrative and rekindle its associated neural nets. The therapist's job is to help this child create a better story for herself—as a survivor, a Pocahontas determined to get back home, a girl who knows her own powers even if nobody else sees them—and encourage her to utilize the new narrative while tolerating the inevitable frustrations as part of the journey.

New narratives help children reorganize how they respond to emotions as they try to make sense of the world and organize their efforts to establish realistic goals. Because narratives provide a way to organize their history over the course of time, they link children with other people and promote an understanding of social context. Part of the story may include autobiographical memories that tell children they have been and continue to be lovable and worthy people. Each time the memories are recalled in therapy, they reactivate the neurodynamics supporting them, strengthening the connections between those neurons. The memories also change with each telling, acquiring something of the present's mood and context. In this way other neurons are enlisted to the therapeutic cause, making those memories more complex and enduring.

Narratives serve to organize how children direct their behavior in the future and modulate their current emotional experience (Siegel, 1999). In the listening and the telling and retelling of a cocreated history, the therapist and child may recapture some of the lucid moments of early childhood, when the parent imitates the child's smile or facial expression and gives it back to the child, as if to say "This is my impression of who you are."

These narrative enactments can be understood as patterns of behavior and communication that steer decision making and communication (Baddeley, 1994). Siegel (1999) describes how children use narratives to navigate through the world, tapping into both implicit and explicit memories:

> Narratives reveal how representations from one system can clearly intertwine with another, thus the mental models of implicit memory help organize the themes of how the details of explicit autobiographical memory are expressed within a life story. Though we can never see mental models directly, their manifestations in narratives allows us to get a view of at least the shadow they cast on the output of other systems of the mind. (p. 63)

Narratives are multilayered because children experience innumerable events in their lives. The contexts for their experiences continue to change, and no single narrative underlies their experience. Because they continue to interact with multiple people, the context of those interactions and children's expectations play a role in the narratives they use. The fluid and changeable nature of social experiences means that children remember themselves through narratives in constantly changing social contexts.

Coconstructing narratives is part of the business of child therapy. Instead of supporting a child in her tendency to be pessimistic around peers, the therapist should help her integrate new social experiences into a constructive narrative. Therapists can take advantage of the fact that memories are revised each time they are retrieved. At the synaptic level, retrieving a memory alters synaptic connections between neurons. On another level, the memory is brought up in a supportive environment fused with comforting feelings, and the new narrative is used to describe the memory and reinterpret it, change it. The memory, in essence, is rewritten from the vantage point of the present.

Language is a primary tool in integrating altered neurodynamic patterns based on new narratives. Primarily a left-hemisphere function, language used in the service of positive and adaptive narratives changes the brain. Originally, narratives are self-stories shaped by interactions with parents, peers, and the context of one's culture. When those narratives do not serve children or adolescents well, the therapist's job is to help them reconstruct those narratives so that the associated neural nets allow them to minimize anxiety, depression, or other psychological problems.

Cognitive therapists identify unrealistically negative thinking and negative self-statements as psychologically destructive (Beck, 1976; Ellis, 1962/1996). Yet narratives are not dependent on one hemisphere or the other. A narrative that is too left-sided has no context and is incoherent. An overly right-hemispheric narrative is impoverished linguistically and makes no sense. How children explain their world and their place in it has a profound effect on their emotional experience.

Narratives in therapy provide the psychological and neurodynamic infrastructure for mental health. The autobiographical narrative weaves together feelings, thoughts, sensations, and actions in ways that organize the internal and external world (Cozolino, 2002). The flip side to Hebbian learning is that every time we do, think, feel, read, or say something new, we are changing our neurodynamics. Therapy utilizes this principle to modify clients' neurodynamics by remodeling the narratives. Say a child is often melancholy and preoccupied with having few friends; she believes other kids are happier and are shunning her. The therapist can remodel some elementary themes as a foundation for a new narrative based on the belief that the client is actually *shy*. The therapist might tell the child that shyness is like a feeling, it comes and goes, like a wandering cat in the neighborhood that can be invited to come in or invited to stay out. If the child takes in this news that shyness and identity are two different things, and shyness is something one can do something about, her neurodynamics will change. With practice, some risk taking, and the therapist's support and patience, the child's support system can grow. New narratives build bridges and integrate neural networks in the present time.

New narratives ordinarily should include themes such as optimism, hopefulness, tenacity, and positive self-perception. A good sense of humor can promote resiliency in the face of adversity. Narratives with these characteristics foster the neural circuitry that becomes the default mode, or attractor, for positive affect. The capacity to recover from negative emotional states is an important aspect of resiliency. Richard Davidson (2000), a pioneer in research on cerebral asymmetry and mood states, proposed that those individuals who generally maintain positive mood states and well-being in the face of the adversity are more resilient and tend to activate their left frontal lobes. Encountering adversity, these individuals typically bounce back to what appears to be this neuropsychological default mode of functioning. Narratives can help clients effect this kind of shift. Given the inherent malleability of memory, negative right-hemisphere-biased memories that constitute the bricks and mortar of old narratives can be remodeled, the old narrative balanced with more nuanced and neurodynamically integrated versions. The therapist can also help children's families create new narratives with more positive attribution biases.

The human brain seems to have an insatiable appetite for stories. The popularity of Hollywood (and Bollywood), of novels, sporting events, the soap opera (which seems to have emerged as a ubiquitous genre on world television) is not an accident. A good story sells. When a parent dies, one of the dilemmas facing the bereaved child is that a lot of her story dies with the parent; there is no one else with whom to cocreate the past. Because these coconstructed narratives preserve some of the most dearly held characters and elements of the past, and because therapy almost always challenges the child to change the narrative to one degree or another, therapy always stirs up feelings, often strong ones, in child clients and other family members. We now turn to a consideration of how to use these important reactions therapeutically.

MANAGING AFFECT

In object-relations theory, the infant's internal life emerges out of the baby's capacity to distinguish, at least transiently, between self and mother. Given a primitive sense of "me" and "not-me," the baby is set up to start fantasizing (an activity many of us go on to give considerable time to throughout our lives). Affect, fantasy, and internalized representations of repeating patterns of interactions with caretakers are bound up together in the formation of schemata theorists call "objects." In infants, emotions sharply distinguish between "good" objects and "bad" ones. A "good" breast provides milk; it is associated with satiation and is loved. A "bad" breast withholds milk when it is wanted; it makes the infant scream with discomfort, and is hated and envied (Klein, 1975). These emotions are extended from part objects, such as the breast, to whole objects, such as the mother, as the child's neurodynamics knit together the impressions from the various senses, and the cortex improves coordination of diverse inputs from all over the brain. Very young infants who want to devour or utterly reject the breast go on to have similar feelings about their mothers. As rage at the bad objects subsides, it normally turns to fear of recrimination or rejection by the object. Although these primitive experiences get cross-referenced with later and more reality-based ones, they never quite lose either their autonomy or their emotional power (Mitchell & Black, 1995). For psychodynamic therapists, this conceptualization of the emotional and subjective aspects of early relationships serves as a way of understanding why patients sometimes act as they do.

Good-enough mothering helps children put some of these very different emotional experiences of the subjective self together in one relationship. Winnicott talks about the importance of such a mother being able to withstand her "ruthless" baby. As she does so, the infant gets the idea that the mother is truly separate from her and that her own feelings and thoughts may not be real in the same way she is. The good versions of these experiences help children soothe and comfort themselves and allow them to feel that they can survive on their own. When children are uncertain or stressed and acutely in contact with their bad self-objects, their mothers' steadiness and empathic skill offers a holding environment they slowly take in as part of themselves. As they venture out into the world, they can, to some extent, take with them an internalized good-enough mother.

Therapists are called in when this affect-taming process needs helping along or when something major has gone wrong with it, and the child is still exposed to internalized terrors and rages. Alan Schore (1994, 2003) has written extensively on the need for therapists to aid children in *affect regulation*. He maintains that "dysregulated" neural systems underlie psychopathology. Therapists help children reregulate affect by assisting them to experience increasing tolerance to levels of positive and negative affect.

Specialized approaches to treatment are often useful in these situations. Behavior therapists, for example, help children manage their affects by using graduated exposure to anxiety-provoking situations such as phobias. Joseph Wolpe, in *Psychotherapy by Reciprocal Inhibition* (1958), helped disseminate the use of systematic desensitization. He proposed that patients combine exposure to the feared stimulus with relaxation exercises to control stress, and suggested that therapists encourage and support patients in meeting the challenge of extinguishing fear.

Therapists can help parents find their own way of encouraging children's explorations and facilitating the expansion of their social world. Sometimes talking with parents about the lessons of the attachment research helps. Most parents readily grasp the significance of this research on the persistence of attachment styles and affect regulation patterns into adulthood. Improved parental caregiving, coaching skills, and modeling in dealing with their children's inevitable disappointments and hurt feelings makes the job of parenting easier and much more gratifying. Parents also usually like to know that the therapist is not just there to be a good guy, like a favorite uncle, who gets to play with the child and has nothing to do with the harder matters of child raising. Good therapists, like good-enough mothers, require that children challenge themselves to confront maladaptive ways of dealing with the world. Doing this typically brings up strong disturbing feelings that inhibit children from taking the risks required to make changes. It is the therapist's job to gently encourage the toleration of bad-object feelings and anxieties.

Affect regulation requires and also helps construct cortical circuits that foster adaptation and maintenance of a sense of personal continuity (Cozolino, 2002; Schore, 1994). Such regulation involves integrating emotions and information. Children learn that they can tolerate intense affects and anticipate both eventual relief from the stress and also the rewarding feelings of mastering adversity. Conarrativizing these brain-building messages can employ different media. The medium can be explicitly conversational, an acted out drama between two action figures, or a by-product of haggling over the sale of a piece of property in Monopoly.

The part of the frontal lobes that lies behind the eyes—the orbitofrontal cortex—is important territory for the child therapist, in that it is the module where highly processed and affect-ladened information converge. In addition, the OFC adds to the neurodynamic process a stream of information from the limbic areas about the affective significance of the experience (Schoenbaum Chiba, & Gallagher, 2003a). The OFC also plays a significant role in controlling behavior during situations of conflict—for example, where the child's values and incentives are put under pressure and revision is being considered (Schoenbaum, Setlow, Nugent, Saddoris, & Gallagher, 2003b). Finally, the OFC reviews and monitors performance, detecting conflict and mistakes as well as how we are feeling about our experiences as they unfold (Carter et al., 2000).

The attachment styles discussed in Chapter 3 represent schemata for regulating affect. The concept of schemata is relevant to both psychodynamic and cognitive psychology. Schemata are created out of the infant's repeating experience as that experience changes the brain and becomes internally represented. Because they are based in interactions that typically have a beginning, middle and end, time and sequence—what follows what—are important elements in most schemata (Beebe & Lachmann, 2002). Schemata allow children to assimilate new information rapidly, by providing an organizational infrastructure that can deal with incoming stimuli. Because emotions prime many different neurodynamic systems, bringing them, as it were, to attention, the formation of schemata is heavily influenced by mood. Attachment styles predispose us to react to new situations in characteristic ways. They set the terms for what we will allow ourselves to think, remember, feel, and do—without even having to think about it (see Wallin, 2007, for an interesting discussion of this rule-setting aspect of attachment). From the outset, relatedness and emotion are tightly coupled with each other, and attachment schemata are rules for regulating affect in such a way that it works in a relationship. According to this view, schemata are similar to the defense mechanisms of psychoanalytic theory. Like Piagetian assimilation, schemata allow us to digest incoming experience without unduly undermining the equilibrium of existing schemata (Piaget & Inhelder, 1969).

Children develop multiple schemata and apply them simultaneously and nonconsciously. Schemata provide feedback to children on their behavior and help them learn from experience. If the experience conflicts with the existing schematic defenses and therefore cannot be assimilated easily, children may try to reject the experience in some way (through, e.g., denial or a flagrant confabulatory explanation) or accommodate to it, allowing the experience to alter their regulatory cognitive and emotional rules. The dialectic between assimilation and accommodation sends a ripple effect through the self system. The brain's capacity for maintaining multiple parallel channels enables maturing children to deal with threats and also with changing social situations; their defenses allow them to do so somewhat on their terms and with a sense of not being too far from their secure "home base."

The organization of these affect-regulatory schemata can be thought of as part of the continually evolving infrastructure of children's sense of identity. The self is not a static structure; rather it is a self-organizing process that maintains a sense of authorship and continuity while allowing for adaptive change (Arden, 1996). Flexible defense systems and flexible cognitive structures enable children to perceive and make use of new narratives.

The Piagetian paradigm of cognitive development and the object-relational paradigm of the synthesis of affective elements are complementary. For healthy development, both kinds of development require ongoing flexibility, an openness to variable experiences of the self, and the capacity to be altered by environmental stimulation. A third vantage point, systems theory, reminds us that children develop within multiple contexts. Within a family, children learn how to define their identity by being part of a group from which they also differ in certain important ways. Family therapists help family members develop autonomy, bringing more flexibility to what can otherwise become a rigid system. Each member ideally develops a balance between autonomy and interdependence (Bowen, 1978). Attachment theorists would describe this process as enhancing the security of the attachment styles of some or all members of the family.

Children, like adults, are constantly in the process of maintaining and revising their emotional and cognitive schemata. Children change the rules that govern their regulation of emotions. They can increase their control over emotions by intentionally reapprising them (Ochsner, 2006). Even the process of naming felt emotions can calm the amygdala (Harira, Bookheimer, & Mazziotta, 2000). This process activates the prefrontal lobes and puts the brakes on the tendency of the amygdala to overreact. In terms of frontal lobe activation, talking, naming, and narrativizing with a therapist calls for some integration of right-hemispheric emotional processing with the left hemisphere's language and positive-affective capacities.

Within the transference relationship, the therapist teaches and supports children's ability to regulate affect. The OFC's governance of the activating properties of the sympathetic nervous system and the relaxation-oriented ones of the parasympathetic nervous system are enhanced by regulating emotions. Children need enough sympathetic arousal to experience a "safe emergency" in the therapeutic alliance—for example, allowing themselves to feel deeply insecure for some moments with the therapist—while also experiencing a growing confidence that they can apply the parasympathetic brakes on this arousal when they feel they have to. This typically comes about through play bolstered by the many subtle ways therapists have of letting the child patient know that control over the hour is shared between both parties.

Therapists who simply facilitate parasympathetic inhibition without also allowing some exposure to periods of sympathetic arousal are missing opportunities to help the child patient change. This is one of the great lessons of the cognitive behavioral research on exposure in panic treatment (Zuercher-White, 1998) and exposure-response-prevention in the treatment of obsessive-compulsive disorder (Kaiser-Permanente, 2001b): An effective balance between the sympathetic and parasympathetic systems produces lasting change. When children feel secure in the therapist's attunement, and both parties share the experience of a "safe emergency" in the therapeutic alliance or the narrative, the neurodynamics of healthy affect regulation are invigorated.

The task of therapy is to integrate the processes of neurodynamic subsystems so that they can be regulated effectively. Freud's concept of making the unconscious conscious has some relevance here, but insight alone is not sufficient to produce change. When treating specific disorders, such as depression and anxiety, therapists must help children regulate affect within the parameters of evidence-based practice, as we emphasize in the later chapters of this book.

The therapeutic relationship replicates many aspects of an attachment relationship, including role modeling, empathy, bi-directional regulation, coconstructing narratives, and challenging and testing affect regulatory skills in a relationship that has some level of security. With good-enough parenting, children develop the capacity for flexibility and stability—in short, the power to self-organize (Arden, 1996). Without a good-enough parental relationship, children are prone to inflexibility, dysregulated emotions, and rigidity and are vulnerable to serious psychological problems. Even in the worst cases of institutional neglect, however, many children retain the capacity to use a good relationship to repair the effects of the past on their neurodynamics. Children who have not been exposed to trauma, and whose parents are (or are almost) "good enough" generally know how to use good relationships with teachers, therapists, or other adults in their lives. These relationships are materials the child uses to build the brain structures that will one day take the place of home.

THEORY OF MIND

Affect regulation is a prerequisite to effective communication with others. So too is the capacity to build reasonably accurate mental models of what another person is thinking and feeling. This modeling is known as theory of mind (ToM). Theory of mind is the ability to attribute mental states— intents, desires, fantasies, knowledge—to self and others. As originally defined, ToM enables one to understand that mental states can be the cause of—and thus be used to explain and predict—others' behavior (Premack, & Woodruff, 1978). This capacity suggests the existence of an even more fundamental insight: the recognition that the mind is a generator of representations and the understanding that others' mental representations of the world do not necessarily reflect reality and can differ from one's own (Courtin, 2000; Courtin & Melot, 2005).

ToM is an accomplishment of early childhood development. By age 4, cognition has evolved from a state of primary egocentrism toward a new equilibrium capable of the most elementary principle required for the eventual attainment of a theory of mind: the knowledge that other people are separate and do not know or look at the same things we know and see (Piaget, 1951, 1952). Almost all children develop some capacity for empathy; many show it before age 4. They will build on this skill throughout their lives, adding in progressively higher levels of cognitive and psychological complexity (Rochat, 2002).

To demonstrate differences between species and brain size, researchers placed various animals in front of a mirror to determine if they were capable of recognizing themselves. Dogs barked at their reflection in the mirror as if they were faced with another dog invading their territory. Only apes and to a lesser extent certain species of monkeys were able to recognize themselves (Gallup, 1997). Researchers concluded that it is an expanded prefrontal cortex that differentiates species that possess this capacity for self-awareness.

ToM skills contribute to greater success in navigating through the social world. One way to illustrate how critical ToM is to a child is to note the way that socially inept children stumble through life without developing a social support system. They are isolated socially and tend to have little success developing empathetic relationships.

Studies utilizing positron emission tomography (PET) and functional magnetic resonance imaging (f MRI) scans on normals have revealed that the ToM capacity is dependent on areas of the medial and lateral inferior aspects of the PFC. These same areas are activated when subjects are asked to focus on their internal mental states as opposed to external reality (Firth & Firth, 1999).

ToM Deficiencies and Autistic Spectrum Disorders

Different attachment experiences influence the development of both these reflective skills and a ToM (Fonagy & Target, 2006). The ability to create a model of another person's mind may be mediated both by the right hemisphere and by the attachment experiences during which the neurocircutry of that hemisphere undergoes intensive development (Siegel, 1999). As children begin to move in a progressively more complex world of relationships, they accommodate new experiences to their existing schemata and, over time, gain the skills of ToM. Without it, children relate to other people as if they were objects.

ToM skills are generally absent in children with autism and Asperger's disorders. ToM may be dependent on a special kind of neuron, called *mirror neurons* (Rizzolatti, Fadiga, & Gallese, 2001; Rizzolatti, Fadiga, Gallese, & Fogassi, 1996). Generally children *without* autism or Asperger's disorder develop the capacity to empathize with another person, which is dependent on the mirror neuron system. Research using fMRI imaging has shown that young teens with autism, compared to normal teens, show deficiencies in PFC mirror neuron activity when reading and imitating facial expressions.

One of the earliest diagnostic indicators of autism is the avoidance of eye contact. Studies have shown less activation in the brain's face-reading area with people diagnosed with autism when they (albeit infrequently) look at someone. Subjects who showed diminished activity in the brain's fusiform area when looking at faces were more likely to have autism. Interestingly, autistic children show activity in this area when they look at a cherished object or even just a pattern, but not a person. When autistic people do look at the eyes of another, their amygdalas become hyper-activated. They quickly avert their own gaze to stare at the other person's lips or chins. When nonautistic people view faces, they use networks that are collectively called the "social brain"; they use these same networks when looking at pictures of faces that are right-side up. When looking at pictures that are upside-down, they use neurodynamic systems associated with identifying objects. Autistic subjects use these "object" systems when viewing objects *or* faces (Pierce & Courchesne, 2000). There is a range of capacities across the autistic spectrum disorders (ASD) with respect to developing a ToM. Autistic patients have been noted to have major deficits mentalizing about social relationships (Fletcher et al., 1995). Asperger's patients have been noted to process ToM tasks in their left-frontal region (Happé et al., 1996).

By 18 months of age, most children engage in behaviors that indicate a developing ToM. Three behaviors common to most normal children and uncommon among children with ASDs include:

1. **Pointing.** Directing another person's attention to an object
2. **Gaze pointing.** Looking in the same direction as an adult
3. **Pretend play.** Imagining objects that serve as a symbol for other objects

The absence of these three behaviors suggests the development of an ASD (Baron-Cohen, Allen, & Gillberg, 1992), but the presence of these capacities is not a foolproof rule-out indicator, as some children who display these behaviors later do develop ASDs (Baird et al., 2001). Among these children, one or more genes may become active after the second birthday to create the brain state that prevents normal development (Kagan & Herschowitz, 2005). The criteria for the diagnosis of autism include:

1. Severe impairment in reciprocal social relatedness
2. Severe impairment in communication, including language
3. Restricted, repetitive interests, activities, and monotonous behavior patterns

When differentiating autism and Asperger's disorder from other child-hood disorders, it is important to keep in mind that autism involves *severe* dysfunctions in all three of these areas.

Children with Asperger's disorder show deficits in social interaction based on a lack of empathy. These children can communicate, albeit in a one-sided way, about a topic they are completely absorbed with and possess keen knowledge of (Aronowitz et al., 1997). Overall, the general consensus is that Asperger's disorder is a less severe form of autism. In both disorders, patients show deficits in reading facial expressions, espe-cially in reading fear (Pelphrey et al., 2002).

Because the amygdalas of children with autism and Asperger's seem to overactivate when they are asked to look into the eyes of another person and judge what they might be thinking, some have argued for an amygdala theory of autism (Baron-Cohen, 2000). A number of other abnormalities are also common with ASDs including hypometabolism in the limbic areas and the cingulate cortex (Haznedar et al., 2000), reduced corpus callosum size (Egaas, Courchesne, & Saitoh, 1995), and abnormal growth and pruning of neurons in the cortex and limbic regions (Courchesne, Carper, & Ashoomoff, 2003). Based on a magnetic resonance imaging analysis of preadolescent autistic children compared to controls, autistic children showed abnormal patterns in the superior frontal sulcus (the area asso-ciated with working memory, language, affect, and gaze) (Levitt et al., 2003). Other studies have shown that some autistic patients have smaller neurons with shorter dendritic extensions and structural abnor-malities in the columns of the prefrontal and temporal complex (Casanova, Buxhoeveden, Switala, & Roy, 2002).

The term *dyssemia* has been used to describe people who have difficulty with the complex synchrony of communication that often involves being attentive to nonverbal cues and even tones in another's voice and prosody. These people have a great deal of difficulty connecting to other people and as a result seem out of sync with them (Nowicki & Duke, 2002). Although people with autism and Asperger's syndrome have severe deficits in these areas as well, their deficits result from neurological dysfunctions. According to Stephen Nowicki (quoted in Goleman, 2006, p. 92), 85% of those with dyssemia develop the disorder because of a failure to learn how to read and respond to nonverbal signals. A common cause seems to be a lack of adequate practice interacting with families or peers due to social isolation or alexithymia. However, approximately 10% of these children develop dyssemia because trauma short-circuited the necessary social learning. Only 5% of this population has a diagnosable neurological disorder.

The development of social skills acquires a growing momentum and significance during the latency period and adolescence. In optimal development, peer relationships become of paramount importance. Social skills, ToM, affect regulation, and a sense of personal identity during adolescence are critical skills for the normal developmental pathway we discuss in the next chapter.

CHAPTER 5

Adolescence

A 16-year-old boy . . . in his own words a "loner" and a "risk merchant," tells me in a session about the moment, at age ten, when he eventually learned to swim after having been terrified of water: "I knew I was safer out of my depth because even though I couldn't stand, there was more water to hold me up. . . ." Standing within his depth, apparently in control, was the omnipotence born of anxiety; the opposite of omnipotence here was not impotence, as he had feared, but his being able to entrust himself to the water.

—Adam Phillips

THROUGHOUT MOST OF recorded history, adolescence has been thought of as a relatively short period of time between puberty and the assumption of adult roles. In postmodern western society, however, the period has been extended into the early 20s. Regardless, adolescents are asked to do many things, such as go to war, before they are through the transition.

The concept of adolescence as a period of storm and stress became a stereotype in twentieth-century America through films and rock songs that in effect made adolescence a subculture. The stereotype was buttressed by the scholarly contributions of G. Stanley Hall and Anna Freud. A. Freud promoted the idea that adolescence represented a period of internal disharmony and intrapsychic disequilibrium between the forces of the instinctual demands of the id and ego. From this psychoanalytic perspective, adolescents struggle with parents to develop a sense of identity by using defense mechanisms such as reaction formation, displacement, and withdrawal.

In recent years, the idea of adolescent disharmony has been revised. A more balanced view considers adolescence as a period of biological, cognitive, emotional, and social reorganization with the main goal of adapting to adulthood (Susman & Rogel, 2004). Most normal adolescents do not fit the psychoanalytic stereotype. Because there are multiple dimensions to this transition, contemporary researchers and theorists employ a dynamic model that emphasizes complex interactions among the psychological, biological, and social domains that distinguish young people in this period. Family, peers, school, and neighborhood are settings that call on adolescents to respond in different ways, challenging the teens' sense of self and ego-organization and pushing the envelope on the teen's neuroplastic accommodations to the environment.

Erikson (1963) was the first to draw attention to the developmental challenge of forming a sense of identity during adolescence. It is during this period that most individuals explore potential roles. By eventually adopting a role—or several—that structures interactions with others, adolescents begin to develop an identity that will carry forward into adulthood (Baumeister & Muraven, 1996). Identity is formed, in part, through an internalized narrative that weaves together all the events in an adolescent's past. This narrative connects the past and the present as it looks ahead to the future. It carries within it moral and ideological themes and gives the adolescent a sense of unity and purpose (McAdams, 1999).

The English word *adolescence* comes from the Latin *adolesco*, which means "to grow up." The definition captures the fact that adolescents are neither children nor adults, although they are at times children and at times expected be very adult. Older adolescents drive automobiles, care for siblings, and not infrequently have children of their own. They are nevertheless told what to do and are often not trusted to act independently.

Many adolescents go to great pains to differentiate themselves from their parents. A father of an adolescent patient said to one of the authors, "Sometimes it seems that the only thing he knows for certain is that he isn't me, and he has to go to extremes to prove it!"

Some adolescents are prone to impulsive decisions and tend to overreact when compared to the adults whom they are expected to emulate. For this reason, adolescence has long been regarded as a developmental period rife with emotional turmoil and behavioral risk taking. The military recruits adolescents not only because of their physical capabilities but also because of their sense of invincibility and willingness to take risks.

HORMONES, GROWTH, AND SEX

Puberty marks the developmental transition from being a child to being able to create one. It is marked by many physical changes, including the accelerated release of growth hormones and increased androgen (sex hormone) production from the adrenals, which in turn switches on the production of estrogen in the ovaries and testosterone in the testes. The secondary sex characteristics that develop during early adolescence in both sexes require significant psychosocial adjustments at a time when egocentrism, interest in peers, and capacities for social appraisal are exquisitely sensitized. These changes occur a year or even two years earlier in girls than in boys.

It is startling to see two 13-year-olds of either sex standing side by side, one with the body of a child; the other, six inches taller, with the body of a young adult. Along with changes in the body's height, weight, and sexual phenotype, there are corresponding surges in sexual interest. Early-maturing girls are the subject of a great deal of attention, may be targets of teasing or harassment, and often are subjected to a destabilizing level of attention during a sensitive period in the development of self-esteem, emotion regulation, and identity formation. During the massive acceleration of growth in adolescence, 50% of adult body weight is achieved. The male larynx, cricothyroid cartilage, and laryngeal muscles enlarge, changes that may result in a period when the voice breaks, usually at about 14 years of age. The adult male voice is usually attained after 15 years of age.

Variations in the levels of adrenal androgens, such as Dehydroepi-androsterone (DHEA) and its sulfate, DHEAS, which begin to rise during adrenarche, have been associated with an increase in problem behaviors. For example, girls with lower concentrations of DHEAS who experience more negative life events can be more aggressive than female peers with fewer negative life events. Girls with premature adrenarche who also have higher adrenal androgens have been reported to be more anxious than girls who develop on a normal schedule. Finally, higher levels of DHEA predict the onset of the first episode of major depression in girls (Susman & Rogel, 2004). Rapid hormonal increases in females also are correlated with the onset of major depressive disorder. Given that hormonal levels usually moderate in late adolescence and adulthood, and that not all girls become depressed, researchers have suggested that other moderating variables must be involved. Maternal depression and genetic predisposition are likely very significant variables (Angold, Worthman, & Costello, 2003; see Graber, 2004, for a review).

Much attention has been focused on the issue of early-maturing adolescents because they experience psychological problems disproportionately. Early-maturing girls have been reported to engage in more acting-out behaviors than girls who mature on a normal calendar. They spend more time with older boys and are more likely to engage in early sex. They also generally report more negative emotions and tend to have internalizing disorders, such as depression, than girls who mature on time or late (see Susman & Rogel, 2004, for a review).

Early-maturing boys have been reported to have a higher incidence of antisocial behavior and substance abuse. In general, early-maturing boys and girls report more contact with deviant peers. The timing of puberty affects self and body image in all youth. Generally, early-maturing girls have been reported to be dissatisfied with their appearance, body image, and physical characteristics. Not surprisingly, given the importance of cultural attitudes toward sexuality and the heightened importance of peer assessment, attitudes toward the schedule of maturation vary among different ethnic groups. Hispanic girls report greater body-image satisfaction if they develop on time with other girls. African American boys and girls report markedly less satisfaction if they mature late. Asian American boys and girls who mature late report relatively less dissatisfaction with their body image than adolescents in other groups (see Susman & Rogel, 2004, for a review).

Sleep is a neurodynamically regulated behavior pattern that also begins to change around puberty and early adolescence. Changes in stages 3 and 4 (non–rapid-eye-movement [REM]) sleep accompany increases in rapid growth. Changes in REM sleep appear related to puberty and sex hormones (Dahl, Tubnick, al-Shabbout, & Ryan, 1997). Adolescents also experience a shift in circadian rhythms, staying up later in the evening and waking up later in the morning (Carskadon, 1999). Sleep loss induced by conflicts between this shift and domestic or school schedules is likely to affect adolescents' mood, motivation, and attention. Many adolescents catch up on sleep loss during the weekends, a practice that contributes to a delay in developing a mature circadian rhythm.

GENDER AND THE BRAIN

The asymmetrical development of the two hemispheres is less pronounced in females than males. This important gender difference is a long-standing one, as it shows up in the fossilized skulls of our evolutionary ancestors. Male and female brains also differ in the thickness of the cerebral cortex. In males, the right frontal lobe is thicker than the left, a difference that is less pronounced in females. This gender difference also is seen in several other mammals (Glick, Meibach, Cox, & Maayani, 1979; Glick, Ross, & Hough, 1982). Again, the female pattern suggests more balance in the hemispherically specialized functions and greater facility in integrating them. Females also have a greater density of neurons in two layers of the temporal lobes. This area is thought to be involved in receiving input from the auditory system and appears to support enhanced language skills (Witelson, Glezer, & Kigar, 1995).

Males typically have more pronounced functional differences between the frontal lobes than do females. Goldberg and colleagues devised tests to examine the psychobehavioral implications of these differences. One study differentiated male from female decision-making styles (Goldberg, 2001). The researchers found that males tend to make *context-dependent decisions*—i.e., choices that depend on the context of the subject's stable, preexisting preferences. Females, by contrast, make decisions that are *context-independent*—i.e., decisions based on features of the particular situation and hence are less predictable than those of the typical male. Males and females also appear to react differently to frontal lobe damage. Males with right frontal lobe damage show an exaggeration of the typically male context-dependent decision-making style, while males with left frontal lobe damage use an extremely context-independent decision-making style (Goldberg, 2001). These studies suggest that the right and left frontal lobes in males make very different contributions to the decision-making process.

Females with frontal lobe damage do not show this pattern. Damage to *either* the left or the right frontal lobe increases context-dependent behaviors. This is in contrast to neurologically normal women who show context-independent behavior. (A female neuroscientist we know summarizes these studies by noting that normal men behave like brain-damaged women). Male right-handers who have a preference for context-dependent decisions show a particular activation of their left prefrontal cortex (PFC) while doing a task. However, males who have a preference for context-independent decision making show activation of their right PFC. In general, females show less asymmetry. Right-handed females with a preference toward context-independent decision making show bilateral activation of their PFC. Females with a preference toward context-dependent decision making show a bilateral activation of their posterior cortex.

PREFRONTAL CORTEX EXPANSION

More than 100 years ago, the eminent neuroanatomist Hughlings Jackson introduced his law of evolution and dissolution (Jackson, 1884/1932). According to Jackson, the phylogenetically youngest parts of the brain are the first to succumb to brain diseases. Goldberg (2001) notes that because of the exceptional richness of their connections, the frontal lobes are especially vulnerable to neurological injury. Because of this vulnerability, frontal lobe lesions are not necessary for frontal lobe dysfunction to occur. Frontal lobe dysfunction can result from distant, diffuse, or distributed lesions. For example, researchers have found that disruptions in cerebral blood flow in the frontal lobes can occur as a result of tumors outside this region (Lilja, Hagstdius, Risberg, Salford, & Smith, 1992).

The brain changes in some dramatic ways in adolescence. Although 95% of the brain has developed by age 6, its next maturational spurt is in early adolescence. The most significant myelination occurs in the PFC. The PFC, and especially the dorsolateral prefrontal cortex (DLPFC), are at the forefront of the expansion of the frontal lobes in adolescence, enhancing working memory and decision-making skills. PFC myelination tends to continue through the early 20s and is matched step for step by changes in adolescents' social capacities and interests (Nelson, Leibenluft, McClure, & Pine, 2005). Three major neural developmental changes occur in the teenage years:

1. A significant development of the PFC
2. A major enhancement of connectivity among parts of the brain as evidenced by increased white matter
3. An increase in synaptic pruning (cutting back on unused or superfluous neurons)

The development of the PFC manifests in the adolescent's attainment of a new and higher-order cognitive process than is seen in childhood. The orbitofrontal cortex (OFC) helps make decisions based on values and emotional information and options. The DLPFC gets involved in decision making and helps make decisions when there are multiple sources of information; it can recruit various other areas of the brain for this task when needed. The ventral and anterior cingulate cortex activate when necessary to sort through conflicting options, acting like an error recognition system (Krawczyk, 2002). The DLPFC processes cognitions pertaining to the formulation of future goals. When encountering conflicting emotional conditions, the DLPFC recruits the ventromedial PFC (of which the OFC is part) for input.

As an illustration of how important the ventromedial PFC is as a mediator between emotional urges and practical demands in a social context, the famous case of Phineas Gage was described in *Brain-Based Therapy with Adults* (the first volume in this series) and in the appendix. The extensive damage to his ventromedial PFC left Gage with little or no ability to suppress emotional impulses, radically altering his personality and ultimately his life. Healthy development of the OFC is particularly critical for the development of affect regulation. The DLPFC apparently matures later than does the OFC (Thompson et al., 2000). In fact, from an evolutionary perspective, the DLPFC is the most recent system to develop in the human brain (Fuster, 2000).

Long-term planning, prioritizing values, and matching conduct and social standards in any given social situation are all skills learned (or not) during adolescence. We could not negotiate these developmental hurdles without the DLPFC. Together with the OFC, the DLPFC acts as a general synthesizer of experience, self-evaluation, and emotion regulation (see Keating, 2004, for a review).

Compared to adult subjects, adolescents show significantly more activity in the DLPFC in functional magnetic resonance imaging studies (Luna et al., 2002). Presumably this occurs because when skills are in intense development, the neurodynamic modules that are most important in supporting them must work harder. Once the skills are well learned, the neurodynamic process becomes more effortless and efficient. Regarding the different portions of the PFC, Monica Luciana (2006) of the University of Minnesota writes:

> Overall, the pattern of findings . . . suggest that different PFC regions reach functional maturity at different rates, with the ventromedial region maturing prior to the dorsal lateral region, which is responsible for the highest level executive control over information processing. (2006, p. 315)

The second important change in the brain during adolescence is an increase in white matter, also referred to as *myelination*. This process involves coating of the neuronal axons with a sheath of fatty oligodendroglia cells. Myelination promotes neural conductivity in the same way that the plastic or rubber coating of electrical cords enhances electrical conductivity. The importance of myelination becomes painfully obvious in individuals suffering from demyelinating diseases such as multiple sclerosis. The increase in oligodendroglial cells that make up the myelin sheaths in such cortical areas as the frontal lobes is consistent with the major psychological changes that characterize adolescence. These new skills require enhanced processing efficiency (Spear, 2000). They assist adolescents struggling with developing a social identity, separating from the family, and building a personal belief system.

Synaptic pruning helps the adolescent brain work more efficiently by cutting out the clutter. This experience-dependent process also helps strengthen, reshape, and develop needed synaptic connections. These contextual changes enhance the flexibility and neuroplasticity of the adolescent's brain. In periods of prolific synaptic formation and pruning, such as infancy and adolescence, these contextual changes are adaptive and experience dependent (Lewis, 1999).

Teenagers such as the Adam Phillips's patient, quoted at the beginning of this chapter, need to learn to trust themselves as independent agents in the world (Phillips, 1993). In the process of learning this exhilarating lesson, they also inevitably find themselves in risky situations, often as a result of inadequate planning. Teens need to learn through experience the concept that things can go wrong. As they acquire episodic memories of things going badly, these memories prompt the newly pruned PFC and anterior cingulate to activate and start problem solving. Activation of a more heavily myelineated DLPFC also enables better planning and more analytic processing. As adolescents develop the capacity to grasp the emotional gist of a situation, their ability to manage their emotional reaction to it also improves, in part through a more efficient OFC (Keating, 2004).

PSYCHOLOGICAL DEVELOPMENT

The transition into adolescence from middle childhood involves a leap forward in cognitive and emotional regulatory skills. An example is the adolescent's newfound ability to engage in deductive reasoning. Early adolescents (ages 11 and 12) are less likely to require physical evidence to solve problems than are late-latency-age children. Young teens can solve problems and make predictions based on logic and internal hypothesis-testing alone (Morris & Sloutsky, 2001). As Keating has pointed out, it is not as if children are incapable of logic or that there is a single developmental pathway. Rather, adolescents develop a deeper version of natural logic (Keating, 2004).

Generally, cognitive processing efficiency, working memory, and higher levels of reasoning flourish in the teenage years. These PFC-based skills are critical for the emerging ability to create and manipulate concepts. Linking ideas and applying them to novel content, a hallmark of cognitive flexibility, is increasingly expected and rewarded in relationships with friends and at school. Thinking divergently and reflectively requires a new kind of cross-modal integration in the brain. Most of all, adolescents are required to use their burgeoning talent for mentalizing (Fonagy & Target, 2006), or *metacognition*, the thinking about emotions and ideas. The meaning of an experience and its relationship to personal identity in this period becomes semi-independent of the moment. A child who did not enjoy math in elementary school becomes an adolescent who says "I'm just not good at it." Like Phillips's 16-year-old at the outset of this chapter, the adolescent can look back and recall what it was like to think like a child, while simultaneously maintaining the new perspective about how he thinks now. Feelings about parents that were once more determined by the gratifications and frustrations of the moment meld together into more durable images of Mom and Dad.

For adolescents, metacognition is a moving target, which is one reason why adults distrust adolescents' decision-making capacities. For many years, researchers attributed the tendency of some adolescents to abuse drugs, practice unsafe sex, speed on city streets, and so on to poor cognitive skills. There is now substantial evidence that teens engage in these activities *despite* the knowledge that these activities are unsafe. Adolescents' actions are still tightly coupled with their emotions and their likes and dislikes (Steinberg et al., 2006) and they are more likely than adults to do something because they feel like it, or a friend they were with felt like it. They learn to guide their behavior and manage their emotions largely independent of adult supervision.

The adolescent's experiences of emotion and impulse intensify simultaneously with the escalation in the demands parents and peers put on the teen to modulate them. Perhaps at no time since the formative period of infantile attachment is the "social brain" so besieged by internal and environmental pressures. In fact, many emerging neurodevelopmental skills of teenagers continue to be much influenced by early attachment. Teens with secure attachment styles are better able to negotiate the complexities of adolescent group life than those with anxious attachment histories. They tend to be more involved in discussions, draw the attention of others in positive ways, and are effective negotiators and more persuasive advocates (Sroufe et al., 2005).

Attachment schemata in adolescents affect a range of developmental outcomes, especially those having to do with intimacy and trust issues. For males, the combination of early disruption in attachment and low support from available men is a powerfully bad combination (Sroufe et al., 2005). Many aspects of psychopathology in adolescents can be attributed to difficulties managing affect and behavior under the steady pressures of familial, academic, and peer expectations (Steinberg et al., 2006). Robert Kegan (1994) captures the expectations one set of parents harbor toward their teenage son, Matty:

> He is looking more like a young man, talking more like a young man, and demanding the greater freedoms of a young man. Although they may not exactly know it, they believe that if they are to see him more as a man than as a child, they should be able to experience him on the other side of a relationship that no longer requires them to regulate an unsocialized, self-interested

creature who needs their behavioral limits and who is constantly testing whether they will effectively keep playing and keep winning a game of control. Their expectation is that *Matty's own relationship to what he knows they care about will allow them to feel themselves included in shared bonds of mutual trust and concern.* (p. 24, italics added)

Development and Social Change

Adjusting to a changing society while simultaneously transitioning into adulthood describes the arc of adolescent experience. For contemporary adolescents, even "nature"—that is, the relatively fixed factors of biology—appears to be in flux: over the course of a relatively brief historical period, puberty is occurring earlier in childhood. The precocious appearance of secondary sex characteristics in pubescent children is associated with the earlier onset of dating, romantic involvement, and sexual experimentation.

Rapid social change not only provokes greater conflict with parents who try to monitor their teen's values and behaviors, it may also overtax the child's neurodynamic capacities for handling emotions, planning, and delaying gratification. Moreover, adolescents are exposed daily to a media that knows that "sex sells." Sexually provocative images and lyrics with themes of challenging authority stoke the potential for family conflict. A backlash to these aspects of contemporary culture can be seen in the resurgence of conservative religions and the emphasis on the politics of "family values." As a consequence of these bifurcations in society, contemporary adolescents have fewer external resources to draw on.

Adolescence, a period of developmental flux occurring in a social context that is itself in transition, is characterized by the emergence of particular psychological problems. Based on a review of the research on adolescent psychopathology, Steinberg and colleagues (2006) have reached four major conclusions:

1. There has been a notable increase in the prevalence rates of certain types of adolescent psychopathology, including depression, eating disorders, social anxiety, psychosis, and substance abuse.
2. There are changes in how these problems manifest themselves. For example, in depression, feelings of hopelessness become a more salient feature.
3. New patterns of gender differences in psychopathology have emerged. For example, prior to puberty, the depression rates between boys and girls is similar but by middle adolescence, depression is twice as common among girls as it is among boys.

4. Prevalence rates have changed over time. There has been a fivefold increase in major depression, and the increase may be even higher among adolescent girls (Angold, Costello, & Worthman, (1998). There has been an alarming increase in completed suicides among adolescents over the past thirty years.

These findings will not surprise therapists who work with adolescents. Problems such as eating disorders, self-harming behavior (including cutting, burning, and suicidality), sexual victimization, binge drinking and substance use, and acute depressions once seemed relatively rare, but they are no longer so in current clinical practice. Many adolescents seem to be attempting the high-wire act of maintaining multiple selves at the same time that they are testing their independence from their parents. Many lack social nets that are strong enough to catch them if they fall. The various aspects of the new selves of these teens sometimes seem as if they were separate identities (Harter, Bresnick, Bouchey, & Whitsell, 1997), not only to us but to our teenaged patients as well. The challenge for therapists is to maintain a flexible and adaptive holding environment for these teens, while working to maximize the security of the adolescents' family and social relationships.

Social skills, peer relationships, and emotional regulatory skills are interlinked. Research suggests that rejection or a lack of peer relationships should raise a warning flag for teachers, parents, and therapists (Rubin, Bukowski, & Parker, 1998). Academic competence is another important predictor of adolescent psychopathology. Perhaps grasping the links between attachment, school performance, cognitive development, and emotion regulation, some school systems and community programs have created programs to improve the positive bonding of teenagers to their schools. The Seattle Social Development Project, for example, offered multifaceted interventions to elementary school students. When students who were involved in the project reached high school, they bonded more positively to their schools and were at lower psychosocial risk than controls (Hawkins, Smith, Hill, Kosterman, & Abbott, 2003).

Adolescents who are bullied and victimized (as well as actually traumatized) are at risk for developing internalized symptoms. Close friendships buffer the effects of victimization. Socially successful teens are better able to endure problems arising from interactions with the larger peer group (see Graber, 2004, for a review). The teen's capacity to form and utilize close friendships in adolescence develops out of the security of their early attachments. But even as peer relationships take on more importance for teenagers, their success in navigating the complex relational world continues to be highly influenced by their parents.

PARENTING

Parenting an adolescent is in some ways the last act in a three-act play titled "Attachment." Adolescents are as much in need of good-enough parenting as are younger children, but the demands of successfully parenting teenagers are different from those required of parents of the latency aged child. Like toddlers, adolescents need love, empathy, and limit setting, a combination of firmness and flexibility that feeds the teen's potential for self-organization. Few statements have summed up the contradictory set of demands faced by parents of teens better than Anthony Wolfe's title of his (2002) popular book: *Get Out of My Life, But First Could You Drive Me and Cheryl to the Mall?*

Parenting is the key mediator of adolescent life experiences. Diana Baumrind (1978, 1991) described a set of parenting styles and researched them over the last 30 years. The categories include:

- Authoritarian
- Permissive
  - Indulgent
  - Indifferent
- Authoritative

The classic stern, strict, harsh, and punitive guardian is the authoritarian type. These parents impose their will and opinions on their children without discussion or compromise. Obedience is simply expected, and anything else is unacceptable. At the other end of the spectrum are permissive parents who make few demands on their children and rarely seek to control their behavior. The two subtypes of this laissez-faire approach are the indulgent and the indifferent. Indulgent parents may be very supportive and optimally encourage a great deal of independence in their children. Therapists see the negative psychological consequences of this approach in children who seem at once entitled and insecure. Indifferent or neglectful parents are neither supportive nor controlling. They are basically disengaged and their children often seem socially avoidant or very preoccupied with issues of self esteem.

Authoritative parents retain a sense of authority while being warm and supportive. They are clear about rules and expectations, reward appropriate behavior, and enforce consequences for inappropriate behavior. They are flexible, open to discussing opinions, listen to the child's side of things in a conflict, and encourage reasoning. This style of parenting supports teenagers in developing prosocial behaviors, independence, responsibility, and creativity.

The authoritative parent has been shown to have a benevolent influence on general development. In contrast, the authoritarian and permissive parenting styles, on average, negatively affect development. Families with little warmth or structure and with high levels of hostility significantly exacerbate the risk of adolescent psychopathology (Steinberg et al., 2006). The authoritative style recently has been referred to as the *inductive* style because it is associated with actively engaging children to reason about feeling states. The inductive style promotes the development of empathy and increased morality. This style of parenting is analogous to the secure type of attachment relationship. Both promote empathy, effective emotion regulation, a sense of security, and a sense of curiosity about the world and the associated prefrontal circuitry that makes these personal qualities possible.

Although parental authoritativeness/inductiveness attends to children's needs, at the same time this style demands age-appropriate levels of self-regulation. The authoritarian style ignores children's needs and developmentally mediated levels of competence and undermines the development of affect regulation. Baumrind (1991) followed children raised by authoritative, authoritarian, and permissive parents from preschool through adolescence. Adolescents who have indulgent parents tend to be irresponsible, immature, and conforming to peers. Children and adolescents with indifferent parents tend to be impulsive and at risk for precocious sexual behavior and for early use of alcohol. Authoritarian and neglectful parents have little positive influence on the school performance of children or adolescents. When parents with an authoritative/inductive style get involved in their children's schooling, a positive impact on school performance results.

Baumrind (1991) found that children raised by authoritative parents had many more positive experiences than children whose parents fell into other parenting categories. Responsive yet firm parents were especially important in the development of competent sons. Authoritarian parents had especially negative effects on sons who had low academic performance and low cognitive and social competence. These boys lacked initiative, self-confidence, and leadership skills. In another study, overcontrolling parents maintained and even exacerbated inhibition in their children (Wood, McLeod, Sigman, Hwang, & Chu, 2003). There is also evidence that parenting can have paradoxical consequences if it rewards and encourages children's fearfulness by controlling their activities and solving their problems (Rubin, Burgess, Kennedy, & Steward, 2003). Helping children to avoid challenges subtly promotes anxiety.

Other research links parenting that is rejecting and limited in the expression of personal warmth to the development of anxiety disorders in children (see Wood et al., 2003, for a review). Parents who invalidate or excessively control their adolescent's feelings through withdrawal of love or attempts to induce guilt tend to promote the development of internalizing disorders, such as depression, eating disorders, and identity confusion; and a subjective sense of loneliness and diminished self-efficacy (Barber, 2002). Moreover, authoritarian parents tend to produce children and adolescents who are prone to be passive, dependent, less creative, and less socially adept than other adolescents. They also can be prone to externalizing behaviors. In a Cambridge study of delinquent development in which 400 London adolescent boys were followed longitudinally, it was found that the third most important predictor of convictions for violence (after hyperactivity and poor concentration) was having authoritarian parents (Farrington, 1994).

The neurodynamic consequences of authoritarian or neglectful parenting are generally similar: children do not get exposed to the kind of environmental stimuli that interact with their genetic potential to produce enhanced circuitry for planning and emotion regulation in the PFC. Children of authoritarian parents learn to keep their subjective affective experience out of consciousness and to suppress emotional expressiveness; or else they become rebellious and pseudoindependent. As noted above, children of neglectful parents are likely to remain preoccupied with maintaining a secure base for development. Those who react to this problem with externalizing strategies are at risk for oppositional defiant disorder and conduct disorder, both of which are associated with lower baseline cortisol levels. (Kruesi et al., 1989; Pajer, Gardner, Rubin, Perel, & Neal, 2001). This finding has been replicated across many studies of children with conduct problems, as long as subjects do not also show high comorbid anxiety (in which case the cortisol levels are typically elevated). Insecurely attached children who cope by adopting internalizing strategies typically show *higher* baseline cortisol levels (Ashman et al., 2002; Fox, Howe, & Perez-Edgar, 2006). Children with early-onset conduct disorders and antisocial personality disorders tend to have smaller right temporal and right prefrontal lobes (Kruesi, Casanova, Mannhein, & Johnson-Bilder, 2004).

Fathers make a unique contribution to the development of their children's social skills (Isley, O'Neil, & Parke, 1996). For example, third-graders with responsive and involved fathers were found in one study to be more popular than children whose fathers were not (Henggler, Edwards, Cohen, & Summerville, 1992). Fathers who respond in kind to negative affect from their children are more likely to encourage less socially skilled, less altruistic, more avoidant, and more aggressive behaviors in their children.

Fathers play a significant role in teaching their children how to manage their emotions and as a result influence the degree children are accepted by their peers (Parke & Buriel, 1998). Based on a longitudinal analysis, Gottman, Katz, and Hooven (1996) looked at the impact on children of contrasting paternal emotion-regulation strategies. Children who at age 5 had fathers who accepted their sadness and anger and offered support and assistance, demonstrated greater social competence and academic achievement at age 8. Sons of these fathers demonstrated more competence in dealing with anger and were less aggressive overall. Teachers independently rated daughters of these fathers as more competent, and these girls also did better academically.

In children and adolescents, affect management skills are linked to the family's style of expressing emotions and to the youngsters' understanding of their own emotional reactions. As teenagers learn to name emotions with their left PFC and understand what it is about the context that gives rise to these affects, family members, especially the parents, model how to manage and express feelings. Teens' emerging ability to manage emotions constructively is correlated with how constructively parents support and accept them (Parke & Buriel, 1998). If parents demonstrate a willingness to discuss emotions, teens' awareness and understanding of their emotions and others' increases. For example, Cassidy and colleagues (Cassidy, et al., 1992) found that children who were more accepted by their peers were also better able to acknowledge emotions, name them, describe their causes, and expect that their parents would respond appropriately to their emotional expression.

High levels of positive affect in families is linked with popularity with peers; negative parental affect is associated with lower levels of peer acceptance (Isley et al., 1996; see Parke & Buriel, 1998, for a review). Hebbian plasticity no doubt lurks behind this phenomenon: the more neurons fire together, the more likely it is that they will fire together again. Families that promote positive emotional expressions cultivate the circuits of positive affective experience in the brains of their child and teenaged family members. Positive moods become the default mode, and this emotional tone promotes more resilient and socially skilled children and adolescents.

The neurodevelopmental consequences of different parenting styles makes it a good practice for therapists to promote the inductive style in their work with parents. The extent to which this goal is practical, given the individuals involved, is a matter of clinical judgment. There are clinical syndromes—for example, anorexia and borderline personality disorder—that are likely to require the involvement not only of parents but physicians, nutritionists, teachers, and others. On the other hand, most experienced clinicians can tell compelling stories about adolescent patients who have successfully moved into young adulthood seemingly *despite* their parents. For most of these teens, an attachment to another, healthier adult— whether that person is a therapist, a teacher, an uncle, or someone else— has been critically important. Where the therapist makes the judgment that it is likely to be more productive to treat the teenager individually rather than within the family system, it is important to bear in mind that the therapeutic relationship with the teen should incorporate many of the characteristics of inductive parenting. That is, therapists should set out treatment guidelines and the reasons for them, encourage positive experiences between themselves and the patient, and stimulate discussion about how the adolescent feels about what's going on at home and in the outside world. It should be made explicit that the teen may develop different feelings about the treatment as it progresses, and the expression of any negative feelings is welcome. The repair of ruptures in a relationship is often the experience that makes a therapy successful in mending an underlying attachment style, and in giving the adolescent the self-confidence to try to float, like Phillips's adolescent at the beginning of this chapter. As we illustrate in the chapters on the specific disorders, an active, empathetic, and authoritative therapeutic approach informed by both neuroscience and evidence-based practice gets the best outcomes.

When possible, it is a good idea to maintain a partnership with the parents, vis-à-vis the treatment. The concept of *nonshared environments*— i.e., that every individual has a unique experience even in shared settings where there is quite a lot in common, as there is between family members— should be introduced. Studies in behavioral genetics indicate the extent to which children in the same families often have very different experiences. Even in genetically identical twins, one may develop a psychological disorder, the other not, as a product of invisible differences in epigenetic factors and environment. Researchers repeatedly have had to acknowledge this phenomenon (Loehlin, Neiderhiser, & Reiss, 2005; Reiss, Neiderhiser, Hetherington, & Plomin, 2000]) as well as its corollary: children within the same family react to and interpret the family interactions differently. The effects of nonshared environments are even stronger in higher-risk families, such as those with maternal depression and/or lower socioeconomic status (Ashbury, Dunn, Pike, & Plomin, 2003).

Family therapists have incorporated the idea of nonshared environments as a basic assumption in their work and identified some of the commonly differentiated roles, such as "identified patient" or "mascot," in family systems. As an invited guest, the therapist can tease out how each member of the family sees things, and how each of these perspectives makes sense interactively as part of the system. Eventually, the therapist may be in a position to point out how the system is affecting the individuals and try to alter the momentum of the family system's Hebbian dynamics. By clarifying the existing rules and their consequences, and through the naming and working through of each individual's emotional reactions, the family may be able to create a healthier holding environment for the emerging teenager.

CHAPTER 6

Working from the BASE

> I would say this: people grow best where they continuously experience an ingenious blend of support and challenge; the rest is commentary.
>
> —Robert Kegan

IN THIS CHAPTER, we put together the four major elements of brain-based therapy with children: a neurodynamic theory of attunement and empathy, a systematic approach to treatment planning (based on the diagnosis), and the system of clinical strategies that utilize both the therapeutic relationship and evidence-based methods. We refer to the fundamental dimensions of this model as the *BASE*. This stands for:

Brain—the neurodynamic basis for consciousness and behavior
Attunement—the quality of the therapeutic alliance
System—the system of psychological theories and diagnosis
Evidence-based practice—what research has shown works

The BASE concept supports the complex thinking and strategizing that goes on in planning and conducting psychotherapeutic treatment with children and adolescents. In subsequent chapters, we apply this schema to clinical cases and explaining evidenced-based approaches to particular psychological problems.

B IS FOR BRAIN

As noted in Chapter 2, the human infant comes into the world with a number of reflexes and other innate capacities designed to promote bonding. Thus endowed, the baby meets a mother who is biologically primed for her part in the interactions the baby's brain must have to develop more highly object-related skills. Within 48 to 72 hours after birth, infants learn to distinguish their mother's voice (Fifer & Moon, 1994); by 2 to 3 months of age, the baby's endogenous reflexive smile will be replaced by the more socially meaningful social smile. These limbically and cortically mediated reactions sponsor the real nutrient of attachment styles—*interaction* between babies and their primary caretakers. Attachment is a co-created process, like psychotherapy.

THE NEURODYNAMICS OF EMPATHY

After a century of theorizing about the mind as if it were something other than an embodied biological function, and of conducting studies about esoteric neurological minutiae that seemed to overlook the existence of the mind altogether, in the last decade psychotherapists and neuroscientists seem to have learned to speak the same language. This dialogue has come about partly as the result of improvements in the technology of brain imaging, and partly as a result of a consensus about the importance of relationships in both brain development and psychotherapy. Both neuroscientists and clinicians can now *see* the effects of relationships such as psychotherapy on the brain. A topic of great common interest is empathy, the capacity to feel what another individual is feeling when they are hopeless or in love.

Mirror Neurons: A breakthrough event in recent neuroscience, the discovery of *mirror neurons*, has fueled this common interest in empathic experience (Rizzolatti, Fadiga, & Gallese, 2001; Rizzolatti, Fadiga, Gallese, & Fogassi, 1996). Initially discovered in the frontal cortex of macaque monkeys, these specialized cells were subsequently found in the frontal lobes of apes and humans. Mirror neurons are named for their unique habit of firing not just when an individual *engages* in a goal-directed behavior, but also when he or she *observes* someone else engaging in it. That is, the neurodynamics underlying the actions of others are mirrored in our own brains. Note that behavior that is intentional—motivated by emotion or planning—causes these neurons to fire. Iacoboni (2005) has theorized that cortical mirror neurons transmit their interpretation of the intentions of others to the insula, which then transmits this information to the amygdala, triggering body-based feelings.

In monkeys, mirror neurons are found in an area of the frontal lobes known as F5, analogous to Broca's area in the human brain, a module

critical to speech and language. At an earlier point in our common evolutionary history, mirror neuron systems probably were part of the neurodynamics of communicating with the hands (Rizzolatti & Arbib, 1998). As
this gestural proto-language proved advantageous and became commonplace, the possibilities for more highly evolved sound-based communication systems opened up to our ancestors. Advances in the architecture of
the frontal lobes that enabled our ancestors to imitate the goal-directed
behaviors of others (Gallese, 2001) added momentum to this trend. Mirror
neurons and the mimetic behaviors they support became part of this neural
infrastructure for using vocalization as a medium for symbolic meaning
(Arbib, 2002). In the modern brain, listening to the speech of others
activates the neurons that control our tongue muscles.

Mirror neurons have been found in the premotor cortex, the posterior
parietal lobe, the superior temporal sulcus, and the insula. They are
thought to play a part in everything from the almost irresistible urge
we feel to yawn when we observe someone else doing so, to the projective identification of emotions. As these experiences are repeatedly evoked,
the circuits underlying them are reinforced and the overall architecture
of the brain changes. Mirror neurons no doubt play a role in fostering
infants' ability to communicate with, imitate, and understand the intentions of caregivers. They sensitize children to their mother's sadness and
play a role in why the children of depressed mothers often become depressed themselves. Giacomo Rizzolatti, the Italian neuroscientist who led
the team that discovered mirror neurons, noted that these cells "allow us to
grasp the minds of others not through conceptual reasoning but through
direct simulation; by feeling, not by thinking" (quoted in Goleman, 2006).
Mirror neurons are an integral part of what we would call the therapeutic
brain.

The Therapeutic Brain: The empathic potential of specialized cells such as
mirror neurons are just one part of the therapeutic brain. Frontal lobe
structures also support cognitive and emotion-regulation functions vital to
the brain's capacity to generate the interactions it needs to develop. As we
noted in Chapter 5, growing children and adolescents require experience-
dependent cognitive structures for understanding and predicting the
behavior of others. These structures are collectively referred to as mentalizing, metacognition, or a theory of mind (ToM). Normal children develop
aspects of this capacity by age 4. The neural substrate children utilize for
ToM is the same as that used for planning the future (Ramnani & Miall,
2004), and includes the frontal lobes, the amygdala, the insula, and the
anterior cingulate (Siegal & Varley, 2002; see Cozolino, 2006, for a review).

The right OFC is involved in decoding mental states, while the left OFC specializes in reasoning about these states (Sabbagh, 2004). Damasio (2003) points out that empathy is associated with the right hemisphere's somatosensory cortices, a region also associated with integrated mapping of the body. Damage to this area of the brain results in demonstrable loss of empathy for others. Overall there may be three major nodes involved in ToM processing:

1. Medial prefrontal cortex (PFC) for self-related mental states
2. Superior temporal sulcus for goals and outcomes
3. Inferior frontal PFC for actions and goals (Frith & Frith, 1999)

If certain key modules of a child's brain are impaired by insults such as traumatic brain injury, or through disturbed attachment experience, the development of ToM is stunted. The importance of these areas is exemplified by research showing that prenatal abnormal development of the OFC is associated with ToM deficits that seem to underlie the problems autistic children have with social appraisal (Baron-Cohen, 1995).

The frontal-lobe structures that make it possible to conduct complex interactions in attachment relationships are also fundamental to doing therapeutic work with children. In growing up, children may learn from interactions with parents that rage is a dangerous instinct and the person inspiring it can be silenced or banished. The lesson may be that rage leads to abandonment. Or the lesson may be that rage, like other evils in life, can be transformed by goodness. The basis for the transfer of this kind of critical knowledge about conducting an internal life and relationships with other people arises from interactions between parents and children, or children and their therapists. It requires a brain with the capacity to share the emotional experience of another person, think about *why* we feel what we feel, and what motivates others.

The OFC is critical in integrating these processes. Studies measuring OFC activity demonstrate that when this area of the frontal lobes is activated, the person experiences feelings of warmth and love. Mothers participating in functional magnetic resonance imaging studies show activated, OFCs when viewing pictures of their infants but not when looking at pictures of other people. The greater the degree to which the OFC is activated, the stronger the reported feelings. The OFC essentially overwhelms the rest of the brain with these warm feelings (Nitschke et al., 2003).

The OFC is highly connected with several subcortical structures, including the amygdala. These connections tie the OFC in to nonconscious centers of motivation and emotion (Fuster, 1997). The OFC is both a receiver (so to speak) and a transmitter of the neurodynamic data underlying the psychological experience of emotion. The OFC's capacity for planning develops step-for-step with the child's capacity for integrating conscious and nonconscious experiences of emotion. These networks allow children and teens to fiercely desire the attainment of a goal, such as making the A level in Little League, and manage their emotions when they only make the B team. The ability to inhibit impulsive emotions that may conflict with long-range planning is critical. All these functions make the OFC a centerpiece in the therapeutic brain. One of the goals of brain-based therapy is to promote neuroplastic flexibility in the frontal lobe regions. As affect regulatory skills are strengthened, the OFC can more effectively inhibit activation of subcortical areas, including the amygdala. Better OFC control over the reactivity of the subcortical anxiety modules helps children manage fear and make better decisions about risk taking.

An area of the OFC not so poetically referred to as F1 and an area of the anterior cingulate cortex (ACC) referred to as area 24 are thought to be involved in our emotional reactions to others, especially instantaneous feelings of empathy. Hearing a baby cry, for example, can evoke a gut-level response in an adult. Some investigators believe these networks are also part of the neural basis for love because they activate when we find a person attractive or we see a picture of a loved one (Bartels & Zeki, 2000).

Spindle Cells: Both F1 in the OFC and area 24 in the ACC are rich in a second kind of specialized neuron, the *spindle cell*. Spindle cells are more abundant in humans than in any other mammals. Humans have 1,000 times more spindle cells than do chimps, our closest relatives. Spindle cells connect divergent bits of information quickly and efficiently in unique ways (Nimchinsky, Vogt, Morrison, & Hof, 1995; Nimchinsky et al., 1999). Many theorists attribute our capacity to make snap judgments to these cells. They are named for their large bulb (about four times the size of the bulb of the average neuron) at one end and their spindly extension at the other. These peculiarities are thought to facilitate high-velocity transmission; hence the "snap" in snap judgment. Their central location and rich interconnectedness suggest the importance of spindle cells in social relatedness and emotional experience. Spindle cells have abundant synaptic receptors for dopamine, serotonin, and vasopressin—and each of these neurochemicals plays a role in the emergent psychological experience of mood.

Spindle cells maintain connections between the cingulate cortex (where these cells are found in large numbers) and the OFC (Allman, 2001). Insofar as they provide a neurodynamic interface between cognition and emotion, spindle cells help us maintain sustained attention and self-control. They provide the behavioral flexibility to engage in quick but complex problem resolution in emotionally stirring situations (Allman, 2001, 2005). Spindle cells emerge after birth and their growth and development appears to be dependent on experiential stimulation. Their development also seems to be susceptible to the adverse effects of neglect, abuse, and trauma, which can produce deficits in the abilities organized by the cingulate cortex (see Cozolino, 2006, for a review). Spindle cells are one of the many parts of the brain that participate in the integration of emotionally provocative and conarrativizing experiences in psychotherapy.

The ACC acts as an alarm system for both emotional and physical pain (Eisenberger & Lieberman, 2004) and is sensitive to signs of impending rejection (Lieberman & Eisenberger, 2005). The ACC is activated in such formative social interactions as early attachment, social bonding, and psychotherapy. Damage to the ACC results in decreased empathy and decreased maternal behavior (Brothers et al., 1996). When we or those we love experience pain or social ridicule, the ACC becomes activated (Botvinick et al., 2005). The posterior part of the cingulate cortex has been correlated with autobiographical memories and emotional processing (Critchley et al., 2003). Autobiographical memories in the form of narratives provide the text, as it were, the manifest content, for therapy.

Between the core of the brain, the temporal lobe on the sides, and the parietal lobe in the rear is the *insula*. The insula acts as a conduit between subcortical areas and the cerebral cortex. It sends information from the body, the amygdala, and other brain modules to emotion-regulation networks in the OFC. Insula-OFC processing transforms raw emotional experience through reflective interpretation. The insula contributes an inward somatic dimension to empathy, correcting the purely cerebral view of another person's experience. The combined top-down, bottom-up circuitry results in a more accurate empathy (Carr, Iacoboni, Dubeau, Mazziotta, & Lenzi, 2003). Differences in the efficiency of these brain processes may be what discriminates average from exceptional psychotherapists.

Facial Expression: In addition to the interplay of the OFC, the ACC, and the insula-OFC networks, important neurodynamic modules are activated by a smile, a frown, or an expression of fear. Facial expression communicates a wealth of information. The movement and position of the eyelids and the whites of the eyes (the sclera) alone convey important information quickly and nonconsciously. In one study, researchers exposed subjects to various photographs of the eyes. The photographs featured differing ratios of the pupil-to-sclera characteristic of different emotional states—some happy, some fearful—that were presented too rapidly for research subjects to be consciously aware of what they had seen. Their amygdalas, however, were significantly activated by the fearful eyes (Whalen, Kagan, & Cook, 2004).

The right hemisphere is more adept than the left at reading emotions in the facial expressions of others (Ahern et al., 1991). Patients with right-hemisphere damage are impaired in their ability to read both emotional facial expressions and emotionally expressive body language (Blonder, Bowers, & Heilman, 1991). The left hemisphere lacks the competence of the right side in accurately reading not only the facial expressions of others but also their body postures, gestures, and subtle movements. The right hemisphere reacts to these communications accurately even when they are at odds with what the other person, using their left hemisphere, is communicating verbally. Alexithymics process facial information atypically, using their left hemispheres more than the right side, and activate their medial frontal regions and cingulate gyrus less than do normals (Berthoz, Armony, Blair, & Dolan, 2002).

The right hemisphere processes the gist of a situation and is an invaluable check on the sometimes overly explicit and verbal process of psychotherapy. In child and adolescent treatment, it is also well to remember that the right hemisphere develops more quickly in infancy than does the left, and that nonverbal communication may provide the best clues to the patient's emotional experiences in the preverbal years.

Other neurodynamic networks that are important in processing emotional communications in facial expression are the fusiform gyrus, superior temporal sulcus, and amygdala (Gauthier et al., 2000; Puce, Allison, Gore, & McCarthy, 1995). Amygdalar damage results in deficits in social judgment and in reading faces—especially in estimating another's trustworthiness when there is a discrepancy between verbal and nonverbal communication (Whalen et al., 2004). After the amygdala performs a quick-and-dirty appraisal, a variety of regions in the cortex become activated depending on whether the person is familiar or a stranger. Interestingly, these systems in humans are activated only when faces are right-side up. When subjects are shown pictures of people upside-down, these modules are not activated (Kilts, Egan, Gideon, Ely, & Hoffman, 2003). Instead, systems associated with identifying *objects* are activated (Aguirre et al., 1999). Recall that persons with autism use these same object-oriented systems when visually processing objects and people.

Paul Ekman, a psychologist at the University of California, San Francisco, has done pioneering work on facial expression (Ekman, 1993). Ekman demonstrated that basic facial expressions are universally understood cross-culturally (Ekman & Frieson, 1972). He also demonstrated that activating one of the networks for communicating emotions activates other elements in the system as well. A feedback process occurs simply by making an emotional facial expression. If children are asked to frown or smile, for example, they are likely to report feeling sad or happy, respectively. Contracting the muscles on the right side of the face activates our left hemisphere, and is likely to produce a more positive emotion. Conversely, contracting the muscles on the left side of the face activates the right hemisphere, and is likely to produce a negative shift (Schiff et al., 1992). We are also influenced emotionally by the affective tone of what we are looking at. Researchers have found that subjects looking at a smiling face are likely to feel more positive than those looking at a face that is wearing a frown (Larsen, Kasimatis, & Frey, 1992). Children, not surprisingly, have a preference for happy faces (Leppanen & Hietanen, 2003).

BUILDING POSITIVE AFFECT AND METACOGNITION

As therapists, we read the facial expressions of our child and teen clients and influence them through our own expressions. Using mirror neurons, children are nonconsciously prone to imitate our facial expressions and moods, just as they do with parents and peers. The more often positive emotional states occur in therapy, the more likely it is that children will incorporate them as common moods.

When the brain is at rest, the modules that seem to be idling include the dorsal and ventral parts of the medial PFC and parts of the intraparietal sulcus (Mitchell et al., 2002). These idling circuits seem to become more active when children interact with us or think about what we are trying to communicate. According to Iacoboni and colleagues (2004), these neural systems make up a system that comes to life when we are mulling over relationships. The brains of children are acutely sensitive not only to attachment relationships but also to interpersonal communications in general. Therapists can tap into this sensitivity and help children rewire neural systems to promote ToM, flexibility, positive moods, and resiliency.

A IS FOR ATTUNEMENT

The therapeutic relationship is a focus of all forms of psychotherapy, regardless of the particular orientation. It is made possible by the interplay of neurodynamic elements we reviewed in the last section, and equally by the environmental inputs from the primary caregiving relationships. Winnicott (1965) helped lay the foundation for the concept of *attunement*, which goes beyond the useful (if commonplace) idea that therapists should try to understand the patient's words and actions. In Winnicottian terms, and in the subsequent research of Stern (1985), Beebe and Lachmann (1994, 2002), and other clinically oriented infancy researchers, attunement takes on the sense of a networked reality, one that allows for separateness and also for the incomparable feeling of moments that are completely shared. Infant researchers such as Stern see this experience reoccurring throughout infancy and childhood, and playing a formative role in children's emerging capacities to experience a self, name feelings, and generate rules based on repetitive emotional experiences.

The degree to which we can help child or adolescent patients overcome the effects of ambivalent or avoidant attachment styles depends on many different variables. Optimally, to the extent that a therapeutic contact lasts and becomes an intimate bond, something like "reparenting" can occur. In the present context, this means that children have the opportunity to experience a fairly complete range of both negative and positive feelings for the therapist. As Winnicott repeatedly asserted, the expression of negative, angry, and hateful feelings is often what liberates the child from the bonds of an insecure attachment style. The good-enough therapist who can tolerate these feelings and not reciprocate in kind can help the child revise underlying attachment insecurities.

Beebe and Lachmann (2002) use the term "bidirectional regulation" to describe the complex interactional patterns between infants and caretakers that constitute the earliest examples of attunement:

> Positive as well as aversive interactions can be bidirectionally coordinated. The statistical concept of the probability that one person's behavioral stream can be predicted from that of the other can be translated into the idea that each person can sense whether or not the partner's behavior is related in time to his or her own, that is "coordinated." Sensing that the partner's behavior is coordinated with one's own provides the most fundamental layer of implicit relatedness. This sensing generally goes on out of awareness; it is most easily noticed when absent. But this sensing can be brought into awareness under certain conditions. This concept of bidirectional coordination defines one use of the term co-construction, that is, that all interactions are co-constructed by both people. (2002, p. 210–211)

EDDIE

Attunement, or "bidirectonal coordination," in a relationship changes and develops in the course of child therapies. It has both conscious and nonconscious dimensions, as illustrated in the case of Eddie, a boy one of us began working with when he had just turned eight. Eddie was brought to therapy by his mother and stepfather because of his temper tantrums, and his seemingly calculated humiliations of his little sister. Eddie cussed like a sailor and broke things. He had compulsive symptoms related to his aggressiveness. He consumed all the hot water in the house in the course of long showers and washed his hands so often and so vigorously they looked red and raw. Eddie was smart as a whip and disdainful of anyone who couldn't keep up with his exceptional capacity to learn.

Eddie's first therapy session took place two days after his therapist had taken delivery of a new upholstered chair for the office. Eddie streaked into the room, cased the joint, and announced that he and the therapist were going to play hide and seek. Eddie plunked down in front of one of the upholstered chairs, reached behind himself and lifted the chair over his head; the next thing the therapist knew, Eddie was actually inside the chair. He had ripped out the cheese-cloth covering on the bottom of the chair in the course of making himself disappear. Except for the therapist, the room looked empty, but laughter was coming from inside the chair.

Over the course of the next weeks and months, Eddie laid siege to the office, the play materials, and often the therapist's person. The relationship fluctuated between the limit-setting characteristic of a parent–child relationship and a reflective one typical of child therapy. The therapist made some progress in establishing a therapeutic alliance with Eddie, partially dislodging him from his habitual mode of communicating through action (just an exaggeration of what normal 8-year-olds do). Eddie showed progress in using words, although sometimes his speech, like a sports announcer's, was simply a narrative following the ongoing stream of movement.

The next hurdle in treatment was establishing a relationship in which one of the central activities was talking about feelings and repairing therapeutic ruptures. Rupture repair characterizes successful therapies with adults (Safran & Muran, 2003), and it is, if anything, even more important in child work. Perhaps no activity in therapy relies more on the therapist's attunement to the child's affects and defenses. As the hours with Eddie went by, there were many opportunities to practice it, for example:

Eddie made a paper chain and tied it to the doorknob of a closet in the office. He told the therapist to start turning it so he could jump rope. Eddie jumped in the arc of the swinging paper chain two or three times. He jumped on the chain and broke it. He and the therapist repaired it together. They resumed the game for a moment and then Eddie deliberately broke the chain again.

T: "Eddie, it seems like you're upset about something. I guess it's hard to just tell me about it."

E: "You're stupid!" he said with a smile.

They fixed the chain again and Eddie, bossing the therapist around, had him turn it at different heights and at differing speeds. He rolled through the chain and crashed it down. He got up and swore and ripped the chain further, then tried to hit the therapist with it.

T: "I don't want to be hit, stop. You're upset about something that happened and now about the chain too. But sometimes when you get upset, you get so much stuff going that I can't think about what the feelings are, and I don't think you can either. Let's talk about it and try to figure it out."

Eddie hit the therapist with the chain hard enough to make him feel spontaneously angry.

T: "I said stop it. I'm not going to let you do that."

E: "Sorry!" he said, laughed anxiously, and retreated a few steps.

T: "That made me mad, Eddie, and you know it. You look worried about what I'm going to do about it. Let's calm down and talk this out."

He smiled, seemed to come toward the therapist and yet stay where he was at the same time. He looked at him attentively.

T: "You're checking it out to see if I'm still angry at you, huh? Well, I'm not angry anymore but when so much gets going on in here, I feel like it makes it hard for me to understand your feelings or to help you. You know what I mean?"

The therapist, in addition to conducting a running commentary on the process, modeled for Eddie how development helps us tame narcissistic slights and feel safer. He showed Eddie how to use words to label feelings and interpret actions, transferring right hemispheric and limbic experience to the left PFC, which is more positive. Eddie did his part in the therapy dyad by closely attending to another important modality in interpersonal communication—facial expression—and using cues in the therapist's expression to modulate the interaction.

As further hours went by, Eddie showed signs of developing an interest in the therapist's life outside the office. When the therapist informed him that he would be taking a vacation at the end of the summer, Eddie asked if the therapist had any pets, and volunteered to take care of them. The therapist told Eddie that he did indeed have a pet, an old and irascible parrot. Eddie became interested in parrots and did some research about them. He drew pictures of them during the hour. He got jobs watering lawns during the summer and caring for the pets of neighbors when they were away for short periods. He kept asking about the impending vacation and earnestly asking the therapist about babysitting the old parrot. These discussions were interspersed with a give-and-take that had become routine in the hours, around themes of aggression, testing, and anxiety about the repercussions of destructiveness.

Without planning to do so, the therapist after one of these discussions told Eddie that he just wouldn't be comfortable entrusting to him anything that meant as much to him as that old bird. Eddie was silent and uncharacteristically still. He looked at the therapist solemnly and nodded. He got it. He understood that the therapist was outside his aggressive fantasies yet was attuned enough to them that he could see what it was that Eddie was worried about. From there they could embark on some tentative discussions of Eddie's memories of early abuse.

Attunement and Metacognition

Attunement with a child involves coherent, often nonconscious, interaction between the therapist's thoughts and emotions and those of the child. The therapist understands and empathizes with the child's view of his or her predicament (not infrequently including feelings about having to come for therapy). From an emotional perspective, the therapist feels some version of what the child or teen feels and communicates it back in the form of "this is how I see you" (Preston & deWaal, 2002). By paying close attention to the transference dynamics in the relationship, the therapist can infer the child or teen's nonconscious and habitual patterns of relating. Secondarily the therapist can create some markers differentiating between what happens in the therapeutic relationship and the child's habitual patterns of relating to others. On a conscious level, the therapist can help the child understand how past experience and beliefs do or do not match up to current experience and create new narratives where change is called for.

Attunement brings nonconscious processing between the child and the therapist to the forefront, and engages the empathetic neural networks in the brains of both parties—from mirror neurons and spindle cells to the cortical cognitive and affective capacities underlying a theory of mind. The task of therapy is the repair of attachment difficulties. The child's characterological reactions convey implicit memories of attachment experiences that are difficult to describe but are enacted behaviorally across a range of situations. Therapists soon learn that even the most brilliant and concise interpretation is not sufficient to produce change in these schemata. A combination of empathy and gentle encouragement that is sustained over time typically can do so. It challenges the child to question and abandon less secure representations of what a relationship is and what it can do. New representations of self and others, which eventually transform the old ones, develop out of this kind of interaction.

Establishing attunement is more difficult with some children than with others. Sexually abused children and/or adolescents may be either disconcertingly open and needy or very cautious and defensive with their therapists. A therapist who lacks warmth and empathy, or who appears uninterested or indifferent about reports of abuse, can cause a child to experience further humiliation and shame and reinforce insecure attachment schemata. In some cases, the therapist may fear having to report child abuse to an outside agency or may be uncomfortable talking about sexual issues.

Staying attuned with a child or adolescent involves shared attention, mutual positive feelings, and in-sync body language. It frequently involves the judicious sharing of the therapist's feelings about what's going on in the hour, and looking for opportunities to repair ruptures in the relationship by fully attending to the child's feelings and attempts to manage them. A stream of nonverbal communication accompanies the language. The tempo of naturally coupled movements increases positive feelings (Bernieri & Rosenthal [1991] reported in Goleman, 2006). Two people in conversation can develop better rapport by naturally matching the rhythm of inhaling and exhaling (McFarland, 2001). Empathy grows out of such shared embodied states of attunement.

S IS FOR SYSTEMS

The two people in the therapeutic relationship form a complex system and each, in turn, is connected to other systems (both real and conceptual), in something like the way that individual neurons are part of hierarchically organized modules in the brains of the two individuals. Conceptualizing and carrying out psychotherapy with younger patients requires therapists to think explicitly about some of these systems; others remain implicit and in the background but affect the course of treatment nonetheless.

THE FAMILY SYSTEM

Any assessment of a child or an adolescent necessarily involves an assessment of the family system. Therapists must keenly observe how family members interact and how affects are handled in the family. How children respond to parent(s) and siblings tells much about their development. The family's mood and the affective style of the parents is particularly important. A depressed mother should cause us to look for a similar disorder and an insecure attachment style in the child.

Because children adapt to their parents' attachment style, work with parents is almost always indicated with children under the age of 12. In most cases, children do not come to treatment on their own and the primary alliance typically is with the parents. Parents who are clinically depressed or anxious may be candidates for their own treatment. Sometimes they respond to therapist suggestions that appear to be aimed at the child's well-being. By empathizing with parents about the difficulties of parenting, helping them reframe their feelings of failure for having a child in treatment, and encouraging them to restart activities that they used to enjoy (such as a spiritual practice or a physical exercise regimen), child therapists can be enormously helpful to parents. Therapists who talk hopefully about the outcome of treatment, remind parents about their child's positive qualities, and encourage them to plan activities the family enjoys help shift the family system into more positive affective territory.

SOCIAL SYSTEMS

The social system surrounding the therapeutic dyad may stay in the background or be impossible to ignore in its effects on the child and family system and the treatment. Economic, educational, public safety, and other critical resources are distributed inequitably and are silent partners in child development. Racism is a factor that inevitably affects children of color, and ethnic and religious factors play an important role in development as well. The protective factors that shield children from traumatic experiences vary, but in all ethnic, religious, and racial subsystems in our society (and probably in all societies), young people are more vulnerable. Protective factors in the family and society generally too often fail to shield children from abusive behavior. As a result, trauma is more common among the child population than we would like to believe. It is part of a systematic approach to child treatment to inquire about the occurrence of traumatic events in the lives of children (and the lives of their parents) as soon as there is sufficient rapport to support the question.

Trauma has long-lasting effects on many of the children exposed to it. Felitti and colleagues constructed a sample of 13,000 adults who had been medically assessed at Kaiser Permanente (Felitti, et al., 1998). Participants were independently surveyed regarding the experience of "adverse child-hood events," such as sexual abuse or witnessing the physical abuse of a parent. Investigators compared the incidence of such events with subjects' later development of adult psychiatric and medical health problems, and adjusted for demographic factors to obtain a clearer sense of the relationship between early trauma and later psychiatric and medical pathology. The results were startling. More than half of the sample reported at least one, and one-fourth reported two or more categories of childhood exposures. Subjects who had experienced four or more categories of childhood expo-sure, compared to those who had experienced none, had a 4- to 12-fold increased risk for alcoholism, drug abuse, depression, and suicide attempts. Subjects who as children had witnessed parental spousal abuse had a fourfold increased risk for later ischemic heart disease (Felitti, et al., 1998).

Child and family therapy can help ameliorate or even prevent this pattern of intergenerational transmission of psychobehavioral and medical pathology—but in many cases psychotherapy alone may not be sufficient. For this reason the assessing therapist must think systematically about including other needed resources and how the family can obtain them. Access to pediatric, educational, and social services varies from one social subsystem to another, but Felitti's Adverse Childhood Events Study makes it all too clear how important it is for therapists to do their utmost to help patients connect with the services they need. Given the incidence of adverse events, it is a necessary element in the assessment to screen for them, and to work with parents and the system of care to provide appropriate interventions.

Where the child's age and developmental level permit, it is a good practice to interview the child alone for some part of the initial assessment. This separation is likely to prime the child's attachment schemata and provide useful information for treatment planning. How does the child handle this "strange" situation, and how do parents and children deal with the reunion that takes place when the therapist invites them back into the room? If the separation has provoked some rupture in the relationship between either parent and child or child and therapist, it is a good time to point out that repairing problems like this are what therapy is all about. Repairing ruptures teaches important emotion-regulation skills and changes the brain.

An important part of being systematic in child therapy is helping the family understand what is expected of the various parties in the treatment and how the therapy will work. In the mental health system where the authors work, often several people are involved besides the therapist, the child, and the parents. Child therapists routinely gather information from multiple sources. Pediatricians and other medical specialists may be involved and therapists also work with counselors, teachers, and educational psychologists in the school setting. Extended family members also may become involved in the treatment to one degree or another.

DIAGNOSTIC SYSTEMS

Making a plan to achieve the goals of therapy and how they are likely to be met will vary depending on the therapist's specific situation. The psychotherapy outcome literature has demonstrated that diagnosis is not an especially useful foundation on which to build a psychotherapeutic treatment plan (Lambert & Barley, 2002). DSM diagnoses are, however, a necessary and useful tool for therapists and mental health professionals collaborating with psychiatrists or other providers, or where third-party reimbursements or clients are involved. Greenspan (1996, pp. 17–22) suggests some good overall principles that make diagnosis a more useful process:

1. Generate a collaborative process for all involved.
2. Use an integrated developmental model.
3. Utilize multiple sources of information.
4. Attend closely to interactions with the parents.
5. Get a sense of the child's developmental history.
6. Learn how the child organizes experience and what the child's functional and cognitive abilities are.
7. Determine the child's current competencies and strengths.
8. Discover what needs the most attention in the child's development.

At Kaiser Permanente we use a standard child evaluation form that assesses these factors:

1. Identifying information and referral source:
2. Presenting problem:
   • Mood:
   • Conduct:
   • Interpersonal contacts outside the family:
   • Academic:
   • Self-regulatory:
   • Other:

3. Psychosocial history:
   - Family structure (siblings, etc.):
   - Pregnancy:
   - Temperament:
   - Attachment issues:
   - Early developmental landmarks:
   - Trauma, health:
   - School performance:
   - History of current problem:
4. Patient's prior psychiatric history:
   - Outpatient therapy:
   - Inpatient treatment:
5. Family history/impressions:
   - Biological mother:
   - Biological father:
   - Sibling:
6. Past medical history:
7. Substance abuse screening:
   - During pregnancy:
   - Current drinks/drugs per day:
   - Other history:
8. Mental status examination:
   - Appearance (grooming, head size, bruises, etc.):
   - Behavior (energy, affect, lateralization or speed of movements):
   - Demeanor/facial expression/manner:
   - Speech (coherence, irregularities):
   - Mood (anxious, depressed, elated):
   - Affect:
   - Thought process (focused; tangential; disorganized):
   - Thought content (preoccupied, morbid, bizarre):
   - Attention (distractible, clouded):
   - Impulse control (inhibited, impulsive):
   - Insight (reflective, ToM):
   - Judgment (i.e. keen sense of logic and cause and effect):
9. Self-harms:
   - Cutting/burning:
   - Suicide attempts:
   - Current thoughts:
   - Plans:
   - Family history:
   - Peer history:

- Access to means (firearms in house?):
- Other risk issues: _____
- Overall assessment of risk: _____
10. *DSM-IV* diagnosis: I: II: III:
11. Goals of treatment:
    - Parents:
    - Child/adolescent:
    - Brain-based:
12. Treatment plan:
    - Expectations of therapist:
    - Expectations of parent:
    - Expectations of child:
    - Other clinicians/services:
    - Educational services:

Finally, part of a systematic approach in some child and adolescent cases requires consideration of a medication evaluation. In Chapters 7–9 we will deal in detail with medications commonly used in the treatment of OCD, ADHD, and depression. For the present, it should be mentioned that all child therapists should have a relationship with an expert child psychiatrist or behavioral pediatrician. Prescribing for teens and adolescents is still more of an art than a science. How antidepressants work on the brain is slowly becoming understood, and there are special concerns about their effects on the developing brain. All too little solid evidence is available about the long-term effects of these agents. Nevertheless, most experienced clinicians have concluded that antidepressants are on balance helpful with major depression and in some cases indispensable (Raeburn, 2007).

CONCEPTUAL SYSTEMS

Once a coherent diagnostic picture emerges, the therapist uses a psychological framework and conceptual system to formulate the case and treatment plan. A brain-based approach is a good overall framework, because the effectiveness of developmental, cognitive, expressive, psychodynamic, and cognitive-behavioral methods depends on their power to affect the brain in a positive manner. Not all psychotherapeutic methods actually do this. For example, a not uncommon event in therapy with an adolescent is that the teen tries to recruit the therapist to join in being critical of the parents because they are trying to set limits. Therapeutic attunement (in the sense of a completely congruent stance) with the adolescent is not likely to produce any neurodynamic, cognitive, or emotional change in the patient.

Effective therapy involves disrupting the powerful neurodynamically based attractors of moods, cognitions, and emotion regulation. Therapists can implement this principle in any one of several ways: they may point out that the rules actually seem pretty reasonable or, if not reasonable, may be motivated by the parents' concern. It may be useful to mirror the patient's viewpoint in a Rogerian way ("So the way you see it is that . . . "). Utilizing the adolescent's developing capacity to look at things from various angles, the therapist might find it useful to ask the teen to adopt for a moment the parents' point of view. What *do* these people feel and what *are* they thinking that makes them say and do these things? It can also be effective to work "in the transference," focusing on the teen's feelings about the therapist not supporting their view, and on repairing the rupture in the therapeutic relationship that has occurred as a result. Whatever seems clinically indicated at the time, it is typically a mistake to remain silent or to actively join an adolescent's attacks on their parents.

Often enough, as therapists we are called on to be aware of more than one way of thinking about our work as it is unfolding with children and adolescents. When we are playing with a child, for example, we are expected to be fully engaged in the play, using our mirror neurons and our PFCs to grasp how the child is seeing things and how the action is driven by certain themes and patterns of affect regulation. Some of the communication is verbal; much of it is in the child's (and our own) facial expressions, tone of voice, and body language. While our left frontal lobe is thinking of something to say, the right side is putting together the nonverbal communication. Both sides are called on to look at the play as a dream-work, as an activity with important symbolic and nonverbal elements that can be verbalized, utilizing integrated right-left and top-bottom processing in the brain. Yet we are also always in the role of an alternative adult. The therapeutic relationship presents an opportunity to modify neural networks that mediate thoughts and feelings previously associated with repetitive conflicts by modeling, coconstructing new narratives, and challenging the client to come out from behind the barricades and start (or stop) taking risks.

As we noted in Chapter 2, moderate stress facilitates neuroplasticity and promotes new learning, whereas extreme stress and trauma have a corrosive effect on the brain and can lead to dissociation. The role of psychotherapy is to promote durable growth and work against dissociation by integrating disparate states and self-representations (Cozolino, 2002; Grigsby & Stevens, 2000). Depending on children's level of functioning, the goal of therapy may be to stabilize them in a secure attached state, verbalize implicit emotional reactions, and rely on neuroplasticity to promote new and healthy traits. Good-enough therapists elicit more positive transference, and are also better prepared to deal with ruptures in the therapeutic relationship. Being a good-enough therapist means struggling against whatever qualities we, as therapists, may have in common with the uninvolved mothers of avoidantly attached children and with the inconsistent ones of the ambivalently attached children. A systematic way of proceeding helps ensure that we will remain genuinely attuned to the child—not always doing what the child would wish us to do, but doing what is in the child's best interests as we understand them.

E IS FOR EVIDENCE-BASED

Evidence-based treatments (EBTs) is a term that is applied to therapeutic approaches that meet the American Psychological Association's (1995) standards for empirical validation. In the clinics in which we work, EBTs are known collectively as "best practices" and are offered in formats ranging from one-session classes to ongoing groups designed for patients with diagnostically related problems. Within our system, best practices have become mainstream. Kaiser Permanente's Best Practices workgroups look for effective ways of treating the system's 3 million Northern California members in its 25 psychiatry clinics and 5 chemical dependency day-treatment programs. Where the scientific evidence does not warrant a practice guideline, clinical recommendations and clinical resources have been published to help clinicians understand a consensus expert approach. Publications on attention-deficit hyperactivity disorder in children, adolescent depression, adolescent eating disorders, childhood obsessive-compulsive disorder, and social anxiety disorder set out EBT approaches that clinicians may wish to consider in treating these problems (Kaiser Permanente, 2001a, 2001b, 2003, 2004, 2005, 2008).

One of us (LL) leads the Best Practices program and the other (JA) has organized a program for training postdoctoral psychology residents and psychology, social work, and marriage and family therapy interns utilizing the Best Practices literature as the curriculum. Each year over 100 psychology postdoctoral residents and interns are trained in the Best Practices model.

Although voluminous literature exists on EBTs for many different psychological problems, practical considerations limit us to a sampling of these approaches rather than an encyclopedic overview. We have chosen to do this for two reasons. The first is that the mission of this book (and its companion volume on adults) is to look at the issue of therapeutic effectiveness in a new way, based on an understanding of how the brain works. The discovery that these approaches are effective in treating common psychological problems is by no means just a happy accident (as was the case with many psychotropic medications), but rather the product of concerted research. Astonishingly, this research has had almost nothing to do with the brain or how the brain actually works. Much of the discussion in this book and its companion volume is devoted to closing the gap between neuroscience and psychotherapeutic research and practice.

A second reason we have limited our discussion of the EBTs relevant to child practice is that understanding something about the brain changes the standards for what constitutes effectiveness. Neuroscience helps clarify the fact that technique is only one part of what matters in therapy. The person of the patient, for example, is more important than method in determining outcome, and the person of the therapist is every bit as important as whether or not a particular technique is used in the treatment. Many things make therapy effective, and our acronym, BASE, captures most of what is relevant to success. In subsequent chapters we have limited our presentation of EBTs to those problems most commonly seen in child work— ADHD, depression, and anxiety—and apply the brain-based approach to each. These problems make up the bulk of current referrals for child mental health services.

CHAPTER 7

Disorders of Attention and Self-Regulation

Tommy's mother pushes her fingers through her hair. "I wish I could give up on you," she says, "I wish I could just let you fail and not give it a second thought."

"So do I," Tommy says glumly.

—E.M. Hallowell and J.J. Ratey

ATTENTION-DEFICIT DISORDER (ADD), with or without hyperactivity, is the most commonly diagnosed childhood psychological disorder. The diagnosis is not without controversy. Some see attention-deficit diagnoses as little more than a label, one that has been overused since the 1980s (Barkley, 1997a). While physicians are blasted for "giving speed" to kids, at a Kaiser Permanente Medical Center we noticed a surge of people *seeking* a diagnosis of ADD following a segment about it on *Oprah*. A well-known Bay Area psychiatrist specializing in ADD ran ads in the *San Francisco Chronicle* featuring screening questions that read more like astrology than science. Many of the items could have been positively endorsed by almost anyone.

Scores of people seem to be shopping for a diagnosis that explains why they cannot muster the focused attention necessary to achieve their goals. Parents look for reasons to explain why their child "never listens" or does not finish homework. For some, a diagnosis of ADD seems to lighten the burden of personal responsibility.

In fact, ADD is a serious affliction that should never be diagnosed casually. Over the last 40 years, many descriptive terms have been used for the spectrum of symptoms associated with ADD/ADHD (attention-deficit hyperactivity disorder), including hyperactive child syndrome, hyperkinesias, hyperkinetic disorder, minimal brain function, and hyperkinetic disorder in childhood. The syndrome is considered chronic, and there is no cure. It has been shown to have a high genetic concordance, with significant neuroanatomical and neurophysiological correlates. From a brain-based perspective, it would seem that the syndrome is misnamed; ADD is a disorder not only of attention but of the executive brain. It adversely affects relationships, impulse control, working memory, and judgment. If individual psychological development is the product of interactions between genetically influenced structure and responsiveness to the environment, ADD is at the far structural end of the spectrum.

DIAGNOSIS

There are two main varieties of this disorder, the impulsive type and the distractible type. Many children share characteristics of both, ranging from low on both factors, to low on one and high on the other, to high on both impulsivity *and* distractibility. Children with predominantly distractible symptoms have difficulties concentrating on any one thing. Easily beguiled by the stimuli in their surroundings, these children are prone to miss details and make mistakes. They may get bored quickly by tasks they do not relish, such as homework, and exhibit tenacious capacities for attending to things they enjoy. It is hard for an ADD/ADHD child to maintain the neural networks involved in paying the kind of sustained attention needed to start and complete a task.

The *Diagnostic and Statistical Manual of Mental Disorders* (*DSM*) provides some additional behavioral signs of attentional problems characteristic of ADD:

- Does not seem to listen when spoken to directly
- Often does not follow through on directions and fails to finish tasks
- Frequently has trouble organizing tasks and activities
- Frequently avoids activities that require sustained mental effort
- Loses things
- Gets distracted by extraneous noise
- Forgets even routine daily activities

Children are often brought in by exasperated parents who have read about the diagnosis and are convinced their child must have it. In our experience, a third or more of the children labeled with ADD are mis-diagnosed. One good practical rule of thumb in assessing children for ADD is that everything *but* ADD should be ruled out first. Children with self-regulatory issues arising from different causes are quite likely to be misdiagnosed with ADD. Pervasive developmental disabilities and children with a psychotic process distracted by voices also have problems attending and self-regulating. In contrast to these conditions, however, ADD kids respond more to external cues than to internal ones. Their self-regulatory capacities are so impaired that they are unduly influenced by environmental stimuli. The primary diagnostic question becomes: is the self-regulatory problem *reactive* (in which case, the problem is not ADD) or is it *neurodynamic*?

Many ADD children, especially those with the inattentive type of the disorder, are sad and ashamed of their inability to meet the developmental landmarks their peers pass with ease. With ADD, problems with parents typically occur after the early attachment period and more in the toddler phase, when children are expected to start showing capacities for self-regulation. Clinicians evaluating a child for possible ADD/ ADHD should attend to the child's level of *impulsivity* in addition to inattention. Impulsive children act and react quickly, without thinking of the consequences of their actions. Again, these are capacities that rely on cortical (particularly the PFC) networks that develop across childhood and well into adulthood, so assessment requires that the clinician have a good sense of age-appropriate norms for planning, foresight, and aim-oriented behavior. Whereas children with conduct problems may react the way they do because attachment issues, overcorrection, or inconsistent parenting predispose them to feel less empathy and to care less about being liked and approved of by others, these are not causal elements for ADD.

Impulsivity in ADD children may be apparent from speech (deficits in stopping thoughts from becoming speech), in big-muscle behavior (running out into the street without looking), and in behavioral choices (hitting, butting in line). The concept of cause and effect does not easily get integrated into the executive process for self-regulation or planning for these children. Although a little girl may have been told many times that being part of a group requires her to "wait your turn," for example, the wiring in her executive and social brain does not accommodate well to the lesson. "I have to tell him the same thing over and over," one mother said, "and every time it's as if I'd never said it before. I could say it a thousand times, and it's still like the first time I've said it." The DSM also mentions that impulsive children and adolescents are prone to blurt out answers before the speaker has completed the question and habitually interrupt or intrude on others.

The impulsivity characteristic of ADD/ADHD children may arise because of atypical development in the frontal lobe regulatory systems in the brain. As we discussed in Chapter 6, these systems develop over time and are shaped by how children experience the demands placed on them. Even young children can be considered and observed to be "temperamentally difficult," a description that includes some who may later turn out to develop ADD/ADHD. The proportion of erratic eating and sleeping habits seems to be higher in young children who later develop the syndrome, as does their sensitivity to noise and other stimuli.

Toddlers who will later demonstrate the full syndrome are more likely to have very "terrible twos," engage in power struggles with caregivers, and have meltdowns and tantrums. One pre-ADD toddler of our acquaintance leapt off his parents' bedroom deck into the branches of a huge oak tree, made his way down to the ground, and was a half block away before his startled mother realized he was no longer in the house and caught up with him. Preschool is often difficult for children with ADD. They are typically identified by teachers and other parents as distractible, unsocialized, impulsive, and hard to control; not infrequently their daycare providers quit or their preschool asks them to leave. The ADD syndrome overtaxes adult caregivers. By school age, impulsivity takes on additional social dimensions outside the family. ADD kids require undue (or impractical) levels of supervision in the classroom, get into fights, act like "babies," and are considered "poor losers" by their peers. By adolescence, impulsivity and self-regulation often become even more problematic: drinking and drug use, sexual permissiveness and aggressivity, and confrontations with authorities over their impulsivity are common.

In addition to inattention and impulsivity, a third factor that must be dealt with in an evaluation is whether the child has symptoms of *hyperactivity* (a factor, like attention, that can be evaluated only in the context of developmental norms). Excessive movements range from being unable to stay seated for more than a few minutes, to incessant movements of the hands and feet, to rapid-fire speech. One ADD boy described the psychological experience accompanying hyperactivity as "words come out before my brain starts to work." Not infrequently, hyperactive children will initiate and try to maintain several activities at the same time. The DSM lists two more frequently observed characteristics of these hyperactive children and adolescents: in latency, running or climbing excessively where it is not appropriate to do so; and great difficulty playing quietly or engaging in leisure-time activities. Once again, these issues are better understood in the general context of neurodynamically impaired self-regulatory functions than as a learned behavioral or conduct disorder.

There is evidence that children who develop the full ADHD syndrome are unusually active even in utero. After birth, they may start climbing out of the crib as soon as they are physically able to do so, or head for a staircase faster than their parents can intercept them. As soon as they can walk, they try to run. The development of fine-motor skills is delayed. As latency-age children, they are messier than their peers and cannot sit still. Teachers have problems controlling them in the classroom—"I can't make Danny stay at his desk"—but the actual problem is that these children have trouble controlling themselves. As we discuss later in this chapter, such characteristics have profound effects on children's relationships, especially the primary relationship with parents.

Many children diagnosed with ADHD during childhood improve as they grow older, but 60% continue to meet the criteria in adulthood (Kessler et al., 2005). By this standard, the disorder is considered chronic. The number of adults with some form of ADHD who nevertheless lead successful and satisfying lives is testimony to the fact that activity levels can be suppressed and modified through neuroplasticity; impulsivity can be tamed to some extent, and the attentional faculty can be developed through structure and practice.

PREVALENCE AND COMORBIDITIES

ADHD affects between 3% and 10% of children. The disorder has been estimated to be anywhere from four to nine times more common among boys than girls (American Psychiatric Association Task Force on *DSM-IV*, 2000). This finding may be due to the fact that the diagnosis is missed more easily among girls (who do not express as much hyperactivity or impulsivity as do boys). The female brain tends to be less hemispherically lateralized than its male counterpart, which may partially compensate for ADHD's neurodynamics. About one-third of the ADD population develops an anxiety disorder, and about 1 child in 5 with an anxiety disorder has some form of ADHD (Kaiser Permanente, 2004). From adolescence on, ADD sufferers are overrepresented in the substance-abusing population. Up to 25% of the population diagnosed in childhood with some form of ADD is later diagnosed as bipolar. This coincidence of diagnoses may be a real phenomenon or an artifact of the difficulty in accurately diagnosing ADD. The impulsive and inattentive symptoms of bipolar disorder mimic those of ADHD, but ADHD symptoms are more stable and persistent. In children, the cycle of mood swings characteristic of bipolar disorder may not be as noticeable.

Roughly 3 people in 4 who have ADD also will be diagnosed with depression at some point in their lives. This figure may represent a true comorbidity, given the fact that ADD has debilitating social and performance effects. For most ADD children, the disorder results in chronic stress (with the neurodynamic consequences of elevated cortisol we have already discussed) and negatively impacts relationships that help normal children achieve stable affect regulation. Depressive symptoms in childhood include moodiness, irritability, and inattentiveness—symptoms that may resemble ADD. ADD is also comorbid at higher-than-expected rates with obsessive-compulsive disorder and learning disabilities. Learning disabilities may overlap at some points with those of ADD; both are brain-based deficits affecting the manner in which a person of average or greater intelligence receives and processes information. Very high percentages of children diagnosed with oppositional defiant disorder (65%) and Tourette's syndrome (50%) are also diagnosed with ADD (Kaiser Permanente, 2004). These extremely high comorbidites may be inflated by diagnostic error.

Anastopolous and colleagues (2006) suggest that the high coincidence of ADD and oppositional or conduct disorders actually stems from the problems these children have with internalizing regulatory schemas and the failure of family and social systems to help them do so. An interesting meta-analysis of ADHD outcomes studies (Corwin et al., 2004; Lee, Mulsow, & Reifman, 2003) suggests that ADHD per se makes only moderate contributions to the adolescent risk-taking behaviors associated with conduct and oppositional defiant disorders. The implication is that the experience of having a self-regulatory problem such as ADD increases children's vulnerability in multiple ways and significantly raises the bar for those trying to help them grow up. Indirect testimony to how challenging it is to parent these vulnerable children comes from a study showing that ADD kids exposed to stressors are significantly more likely than others to later develop conduct disorder, oppositional defiant disorder, antisocial behavior, and major depression (Barkley, 2003). Adolescents with ADHD are at elevated risk for repeating a grade, getting suspended from school, earning lower grades than they are capable of, experiencing social rejection, engaging in risky behavior, sleeping poorly, and, relative to controls, possessing a less accurate sense of time (see Corwin et al., 2004, for a review).

ASSESSMENT

As the preceding discussion illustrates, many of the symptoms character-izing ADHD mimic or co-occur with the symptoms of other disorders. Differential diagnosis is especially important with adolescents because other disorders often mask ADHD and the problems that result from it. Given the high rate of comorbidity (40%–60%) in ADHD adolescents, clinicians, particularly physicians, may be more inclined to diagnose and treat the disorders comorbid with ADHD than to evaluate and treat ADHD symptomatology. As noted, the most common comorbid conditions are depression, disruptive behavior disorders, anxiety, and learning dis-abilities. To capture the diversity and degree of impairment caused by ADHD symptoms, a multifaceted evaluation is important. *This means obtaining measures of the child or adolescent's emotional and behavioral function-ing in the home, social, and academic settings.* Before beginning treatment, the therapist should work with the parents to be sure that a physician completes a physical exam and medical history. Medical conditions such as seizures, thyroid problems, central nervous system lesions, ele-vated lead, low iron, or medication side effects must be ruled out. The evaluations also should include hearing and vision tests.

LATENCY CHILDREN AND PREADOLESCENTS

Therapists typically begin the assessment of ADHD by meeting with the parent or parents of the child. Five screening questions are useful in getting an idea of whether a preadolescent child has ADHD (Kaiser Permanente, 2004):

1. Does your child have difficulty following through on instructions and have trouble finishing schoolwork, homework, or chores?
2. Does he or she have trouble organizing his or her work or time, seem forgetful, and have difficulty listening to others?
3. Is your child easily distracted by such things as noises, conversations, or even by his or her own thoughts (e.g., daydreaming)?
4. Does your child run or climb around excessively in situations where it is inappropriate to do so?
5. Does your child often act before thinking or have trouble waiting his or her turn? Does your child blurt out things he or she may regret later, or make careless mistakes because of rushing?

Kaiser's ADHD Best Practices recommends beginning the assessment of preadolescent children in a group setting—a procedure that is not practical for therapists in private practice. The advantage of this method is that it gives the evaluator access to an important source of unbiased information about the child's behavior in a more natural setting than seeing the child alone or with parents. The Kaiser program also has developed a set of standardized forms for collecting the input of teachers, for collecting developmental information from parents, and for assessing the child's pre- and posttreatment functioning on a standard measure (the Achenbach Child Behavior Checklist [CBCL] for parents and Teacher Report Form [TRF] for teachers; Kaiser Permanente, 2004).

ADOLESCENTS

The diagnosis of ADHD is often missed in children over 12 because symptoms are somewhat different for this group than for preadolescents. In addition, the interactions among development, mood, behavior, and substance abuse make diagnosing adolescents more challenging. These points should be kept in mind:

- There is a *decrease* in hyperactivity in adolescence but an *increase* in internal restlessness.
- Inattentiveness does not improve with age, but the demands on the adolescent increase—as the bar is raised academically, and teenagers' attentional, organizational, and time-management skills are severely tested. Conflicts with parents are likely to increase.
- The ADHD-inattentive subtype is often missed or ignored during earlier childhood and becomes noticeable only in adolescence.
- Adolescents tend to underreport or minimize ADHD symptoms. Collateral opinions and input (e.g., from teachers) are necessary to conduct an adequate evaluation.
- Adolescent ADHD girls are less likely than their male counterparts to be disruptive and are more likely to have attention and organizational difficulties. Girls have been reported to have elevated rates of unintended pregnancy and depression (Corwin, Kanitkar, Schwebach & Muslow, 2004).

ETIOLOGY AND NEURODYNAMICS

Important neurochemical, neuroanatomical, and neurophysiological abnormalities underlie ADD symptoms in children. Genetics makes a very significant contribution to the disorder; ADD's heritability coefficient is .67 (out of a possible 1.0). If a child has ADD, there is a 55% chance that one of the parents does too (Robin, 2007). In a few cases, the syndrome may be the result of insult to neural pathways from any one of a number of sources.

Barkley (1997, 2003) argues that beneath the inattention, impulsivity, and hyperactivity of ADHD is an underlying deficit in the executive brain's capacity to control behavior. In Barkley's formulation, ADD affects two of the four key executive functions:

1. Self-regulation of affect, motivation, and arousal
2. The capacity to match the contents of working memory with appropriate existing behavioral response patterns and then recombine these elements into new responses

Deficits in these executive functions, according to Barkley, leave the ADD/ADHD child vulnerable to making poorly formulated responses to environmental stimulation.

In both the family and at school, ADD children are at a disadvantage when confronted with processes that require sophisticated emotion regulation or sustained cognitive attention. Anastopoulos, Rhoads, and Farley (2006) see disrupted parenting, the idiosyncrasies of parental personalities, family stressors, the child's defiance, and social aggression as flash points between this environmental sensitivity and limitations in the interpersonal environment that fall short of the standard of "good enough for these children."

Attention is a flashlight we shine inward to illuminate our psychological and perceptual processes and outward to highlight details of the external world we wish to focus on. Goldberg (2001) has noted that the prefrontal cortex (PFC) is the area of the brain directing the flashlight's beam. He describes a looplike process involving the PFC, the ventral brain stem, and the posterior cortex. A breakdown or failure of mutual regulation anywhere along this loop impairs self-regulation and can lead to ADD.

Imaging studies of the brains of ADD children show consistent neurodynamic features of the disorder. These studies suggest involvement of the PFC, portions of the basal ganglia, and the cerebellum at the back of the brain (see Giedd, Shaw, Wallace, Gogtay, & Lenroot, 2006, for a review). In individuals with ADHD, the right frontal lobe is consistently shown to be smaller. An attentional alerting system has been associated with the right frontal and parietal lobes, and warning signals that modulate alertness are thought to involve norepinephrine (Marrocco & Davidson, 1998). Consistent with the classic symptoms of the disorder, children with ADHD have been shown to have right-frontal, cingulate, and basal ganglia deficits (Casey et al., 1997).

Other imaging studies have found atypical hemispheric volume in ADD children (Hynd, Semrud-Clikeman, Lorys, Novey, & Eliopulos, 1990) and a smaller-than-typical corpus callosum (Hynd et al., 1991). These findings suggest problems with integration of left- and right-hemispheric functions. Studies also have confirmed that these neuroanatomical differences are consistent across the span of development from childhood to adulthood (Wender, Reinherr, Wood, & Ward, 1985). These findings, together with the fact that the same medications are useful to patients regardless of age, buttress the theory that what we are seeing in child and adult patients are a brain-based processes.

Children and adolescents with ADHD have been reported to have smaller volumes in the right PFC, right anterior white matter, right caudate nucleus, and anterior portion of the corpus callosum than children without ADHD (Giedd, Blumenthal, Molloy, & Castellanos, 2001; Rubia et al., 1999). In twin studies, the identical twin with ADHD has been shown to have a smaller caudate volume than the unaffected twin (Castellanos et al., 2003).

To account for genetic contributions to the disorder, some researchers have identified one or two D4 dopamine receptors (DRD4)–repeat alleles correlated with siblings with ADD/ADHD (Madras, Miller, & Fischman, 2002). Methylphenidate (Ritalin) slows the reuptake of dopamine in the synaptic cleft by blocking the dopamine transporter molecule (Roman et al., 2002).

WORKING MEMORY

Working memory is the term used to describe the set of functions that hold incoming perceptual impulses and conscious cognitive contents in awareness for approximately 30 seconds. During this brief interval, the contents of working memory may be coded for longer-term storage or allowed to dissipate (see Appendix for a more complete discussion). The dorso lateral PFC (DLPFC) plays a crucial role in working memory and is richly endowed with dopamine receptors to support this function. Dopamine helps bias cortical cells to respond to strong inputs and alerts the system to focus attention on active goals instead of distracting stimuli. Dopamine is an important neurophysiological component in the working memory system that participates in holding information and experience pertinent to the task at hand. According to Barkley (1997), two working memory subsystems are important in considering the etiology of ADHD: nonverbal working memory, which holds information in the mind while a response is being formulated; and verbal working memory, which holds memory traces of both interpersonal and private speech. Both these systems are disrupted in ADHD, according to Barkley. Some support for this theory comes from imaging studies of ADHD patients that show reduced volume in the right PFC (Casey et al., 1997), an area of the brain that is involved in working memory functions. Ritalin and other stimulants also act on receptors in this region of the brain (Arnstein, 1998).

ATTENTION AND RELATEDNESS

Children who possess more attentional control than children with ADD/ADHD demonstrate more positive affect, empathy, social competence, and a more developed conscience (Eisenberg, Fabes, Guthrie, & Reiser, 2000; Kochanska, Murray, & Harlan, 2000). Preschoolers who can delay gratification develop competent coping skills by adolescence (Shoda, Mischel, & Peake, 1990). By age 30, they show the ability to cope competently with rejection (Ayduk et al., 2000). In adolescence, positive peer relationships provide a buffer for adolescents with ADHD. Positive rating by peers is a powerful predictor of favorable educational and substance abuse outcomes (Lambert, 1998). Derryberry and Tucker (2006) report studies showing that students with good attentional skills use more complex and efficient strategies in coping, planning, and positive appraisal. Those with poor attention tend to use simpler and less efficient strategies, such as denial, disengagement, and venting.

In their search for self-regulation and positive regard, ADHD children can overtax everyone around them, especially their parents. They are harder to take care of than ordinary children. As a result, whatever weaknesses may exist in the parent's own attachment schema will be brought to the fore rapidly and repeatedly in raising these children. Parents with insecure attachment styles are prone to slip into patterns of avoidance with their child, and those with an ambivalent schema are liable to become aggressive and negative. Disorganized parents are much more likely to be provoked (as they see it) into physical abuse or to experience major psychiatric problems in the course of family life. All these factors play into the ADD/ADHD child's own problems forming effective emotional regulatory neurodynamic attractors and a stable self-image.

TREATMENT OF ADD/ADHD

Like many other categories of psychiatric nosology, ADD underwent a transformation in the 1970s. Interest in the disorder was spurred by publication of the third edition of the *Diagnostic and Statistical Manual of*

Mental Disorders (American Psychiatric Association, 1980). Clear-cut criteria for the disorder were developed, facilitating research on specific methods for the palliating symptoms. Medication was identified as an essential component in the effective treatment of ADD as well as bipolar disorder and psychosis. More than 2,000 studies relevant to the disorder were published in the course of the 1980s.

PSYCHOPHARMACOLOGICAL TREATMENT

Medication is the single most effective treatment in ameliorating the core symptoms of ADHD. If children and parents comply with the prescribed regimen, medication can produce significant symptomatic improvement. Stimulants such as Ritalin, alpha blockers, and a relatively new medication, atomoxetine (Strattera), are approved for use with ADHD. Most studies indicate that the stimulants are the most effective of these medications— and that they are perhaps the most problematic as well (Kaiser Permanente, 2004).

Stimulants: The stimulant medications typically prescribed for ADHD in children and adolescents are the methylphenidates, Adderall, and dextroamphetamine. They reduce ADHD symptoms 70% to 80% of the time and if one type of these agents does not work, there is a reasonably good chance that one of the other two will. The overall effectiveness of stimulants in treating ADHD symptoms is approximately 90% in terms of reduction of the target symptoms of inattention, distractibility, impulsivity, and hyperactivity (Elia, 1991). They are also effective, although less reliably so, in reducing aggression and enhancing peer interactions, academic performance, and self-esteem. Stimulants alter brain activity, especially in the striatum (Vaidya et al., 1998) and in the dopaminergic circuits of working memory. PET (positron emission tomography) imaging studies are consistent with these observations (Volkow et al., 1998).

Stimulants, the medicines most likely to affect the symptoms of ADHD, require skillful management. They are readily abused, and not necessarily by the patient. Stimulants do not produce the same "jolt" of arousal in those with the diagnosis as in those without it. However, family members (including parents) and friends are all too frequently tempted to take the medications intended for the patient. These medications also have street value. Refills should be monitored by the physician to make sure the drugs are not being overused. Stimulants also can produce unpleasant side effects in ADD sufferers, including tics, reduced appetite, insomnia, and irritability (Kaiser Permanente, 2004). Although most ADHD sufferers respond to mediation therapeutically, therapists regularly hear reports from ADD patients that stimulant medication increases their energy, jitteriness, insomnia, and irritability to uncomfortable levels.

Because of these considerations and the lack of longitudinal research on the effects of stimulants on developing nervous systems, therapists should understand that initiating a course of stimulant medication for children or teens is a serious matter. To check the accuracy of the diagnosis, and to limit the use of stimulants to cases where they are clearly beneficial, it is a good practice to ask parents, teachers, and other adults who know the child or adolescent well to participate in a drug study. In this trial, the child is given a stimulant at a low dose in week 1, no medication in week 2, and a moderate-high dose in week 3. Each week, the teacher fills out an inventory of ADHD symptom intensity, blind to the dose the child is taking. The parent then returns with the results of the teacher's ratings, and the physician decides whether continuing the medication is warranted.

Antidepressants: The tricyclic antidepressants are the second most commonly studied and used class of medications for ADD/ADHD. These agents appear to have greater effects on impulsivity and hyperactivity than on attention. Tricyclics are particularly useful for children who report excessive side effects from stimulants. Tricyclics often take one to several weeks to reduce ADHD symptoms. The three most commonly used tricyclics are imipramine, desipramine, and nortriptyline.

A major drawback of the tricyclics is that 5% to 10% of the population do not metabolize the drugs effectively, and toxic blood levels of the drugs can build up (Kaiser Permanente, 2004). A blood level should be taken soon after the start of the medication and medication rechecks conducted at 4- to 6-week intervals to assess the medication response and side effects. Tricyclics, primarily desipramine, have been associated with a few cases of cardiac deaths due to arrhythmias (Gutgesell et al., 1999). However, planned and accidental overdoses are the biggest risk with tricyclics, and it is not a good practice to use them in cases where there is any indication of suicidality in patients.

Other Medications: Bupropion (Wellbutrin), a "mixed" antidepressant, and alpha blockers such as clonidine and guanfacine are also used to relieve the symptoms of ADD, especially in children with extreme hyperactivity. Atomoxetine, mentioned earlier, is a relatively new arrival on the scene. It is in a new class of medications called specific norepinephrine reuptake inhibitors. As low levels of norepinephrine have been associated with ADHD, there were good neurodynamic reasons to be sanguine about the drug's therapeutic value. Indeed, a number of studies have indicated that Atomoxetine is beneficial for ADHD, and it appears to improve ADHD symptoms (Michelson, 2002). Its main side effects in children are decreased appetite, weight loss, somnolence, gastrointestinal upset, headache, and irritability. These problems commonly improve over several weeks. The medication can interact with selective serotonin reuptake inhibitors and albuterol, used in the treatment of asthma. Because clinical experience with the medication suggests that atomoxetine is not as effective as stimulants, Kaiser Permanente (2004) considers it a second-line medication to be used in cases of stimulant failures.

MULTIMODAL TREATMENT

In research trials, psychotherapy, particularly of the generic, psycho-dynamic variety, has not been found to be very effective for ADHD suf-ferers. The research track record of cognitive behavioral therapy is also spotty. In a review of 47 efficacy studies of treatments for ADHD, behav-ioral parent training and behavioral interventions with adolescents were found to be efficacious; cognitive interventions were not (Pelham, Wheeler, & Chronis, 1998). Among psychosocial approaches, family therapy and classroom interventions were found to be efficacious and practical (Smith, Waschbusch, Willoughby, & Evans, 2000).

A landmark study on ADD/ADHD was undertaken in the 1990s. The Multimodal Treatment Study looked at which combinations of treatments are most effective for helping children with the disorder. It found that combined medication management and behavioral treatment was no more effective than medication alone (Arnold et al., 1997; MTA Cooperative Group, 1999). The behavioral treatment component of the study included parent training, child-focused summer treatment programs, and school-based intervention. Controversy continues to surround the interpretation of the findings about integrated treatment (Conners et al., 2001).

An advantage of seeing ADHD children in a clinic context is that it often facilitates the provision of the multimodal treatment appropriate to the disorder's multiple dimensions. At Kaiser Permanente, families with a preadolescent child assessed as having ADHD are referred to the Pediatrics Department for the initiation of psychopharmacological treatment. At the same time, parents and children start a group treatment program focusing on behavioral enhancement of parenting skills. Given the self-regulatory nature of the problem, the treatment focus is on changing the environment so that it supplements the skills the child lacks internally. Parents are also invited to join an ADHD Parents Support Group while their child participates in a socialization group. Children get skills training in conflict and anger management, and are seen with their parents in a medication group held jointly with the Pediatrics Department.

William Pelham and his colleagues (1998) at the Western Psychiatric Institute in Pittsburgh developed an effective multimodal treatment program tailored to the complexity of ADHD. James Swanson, Linda Pfiffner, and Keith McBurnett and Dennis Cantell developed a similar program at the University of California, Irvine. The programs include parent training, classroom implementation of behavior modification techniques, social skills training, and psychopharmacological therapy.

For clinicians in private practice, it is essential to have a good working relationship with a behavioral pediatrician or a child psychiatrist who is experienced in working with ADD. Although there are advantages to being part of a clinic practice when working with ADD/ADHD children, the private setting may offer unparalleled opportunities for providing support for parents. Such support is a crucial part of the work with ADHD youngsters. In addition, private practitioners may have more time to work with teachers, helping to keep the ADHD child mainstreamed and exposed to consistent messages at home, in therapy, and at school.

TREATING PARENTS AND FAMILIES

Longitudinal studies have shown that ADHD families are more unstable and have a higher divorce rate than non-ADHD families (Kaiser Permanente, 2004). ADHD places extremely high demands on the parent that may result in the breakdown of more or less secure attachment schemata into insecure parts. Thus, virtually all parents of a child with this disorder can benefit from an informed supportive relationship with a therapist. If the parent has the resources to pay for it, individual therapy to support his or her metacognitive capacities can be an effective way of helping the child.

A good treatment relationship with a parent or family begins with understanding their problems and how they have tried to solve them. As an alliance is being built, the therapist educates families about the neurological and genetic roots of the disorder and its limiting effects on a child's ability to utilize parental and peer relationships. The therapist presents, in neutral terms, ways in which an ADHD child typically engenders negativity, anxiety, depression, and avoidance in the parent. Throughout this discussion, the therapist must balance being honest about the chronic nature of the disorder (and the palliative nature of treatment) with the importance of engendering hope about change and improvement.

A therapeutic approach based on knowledge about neurodevelopment and the power of behavioral therapy—and one offering practical suggestions for improvement in the context of a supportive relationship—is a good fit for most parents. Brain-based therapy is the theoretical basis for talking with parents about the importance of their role in helping their child ameliorate the emotional, attentional, and social consequences of this neurodynamic disorder. Therapists can empathize with the child's problems with regard to managing high levels of impulsivity and distractibility, while also being attuned to the difficulties of shaping the behavior of this child as he or she grows up.

For most parents, it is a relief to discover that other parents of ADHD children also fall into the habit of taking a coercive, harshly critical stance toward their child. It may be even more relieving to be told that bad parenting is not what causes ADHD. These messages can change family dynamics. Parents discover that it is possible to change their negative interactions with their child and that doing so somewhat lessens the child's symptomology.

From this overview, the discussion with parents gets down to the brass tacks of improving brain-based behavioral, attentional, and emotion-regulation performance. It is important for the therapist to assess the degree to which parents are aware of and are using commonsensical parent practices. For example, in regard to making demands and giving instructions, are the parents limiting directives to those on which they intend to follow through? Are the directives and instructions short, simple, and clear enough that a child with attentional problems can retain them in working memory? Are they issued when there are relatively few distractions and when the parent and the child are looking each other in the eye? Does the parent have the child repeat important demands and instructions back to her, to be sure the youngster understands? Finally, has a reasonable and consistent schedule of activities been worked into the family's implicit memory rhythms?

The Kaiser ADHD guideline (2004) advises that "organization and problem-solving skills should be taught as one would teach a child to ride a bike or learn to swim"; in other words, with the expectation that it will take time to master these skills and that shouting does not help the slow learning process. Children learn best when parents patiently teach them skills, including the skills needed to conduct good relationships, with a supportive attitude (no yelling, criticizing, embarrassing, teasing, or degrading). If the parent seems deficient in basic parenting skills, a referral to a training program should be considered as an adjunct to treating the ADD child. Parent education programs including readings and education about

ADHD and behavior management increase parental skills (Weinberg, 1999). In addition to lowering the parents' stress levels, such programs also can reduce the oppositional behavior of ADHD children (Danforth, 1998).

In the collateral or family component of treating an ADD/ADHD child, the therapist and the family look for the emotional or situational triggers that lead to problem behaviors. It is important to start reintroducing the power of positive attention, which in many families has been all but completely sacrificed to more coercive tactics for maintaining control. ADD parents are tired of being hurt, disappointed, humiliated, and even frightened by their child. Because so many of the interactions are negative by the time parents seek help, parents may be actively avoiding the child or coming to interactions ready to be critical, defensive, or controlling. One way to support the reintroduction of positive interactions is to discuss the concept of "negative reinforcement."

The Parent Management Training approach is a well-researched intervention that involves step-by-step social skills training (Kazdin, 1997). The key to this approach is to train parents to alter and shape their behavior and that of their children. Parents are directed to identify unwanted behaviors, such as aggression, and shape those behaviors in the direction of prosocial and interpersonal skills. The program is especially effective with children with ADHD and conduct disorders (Kazdin & Weisz, 1998).

Negative reinforcement often is thought to be synonymous with punishment, but actually it is quite different. It involves learning to avoid a negative consequence. Discovering that we can avoid getting into bad morning commute traffic by leaving for work 30 minutes earlier (and then changing our behavior so that we get out of the house on time) is an example of internalized negative reinforcement. In raising an ADD child, both child and parent tend to become negative reinforcement experts. Parents know they can avoid angry power struggles with children by letting children have their way. Children know they can get their parents off their backs by having a tantrum. This kind of standoff between negative reinforcement experts powerfully reinforces the behavioral schemata typical of ADD in the child's developing brain.

In working with parents, it is important to bring this pattern to their awareness and offer them viable alternatives. Anastopoulos and colleagues (2006) offer some useful techniques for encouraging parents to resurrect a neglected aspect of the parent-child relationship: positive reinforcement. In Beckian terms, parents actually encourage noncompliance by selectively attending to it (as an attractor) and discourage compliance by ignoring it (extinction). In other words, although ADHD is a self-regulatory disorder determined by neurodynamic attractors rarely accessible to therapeutic change, ADHD children, no less than other children, develop particular character styles that can be reworked in the interpersonal process of psychotherapy. Anastopoulos and colleagues suggest that therapists work with parents to set up periods during the day when they temporarily give up trying to control all but the child's potentially dangerous behaviors. During this time and throughout the day, parents are encouraged to reflect on things about their child that they regard positively. This "positive attending" approach works not only because children often respond to it, but also because it breaks up the parents' selectively attending to impulsivity and not staying on schedules. From a cognitive behavioral therapy point of view, this approach disputes a parent's core belief that "he never does anything I tell him to do."

Using specific, immediate, and consistent shaping tools to express appreciation boosts the efficacy of this parenting approach. Setting up a positive reward system is appropriate for the limited capacity of ADHD children to attend to ordinary emotional incentives. More tangible rewards often get their attention, engaging the PFC and the ventral brain stem. Behaviors that are rewarded repeatedly cause new attractors to be created in these circuits.

In working on positive attending, the therapist may ask parents to create two lists. The first notes the privileges and activities their child most enjoys; the second lists the parents' goals for improving the child's behavior (such as completing household chores, getting ready for school on time in the morning). Typically, parental goals include improved compliance in tasks the child *refuses* to do or avoids and also completion of tasks left undone through inattention. With the therapist's help, the parents prioritize the tasks and assign a point value, or "cost," to each one based on its importance and difficulty. Then the privileges and other positive reinforcements the parents come up with are rank-ordered and assigned a "currency" point value.

Anastopoulos and colleagues suggest using poker chips for transactions with latency and preadolescent children as currency to redeem privileges and other positive reinforcements. For older kids, the point "balance" may be kept on paper or in a check register. At the outset, the token economy is utilized for positive reinforcement only, never for punishment. After the system has been implemented and debugged, it is gradually extended to include making noncompliance more aversive (Anastopoulos et al., 2006).

Gradually, the therapist encourages parents to use positive attending more generally with the child. This approach makes sense in terms of behaviorism and in terms of the emphasis in the attachment literature on the benefits of security and consistent expectations. Parents make a point of noticing and liberally rewarding secure attachment behaviors, such as independent play. This works only when parents actually feel appreciative or affectionate toward the child and not when used as a more subtle form of avoiding or dismissing the child—a distinction children will likely pick up on and react to. When the child allows her mother to go about her business of making the phone call to arrange a playdate, for example, both negative and positive reinforcement are being used to shape the child's behavior. Seeing positive attending have good effects reminds the parent of a basic aspect of the attachment relationship: evolution has built into all of us a default response of accommodating to perceived parental feeling.

WORKING WITH SCHOOLS

Effective treatment for the ADD child also involves contact with professionals in the child's school setting. Teaching an ADD child while trying to give other kids their due is a very difficult job (especially since, in a classroom of 30 children, an average of 3 of them will have the disorder). Teachers are often hungry for tips from therapists about how best to help children with problems attending and controlling impulses. Attentional and self-regulatory skills can be taught by:

- Breaking down tasks into small components
- Teaching strategies for organizing time
- Promoting routines and structured environments
- Using multimodal sensory stimuli including shapes, colors, and textures to help children learn organizational skills
- Minimizing distractions
- Engaging children during periods of frustration to promote staying on task

These pedagogical guidelines have been widely embraced in the literature (Harwood et al., 2008). Following them consistently and over a period of time is an effective way of promoting better executive skills. Parents and caregivers also need to know their children's legal rights (e.g., entitlements to an individualized educational plan [IEP]) and how to access school and community resources—and they need support to navigate this process.

PROGNOSIS

The long-term prognosis for untreated ADHD is guarded at best. From infancy on, ADD children struggle with issues of self-regulation. Children with the disorder tend to have more personal and interpersonal problems and a higher likelihood of engaging in antisocial behaviors and substance abuse, and are more likely to develop serious comorbid conditions, such as conduct disorders. ADHD is not a benign condition. The majority of individuals diagnosed in childhood still exhibit symptoms in adulthood, and a disproportionate number will go on to face the challenges of parenting an ADD child themselves. As the Kaiser guideline concludes, however: "Research has indicated that prognosis is significantly affected by additive interactions among the following factors: treatment, individual variables, ecologic and familial characteristics" (Kaiser Permanente, 2004, p. 8). When parents, teachers, pediatricians, therapists, and other significant adults team up, the child's chances for a better life expand.

KYLE: THE BASE

Kyle is a chunky 12-year-old boy who was brought to the Psychiatry Department for an evaluation. His grades had been dropping because of missing assignments and low test scores. His school had completed an individualized educational plan and recommended that he be evaluated for medication. As part of the department routine, Kyle was screened by our child and family team before being referred for a medication evaluation appointment. Kyle was evaluated by Barbara, a predoctoral psychology intern.

The interview began with Kyle's parents complaining that they were fed up with Kyle's school performance and his attitude at home. All he seemed to do at school was talk to his friends. Despite their repeated requests, he never seemed to be able to write down or remember homework assignments and would lie about the homework to his parents. When he did do homework, it was sloppy and incomplete. The parents could not understand why Kyle did not seem to care. "He's just so disorganized," Kyle's mother said, "but he gets mad at us and it's a huge hassle when we remind him of things or try to correct him."

Family arguments erupted not only about homework but chores as well. Glued to the video games on the computer in his room, Kyle's usual response to being asked to do something, such as take the dog for a walk, was "in a minute," but few chores were completed without the discussion escalating into yelling and arguing. "I don't like his attitude," Kyle's dad chimed in. "He's sarcastic, he calls us stupid, and he's got disrespect written all over his face. Oh, and he can't seem to stop himself from messing with his little brother." Both parents agreed that Kyle could not seem to resist trying to get a rise out of his brother by taking his things, calling him names, and impulsively hitting or pinching him.

Although it initially seemed that both parents were in agreement, as the discussion continued, some differences emerged. The father's work required him to be out of town a lot, and the mother tended to save up grievances while he was gone and then ask the father to punish Kyle when he returned. The father thought the mother was too strict. "The fact is, I never did that well in school either," the father said. "Martha is so organized compared to me, but she gets really uptight about it too."

Although Kyle had always been a restless and impulsive child with lots of energy, he did fine in school until fifth grade. It was in sixth grade that things started to change, as he did less and less work, got more disorganized, and started getting into conflicts about his absorption in video games. One of his teachers that year commented on the fact that Kyle seemed inattentive and asked if he had ever been evaluated for ADHD.

Later that day, Barbara presented the case to her supervisor, Gail. Barbara wondered if a quick medication evaluation was indicated. Gail suggested that they think about it, starting from the BASE perspective. She talked with Barbara about beginning their discussion of the diagnostic question from the point of view of what areas in the brain are associated with ADHD. "The current thinking is that the diagnosis itself is kind of a misnomer," Gail said. "Inattention is just part of the picture. What we see with Kyle is that, yeah, he's inattentive in class and not paying enough attention to getting his homework or test preparation organized. But he used to do okay with this; it seems like it's more like the bar has been raised on him and he just can't get over it anymore. Besides, there's a lot of impulsivity here as well. The way he talks to his parents and picks on his little brother sounds classic ADHD—it's out of his mouth or he's got his hands on his brother before he even really thinks about it. So this is bigger than just an attention deficit, and we're not seeing that much hyperactivity. It's really a problem with the whole package of self-regulation, which is a frontal lobe function. At least this is a strong possibility. Let's do some assessment."

Barbara administered the Achenbach. The results supported her diagnostic impression of ADHD from the family meeting. She had a second individual meeting with Kyle, who seemed a little less sullen and defensive than he had in the family meeting. He complained that all his parents did was yell at him, and he needed a bigger allowance. He also disclosed that a kid at school was bullying him and calling him a retard. The day before yesterday, the boy had done it in front of a bunch of other kids and they had all laughed. Kyle looked vulnerable and miserable.

Barbara called the school and spoke to two of Kyle's teachers. One of them seemed as angry and fed up with Kyle "acting immature" as his parents were. "I've seen this type of kid before; he'll end up in the continuation high school." The other teacher, who seemed to have had more experience with ADHD kids, said she was relieved that the parents had finally acted on the feedback they had been getting. She said it seemed to her from the limited contact she had had with the parents that they had "kind of given up on the kid."

Having thought through things from the point of view of the neurodynamics and worked on building her attunement with her client, Barbara scheduled a medication evaluation with a child psychiatrist. The psychiatrist met with Kyle and the family, reviewed Barbara's notes on the case, and wrote a prescription for initiating Ritalin treatment. He scheduled another appointment for the family to come back in 2 weeks.

In their next supervision session, Barbara said that she felt she needed to do more work on the alliance with both Kyle and the parents. "I think that's a very good idea," Gail said. "Meds can make so much difference with kids like this that everybody's boat floats a little higher in the water and you can use the optimism to make some changes."

Barbara continued to meet individually with Kyle and talk about strategies for dealing with the bully, since that had become something he worried about, and also started talking with him about some strategies for getting his homework situation more together. He liked the idea of getting a cell phone with an organizer in it. Barbara said she would suggest it to his parents, but commented she thought they would want to see some return on their investment in one of these gadgets. Unexpectedly, Kyle started to cry. He talked about how lousy he felt about himself for being "such a loser. I don't blame everybody for hating me like they do."

Barbara told Gail that the focus in the family meetings actually had shifted somewhat away from Kyle and toward the marriage. It seemed that Kyle's father was verbally abusive not only to Kyle but to his wife as well. "It was like all the sudden, whoa! The mother says she doesn't blame Kyle for trying to get into his room and close his door as soon as he's in the house. She wishes she could do that too!"

Gail recommended that Barbara see if she could get Kyle's father interested in an anger management class. She presented this recommendation as a way to help Kyle and lower the family's temperature a bit, so he did not feel that he had to hide out in his room to escape the volatile household atmosphere. Gail met with the parents to talk about creating a structured and consistent series of expectations with rewards to cultivate discipline and attention. She explained that Kyle's problem was not their fault; he was a kid who needed extra help. Because his brain had some challenges in keeping things organized and not letting his mouth or his hands get ahead of his thinking, he needed more structure and limit-setting support from the environment. The parents agreed to a plan whereby Kyle could earn points toward a new video game by bringing his homework home every day, completing it, and getting it turned in on time. Kyle's mother said she would take responsibility for checking with his teachers each week. Barbara suggested that after they got some positive rewards started, they would talk about building in negative consequences for not complying with expectations.

Meanwhile Barbara worked hard to build her attunement with Kyle. She found a support group for kids with ADD and got Kyle into it. In the group, he discovered how his peers learned to expand their attentional skills and gained self-esteem. Suddenly he was not just a loser; he was a kid with a problem that had a name, and there were many other kids who had the same issues.

After the Ritalin kicked in, things changed quite rapidly for Kyle. Getting his homework done became less of a problem and his grades started to go up. The teasing stopped at school. He got invited to another kid's birthday party for the first time in three years. Barbara went to the school's next IEP meeting to support her patient and answer any questions about the treatment plan. She was able to work out a partnership between the family and the school for remediation.

Kyle's self-esteem gradually rose, and his grades stayed in an acceptable range. Out of the blue, Kyle's father started talking about how happy he was to have his son back and how he wished they had done this years ago. He thought he had a lot of the same problems that Kyle did, and wondered if maybe he had the adult version of ADHD.

For the time being, everybody was feeling a lot better, but Barbara was very clear with the family that there were no magic solutions for this problem. The improvements were likely to be only as durable as the changes they had put in place, and these might need tune-ups from time to time in the future.

CHAPTER 8

Anxiety in Children and Adolescents

Based on the way our brains operate, evolution appears to have been far more interested in keeping us alive than making us happy.

—Lou Cozolino

WITH THE EXCEPTION of attention-deficit disorder, anxiety disorders are the most commonly occurring psychological disorders among children and adolescents. Incidence estimates range from 4% to 19% of the population under the age of 18 (Costello & Angold, 1995; Ford, Goodman, & Meltzer, 2003). In real-world practice, anxiety disorders commonly co-occur with other disorders, such as depression. The presence of an anxiety disorder during childhood increases the risk of developing anxiety or other disorders such as depression later in life. The anxiety disorders that most commonly occur in childhood and adolescence are:

- **Generalized anxiety disorder (GAD).** Youths with GAD worry excessively about their future, health, family, friends, and safety.
- **Separation anxiety disorder.** Children with separation anxiety disorder excessively fear being separated from home or parents. As these children enter school, they worry about parents' health and safety. They may have difficulty sleeping without their parents and may refuse to go to school because of somatic complaints, such as headaches or stomachaches.

- **Panic disorder (PD).** Adolescence is a peak period for the onset of PD. Adolescents with PD spontaneously experience recurring episodes, or "attacks," of intense fear, which include somatic symptoms such as racing heart, shortness of breath, and chest pain. These symptoms result in a fear of dying or going crazy.
- **Social anxiety disorder (SAD).** Again, adolescence is a peak period of onset. Adolescents with SAD show excessive fear or discomfort in social or performance situations. They fear negative appraisals by other people, based on worries about some character defect (such as stupidity) or the fear that they will do something embarrassing.
- **Specific phobias.** Phobias involve intense fear of a specific thing (such as spiders) or situations (such as being up high). Phobic children or adolescents are prone to avoid these objects and circumstances.

DISPOSITIONAL FACTORS

TEMPERAMENT

An overdeveloped capacity for behavioral inhibition, as expressed in traits such as shyness, withdrawal, and emotional restraint, appear to be risk factors for anxiety disorders and depression. A trait referred to as *anxiety sensitivity* appears to be a risk factor specifically for panic disorder in adolescents (Kaiser Permanente, 2001a). Anxiety sensitivity involves the tendency to believe that physical symptoms of anxiety, such as shortness of breath, an increased heart rate, and physical shakiness, will result in acutely negative psychological and/or physical consequences.

Longitudinal studies have demonstrated a link between anxiety sensitivity and panic disorder. For example, European Americans, Asian Americans, African Americans, and Hispanics with this trait also have a tendency to develop panic disorder (Hayward, Killen, Kraemer, & Taylor, 2000). Among these four ethnic groups, panic symptoms are most severe for European American youths, while Hispanic and Asian youths report higher overall anxiety sensitivity (Weems, Hayward, Killen, & Taylor, 2002).

Rothbart and Posner (2006) point out that strong approach tendencies may contribute to positive feelings in some children and impulsivity in others. Infants with strong approach tendencies show positive anticipation and impulsivity along with anger/frustration and aggression at 7 years of age. These children tend to be low in attentional control. They also experience intense pleasure in approach behaviors. In contrast, expressions of fear in early childhood are related to relatively weak approach behavior and internalizing behavior; these children try to maximize their self-calming and withdrawal behavior in an apparent effort to feel more secure. Approach tendencies are an "accelerator"; the inhibitory tendencies are the "brakes." Strong accelerative tendencies may weaken the influence of inhibitory control (Rothbart & Derryberry, 2002). The balance between these two tendencies is critical to healthy development. Appropriately realistic levels of fear help moderate the two opposing tendencies. Rothbart and Posner (2006) write:

> Fear appears to take on an important and inhibitory role constraining the development of externalizing, and contributing to the development of conscience. (p. 477)

Temperamental inhibition has been associated with the later development of anxiety disorders. For example, Kagan, Snidman, Zentner, and Peterson (1999) followed a group of 4-month-olds who were observed to react at high or low extremes in terms of motor activity and negative emotional response to novel stimuli. Assessed again at age 7, these highly reactive children showed significantly more anxiety symptoms. Similarly, Goodwin, Fergusson, and Horwood (2004) found that anxious/withdrawn behavior ("internalizing") at age 8 was associated with later major depression.

NEURODYNAMIC FACTORS

In children with GAD, the size of the amygdala is larger than it is in their less anxious peers (DeBellis et al., 2000). Anxious girls between ages 8 and 11 assessed by electroencephalogram were found to have greater right-frontal asymmetry and more dominant right processing than a nonanxious control group (Baving, Laucht, & Schmidt, 2002).

The inhibiting tendencies of shyness, caution, and emotional restraint are associated with high arousal of the sympathetic nervous system. In combination with an amygdala that is more than usually robust, these children may have a neurodynamic potential for anxiety, a potential that is difficult to change without considerable environmental support. Elevated levels of cortisol during childhood—a frequent concomitant of this constellation of temperamental and physiological characteristics—contribute to problems later in life. Cortisol has a normal diurnal cycle, peaking in the morning and tapering off during the day. Essex and colleagues (2002) showed that higher later-afternoon cortisol levels predict behavioral

Table 8.1

Neurodynamic Correlates of OCD, SAD, and Anxiety Not Otherwise Specified

Disorder	Brain Module/ Process	Abnormality	Effect on Functioning
Obsessive-compulsive disorder	Basal ganglia	Increased volume	Diminished filtering and inhibition of stimuli to prefrontal cortex
	Orbitofrontal cortex and anterior cingulate gyrus	Inhibition of globus pallidus, releasing increased activity in thalamus	Increased activity in frontal cortex, associated with overthinking
Social anxiety disorder	Right frontal cortex	Atypical slow arousal and then prolonged elevation	Experience of discomfort and arousal
Anxiety not otherwise specified	Amygdala	Enlarged volume	More intense arousal requiring more cortical override
	Right frontal cortex	EEG asymmetry	Disturbed emotion regulation

problems 1 to 2 years later. Similarly, Goodyer, Herbert, Tamplin, and Altham (2000) showed that spiking cortisol predicts the onset of depression within a few months. Table 8.1 summarizes the neurodynamic correlates for obsessive-compulsive disorder (OCD), social anxiety disorder (SAD), and anxiety not otherwise specified.

SARA: The BASE

Sara, age 15, burst into the nurse's office at school complaining of heart palpitations and feeling like she was having a heart attack. The nurse listened to her heart and found no irregularities. Sara's pulse was elevated to 130, she was sweating profusely, her whole body was trembling, and in a breathless, pressured voice she told the nurse she was scared she was going to die. Almost as soon as she sat down on the examination table, she sprang up and started pacing. The nurse called the school counselor. Together they agreed that Sara was probably having a panic attack. When they conveyed their opinion to Sara, however, she would have none of it. She demanded to see "real doctors."

Sara's parents picked her up and took her to the emergency room. The physician there checked her out and told Sara and her parents that she concurred with the people at school; Sara *was* panicking, not having a heart attack. The doctor told the family that people often came to the ER because of panic, and it was a very real problem, but it would not kill her. The physician referred Sara and her parents to the Psychiatry Department, and her parents reluctantly agreed to a drop-in appointment.

During the psychiatry intake with a social work intern, Sara revealed that she had been trying to keep her weight down and was eating as little as possible and filling up on Diet Coke. She said that she always was "on the nervous side." She worried that the girls at school who were getting asked out on dates were slim and attractive—they looked like models. When Anna, the intern, asked her if she worried about anything else, Sara said she worried about her grades, whether her brother would get into the college he wanted, about her dog's advanced age, and that her father was so stressed out and smoked.

Sara's parents requested some medication to help their daughter "calm down." They did not like the fact that Anna was so young, that she wasn't an M.D., and that Anna said she would need to confer with her supervisor about the request for medication. Anna asked for a special consultation with her supervisor, Margaret, because the case seemed urgent. She wondered whether Sara suffered from an eating disorder and wanted to get permission to book an urgent medication appointment. Anna reported, however, that she had screened for anorexia and bulimia and found no frank symptoms of either. Margaret suggested that Anna remain attentive to any signs of an eating disorder at the next appointment.

Margaret smiled at Anna and told her to calm down. "What you're probably feeling is contagious anxiety," she said, "and it's actually useful in making the diagnosis. If you think about it, what's really the emergency here? This girl has been screened medically, and they ruled out the heart problem. It's really just that the patient is able to transfer her anxiety to you. It's not Sara's heart; it's her head that's the problem."

Anna relaxed a little and agreed to use the BASE to think about a treatment plan that made sense. "Two things jump out at me about this girl," Margaret said. "One is Sara's temperament—she says she's always been anxious—and the other is her intake of caffeinated soda. For starters, I'd suggest talking with her about how her diet and her temperament are interacting at this point. She's got her neurochemistry out of balance and she's way too hyped up. A more balanced diet will help get her neurotransmitters back into some kind of equilibrium." Otherwise, the next level of treatment could only limp forward.

After giving some consideration to the neurodynamic elements of Sara's condition, Anna and Margaret talked about the second element of the BASE, the alliance. "Frankly, I don't think a lot of her parents," Anna said. "They're pretty useless. They seemed almost more anxious than she was, and they certainly don't think much of me." Margaret empathized with the countertransference. She said that the cognitive process that goes with anxiety is pretty much limited to fight or flight, and our brains are ideally adapted for the social transmission of anxiety. As Anna helped the parents through this crisis, she would no doubt see more likable parts of the couple. In the meantime, as in all child treatment, therapy was unlikely to progress without the parents' support.

Margaret looked at the intake form and noted that the father was an attorney and the mother a certified public accountant. "They're educated people," she said. "Maybe they'll respond to information; their reaction to you also suggests they would feel comfortable with a physician or psychologist. We can arrange that!" Anna and Margaret brainstormed about interventions designed to increase the parents' engagement in the treatment. Margaret proposed that Sara use Prochaska's stage-of-change method and think about where the parents were in terms of the early stages: *precontemplative* (before there is really any motivation present or much thought given to how to change) or *contemplative* (ambivalent motivation and looking for more information before reaching a decision) (Prochaska & Norcross, 2002). "I don't know that they're thinking at all," Anna said. "They're so anxious at this point." "So let's go with that," Margaret said. "The goal will be to move them up one stage from precontemplation and get them to consider the fact that they need to do something more than wish for a magic pill and hide their heads in the sand about their daughter."

Margaret gave Anna some literature about panic, including Kaiser's panic practice guideline, and suggested she also Google panic disorder on the Web. She needed some solid and accurate sources of information that would be understandable to a layperson. The parents and Sara needed to know what the disorder was and why the treatment made sense. Next Margaret and Anna agreed to refer the family to a psychiatrist who had experience with panic and recognized that anxiolytics are rarely the treatment of choice for the disorder. The M.D. would support Anna's treatment plan and could help cement the alliance.

Building attunement required instilling a sense of a holding environment that carried with it hope, commitment, and empathy. When Anna met with the parents again, she gave them the referral they wanted and laid out a treatment plan that was consistent with evidence-based practice. This included psychoeducation about the brain, the possible contribution of Sara's current nutritional patterns, and the importance of diminishing Sara's avoidance and increasing her comfort with the sensations of anxiety. When she met with Sara again, Anna was pleasantly surprised that the teen had no problem getting on board with the treatment. She liked Anna and expressed some confidence that this was a person who could help her prevent another "attack."

Sara agreed to try restructuring her ideas about what the physical signs of anxiety really meant. Due to the power of a fear-conditioned amygdala, it is important that patients get some help in clarifying their thoughts and making them more realistic (a process known in CBT as "cognitive restructuring") prior to the part of the treatment that involves exposure to what the person fears. Any cognitive restructuring format that at least includes identification of automatic thoughts, hot thoughts, and alternative thoughts and interpretations should be helpful. Cognitive restructuring provides the basis for processing in a different way what comes out of the exposure. It directs cortical attentional processes onto the fluctuating content of working memory. In a person with highly developed neurodynamic attractors for panic, it seems that even as new experience enters the brain through nonconscious processing and working memory, it is already being distorted by fear-based affects.

Talking about the brain was one thing; but Sara really only got the message after Anna had linked the discussion about the sensations of panic with exercises that induced some of its actual physical signs. She had Sara breathe faster and faster until she was panting, and then repeatedly stand up and sit down in her chair until she was feeling light-headed. Sara described the physical sensations, and Anna reminded her of why she was having these reactions. Anna had Sara sit in her chair and whirled it around until the girl got dizzy; then they stopped and talked about how it felt. The two left the office, and Anna had Sara run up and down the clinic steps four times, until she was breathless and her heart was racing. Repetition of exposures is important; it builds new neural nets and new system attractors. These exercises helped Sara learn to tolerate the physical sensations she had previously overreacted to and replaced her old interpretations of them with a sense of normalcy. In neurodynamic terms, the two had helped decondition Sara's amygdala and strengthened the left hemisphere's modulation of amygdalar activation.

It was appropriate that Anna introduced these physical elements—through a technique called *interoceptive exposure* (or exposure to stimuli arising within the body) *after* cognitive restructuring had begun (Barlow, Craske, Cerny, & Klosko, 1989; Craske, Meadows, & Barlow, 1994). Simultaneous restructuring and interoceptive exposure helps the patient challenge cognitions arising from exposure (Zuercher-White, 1997). Psychoeducation helps the patient understand why it is helpful. Panic can be thought of as a *phobia of internal bodily sensations*. Interoceptive exposure helps clients habituate to these sensations. The technique also can be taught in a group format, where patients try out new skills and see peers succeeding with them.

CHILD AND ADOLESCENT OBSESSIVE-COMPULSIVE DISORDER

Obsessive-compulsive disorder is characterized by *obsessions*—persistent and intrusive ideas, thoughts, images, or impulses—and *compulsions*—physical or mental acts designed to neutralize the obsessions. Many patients try to avoid stimuli and situations that could trigger their obsessions. Children and adolescents with OCD typically are anxious and feel tense, guilty, irritable, and frustrated as a result of the disorder. When asked, many seem unable to identify a threat other than the obsessive thought or impulse. Some researchers report the counterintuitive finding that girls have more aggressive obsessions while boys have more sexual and symmetry obsessions (see Bessette 2004, for a review). Many OCD sufferers feel they have to engage in a stereotyped compulsive ritual to restore a sense of calm and well-being, experiencing a great relief— a "just-so" feeling state—when the ritual is completed. Obsessions are experienced as intrusive and involuntary, while compulsive activity feels more voluntary, although it often follows very strict idiosyncratic rules.

DIAGNOSIS

Not every child or adolescent with rituals has OCD—for example, the adolescent who when home alone checks the locks several times or the girl who always leaves her closet door slightly ajar before bedtime is not exhibiting OCD. The diagnosis requires that the obsessions or compulsions cause significant distress, consume 1 hour or more a day, or significantly interfere with the person's normal routine or functioning.

Although there is a remarkable heterogeneity of OCD symptoms, common child and adolescent obsessions (and their corresponding compulsions) are:

- **Contamination.** Obsessive fear of contamination by dirt, germs, or toxic substances, coupled with avoidance of the feared substances and compulsive washing when these objects have been touched.
- **Hypochondriasis.** Obsessive fear of ill health and a compulsion to obtain medical reassurance repeatedly.
- **Pathological doubt.** Obsessive worry of forgetting to do something that will result in a terrible event. The paired compulsion involves constant checking—for example, checking the door to prevent a killer from coming in through the unlocked door.
- **Fear of disasters.** Obsessive fear of imagined disasters paired with the compulsion to perform rituals, such as keeping objects or events in a certain order or place.
- **Aggressive or sexual imagery.** Dread of performing vividly terrible aggressive or sexual acts, or intrusive thoughts of an aggressive or sexual nature. Repeated confessions, repeatedly seeking reassurance, phobic avoidance of potential weapons (such as knives), and mental counting or praying rituals are common reciprocal compulsions.
- **Obsessional slowness.** Extreme slowness in behavior due to counting or ordering.

INCIDENCE AND AGE OF ONSET

The years of middle childhood and early adolescence are peak periods of onset for OCD disorder. Boys develop symptoms earlier (the average age being 9), but overall more girls (whose average age of onset is 13) have the disorder. It is estimated that 80% of all OCD cases have their onset in childhood and adolescence (Geller et al., 2001; Kaiser Permanente, 2001b). There are some differences between childhood-onset and adult-onset OCD. The early-onset form has a stronger familial loading and high comorbidity with tics and Tourette's disorder. Childhood OCD is more prevalent among males (Geller et al., 1998), although, more females ultimately develop the disorder (Kaiser Permanente, 2001b).

COMORBIDITIES

Almost 3 out of 4 adolescents with OCD have at least one comorbid disorder, such as tics, Tourette's disorder, or attention-deficit hyperactivity disorder (Geller et al., 2002). There is a close association between tic disorders, Tourette's, and OCD. Between 20% to 30% of OCD patients have or have had tics; 5% to 7% have Tourette's; and 35% to 50% of Tourette's patients have OCD. Tourette's disorder consists of behaviors involving grunting, blinking, or repeating words and gestures that seem to be provoked more by physical sensations than anxiety, but there are often concurrent OCD rituals as well (Kaiser Permanente, 2001b).

Other disorders commonly found with child and adolescent OCD are:

- Other anxiety disorders
- Depressive disorders
- Attention-deficit disorder
- Disruptive behavior disorders
- Learning disabilities
- Developmental delays

Children with OCD frequently exhibit neuropsychological deficits along with executive-function deficits in performing tasks that require planning. Problems such as dysgraphia, dyscalculia, poor expressive written language, and reduced processing speed and efficiency frequently coexist with a diagnosis of OCD (Kaiser Permanente, 2001b).

ASSESSMENT

Because they rarely see clearly obsessive children or teens in their practice, many child and family therapists are surprised to discover that OCD is a fairly common disorder. An estimated 4 to 6 million people of all ages in the United States have the disorder, making it almost as common as asthma and diabetes (Nymberg & van Noppen, 1994). Whether masked by the presence of a comorbidy or by the youngsters' reluctance to talk about their symptoms, the diagnosis of OCD is often missed even by experienced clinicians. Youngsters often hide their symptoms because they are ashamed of them or are fearful that the symptoms say something ominous about their mental health. In assessing *any* child for whom anxiety is an issue, Kaiser Permanente (2001b) recommends asking these OCD screening questions:

- Are you thinking things and doing things that you would like to stop but can't?
- Are there worries you can't kick out of your mind even though they may seem silly to other people?

- Do you have certain actions or routines that aren't really necessary, seem foolish, or make you feel crazy but you do them anyway?

It is a good practice to conduct an assessment of potential OCD in the context of a more general mental health assessment. The therapist should ask about the presenting problem along with the child's developmental history, use of substances, medical health, and current medications. The child's temperament, family history, and possible comorbid symptoms (tics, symptoms of other anxiety disorders, depression, and ADHD) are all of interest. OCD may present in mild and disguised forms; it also can be disabling in terms of the time, mental energy, and stress associated with the disorder.

Looking for opportunities for prevention and intervention in these screening situations can be invaluable to the families. Information-processing biases and magical thinking are sometimes clues to the existence of the disorder. It seems to take 4 to 6 months from the onset of ritualizing before the parents become aware of it. Asking parents these screening questions may help bring some observations more sharply into their awareness:

- Does your child seem to need to keep things in order?
- Do you think he or she washes him- or herself a lot more than other children?

Adding a psychoeducational component to the assessment process often helps the family generate a different understanding of the problem. Reframing and naming symptoms as part of a disorder—as opposed to just attributing it to a moral or character defect—can offer relief and set the stage for the treatment interventions. As with panic disorder, cognitive restructuring of OCD provides the basis for processing in a different way what comes out of the exposure component of treatment.

A valuable OCD assessment instrument for children between ages 6 and 17 is the Children's Yale-Brown Obsessive Compulsive Scale (CY-BOCS; Goodman et al., 1989a, 1989b; March & Mulle, 1998). The CY-BOCS includes a symptom checklist and assesses the time consumed by obsessions and compulsions, along with several other measures of severity, including the child's distress, resistance, and perceived control over the symptoms. The CY-BOCS can be given between the first and the second assessment interview and results discussed as the starting point of the second appointment (Kaiser Permanente, 2001b).

ETIOLOGY AND NEURODYNAMICS

Neuroanatomical, neurochemical (neurotransmitter), and genetic abnormalities have been proposed as causes of OCD. Sufferers consistently show deficiencies in executive functions, visuospatial ability, and nonverbal memory. Imaging studies have shown circulatory abnormalities suggesting dysfunction in the fronto-striatal-thalamic-cortical network. Neurotransmitter abnormalities such as these appear to normalize after successful treatment with selective serotonin reuptake inhibitors (SSRIs) and behavior therapy (Kaiser Permanente, 2001b). Onset of the disorder also has been seen as an effect of brain trauma, toxins, and infections (e.g., Sydenham's chorea). There may well be multiple causes for the disorder.

Giedd and colleagues (2006) summarize the contributions from neuroscience research on the brain-based features of OCD as follows:

> Most theorists hold that OCD is the result of imbalance in the corticostriatal-thalamic circuitry. Specifically, the basal ganglia fail to provide sensory gating by filtering and suppressing input from frontal cortical regions. Thus, a "hyperactive" orbital frontal cortex and anterior cingulate gyrus send outputs to the caudate and nucleus accumbens, which in turn inhibit the globus pallidus, halting its tonic discharge to the thalamus. The cessation of pallidal inhibitory activity releases the thalamus, and the thalamus feeds this excessive activity foreword to the frontal cortical regions, completing a cycle. (p. 163)

As is the case with other psychiatric disorders, such as depression, the evolving neuroscientific view suggests that the OCD experience is a product of dysregulations between activating and inhibitory neurodynamic modules (Grigsby & Stevens, 2000). The cause may be excessive excitement or inadequate inhibition, just as a runaway truck may be the product of failed brakes or a jammed throttle. Using positron emission tomography (PET) technology, Saxena and colleagues have shown that the treatment of OCD with paroxetine (Paxil) leads to a partial normalization of the increased orbitofrontal and caudate hypermetabolism (Saxena et al., 1999); that the medication helps put on the brakes and restore the neurodynamic equilibrium. Helping OCD sufferers and their parents understand the neurodynamic components of the disorder often allows the family to destigmatize the problem and understand why the treatment, especially the exposure-response-prevention component, makes sense.

A small subset of children presenting with sudden-onset OCD symptoms have been found to suffer from pediatric autoimmune neuropsychiatric disorders associated with streptococcal infections (PANDAS). In

PANDAS, the antistreptococcal antibodies marshaled in response to the infection end up attacking neurons in the basal ganglia instead of the infection itself. This relatively straightforward theory becomes more interesting by virtue of the recent discovery of a correlation between the incidence of OCD and childhood PANDAS in certain families, suggesting that PANDAS may release a genetic potential for developing the disorder. One study found that of 54 PANDAS children, 26% had a least one first-degree relative with OCD, and 11% had a parent diagnosed with OCD personality disorder. A study of 600 adolescents in Hawaii found that teens identifying as indigenous Hawaiians had a twofold greater risk than other ethnic groups of developing OCD. This population also has a higher risk of developing rheumatic fever, which is associated with PANDAS (Lougee, Perlmutter, Nicholson, Garvey, & Swedo, 2000). There is significantly increased basal ganglia volume in PANDAS individuals (Leonard & Swedo, 2001). Based on these findings, some researchers have wondered whether other forms of OCD overall also may be "released" by an autoimmune disorder (Bessette, 2004). This assumption is currently only speculative. Many children with OCD do not have a streptococcal infection. The PANDAS do, however, highlight once again the role of the basal ganglia in OCD. In many other species, similar structures primarily function to regulate motor control but, like much else in the human brain, evolutionary changes in systems such as the OFC have resulted in systemic change throughout the brain. The basal ganglia are now thought to play a part in cognition, emotion regulation, and learning.

FAMILY DYNAMICS AND PERSONALITY FACTORS

As therapists, we are likely to focus on the psychological and family-system concomitants of OCD. Harsh disciplinary practices, religious scrupulosity, and critical events—such as a disastrous coincidence between a child's wish that a sibling would die and the sibling's actual demise—are thought to be possible antecedents of OCD. Family issues affect and are affected by a child's OCD. Children with OCD may be very dependent and embedded within the family system. High levels of family conflict combined with parent-child enmeshment is associated with childhood OCD (Freeman et al., 2003).

Cognitive risk factors for OCD include a tendency to overperceive threat and overestimate one's control over a situation. People with OCD tend to exhibit a lower threshold for tolerating uncertainty. Personality characteristics such as extroversion, agreeableness, flexible coping style, balanced attribution style, ego strength, positive self-concept, openness to treatment, and insightfulness are considered protective factors (Bessette, 2004). Cognitive factors associated with the *maintenance* of OCD are:

- The child or teen feels empowered to bring about or prevent harm.
- They have the conviction that thought equals action.
- They have the belief that thoughts or passing impulses reflect a person's true character.

TREATING OCD

Planning a course of treatment with the child and family based on their own targeted and "most disruptive symptoms" list encourages a solid treatment alliance. The list typically includes managing the child, coping with the stress and family disruption surrounding the OCD, and participating in and supporting the child's treatment. The modalities that have been shown to have specific efficacy in the treatment of OCD in adults, adolescents, and children are cognitive behavioral therapy (CBT) and pharmacotherapy (specifically SSRIs; O'Connor et al., 2006). Although OCD tends to be a chronic disorder, both psychological and psychopharmacological modalities usually improve the symptomatic obsessions and compulsions. Moreover, PET scans of OCD patients look normal after successful SSRI *or* CBT treatment compared to the abnormalities in cerebral glucose metabolism that characterize the pretreatment state of the brain (Baxter et al., 1992).

Cognitive Behavioral Therapy: Although the evidence supporting the superiority of one form of treatment over another is mixed for many disorders (Norcross, 2002), this is not true of OCD. Cognitive behavioral treatment is effective because it helps reregulate the systematic reactions between different brain modules involved in managing anxiety and error recognition and correction. As is the case in initiating its use in the treatment of other disorders, using CBT for OCD begins with psychoeducation. For parents and adolescent patients, the therapist explains the neurodynamics of OCD in brain-based terms and focuses on why the treatment makes common sense. Using simple language and metaphor, the therapist talks with younger clients about "brain-lock" and "false alarms" set off by the intrusive thought or feeling, the "unwelcome visitor." Sometimes using a disparaging name for the disorder helps externalize it, making it a common enemy to be wrestled with and outfoxed rather than a form of madness or shameful weakness.

For parents and older teens, OCD may best be described as a biopsy-chosocial or stress-management problem (Bessette, 2004). In this model, the brain of a person with OCD is predisposed—possibly for genetic reasons—to produce obsessions and compulsions in reaction to certain life events or experiences. Dysfunctional circuits in the basal ganglia and prefrontal cortex activate and become neural "attractors." A moderately arousing event, such as noticing a bee repeatedly buzzing around and landing on one's sandwich, can throw this neural feedback loop into overdrive. The OCD sufferer interprets an event that a non-OCD person would see as a minor annoyance as the beginning of a horrible contagion. Obsessive thoughts generate more anxiety, reinforcing memories of the incident. The sufferer may then resort to a ritualized compulsion in order to detoxify the current situation and prevent it from happening again. These "safety behaviors" serve to maintain the OCD's neural circuitry. The distress is relieved only temporarily, then the obsessions and compulsive behaviors return.

Psychoeducation about OCD shades into the first stage of treatment proper: cognitive reframing. The therapist customizes the content of the cognitive component of therapy to the patient's obsessions and compulsions. The goal is to prepare patients to tackle the challenging task of exposure and response prevention. For example, if the patient's obsessions have to do with contamination, the cognitive analysis aims to undercut the conviction (e.g. that germs always kill or deform) with dissonant impressions or factual information. Adolescents can see beyond the mere *content* of the obsessions into the *cognitions* underlying the disorder. Naming the faulty assumptions that prop up obsessive thoughts ("fortune telling," "playing God") sets them up for challenges by more realistic thoughts ("We're all in the same boat here about not being sure what will happen next"). Sometimes it is useful to create a map of OCD on paper: where are the obsessions, and what is the location of the compulsions and avoidance behaviors arrayed against them? Where are the points of convergence of the "triggers"? Developing a story can help children or teenagers discover and remember when they are symptom free, when they have been really impacted by the disorder, and when they have resisted and tamed it. Using culturally powerful narratives ("David decks Goliath") or one of the child's favorite narratives from a movie, TV show, or book can bolster the patient's cognitive reframing of OCD and its treatment. One author used the theme "How I ran OCD off my land," as a narrative for the goals and tasks of treatment (March & Mulle, 1998).

Psychoeducation, positive self-support, and cognitive mapping prepare the patient for engagement in the treatment's most effective ingredient:

exposure and response prevention (ERP). The therapist helps the child create a list, or hierarchy, of least-to-most feared situations or objects using a "subjective units of distress scale" (SUDS), where 0 denotes no anxiety and 100 unbearable fear. The SUDS guides the heart of the treatment, which is exposure to the feared stimulus and the gradual deconditioning of the brain's anxiety and error-analysis loops. Exposure typically begins with stimuli that are in the midrange of the hierarchy—items with a SUDS of 40 to 60.

Exposure involves deliberately seeking contact with the feared stimulus. This is combined with *response prevention*, which means that the patient refrains from performing the compulsion usually paired with the obsession. The exposure trial works best if it arouses acute anxiety and lasts until the anxiety subsides. Habituation—a neurobehavioral response—leads to a decrease in the physical and emotional experience of fear. Exposure is critical to the success of the treatment; it also is the element that is most difficult for patients to accept and comply with. Fully a quarter or even a third of patients drop out of treatment to avoid ERP (Kaiser Permanente, 2001b). Therapists may use their own distress in such situations to reinforce their empathy for how hard it is for patients to so directly confront their "unwelcome visitor." But this anxious feeling is not a good reason in itself to stop a therapeutic procedure that has been demonstrated many times to be effective.

Given the "hot" content of some obsessions, countertransference can become a strong deterrent to effective treatment. For example, patients with contamination fears are asked to touch a public toilet seat as exposure without washing their hands afterward. If patients dodge the point of the ERP by simply *delaying* hand washing until they are out of the therapist's sight, the exposure loses effectiveness. The task is to deliberately "contaminate" a patient's body, face, and as many items in the house as possible, giving the prefrontal cortex an opportunity for novel experience and repeated chances to subdue the faulty processing of the brain's anxiety modules. Given that anxiety is a highly communicable reaction, many therapists will have problems not siding with the patient's resistance in this situation.

As in any psychotherapy, the patient and alliance factors trump technique in the CBT treatment of OCD. If an exposure task is too difficult, therapist and patient can agree to take a step down the SUDS hierarchy of intensity or to make the goal *postponing* the compulsive defense for a set interval, say 15 minutes or an hour. In the example just given, the person postpones washing his or her hands (but still uses them for other tasks) for 30 minutes or an hour.

After the exposure experience, therapist and client debrief. Here are some questions to keep in mind for this phase:

- Did you achieve your goal?
- What evidence from the exposure supports your automatic thought?
- Was there any evidence from the exposure experience that challenged your automatic thought?
- Did you use your realistic thought? Was there evidence from your exposure that your realistic thought was true?
- Was there any aspect of the realistic thought that missed the mark? If so, revise it.
- Identify *unexpected* automatic thoughts related to the exposure, and develop a more realistic thought to challenge them.
- What did you learn from the exposure?
- What should the next exposure focus on? It's effective to gradually move up the fear hierarchy.

Tailoring ERP to young clients is an art. It requires coaching children to face a feared object, action, or thought and then to resist the very strong neurodynamic and psychological attractor of engaging in the compulsive behavior. Patients, on some level, magically believe the compulsive action will neutralize the problem. Graded ERP includes therapist-assisted exercises with youngsters where they imagine this exposure without repeating the response and in vivo ERP linked to weekly homework assignments. Response prevention strategies—and the means of supporting oneself through them—should be incorporated as part of treatment. With younger patients, an overarching narrative of young heroes or heroines striving to overcome dark forces with the support of the power of good can sustain them through the process of behavioral procedures that otherwise lack these powerful implicit meanings.

According to the literature, the most effective therapists empathize with the OCD patient's distress. These therapists remain optimistic, inspire trust, firmly maintain the importance of treatment compliance, and try to stay out of power struggles with the patient (Kaiser Permanente, 2001b). Effective therapists behave like the "good-enough" parent who helps children build a secure home base from which to launch out into a purer subjectivity, their curiosity about the world undeterred by their fears.

The ERP component of therapy often requires additional work with the family. Because intense emotional expressions may exacerbate a child's symptoms, helping the family calm down and practice positive, supportive interactions can be extremely important for treatment success. Many families come into treatment caught in a futile cycle of parental attempts to limit the child's suffering by accommodating to the symptoms and providing the child with more and more reassurance. Some parents try to suppress and control the level of conflict when the child is anxious or angry by facilitating the child's compulsive rituals. Other families angrily demand the child give up them up. One goal of involving the family in treatment is to help everyone disengage from the symptoms and in the process reduce the child's confusion and distress.

Psychopharmacological Treatment: Physicians treating an OCD patient should be aware that young patients with mild to moderate OCD often show considerable improvement with psychotherapy alone. In prepubertal children, CBT is the first choice of treatment, even in more severe cases. About 20% of OCD patients who are given a prescription for medication do not respond to the first prescribed agent, and doses must be adjusted often. These changes can be trying for any patient but are especially likely to be so for those with anxiety issues. Giving the parents and the child or teen the alternative of CBT and leaving the door open for future consultation is more likely to lead to positive results (Kaiser Permanente, 2001b).

Severe symptoms and significant interference with functioning and development or failure of an initial course of CBT treatment warrant a trial of pharmacotherapy. Acute anxiety at the beginning of treatment also justifies a trial of medications. Where SSRIs are chosen and depression is also an issue, medications are likely to relieve the depression faster and more completely than the OCD. If tics or extreme lack of insight are present, other medications may be combined with the SSRI. Young patients should be told about the expected benefits and potential side effects of the medication and how long they probably will be taking the drug.

SOCIAL ANXIETY DISORDER

The adolescent or child with social anxiety disorder (SAD) is terrified of committing a social faux pas. Social anxiety disorder "is characterized by fear of negative scrutiny" (Kaiser Permanente, 2008). Social anxiety always occurs in the context of an interaction, even if it is a rehearsed or imagined one. It always involves an observer, even if it is only a figure in one's imagination, watching with amusement, horror, disgust, or disdain. Children and adolescents with SAD may dread eating, reading, or writing in public; going to parties; using public restrooms; or speaking to an audience or an authority figure. Fear usually leads to avoidance. SAD children, sitting invisible and isolated in the classroom, may be noticed only after they start missing school. Their fear is expressed behaviorally (by crying, acting irritably, having tantrums, or shrinking from the sight of unfamiliar people) and physically (by choking, flushing, or shaking; by having palpitations, headaches, and stomachaches). Panic attacks and wanting to die are not uncommon psychological concomitants or symptoms.

SAD adolescents and children often are seen as lonely, fretful, and marginalized (Kaiser Permanente, 2008). They tend to react to social situations by showing deficits in social skills, negative self-appraisals, and states of high physiological arousal (Spence et al., 2000). Anxious children are at greater risk of being rejected by peers when they are withdrawn, inhibited, and submissive and are viewed negatively by their other children and teens (Waas & Graczyk, 2000). Many parents see their SAD child as shy and may react defensively if the anxious behavior is pointed out (much less interpreted as part of a disorder).

In fact, shyness and SAD often are not easily distinguished. One of the keys to sorting out one from the other is to bear in mind that the clinical disorder *impairs the person's ability to learn social and coping skills* and to form social relationships outside the family. SAD therefore becomes more of a factor in the adolescent years, when the child's business is to create a life apart from the family. Unfortunately, by the time many adolescents seek (or are brought to) treatment, the basic disorder, SAD, may have spawned comorbid conduct and oppositional behaviors, such as fighting, truancy, and substance abuse, and psychological symptoms such as suicidal ideation. Adolescents with SAD are more self-conscious, have more problems with transitions (such as middle school to high school), and feel more acutely pressured by peers. But distinguishing normal adolescent concerns from clinically significant ones can be challenging.

The prevalence of SAD in western societies is estimated to range between 6% and 13%, which makes it one of the most common anxiety disorders (Kaiser Permanente, 2008). SAD is more common among females than males. Cross-cultural studies suggest its prevalence is lower in Southeast Asia than in western countries. Because cultural influences permeate the rules that govern social behavior, they are an important consideration in conducting a clinical evaluation. Shyness and embarrassment are universal human experiences; what these states and their physical signals are taken to *mean*, however, varies across cultures and subcultures, genders, and socioeconomic status. About half of SAD sufferers develop symptoms before age 13, and almost all report onset by age 20. Especially for those who develop symptoms early in life, SAD is unlikely to remit without treatment. Early recognition and treatment can arrest the development of a chronic anxiety disorder and also ameliorate the negative consequences that social impairment implies for the developing child (Kaiser Permanente, 2008).

The fourth edition of the *Diagnostic and Statistical Manual of Mental Disorders* (*DSM-IV*) (American Psychiatric Association, 1994) defines SAD as a marked and persistent fear of social or performance situations that expose the person to the social scrutiny of unfamiliar people. To meet criteria for the child or adolescent forms of the disorder, the patient must demonstrate the capacity for age-appropriate social relationships with *familiar* people, and the problematic anxiety must occur in *peer* settings, not just with adults. Exposure to the feared social situation must almost invariably provoke anxiety that may take on the intensity of a situationally bound panic attack. Finally, the person's normal functioning is disrupted or the person experiences marked distress about having these reactions. In individuals under age 18, the duration must be at least 6 months.

As noted, the principal diagnostic problem most clinicians face with this disorder is differentiating SAD from normal shyness and adolescent self-consciousness.

Strategies for social appraisal and ongoing social monitoring are built into our brains. Many neurodevelopmental theorists maintain that our brains evolved principally for the purposes of group life. Our survival and success as individuals depend on being clued into the cues given off by others, especially when they involve anxiety or the disapproval that could signal an impending attack.

Evolution has finely honed our brains and our built-in reflexes for attaching to other human beings and has provided elaborate neurodynamic pathways for appraising the emotional reactions and intentions of others toward us. Each of us has a personal version of this legacy of our evolutionary history built into us, and it has much to do with our ability to think about and regulate emotions. Learning to fit in socially starts immediately postpartum; our survival depends on correctly sensing and skillfully accommodating to how someone is feeling about us. By 1 year of age, a durable internalized working model of how to maintain social equilibrium is established. Without a secure attachment, the young child's neurodynamic capacities for self-soothing and positive forecasting suffer. More primitive fight-or-flight defenses become the neurodynamic attractors called up to combat the anxieties all of us carry within us regarding "What must they think of me?"

In our extroverted culture, displaying such anxieties is not just different, it is inferior. Shyness has gotten a bad name. "Outgoing" is something that seemingly everyone (except the introverts, of course) admires. When it comes to diagnosing SAD, it is good practice for therapists to maintain a perspective that includes cultural, developmental, and behavioral—as well as *DSM-IV*—considerations. The basic somatic signs of social anxiety—trembling, sweating, blushing—are the same in normal shyness and SAD. The cognitive processes (imagined negative evaluation) and behavioral reactions (distress and avoidance) are also often overlapping.

Although shyness often is thought to constitute a risk factor for developing SAD, many children outgrow this trait. In fact, most shy children do not develop an anxiety disorder, and most adolescents with anxiety disorders were not especially shy as children (Kaiser Permanente, 2008). When attempting to diagnose this condition, therapists probably would do best to recognize the subjectivity and lack of reliability that characterizes this diagnosis. In this way, SAD illustrates an important point about everything in the *DSM*: It is not a diagnosis that walks through the door of our office, it is a young person or a family. What we have to offer are not primarily evidenced-based practices for treating that diagnosis but a warm, caring, and skilled relationship that has a brain-changing potential.

COMORBIDITIES

More than half the children and teens diagnosed with SAD also qualify for an additional psychiatric diagnosis, most commonly another anxiety disorder, depression, or substance abuse. Typically, the individual or family seeking help comes in because of the comorbid diagnosis rather than the social anxiety problem. Depression is usually more an effect of SAD rather than its cause (Kaiser Permanente, 2008).

Satisfaction in relationships is tightly coupled with our self-esteem and self-confidence, and what we value in ourselves is closely tied to our sense of how others see and feel about us. The almost inevitable consequence of chronic social anxiety is a decline in the individual's personal confidence, self-worth, and mood. For better *and* for worse, children gradually create an internal model of the self that has been highly influenced by how they are perceived by others—and how they imagine they are perceived. Adverse social experiences play a role, but children are active participants in their social world. When this internalized image of a socially unacceptable self couples with behavioral inhibition, the combination can feed a vicious cycle of fretfulness, dread, avoidance, and gathering deficits in social skills. Clinicians who work with adult patients who present with depression or other forms of anxiety often are struck with the way in which the presenting problem, traced back, began with experiences of social anxiety and presumed social failure.

When outgoing children are faced with novel social situations, they show an initial burst in cortisol levels that rapidly subsides as they engage peers. Such children actually use social interaction for purposes of regulating emotion or anxiety. By contrast, more inhibited children show a weak initial cortisol response that rises (and stays high) as they approach other children (Gunnar et al., 1997). Children with SAD are not as proficient at recognizing faces as other children and are plagued by higher levels of anxiety when looking at the faces of strangers (Simonian, Beidel, Turner, Berkes, & Long, 2001). Children who display high levels of sociability in the first four years of life are more likely to exhibit left-frontal asymmetry on electroencephalograms (Fox et al., 2001). The left prefrontal lobes are critical in our capacity to put positive spin on "what just happened" socially and in generating the words we need to skillfully negotiate encounters. Preschoolers with depressed mothers show greater right-frontal asymmetry and also less empathetic responses to others (Jones et al., 2000).

Graeff, Guimarães, de Andrade, and Deakin (1996) propose two neural pathways (one excitatory and one inhibitory) crucial in the experience of anxiety; both involve serotonin transmission (Argyropoulos, Bell, & Nutt, 2001). Findings of more subtle functional abnormalities are accumulating, showing a highly sensitive fear center in the basal ganglia, the amygdaloid-hippocampal region, and cortical areas such as the prefrontal cortex (Mathew, Coplan, & Gorman, 2001; Tillfors, 2004). Although the utility of SSRIs in treating SAD lends some support to the idea that it is a serotonin-specific problem, the etiology of this disorder is not as simple as this "one-factor" neurotransmitters theory suggests. A lack of balance in the *relationship* among several transmitter systems (serotonin, noradrenalin, dopamine, corticotropin-releasing factor, gamma-aminobutyric acid [GABA], and others) is a more likely etiological factor.

At a higher level of analysis, SAD is a product of neurodynamic attractors. The symptoms of social anxiety disorder are self-perpetuating; that is, neurons that fire together are more likely to fire together again. SAD has consistently been found to run in families, with the more severe variety of the disorder showing the strongest tendency to do so. The role of genetic factors is modest but significant with a possible heritability factor of 0.5 (Kendler, Karkowski, & Prescott, 1999). Most contemporary experts suspect a common genetic background for all the anxiety disorders and several other emotional disorders as well (Kendler, Myers, Prescott, & Neale, 2001). Presumably there are both risk and protective factors that determine the manifestation of social anxiety problems.

TREATING SAD

In a review of 23 efficacy studies of children with phobias and social anxiety disorders, behavioral treatments such as imaginal desensitization, in vivo desensitization, modeling, and self-instruction were found to be efficacious compared to wait-list controls (Ollendick & King, 1998). CBT was found to be effective at 1-year follow-up (Kendall et al., 1997). Treatment of children and adolescents with school phobia with "educational support" was found to be as effective as CBT. Both treatments effectively decrease anxiety and depressive symptoms and increase school attendance (Last, Hansen, & Franco, 1998). Educational support has been compared to contingency management and exposure-based self-control in the treatment of SAD, agoraphobia, and specific phobias. All three treatments were effective by the conclusion of treatment and at 1-year follow-up (Silverman et al., 1999).

In terms of specific methods, CBT and pharmacotherapy yield significant benefit for those suffering from SAD, but neither pharmacologic nor psychosocial interventions meet the needs of *all* patients. Combining exposure and cognitive techniques comprises the most frequently studied treatment for SAD, and 3 out of 4 patients will realize meaningful benefit from this approach (Kaiser Permanente, 2008). Unfortunately, few studies have dealt specifically with treating the childhood version of the disorder.

Cognitive Behavioral Treatment for SAD: As with panic and OCD, CBT makes good neurodynamic sense in thinking about a plan for helping children and teens with SAD, and for the same reasons. SAD comes about as a result of the interaction between biological predispositions in the brain and children's experience, especially their experience in relationships and in regulating anxiety. Neurodynamic attractors interact in a mutually reinforcing way with the "core beliefs" of CBT to produce quite stable maladaptive behavioral and emotion-regulation patterns. CBT helps bring this process to light and CBT therapists offer it in the context of a relationship that both supports and challenges young people through the process of change.

CBT treatment for SAD children and teens means artfully modifying interventions originally designed for adult patients. Exposure, cognitive restructuring, and social skills training are the principal components.

The initial psychoeducational phase of treatment focuses on educating the child and parents about the central components of anxiety—somatic, cognitive, and behavioral—and how specific neurodynamic, cultural, and developmental factors can lead to social anxieties. It is a good practice early in treatment to ask the family about cultural aspects of the experience of which the clinician may otherwise be unaware. With this introduction, clinicians proceed to explain the crucial importance of avoidance in maintaining SAD and why learning to face uncomfortable social situations is part of getting better. Exposure (confrontation of feared situations along a hierarchy) is presented as a tool many people have found invaluable in changing the neural circuitry underlying their behavior and emotional experience. As with panic and OCD treatment, this psychoeducational phase of treatment should not be rushed because it may determine the success of the exposure component that will follow. Psychoeducation gives the prefrontal cortex better tools for processing in a different way that which comes out of the exposure.

A second component of this approach to treatment addresses whatever skills deficits are contributing to social anxiety. The avoidance of social situations reduces the opportunity to observe, practice, and habitualize social skills, perpetuating a vicious cycle. These skill deficits may be very basic indeed. As mentioned, SAD children as a group are significantly less proficient in interpreting the emotional meaning of the facial expressions of others. The developmental line that results in proficiency in this skill begins almost at birth. Meltzoff and others have documented the fact that newborns observe and can mimic the facial expressions of others (Meltzoff & Moore, 1977), and the ability to recognize facial emotion is present by age 3, with adult competency reached by age 10 (Kaiser Permanente, 2008). This skill is very basic in the social life of children from age 2 on. Approaching a peer without perceiving that she is angry may lead to rejection (or worse) rather than a positively reinforcing encounter. If the clinician has any concerns that the child or teenager may have deficits in this area, it is a good practice to include facial affect recognition training in their therapy. Whether young clients lack social skills or are reasonably proficient in this area, inevitably they are burdened by negative appraisals of their performance. Using videotaped exposures and role playing may help them develop more realistic appraisals of the impression they are making on others.

Other Interventions: Group therapy or a group therapy component in individual treatment is often an excellent way to help child and adolescent clients with SAD. It can make the treatment more fun, is an efficient way to conduct cognitive restructuring, and provides an ideal medium for exposure to the situations SAD kids ordinarily avoid. Beidel, Turner, and Morris (2000) developed a treatment protocol aimed at social anxiety, called Social-Effectiveness Therapy for Children (SET-C). Sixty-seven percent of the subjects (ages 8 to 12) no longer met criteria for SAD by the end of treatment, as compared with 5% of controls. The treatment-group members were less anxious, less avoidant of social situations, more skillful in social interactions, and engaged in more social discourse. At 6-month follow-up, 85% of this group did not meet diagnostic criteria. Ferrell, Beidel, and Turner (2004) found similar clinical manifestation of the disorder in a sample of both African American and European-American children; they found that both groups improved equally in treatment. In a 5-year follow-up, Beidel and colleagues found that posttreatment gains were maintained. The authors state that these findings are the more heartening given that childhood social anxiety disorder does not remit without intervention, especially when onset is prior to age 11 (cited in Kaiser Permanente, 2008).

In a group setting, members take turns "starring" in their own exposure or being the "best supporting actor" in the exposure of another member. The content of the situation should be customized to the member's social phobia, and the exposures should be assigned a SUDS score of difficulty before they are attempted. In general, exposures proceed from lower to higher SUDS scores, although the member may wish to pick a situation based on an upcoming real-life social encounter. After the dramatized exposure gets going, the therapist interrupts it every few minutes with the question "SUDS?" and writes down the patient's assessment of his or her level of anxiety at that moment, so they can track the course of anxiety through the encounter after the fact.

Exposures should not be started until patients are equipped with some knowledge of what automatic thoughts have arisen for them in the past in comparable situations and they have had the opportunity to think of realistic thoughts to challenge them. For example, in an upcoming dramatization of giving an oral report in front of a class, the automatic thought that "I'll go blank and I'll look like an idiot" might arise. A realistic challenge to this might be "My mind going blank doesn't equal my being stupid. If I don't know what to say, I can look at my notes or my Power Point presentation." After every exposure, group members are debriefed and the group discusses the evaluation of the experience. The therapist can ask the patient what, if any, lessons were learned from the experience, and the SUDS-based path of the anxiety during the experience becomes fodder for group discussion.

Psychopharmacological Treatment: The International Consensus Group on Depression and Anxiety recommends that an SSRI be used as a first-line agent for children with SAD (Kashdan & Herbert, 2001). Chavira and Stein (2000), however, acknowledge the need for judicious use of medications because of their unknown long-term effects on children and teens. The degree to which adult psychopharmacological data can be generalized to minors is unknown, and the safety of these agents in children has not been established. No medications have been approved by the Food and Drug Administration for treating SAD in children and adolescents, nor have there been any clinical trials of medications specifically looking at their efficacy with SAD in children and adolescents. There are, however, good randomized clinical trials for SSRIs with child and adolescent patients diagnosed with a variety of other anxiety disorders. We recommend medication only after behavioral approaches have been consistently tried and failed.

MONICA: The BASE

During the intake with Lisa, a postdoctoral psychology resident, Monica's parents complained that their daughter recently seemed withdrawn and had feigned illness and refused to go to school on several occasions. Her parents told Lisa that Monica had always been a shy child, but her shyness now seemed as if it was turning into a fear of being around people, especially other kids at school.

When her parents left the room so that Monica and Lisa could talk together alone, Lisa saw an attractive 14-year-old across from her who avoided eye contact and fiddled with her hands. After Lisa made some empathic comments and some conversational overtures, Monica relaxed a bit. She looked up from time to time, but responded to questions with monosyllabic answers and offered no elaboration in response to further prompts. Yes, she had withdrawn increasingly from peers. And yes, she had always been shy. When asked if there was some reason she'd rather stay home than go to school, she responded, "It's easier." She straightened up for a moment and looked Lisa in the eye. "I want to be home schooled. Could you recommend it?"

In supervision with Don later that day, Lisa brought up the home schooling request. Don suggested that they think about the request in terms of the BASE assessment. Lisa said that she was thinking that if Monica's level of avoidance was typical of how she handled dealing with strangers, "she just isn't getting much social experience out of life right now. I mean, I hardly learned anything about her except that it felt like she wanted to run away. I was running out of things to ask her!" Don asked her to think about this reaction and retain the information, to be used later in therapy. "It's so typical of how we react to socially anxious people, isn't it?" he said.

"They want to avoid us, and after the first few minutes of an encounter, the feeling's often mutual. I'm thinking of how this could be like a self-fulfilling prophecy in middle school, which is pretty rough-and-tumble and often competitive socially."

Don talked with Monica about the research on the social brain and how it is key to the development of multiple important psychological functions, such as regulating feelings. He told Lisa that Monica's behavioral withdrawal and heightened anxiety were consistent with literature he'd been reading that associated these characteristics with right-frontal asymmetry in the brain. "Just getting her to talk may help, and it's easy to do."

Talking about the brain and relationships led to some exchanges about the challenges for therapists in staying attuned to young patients with social anxiety problems. They tax the therapist's own social dexterity and capacities for managing our own tendencies to withdraw or get irritated when we're nervous. "It's good to get consultation and talk about your feelings of isolation, fatigue, boredom, and frustration, or whatever else comes up in reaction to the patient's avoidance and withdrawal," Don said. He suggested that with higher-functioning patients, these countertransference feelings may be shared in a limited way. "Remember that social anxiety disorder is at bottom a fear of negative social appraisal, so at some point what you feel toward Monica and her avoidance may have to come up in the therapy." Listening to someone who processes their own feelings talk them out, using both the hemispheres of their brain in regulating and reflecting on emotion as they do so, and then inviting an honest response, may be helpful modeling.

From a psychological systems perspective, both Lisa and Don were thinking that SAD responds better to a specialized approach. What had perhaps began for Monica as introversion was developing into a full-blown disorder. Lisa observed that Monica's avoidance would just perpetuate her anxiety. "So the answer to the home schooling request would be no?" Lisa asked. "Right," Don said. "She needs the opposite to get better."

How to encourage exposure without losing the patient was the next question. Trying to stay attuned to her patient, Lisa did not push exposure too soon, but instead suggested to Monica and her parents that an "extended assessment" would lead to better decisions about treatment. In the meantime, Lisa worked on developing the therapeutic alliance. When she felt it was the right time, Lisa told Monica and her parents that she didn't think home schooling was a good idea, and offered membership in the SAD group she was starting with Don as an alternative. The group included more information about how people overcome SAD through exposure and practice. More importantly, it would offer Lisa an opportunity to create "exposure vignettes" with group members. By tracking her anxiety with the SUDS she could start to transform her social world into a more rewarding and interesting place.

POSTTRAUMATIC STRESS DISORDER

For children exposed to trauma, one of the most important mediating factors include the parents' reaction to the trauma and family support. A catastrophizing reaction by the parent increases the chances that the child who has been exposed to a traumatic event will develop the disorder.

Balanced parental reactions generally have the reverse affect. Not surprisingly, lack of emotional support is associated with developing PTSD after a traumatic experience; positive support seems to help protect children against posttraumatic problems (Kruczek, Salsman, & Vitanz, 2004). Other protective factors are family stability, higher socioeconomic status, and parents demonstrating healthy coping techniques in their own lives. Children in divorced and blended families are at greater statistical risk of sexual abuse and PTSD (Davis & Siegel, 2000). These factors, both positive and negative, make very good sense in terms of what we know about the role of "good enough" parenting in helping children and teens develop and maintain metacognition and good anxiety regulation.

Female gender is a risk factor in childhood, and girls tend to display more intense symptoms of anxiety, depression, and distress after traumatic exposure. These gender differences hold true whether the trauma is personal (e.g., sexual abuse) or widespread and social (the experience of a natural disaster) (Kruczek et al., 2004).

The prevalence of PTSD among adolescents has been estimated to be 6.3% of the population under 18 (Reinhertz, Giaconia, Lefkowitz, Pakic, & Frost, 1993). Given that not all youths who experience a traumatic event develop PTSD, many researchers have proposed that the risk for developing it is related to how the child or teen perceives the trauma (Yule, Perrin, & Smith, 1999), a variable that may be influenced by psychotherapeutic intervention. CBT is the most extensively researched and empirically validated treatment for adolescents who have developed PTSD (Cohen, Berlin, & March, 2000).

DIAGNOSIS

The publication of the *DSM-IV* (American Psychiatric Association, 1994) broadened the definition of PTSD. In addition to including individuals directly exposed to a life-threatening trauma, the diagnostic category includes those *vicariously* involved in a traumatic incident and those traumatized by witnessing what happened to others.

According to *DSM-IV-TR*, the diagnosis of PTSD must involve:

- **Exposure to traumatic event(s)** outside the range of usual experience. The victim experienced or witnessed an event that threatened death, serious injury, or severe physical injury and felt intense fear, helplessness, or horror in reaction to it.
- **Reexperiencing the event(s)**, hyperarousal, numbing, and avoidance in reaction.

PTSD's three main symptom clusters center around traumatic recollections. They include:

1. Reexperiencing in forms such as "flashbacks," nightmares, recurrent and intrusive recollections of the event, including images, thoughts, or other recalled perceptions of it. Sufferers may act or feel as if the trauma were reoccurring in the present through hallucinations, illusions, or dissociative flashbacks.
2. Avoidance, including numbing, involves avoiding thoughts, feelings, or conversations associated with the trauma. The sufferers' memory of the important aspects of the trauma may be blunted. There is a tendency toward feeling detached from others and having a restricted range of affect, including feeling unable to have loving feelings. PTSD sufferers also may feel that their future is limited or ruined by the event(s).
3. Hyperarousal, including difficulty falling or staying asleep and difficulty concentrating during the daytime. Sufferers may be hypervigilant and/or have an exaggerated startle response. They may feel intense distress or physiological reaction at exposure to either internal or external cues symbolizing or resembling an aspect of the traumatic event. Finally, they may have developed pronounced problems managing anger or irritability (American Psychiatric Association, 1994).

If symptoms last less than 1 month after the traumatic event, patients should be diagnosed with acute stress disorder. If symptoms persist beyond 4 weeks, PTSD is the appropriate diagnosis. Children who suffer from PTSD display a different symptom spectrum from that of adults. Stein and Kendell (2003) describe these symptoms common to children:

- Hyperactivity
- Temper tantrums
- Intensified fears, such as being alone or of monsters
- Somatization
- Magical thinking
- School problems
- Revenge thinking
- Reexperiencing in the form of dreams
- Pessimism

PTSD has negative impacts on many areas of patients' lives, including the capacity of mothers with the disorder to form accurate impressions of their newborns (Schechter, 2004). Maternal PTSD generally disrupts the family system and initiates a cycle of fear and confusion, despite attempts by family members to function in a mutually supportive way (Archer & Burnell, 2003). Pregnancy and having a young baby puts women at increased risk for domestic violence and subsequent tramatization (Garmararian et al., 1996). Stein and Kendell regard witnessing domestic violence as a major contributor to unrecognized chronic PTSD. There is also a 30% to 50% overlap between domestic violence and child abuse, the latter being perhaps the most common source of traumatic experience for children and of childhood PTSD (Kaiser Permanente, 2005).

Disassociation is an extreme but not uncommon symptom of the disorder. Allen (2001) describes a spectrum of disassociation he has referred to as a "continuum of detachment." Traumatized people may experience:

- Mild detachment or absorption, involving a breakdown in the ability to notice outside events and extending to an altered sense of self
- Moderate detachment, in which the experience of unreality extends to feelings of depersonalization and derealization and the person observes life and self from afar
- Extreme detachment, involving a state of unresponsiveness; the person appears to be catatonic, with no sense of self or time

Children suffering from PTSD are more likely than children without PTSD to engage in self-harm behaviors such as self-biting, head banging, cutting, starving, and self-burning (van der Kolk, 1996). Many factors can moderate the risk of a child developing PTSD symptoms after exposure to a trauma, including the type of trauma, the extent of the exposure, available social support, and the victim's initial coping style (Pine & Cohen, 2002).

NEURODYNAMICS

Unlike adults with PTSD, the disorder does not seem to be associated with hippocampal changes (DeBillis et al., 1999). A number of other neurodynamic ominous effects, however, do occur. Children suffering from PTSD have smaller intracranial and cerebral volumes when matched with controls, an abnormality that is more prevalent among boys with PTSD than among girls. Also, the corpus callosum that connects the left and right hemispheres of the brain appears to be smaller in PTSD children, and their lateral ventricles are proportionally larger. As with the intracranial effects in this population, changes in the corpus callosum are more common among boys (who are already at risk for the deleterious effects of pronounced lack of hemispheric integration) than among girls. Reduced corpus callosum volume has not been found in other psychiatric disorders, making this a relatively unique abnormality among young PTSD sufferers (Teicher et al., 2004). Some studies have identified abnormal connectivity among brain regions involved in the recollection of traumatic memories among PTSD sufferers, an effect not found among traumatized youth who do not develop the disorder (Lanius et al., 2004). These findings suggest the degree to which trauma may dysregulate the brain and reinforce our sense of how challenging it is for PTSD sufferers to carry on normally complex psychological functioning in many areas of their lives.

Studies of childhood trauma and neglect generally have found elevated cortisol levels in the victims. This effect has been found in children diagnosed with PTSD, in wards in Romanian orphanages, and in maltreated school-children with internalizing problems such as anxiety and depression (see Bremner, 2006, for a review). Carlson and colleagues found that girls with PTSD had higher basal cortisol levels than boys with comparably intense levels of PTSD (Carrion et al., 2002). Klimes-Dougan and colleagues (2001) found that the diurnal cortisol rhythm between male and female adolescents differs.

TREATMENT

For adults suffering from PTSD, research suggests that groups decrease the sufferers' sense of isolation, but too few studies have looked at this intervention with children to fully support a similar conclusion. Group treatment does appear to be a powerful intervention for PTSD among adolescents (Yule, 2001). Group treatment using a CBT approach with psychoeducation can help not only adolescent PTSD sufferers but their parents and teachers as well (Kruczek et al., 2004). One important factor in selecting a group intervention is the potential for retraumatization of a patient through virtual exposure to the trauma of others. No "best prac-tice" for minimizing this risk compares to clinical acumen and sensitivity on the part of the group therapist. Clinical experience argues for regular, more formal assessment of patients' progress, utilizing a simple question-naire administered at the end or the beginning of each group session. A common technique in CBT-driven PTSD groups is cognitive reframing of the automatic thoughts and core beliefs that underlie the interpretation of traumatic events and gradual reexposure through verbalization of the experience. Some therapists use the SUDS method for titrating exposure that was discussed earlier in this chapter. Also, patients who are agora-phobic about some aspect of the experience that reminds them of it can be given homework assignments, which can then be discussed with the whole group. Regardless of the therapeutic method involved, groups can offer many sufferers precious ongoing understanding and support.

Psychoeducation groups are an effective way to teach adolescents about what to expect emotionally as the result of trauma. They provide a means of teaching effective coping strategies for reexposure and ways to reduce reenactment and risk-taking behaviors (see Kruczek et al., 2004, for a review). Psychological debriefing also has been used to provide information about posttraumatic coping and provide an opportunity for the teen to normalize their reactions (Stallard, 2000).

SONYA: The BASE

Sonya is a bright and petite 10-year-old who survived a near-fatal auto accident with her mother. The two suffered nearly identical injuries and were hospitalized for broken ribs and discharged shortly afterward. One of the recommendations for aftercare for Sonya was referral to Child and Family Psychiatry. Initially the mother ignored the referral, but when Sonya began having nightmares and refused to go anywhere in the car, she called the psychiatry clinic where one of us works. Sonya's mother, a single mom, had to return to work and could not stay home with Sonya. Sonya's aunt brought her to the appointment.

One of our postdoctoral psychology residents in the clinic, Kathleen, greeted Sonya and her aunt in the waiting room and invited them both into her office. Sonya looked scared to death. The first thing she said to Kathleen was "If I have to ride in the car again, I'm never coming here again. No one can make me!" Kathleen, buying some time, reflected this back to the little girl, said she understood Sonya was really scared and that she thought she could help with these worries. "So we'll do what we can today and then we'll see." Talking with Sonya's aunt, Kathleen discovered that Sonya's mother was also having nightmares and was too fearful to go anywhere in a car. The mother was not driving and was taking the bus to work, adding almost an hour to her commute each day.

For the moment, Kathleen shelved the logistics of how she could help her client get to the clinic for treatment. She focused instead on the fact that Sonya was also avoiding going to school and had many sympathetic signs of distress, such as stomachaches and tension headaches. In this first appointment, Kathleen did manage to get her young client to start talking about her friends at school, what they were like, who had called her, and how much she missed them. Working with the aunt, Kathleen established a plan to get Sonya to school on the school bus.

Kathleen, usually remarkably organized and sure of herself, struck Doris, her supervisor, as scattered and distracted when they met to talk about the case. Kathleen did not see how she could help if the child could not even get to the clinic for appointments. Doris wondered if Kathleen was feeling a little overwhelmed by the case, not least because she really had *two* patients with PTSD, not one; the mother had seemed like she was very much a part of this, a fourth person in the room during the hour with Sonya and her aunt. After talking about it more, Kathleen agreed that it was unlikely that therapy could reach the girl without getting the mother on board with the treatment—and given the impression they had gotten of the mother's current functioning, this would take some doing.

Kathleen called the aunt at home that evening to talk about how she felt the appointment had gone and to ask her if she would be willing to talk to her sister about how they needed her to come to the next appointment too. Then Kathleen called the mother and tried to establish a relationship. She talked about how the treatment would be very helpful to Sonya, what its goals would be, and how the clinic could, with the mother's help, become part of a team to get things back on track for the family. She shared with the mother what Doris had told her from the perspective of the BASE: It was very important to get things back on track for Sonya as soon as possible because the longer these things went on, the longer they would be likely to last. "Well," Sonya's mother said, "that's kind of obvious, isn't it?"

Kathleen went on to explain how the brain reacts to trauma, and the more often or the longer it goes on reacting that way, the more it gets into a rut. They needed to work together to get Sonya to come to the therapy and back to school. Kathleen told her that she could tell Sonya adored her mother. Sonya was much more likely to start getting her normal life going again if her mother told her that is what she wanted her to do and if the mother would be willing to "walk the walk," and get into therapy herself. Sonya's mother said, in a noticeably small voice, that she wanted to think about this and talk to her sister, but she guessed she could give it a try. The next day the mother called and asked Kathleen to set up an appointment for her with an adult staff therapist experienced in the treatment of PTSD.

In the next meeting with Doris, Doris started by saying "So far what we're doing here should be called ABSE, not BASE, because the issues with attunement and the alliance are paramount, as they often are in crisis cases. But let's take some time to talk about the role of the brain in this disorder because it's important—and at some point you'll want to talk with your clients about this too." Doris discussed the role of the fear-conditioned amygdala in all forms of anxiety and how its overreactivity was essentially hijacking Sonya's frontal lobes to opt for avoidance of fear-producing stimuli—in this case, cars. Likely Sonya's brain was misinterpreting even novel incoming experiences as fearful because of this overactivity.

Reconnecting Sonya with her social networks at school might help rebalance things, as she seemed basically a robust and somewhat extroverted girl with lots of friends. She probably had a premorbid left-hemisphere bias toward being positive, approaching life, and using relationships to help her regulate her feelings. In treatment, imaginal exposure would help the amygdala habituate while her frontal lobes could reengage reality testing. Facts about the brain and "bad trips" could be explained in a simple and almost cartoonish way so that could Sonya understand her feelings about things would change. Eventually Sonya would tell herself that she could get the "smart parts" of her brain to regain control over the "dumb ones." Recalling (or drawing) good experiences Sonya had had in cars and talking realistically about how dangerous it was to ride in them would help get things back in balance. Next Sonya and her therapist would address the issue of avoidance. Both mother and daughter needed to get back into the car and start creating some new memories, leaving the past behind.

CHAPTER 9

Depression in Children
and Adolescents

I'm standing on the edge of some crazy cliff. What I have to do, I have to
catch everybody if they start to go over the cliff—I mean if they're
running and they don't look where they're going I have to come out
from somewhere and *catch* them. That's all I'd do all day. I'd just be the
catcher in the rye and all. I know it's crazy, but that's the only thing I'd
really like to be.

—J.D. Salinger, *The Catcher in the Rye*

THE SCHOOL BUS was crowded with sleepy teenagers early on a spring
morning in Utah. A 15-year-old boy suddenly pulled out a gun, shot
the driver, forced everybody off the bus, and careened away from
the scene. Alerted by a cell phone call, police chased the racing bus through
residential streets and screeched to a halt as the bus ran directly into a
house. Before they could do anything else, a shot rang out and the teenaged
driver had shot himself. Entering the bus, police found the dead boy
holding a clipping of two recently deceased classmates (Horiuchi, Good, &
Kapos, 1996). A month before, two other Salt Lake City high school
students, Caz and Joey, were sharing a lab bench in their honors physics
class. After a fight with his father, Caz hanged himself from a pipe in the
basement. Two weeks later, Joey died instantly after driving his car into a
cement barrier wall at 70 miles an hour.

It has been estimated that in every Utah high school with an enrollment of
2,000 students, there will be, on average, 50 attempted suicides a year (Kahn,
1995). The ratio of attempts to completed suicides in teens is very high
(perhaps as many as 100 attempts for every completed suicide), but national

statistics nevertheless make it clear that a heartbreaking number succeed. According to the Centers for Disease Control and Prevention, suicide is the number three killer of children between the ages of 15 and 18 in the United States, surpassed only by accidents and homicide. It is the fifth most common killer of children between 12 and 15 (Eaton, Kan, Kinchen, et al., 2008)

INCIDENCE AND PREVALENCE

Suicides in childhood and adolescence are the result of depression and interpersonal stress. Estimates of the prevalence of depression in adolescents and children are (as these studies go) fairly consistent. For children, most estimates hover at around 2% of the population (Birmaher et al., 1996); adolescent depression is estimated to range from 6% to 14% (Kessler, Avenevoli, & Ries Merikangas, 2001; Kessler et al., 2005; Shaffer et al., 1996). Research also suggests that the average age of depression onset is earlier than previously thought or actually is occurring earlier than in years past (Klerman & Weissman, 1989). Early depressions frequently persist or recur in adulthood and assume more malignant forms as time goes on (Weissman et al., 1999).

Although about equal numbers of both genders experience childhood depression, girls are more likely to become depressed after early adolescence (and women are twice as likely as men to be depressed as adults). In a meta-analysis of studies using the Children's Depression Inventory, Twenge and Nolen-Hoeksema (2002) found that the gender differences first appear at approximately age 13, with a jump in incidence among girls. Race and sociodemographic status do not affect prevalence, except among Hispanic children. The disparity in the prevalence of depression in the two genders grows dramatically with the passage of time. At age 11, the incidence is 1.79% for boys and 0.31% for girls; at age 15, the ratio shifts to 0.56% for boys and 4.39% for girls. By age 18, 10% of boys experience depression compared to a whopping 21% of girls (Hankin et al., 1998). Galambos (2004) offers three possible explanations for this phenomenon:

1. Girls experience more stressors beginning in adolescence.
2. There are different risk factors for each gender.
3. Girls are more vulnerable to socially-based risk factors peculiar to the teenage years.

DIAGNOSIS

The primary symptoms of childhood depression revolve around sadness, a feeling of hopelessness, and mood changes—just as they do with adults. But depressed children and teens often present clinically in a different way from depressed adults. Depressed children may pretend to be sick, refuse to go to school, cling to a parent, or be preoccupied with catastrophic worries (such as parental death). Latency-age and preadolescent children may sulk, get into trouble in the classroom, be pessimistic and grouchy, and complain that life is unfair. Their parents bring them in for evaluation for these and other complaints. It can be difficult to determine whether a child is just "going through a phase" or is depressed. But if mood-related symptoms become persistent, disruptive, and interfere with social activities, interests, school-work, and family life, youngsters should be assessed for depression.

Depressed adolescents often come in with a kind of über-adolescent attitude, angry, oppositional, and irritable. "Yeah, I'm isolated," a 15-year-old told one of us, "because the world sucks!" Irritable reactions give some degree of protection to a very bright and somewhat overweight 16-year-old who periodically is besieged by feelings of worthlessness and failure. Withdrawal from friends and family members or dropping old friends and hanging out with new more ominous ones may be normal features of adolescent behavior or indicators of a mood disorder. One key to differential diagnosis is whether the symptoms are transient or have become more consistent.

Sadness or irritability is evident in multiple settings with clinically depressed children and teens, not just at home. When severely depressed, teenagers are more likely than adults to exhibit delusions and auditory hallucinations. Depressed teenagers typically have fewer and less intense neurovegetative symptoms and more behavioral problems than do adults (Kaiser Permanente, 2003). The definition from the fourth edition of the *Diagnostic and Statistical Manual of Mental Disorders* (*DSM-IV*) of major depressive disorder—the most commonly diagnosed form of the disorder in children and adolescents—requires that at least five of the following symptoms be present and that the five include at least one of the first two symptoms noted below:

- Depressed (or irritable) mood
- Loss of interest and pleasure
- Significant weight loss
- Insomnia or hypersomnia
- Psychomotor agitation or retardation
- Fatigue or loss of energy
- Feelings of worthlessness or excessive or inappropriate guilt
- Diminished ability to think or concentrate, or indecisiveness
- Recurrent thoughts of death or a specific plan for committing suicide
- Impairment in social or other important areas of functioning

In addition to the *DSM-IV* criteria, clinicians should maintain an index of suspicion for depression if there has been a significant change in a teen's functioning in these areas:

- School performance (such as a decline in grades or cutting classes)
- Reaction to criticism, increased defensiveness or argumentativeness
- Acceptance of support and understanding from friends and family
- Negative self-statements, blaming, and criticism

Self-injuring behaviors, such as cutting and burning; preoccupation with morbid themes, such as death, pain, Satanism, and the occult; and chronic boredom are also important indicators.

Differential Diagnosis

It is especially important to be aware of the possibility of misdiagnosing a depressive episode in teens who have bipolar disorder—either by mistaking major depression for the depressive phase of a bipolar disorder or missing the co-occurrence of the two. Bipolar disorder in its depressive phase can look very much like major depressive disorder. Clinicians may have only history to go on in making the co-occurring diagnosis. They should ask parents about mood cycles or manic symptoms. This is important in general and more so when medications are involved. When given to a person with an underlying bipolar condition, antidepressants can provoke a manic episode. It is good practice for therapists to ask about hypomanic symptoms, especially in cases where a child or teenager is severely depressed, about voices and strange thoughts, and about family members with these problems. Severe depressions characterized by mood-congruent hallucinations and delusions, psychomotor retardation, and pervasive anhedonia often are followed by mania or hypomania. Adolescents with mania may come across as funny and elated. Therapists may find themselves beguiled by how charming or clever or attractive they are. These patients may appear quite grandiose, appear to have boundless energy, and engage in high-risk or hypersexual behavior.

Comorbidities

We are of the opinion that psychiatric diagnosis is on the threshold of a major upgrade. Although the *DSM-III* and *IV* helped solve or minimize some problems, the core dilemma is that there are virtually no "physical findings" available to support any one of the major child or adolescent psychiatric diagnoses, including depression. Since "diagnosis" is at heart a term that makes the most sense in a medical context, this is a problem, to say the least. Nevertheless, the *DSM* is what we have to work with for the time being. Physical findings of the type physicians prefer to rely on in making medical diagnoses may one day be available to therapists and psychiatrists and may well be in the form of brain images.

Perhaps half of adolescents diagnosed with depression have a comorbid condition. In most cases, the comorbid disorder precedes the depressive episode (see Graber, 2004, for a review). About one-third of the people diagnosed with attention-deficit disorder (ADD), for example, also have comorbid depression (Kaiser Permanente, 2003). Boys with the hyperactive/impulsive or combined type of ADD are at higher risk for comorbid depression (Biederman & Faraone, 2004). Both ADD and depression are associated with long-term problems in social functioning, employment, negative self-image, academic achievement, family conflict, and suicide (Barkley 2006; Waslick, Kandel, & Kakouros, 2005). In evaluating postlatency children and all adolescents, therapists should be sure to ask about substance use. Symptoms of substance abuse can mimic those of depressive and bipolar disorders. Finally, mania and hypomania must be distinguished from attention deficit hyperactivity disorder (ADHD) and disruptive behavior disorders, both of which commonly co-occur with depression and bipolar disorder. In bipolar disorder, prominent mood dysregulation accompanies the impulsivity and distractibility commonly seen in ADHD.

ASSESSMENT

Because of the lack of physical findings, the primary tool in assessing child or adolescent depression is the clinical interview. For children under 13, this requires both separate and conjoint meetings with children and parents. Some time to talk with adolescents apart from their families is also indicated. Clinicians should consider the individual's and family's cultural identity and language abilities during the assessment. (If any family member is monolingual in a foreign language, it is good practice to have an independent translator if possible.) The assessment includes evaluation of potential risk factors and the presence of comorbid disorders. The duration and severity of depressive symptoms, as well as previous episodes, should be explored to distinguish differential diagnoses of mood disorders. Where a significant substance abuse problem is apparent, a referral for consultation or treatment with an addiction specialist is a good practice (Kaiser Permanente, 2003). In cases of severe depression or significant risk of suicide, it is also usually wise to try to establish contact with collaterals beyond the nuclear family (e.g., teachers, second-degree relatives, or even friends).

ASSESSING SUICIDALITY

Clinicians are not mind-readers, and our evaluations of potential behavior can be no better than educated guesses. In conducting the evaluation, clinicians should acknowledge the need to keep the teenager safe and discuss the limits to confidentiality and the need to make a safety plan with parents or others if necessary. When conducting an evaluation to determine whether an adolescent is at risk of trying to take his or her life, it is a good practice to set up a meeting with the youth alone and a separate one with the parent(s), if possible. These risk factors should be addressed in the clinical interview:

- Past attempts or gestures
- Current severity of suicidal ideation
- Is there a plan? How specific is it?
- Does the child have access to means of carrying it out?
- Has anyone in the family or social circle killed himself, or tried to?
- Are their acute or chronic psychosocial stressors?
- Is the child or adolescent clinically depressed, bipolar?
- Is there a history of impulsivity, agitation, aggression, and alcohol or drug use?
- Is the adolescent socially isolated or involved with negative peers?
- Are there firearms in the home?

Perhaps half of the adolescents who kill themselves verbalize their intentions to do so within a day of the event (Kaiser Permanente, 2003). Having made a previous suicide attempt greatly increases the chances of another (and probably more successful) attempt, especially in boys. Comorbidities are a significant risk factor—a diagnosis of panic, for example, is associated with suicidal ideation in females, and co-occurring aggressive conduct disorders increase the probability of attempts in boys. Teens who present with mania or hypomania, severe anxiety, psychosis, or intoxication and who are agitated and threatening harm to others are at very high risk. Fifty-three percent of adolescent suicide victims have a diagnosis of substance abuse, and 13% were using alcohol at the time of their death (American Academy of Child and Adolescent Psychiatry, 2001; American Academy of Pediatrics, 2000).

The choice of suicidal method tends to be gender-linked. Boys often chose lethal methods, such as firearms, hanging, or jumping from heights. Overdosing on medication is the most common method among girls. A current situational crisis (such as the breakup of a relationship) or more remote interpersonal events can precipitate an attempt. A recent suicide by a friend (or even an attempt), being pregnant, disciplinary or academic problems at school, parental absence, parents' substance abuse or mental illness, legal problems, debilitating physical disorders, exposure to family violence, abuse, and sexual assault are also common precipitants.

ETIOLOGY

There are myriad suspects in the search for the cause of depressive disorders. Three of the most likely are genes, the adolescent's attachment style, and the brain's response to stress. An additional factor—which we acknowledge just in passing—is that American society itself breeds depression. Our culture seems to become more stressful on a daily basis; some people are more susceptible to stressors than others; and stress is distributed inequitably across the population. Jeanne Miranda (personal communication, 2007), a main author of the Surgeon General's Report on Mental Health and a longtime researcher into the cultural factors underlying depression, looked at Latin American populations that contribute many immigrants to the United States. Among the Latin American populations, the indigenous incidence of the disorder is about one-quarter what it is among native-born U.S. citizens. After they immigrate, the rate among their offspring is about one-half that of U.S. natives. Second-generation offspring, however, suffer from depression at the same rate as the rest of the U.S. population. These data suggest that being American is itself a risk factor for developing depressive disorders.

GENES AND NEURODYNAMICS

Granted that environmental factors, both large and small, influence whether children develop a depressive disorder; genes matter too. Thomas R. Insel, Director of the National Institute of Mental Health (NIMH), has said that, ''People's biological variations set the stage for how they respond to different environmental factors, like stress, that can lead to depression.'' This conclusion is supported by a study funded by NIMH that looked at the incidence of depression among adults who had been abused as children. Those lacking a specific gene variation had twice as many symptoms of severe depression as those who carried the protective variety. The gene carries instructions regarding construction of receptors for a particular type of stress hormone, called corticotropin-releasing hormone (CRH). Receptors are actually proteins in or on cells that act as binding sites for chemical messengers that affect cell function. CRH helps titrate responses to stress by, among other things, regulating neurotransmission (Bradley et al., 2008).

Stanford's Robert Sapolsky (2004) and others argue that the relationship among stress, anxiety, and depression can be measured and demonstrated biologically. The NIMH research on CRH variation discussed above is a case study in how genotype, extreme childhood stress, and neurophysiology interact to produce psychopathology. These researchers found that children responded to stressful events by hyperactivating the CRH system, which increases the risk of later depression. "Our results suggest that genetic differences in signals mediated by CRH may amplify or soften the developmental effects that childhood abuse can have—effects that can raise the risk of depression in adults," according to one of the study's investigators, Kerry Ressler (quoted in Nauert, February 6, 2008, p. 1).

Research clarifies the importance of stress hormones and neurotransmitters in the physiology of depression. Depressed children with a history of abuse have been shown to have lower concentrations of cortisol in the morning. Whereas cortisol in undepressed children without abusive histories declines as the afternoon advances, in depressed, abused children, cortisol actually goes up (Cicchetti & Rogosch, 2001a, b). Stressful events, such as parental conflict, divorce, parental depression, parental medical problems, and conflict with parents, are all risk factors for adolescent depression. Disturbance in body image—which can be provoked by peer teasing or societal reverence for unrealistic body types as the standard of beauty—increases the vulnerability to depression, especially among girls (see Graber, 2004, for a review).

Neurodynamics: For most therapists and educated members of the general public, the dominant brain-based theory of depression is that it is caused by or associated with defects in certain neurotransmitters, the "go-betweens" such as serotonin and norepinephrine, that facilitate communication between neurons. Elements of this model are shown in Figure 9.1.

As we have repeatedly noted, distributed neurodynamic and systemic factors underlie most important psychological states and functions; this is also most likely true for depression as well. Although the neurotransmitter model of depression is descriptively useful—and, as the pharmaceutical industry has demonstrated, an excellent way to get depressed patients to

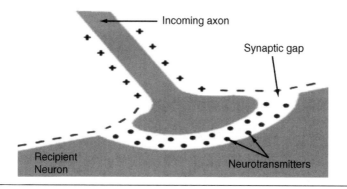

Figure 9.1 Neurotransmitter Model of Mood Physiology

take an antidepressant—recent neuroscience raises significant questions about the model's scientific adequacy. There are logical problems with the idea that low levels of a neurotransmitter such as serotonin or norepinephrine cause despressive disorders. Serotonin is found not only in the brain but throughout the body; there is actually more serotonin in the gut than in the brain. According to John Horgan (1999), "Given the ubiquity of a neurotransmitter such as serotonin and the multiplicity of its functions, it is almost as meaningless to implicate it in depression as it is to implicate blood." (p. 37)

There is an additional problem with the logic of the pharmaceutical companies: simply because an agent helps with a problem does not mean the problem is caused by a deficiency of that agent—for example, the fact that aspirin helps a headache does not mean that headaches are caused by an aspirin deficiency in the brain. Scant direct evidence supports the neurotransmitter hypothesis, despite numerous well-financed attempts to adduce it. Psychiatrist David Burns, winner of the A. E. Bennett Award for Biological Psychiatry for his research on serotonin metabolism, states:

> I spent the first several years of my career doing full-time research on brain serotonin metabolism, but I never saw any convincing evidence that any psychiatric disorder, including depression, results from a deficiency of brain serotonin. In fact, we cannot measure brain serotonin levels in living human beings so there is no way to test their theory. Some neuroscientists would question whether the theory is even viable, since the brain does not function in this way, as a hydraulic system. (Burns, quoted in Lacasse & Leo, 2005)

So if depression is not caused by neurotransmitter deficits, then what? Several imaging studies have found that depressive symptoms are

Table 9.1
Neurodynamic Elements of Depressive Reactions

Neurodynamic Element	Activity Level/ Effect in Depression	Functions Affected
Right prefrontal cortex	Increased activity	Negative affects; global thinking
Left prefrontal cortex	Decreased activity	Positive affects; narrativizing of events, language, and social functions
Anterior cingulate cortex	Decreased activity	Attending to detail
Hippocampus	Diminished volume from neuron death	Memory, retention of detail for long-term storage
Brain-derived neurotropic factor	Decreased levels	Neurogenesis and neuroplasticity
Corticotropin-releasing hormone	Increased levels	Responses to stress hormones and neurotransmitters
Cortisol and adrenaline	Increased levels	Activation of sympathetic nervous system; withdrawal of blood flow from the cortex

associated with increased activation of the right frontal lobe and corresponding inhibition on the left (Baxter et al., 1985, 1989). Making interpretive sense of events and generating positive, optimistic emotions are products of robust left-hemispheric functioning. Much of what we see with depressed patients—their experience of the enthralling power of somber affects, interpretive capacities hobbled by melancholia—is consistent with right-side dominance. Instead of putting details into context, depressed patients seem diverted by a global negative perspective. Right-hemisphere functioning favors global thinking. The ventromedial prefrontal cortex (PFC) also appears to become more active during sadness (Damasio, 1999). The difficulty many depressed patients have attending to detail is reinforced by sharply diminished activity in their anterior cingulate cortex (Lane, 1998). If allowed to go on unchecked, the kindled neural networks of depression are self-perpetuating. The more they fire together without balanced input, the more likely they are to fire again. Table 9.1 presents a list of brain systems thought to be affected by depression.

Imaging studies provide fertile ground for discussions of the links between depressive states and relationship problems. For example, imaging studies of depressed subjects show restricted blood flow to the right-hemisphere modules that make the facial expressions of other people meaningful and interesting to us. Our ability to use the emotional inputs of others to modulate our own emotional states depends to a significant extent on this capacity to read faces. If that capacity is impaired, people become less interesting, and their ability to help us modulate sadness and pessimism fades. When their ability to "face-read" is impaired, teenagers are likely to be that much more thrown back into their internal world of disappointment and despair.

Depression and the Hippocampus: Recent research on depression highlights the role of the hippocampus—the peanut-sized module deep within the temporal lobe that is vital to the encoding of memories and their emotional significance. In this model, the experience of stress causes our hypothalamic-pituitary-adrenal system to turn up the production of the hormone cortisol. Long-term elevation in cortisol shrinks the dendrites and axons of hippocampal neurons and the volume of the hippocampus itself. Some studies have shown a 10% to 20% decline in volume in chronically depressed patients (Sheline et al., 1996). The destructive potency of cortisol's effects on the hippocampus may lie in its power to inhibit the production of a key element in neuroplasticity and neurogenesis. Brain-derived neurotropic factor (BDNF) is a sort of neuro-fertility drug that stimulates the growth of new dendritic branches and releases the reproductive capacity of existing neurons, resulting in the creation of new neurons.

About one-third of the population hosts an unusual variety of the gene that carries the instructions on how to manufacture BDNF (Hariri et al., 2003). People with this allele are even *more* susceptible to the negative effects of stress on BDNF production. Research has documented depleted BDNF levels in the hippocampi and PFCs in the brains of successful suicides (Dwivedi et al., 2003). This BDNF theory of vulnerability predicts what we as therapists so often see: depression running in families. Elevated cortisol levels during depression attack both the hippocampus and the PFC (Brown, Rush, & McEwen, 1999). Cognitive deficits, impairment in working memory, and the diminished capacity to make executive decisions—signal characteristics of depressive disorders in individuals of all ages—are the result.

When the stress response abates, BDNF production resumes and depleted dendrites and axons once again reach out and sprout dendritic foliage. In this model, antidepressant medications stimulate the production of BDNF, enrich neuroplastic capacities, and inhibit the reuptake of neurotransmitters. Fred Gage of the Salk Institute of Biological Studies suggests that the link among selective serotonin reuptake inhibitors, BDNF production, and neurogenesis may be why it takes 3 weeks for antidepressants such as paroxetine (Paxil) to work: this is the amount of time old neurons need to reproduce and their offspring require to get fully wired into complex neurocircuitry (Gage, quoted in Ramin, 2007, p. 90).

There is more to the physiology of clinical depression than is dreamed of in the Prozac model of antidepressant action. New research seems to be improving our aim in designating neural molecular targets associated with depression and other mental disorders. One study examining imbalances in the activity of an enzyme called GSK3β suggested that this enzyme may be closer to the root cause of psychological disorders than are low serotonin levels. In the new study, anxiety- and depression-like behaviors in mice with low levels of serotonin were reversed when scientists blocked GSK3β (Beaulieu et al., 2008).

ATTACHMENT, RELATIONSHIPS, AND MOOD

As we noted in Chapters 3 and 4, attachment styles are "internal working models" of emotion regulation that are highly durable across the span of development. Daniel Siegel (1999), David Wallin (2007), and others see attachment styles as a good way of thinking about overall psychological health. Bowlby (1951, 1969) hypothesized that we are genetically endowed with the propensity to form strong attachments to a caregiver for purposes of survival. Mary Ainsworth demonstrated that infants start life in a psychological state of undifferentiated subjects and objects, in which people are rather interchangeable (Ainsworth, 1969). This changes very quickly. Between 6 and 9 months of age, babies evidence a powerful bond with and preference for their mothers. Ainsworth and colleagues (1978) were among the first to show that the amount of care the mother devotes to her baby is not as important as the *quality* of her attunement to the baby's communications regarding his or her internal state. Some of Ainsworth's most perceptive observations were made in Uganda, but she later robustly confirmed them in Baltimore with a sample of American infants and mothers (Ainsworth, 1978).

Later attachment researchers, such as Mary Main (1995) and Peter Fonagy (2001), were able to show that the "style" of the infant's attachment to the caregiver is important across the developmental life span (see Wallin, 2007, for a review). Infants with mothers who were secure and attuned handled separations well and were able to use the mother as a secure base for exploring the environment when the mother was present. Mothers with insecure attachments tended to elicit attachment styles in their children that were avoidant (where babies behave as if they do not need or prefer the mother), ambivalent (either angry or hypersolicitous of the attachment figure), or, worst of all, disorganized (behaving in an unpredictable and sometimes bizarre way). Main and others demonstrated that these attach-ment schemas (to use Piaget's term) were in place by about 12 months of age and resisted the effects of time. Attachment style is associated with patterns of emotion regulation, serving as a template for relationships. Attachment is the programmer that writes the phenotype of particular styles of emotion regulation into the brain.

Early emotion regulation schematas allow babies to regulate the attach-ment relationship with the mother for survival purposes. The "internal working model" consists of strategies for optimizing the balance among dependency, internal needs, and increasing autonomy. Through the esca-lating expectations of independence in childhood, the brains of children with working models of emotion regulation built on accommodating to insecurity are likely to be more vulnerable to the destructive physiology of stress. An extreme example of these effects can be seen in Romanian orphanages, where infants exhibit all the physical and expressive signs of depression. Consistent attachment is a brain-building nutrient; its absence can prove devastating.

Fonagy and others have asserted that core attachment relationships play a key part in exploiting and shaping the brain's genetically determined neuroplastic capacities. Imagine the impact of an inconsistent or disor-ganized mother on an infant who comes into the world programmed to make attachment work. Accommodating to the primary caregiver is the baby's ultimate survival strategy. The physiology of stress is at work in the baby's brain as it struggles to adapt to an ill-attuned caregiver. Inter-actions between baby and mother yield a sensorimotor model of what one can expect, what variants to the expectation are common, and what constitutes emotional and physiological chaos for the infant. The emerging working model is a set of rules (Wallin, 2007) that tend to be highly durable. Adolescence is a unique opportunity to rework it.

Ideally, children emerge into adolescence with the capacity to conduct Piaget-like "operations" on their own feelings and those of others. Being able to experience some degree of autonomy from our own feelings and moods—possessing a self that has powerful feelings but one only rarely enclosed *within the mood*—allows us to see others more clearly. This faculty, metacognition, is one of the most valuable psychological legacies of normal adolescence. During the teenage years, the developmental metacognitive capacity is likely to experience jolts from many directions: sex and growth hormones, social competition, and narcissistic slights at school and at home. These intensify in adolescence as children move out into the world. Trauma outside the family becomes an increasing threat. The teens' primary venue shifts from the family as the arena of critical relationships to the school, the party, and the street. At the point when children could most use an internal secure base, an ability to stay calm, and the detachment that Main's metacognition can provide, many teens find that this faculty has deserted them entirely. The lack of a relatively detached stance toward strong feelings combines with high levels of stress to make teenagers vulnerable to depression.

The development of the capacity of the left PFC for constructing narratives during the teenage years may be the neuroanatomical basis for Main's metacognition. This capacity makes it possible for teenagers to see and to use the self differently. For secure teens, friendships help them maintain emotional regulation and get on with the business of separating from parents. Those with insecure attachments are likely to feel besieged by stimulation and insult from the outside world. They continue to struggle with the sequelae of insecure attachment styles—trying to regulate their relationships through avoidance, ambivalence, or less well-organized strategies. Their experience is written into their synapses, and tends to make well-learned patterns more permanent, less subject to revision by new experience.

People suffering from depression tend to overgeneralize autobiographical memories (Howe et al., 2006). Kaslow, Adamson, and Collins (2000) identified three cognitive processing areas associated with depression: negative self-schemata, faulty attribution biases, and a sense of helplessness and hopelessness. Cognitive and emotion-regulation schemata that require children to continue to overadapt to frustrating attachment figures leave them at greater risk to the social insults, pessimism, and low self-esteem that are the dark side of adolescent culture.

TREATING CHILDHOOD AND ADOLESCENT DEPRESSION

One way to think about the goals of treating a depressed child or adolescent is to consider the neurodynamic elements likely to be underlying and perpetuating the condition (see Table 9.1). Decreased positive affect, diminished capacity to remember and forecast good stories about life, diminished interest in other people, lowered attention to detail, and chronic stress are all part of the picture. We have many ways of helping—ranging from therapies such as cognitive behavior therapy, which works from the top of the brain down to the limbic areas, to antidepressants, which work from the limbic areas up to the cortex—that repair deficits in ongoing relationships and the attachment styles that nonconsciously influence them.

Treatment begins with an assessment of patients and their families. It includes an evaluation of the cognitive and emotional factors affecting patients' ability to enter into a therapeutic alliance. Adolescents struggling with autonomy concerns may be unable to accept reasonable treatment recommendations made by adults; they may deny that their problems are any different from those of their peers. Where the referral was not the teenager's idea to begin with, just being brought in for an evaluation may be taken as an insult.

Many children and teens present with mild to moderate depression for which there are a variety of promising interventions. In working with more depressed adolescents, a multimodal, integrated treatment plan addressing diverse aspects of the psychosocial environment is likely to be necessary (Kaiser Permanente, 2003). Parental involvement is an enormous advantage in managing a helping relationship. Especially in divorced families, treatment of adolescents and children can become an area of contention between caregiving adults. Single parents struggle with financial problems and the logistics of getting their children (and themselves) to treatment. Despite these complications, it is important to advocate for the best interests of the young patient and, when possible, to support their healthy strivings for autonomy in making treatment decisions.

INFORMED CONSENT AND CONFIDENTIALITY

In most circumstances, parents or legal guardians of a child must consent to treatment. Clinically it is a good practice for therapists to obtain informed consent from both the adolescent and the primary adult(s) at the first meeting and to engage in an honest discussion about the provider–client privilege from both therapeutic and legal perspectives. Adolescents and children do not have the same legal rights to confidentiality as adult clients. Therapists juggle adolescents' need for autonomy and privacy with the obligation to keep them safe. Decisions about whether to disclose something told to us by a teenager in confidence should be based on an assessment of the risks of nondisclosure—and sometimes on our reading of the adolescent's wish that we disclose certain "forbidden" knowledge to others.

Therapists who regularly see adolescents and frequently confront the privacy issue should maintain a current knowledge of the requirements of the Health Insurance Portability and Accountability Act (HIPAA) regarding privacy and the transfer of records. In many states, the law allows minors over the age of 12 to consent to and receive treatment if they are intellectually mature, if they are victims of child abuse, or if denying treatment incurs risks of serious physical or mental harm. Also, in many states, a clinician has the right to deny parents access to clinical information pertinent to their child where disclosure would adversely affect the therapeutic relationship or the teen's well-being (Kaiser Permanente, 2003).

PSYCHOEDUCATION

Family members affected by their child's symptoms benefit from objective information about depression. Treatment abandonment decreases when families are educated about depressive disorders because information cures or ameliorates some of the guilt and blame many parents and teens experience regarding depressive symptoms. Depression tends to run in families, and educating parents about the disorder often helps them recognize their *own* depressive symptoms. If educating parents about depression eventuates in their entering treatment, the referral can be one of the most beneficial effects of the child's treatment (Brent et al., 1997).

PSYCHOTHERAPY

Many varieties of psychotherapy are effective in treating childhood and adolescent depression, and all have common effective ingredients. As with adult patients, the therapeutic relationship is the heart of successful psychotherapy with depressed children and teenagers. "Alliance" does not mean a relationship that is all sweetness and light, or one that avoids important interpersonal conflict. Therapeutic relationships that start well and stay positive all the way through are not, on the whole, as effective as treatments that encounter ruptures in attunement and successfully repair them. Recent work on the importance of attachment schematas suggests that a goal of successful therapy must be the *repair* of the nonconscious attachment schematas that ramify into the complex emotional and relational problems patients bring us (Wallin, 2007). It is not a bad thing to have some relationship ruptures along the way (Safran & Muran, 2003). The energy required to repair relationship ruptures jogs the brain out of deeply set patterns of relating and emotion regulation. The evidence base in psychotherapy research also suggests that technique is a factor in outcome (Norcross, 2001). The interventions discussed next are supported by the research and may be considered "evidence-based" in the treatment of child and adolescent depression.

Cognitive Behavioral Therapy: CBT depression treatment is typically brief and includes homework to practice skill development and build the cognitive and behavioral neural attractors that reinforce change. In a study with randomized assignment comparing CBT, systemic behavior family therapy, and nondirective supportive therapy with depressed adolescents, CBT was found to be the most effective. The systemic behavior family therapy approach was more effective when the mother also had a diagnosis of depression. The supportive therapy approach was found to be ineffective (Brent et al., 1998). CBT may yield faster symptom remission than other treatment modalities, although long-term gains are similar among all these therapies. CBT with adolescent patients employs some of the methods we discussed in the treatment of anxiety disorders:

- Behavioral activation (joining the choir or the Scouts, going to the gym)
- Skill building (role-play in groups, thought experiments in individual work)
- Identifying and modifying automatic thoughts and/or cognitive distortions (either during the hour or by using thought records to capture what goes on outside)
- Changing maladaptive core beliefs (by thinking about realistic alternative beliefs)
- Enhancing interpersonal and social interactions (by initiating social contacts)

Group CBT therapy with children and adolescents may be a preferred practice and a more pragmatic one in agency settings, both because it is efficient and because it permits practicing the social skills important in changing attachment schematas. It is not for everyone. Many depressed teens will refuse to participate in groups, not a few because of feelings of shame about their condition or an underlying social anxiety disorder. Therapists should consider this "resistance" carefully. Adolescent patients may well know better than we do what they need; and teens who refuse groups may need more intensive individual contact with the therapist. For all patients, CBT booster sessions can help prevent relapse, particularly with adolescents whose depression has not been resolved by the end of the group (Clarke, Rohde, Lewinsohn, Hyman, & Seeley, 1999).

Dialectical Behavior Therapy: Dialectical behavior therapy (DBT) was developed by Marsha Linehan and colleagues at the University of Washington as a specific treatment for borderline adults with a history of suicide attempts (Linehan, 1993). Focusing on bolstering emotion regulation, impulse management, managing interpersonal chaos, and confusion about the self, DBT is often well suited to the treatment of adolescents. DBT tends to be more programmatic and multiphasic than other forms of psycho-therapy. It involves participation in a DBT skills training group as well as individual therapy once or twice weekly.

Adolescents engaged in DBT group treatment combined with individual or family sessions show significant decreases in suicidal ideation, signifi-cantly fewer psychiatric hospitalizations, significant reductions in the se-verity of depressive symptoms, and a greater rate of completing treatment than teens receiving non-DBT "treatment as usual" (Miller, Karner, & Kanter, 1998). DBT appears to address what Main called ambivalent or disorganized attachment schematas—those characterized by hyper-sensitivity to the object's whereabouts and state of mind—by bolstering skills in emotion regulation and repairing relationship ruptures. These issues are often the most prominent ones in the treatment of depressed adolescents.

Interpersonal Psychotherapy: Like DBT, interpersonal psychotherapy (IPT) is concerned with the management of affect in interpersonal contexts, and there is evidence that IPT is helpful in the treatment of adolescents with major depressive disorder (Curry, 2001). The four types of interpersonal difficulties treated with IPT are role disputes, extended grief and loss, role transition, and social isolation. Patients in IPT-guided therapies are likely to feel relief in regard to their acute symptoms of depression in the first 6 to 8 weeks of treatment and achieve subsequent improvement in psychosocial functioning after 16 weeks of therapy. IPT also has been shown to be useful as maintenance therapy for patients with recurrent depression (Mufson, Weissman, Moreau, & Garfinkel, 1999).

Family Therapy: Controlled research studies addressing the effectiveness of using family interventions in treating depressed adolescents and chil-dren have concluded that:

- Reducing labile emotion and negative interactions in families is vital to the prevention of relapse in mood disorders.
- Family dysfunction impedes the recovery time for depressed adolescents.
- Parent–child conflicts undermine the successful negotiation of social and psychological tasks.

Helping parents and teenagers develop more effective communication skills that reduce blame and intense affect is a common goal of family interventions (Brent et al., 1998).

Psychodynamic Psychotherapy: Psychodynamic psychotherapy is an insight-oriented approach that recognizes the role of early interpersonal conflict and trauma in the patient's current symptoms, behaviors, and affect. Psychodynamic theorists assert that the dynamics of these early relationships are internalized and reenacted in the present—a premise consistent with attachment theory (Fonagy, 2001). Psychodynamic psychotherapy helps adolescents connect past and present relationships and develop more rewarding coping skills, with concomitant changes in the neurodynamics of the brain. Insight-oriented talk therapy engages depressed adolescents who are in the process of separating from old objects and need help in building integrated identities, values, and relationships. Teens often need a safe place to reflect, talk, and feel listened to and validated while they sort out their lives. In this way, the psychotherapeutic relationship is a crucible for re-forming the attachment schemas of infancy.

Current neuroscience models of memory that emphasize the preponderance of nonconscious functioning everywhere in the brain help frame the limits of "making the unconscious conscious." Regarding the recall of early traumatic events, Howe and colleagues (2006) suggest that because the evidence does not support the view that memories can be stored in the body preverbally, efforts to help young trauma victims recall an event they in truth have no knowledge of may well prove to be countertherapeutic. Because trauma alters neuronal connections in the brain, therapists who require victims to relive traumatic events may unwittingly consolidate the very neurodynamic pathways associated with the traumatic experience.

PSYCHOPHARMACOLOGICAL TREATMENT

Antidepressants were designed and tested on adults, and their impact on the developing brain is not well understood. Both parents and therapists are concerned that the use of medications such as fluoxetine (Prozac) in children and teens may interfere with normal brain development. A meta-analysis of psychosocial interventions including CBT, IPT, and family therapy for depressed adolescents showed that psychosocial treatments compare favorably to placebo control trials and medication treatments (Michael & Crowley, 2002).

Every experienced therapist knows that mediation can be effective in some cases. A large study of combined treatment found that in a sample of 439 adolescents with major depression, a combination of medication and psychotherapy was the most effective treatment (Treatment of Adolescents with Depression Study Team, 2004). The study compared CBT with fluoxetine, currently the only antidepressant approved by the Food and

Drug Administration (FDA) for use with children and adolescents. Of those receiving combined treatment, 71% improved, compared with a 60% improvement rate in the fluoxetine-only group and 43% receiving CBT only. Thirty-four percent of the group that received a placebo also improved. The drug-only intervention raised some safety concerns. Study subjects taking fluoxetine alone had higher rates of suicidal thinking (15%) than those in combination treatment (8%) or those in CBT alone (6%), particularly in the early stages of treatment. Although fluoxetine may speed recovery, this study suggested that adding CBT provides additional safeguards for those vulnerable to suicide.

"Black Box" Warning: The FDA requires all antidepressants to carry a "black box" warning label regarding an increase in suicidal thinking among patients taking the medication. In May 2007, the FDA recommended that the warning be expanded to include young adults from ages 18 to 24. The risk of actual suicide is slightly greater during the first 1 to 2 months of antidepressant treatment. Teens with bipolar disorder, a family history of bipolar disorder, or a history of previous suicide attempts are at heightened risk for suicide when taking antidepressants. Teenagers on antidepressants should be monitored closely for any sign that their depression is worsening. Warning signs include new or intensifying symptoms of agitation, irritability, or anger. Unusual changes in behavior are also red flags. According to FDA guidelines, after starting an antidepressant or changing the dose, adolescent clients should see their psychiatrist or behavioral pediatrician once weekly in the first month, every 2 weeks in the second month, at the end of the 12th week following the initiation of medication, and more often if problems arise.

Relapse Prevention

Given the high rate of relapse, treatment plans for child and adolescent patients should address relapse prevention. Parents and teens need regular reminders about the early warning signs of depression. Families should be informed that depression has a cyclical nature. Parents and teens can anticipate depressive symptoms and develop a plan for utilizing self-care and coping skills.

ALICE and the BASE

A thoughtful and quiet 17-year-old, Alice came to the attention of her high school counselor when he noticed her sitting alone at lunch in the cafeteria. When he invited her to his office, she asked, "Why? What did I do?" When the counselor explained

---

that he just wanted a chat and asked if that was okay, Alice said "Whatever," grabbed her book bag, and hurried out of the cafeteria as if she had just realized she was late for an important engagement. Nevertheless, she appeared in the counselor's office during fifth period, propped her bag in one of the chairs, and slouched down into the other one farthest from the counselor's desk. She avoided eye contact, studying the handle on a desk drawer. The counselor asked her to take the earphones out of her ears. She responded by saying "Clueless people who don't understand . . . call it emo music."

Alice spoke in a soft monotone voice with long pauses between sentences. "What's emo?" the counselor asked. Alice said, "It means emotional music, but that's stupid." The conversation went on like this for a while, with the counselor doing most of the work and Alice responding with minimal information. He did get her to talk a little about what her favorite songs were, and they all sounded sad and unhappy. The conversation was so one-sided, the counselor noticed he was starting to get that familiar tired and sleepy feeling he often felt in the presence of depressed kids. Midway through the interview the counselor decided to press it a bit and asked Alice if she was depressed.

"Why?" she said, looking at him for the first time and smiling sardonically. "Will you send me away? That would be great!"

When pressed for a serious answer, she finally said, "Kinda, I guess."

The counselor had worked with our clinic on several occasions and was able to get Alice to agree to call and make an appointment. He told her he really did not want this to slip through the cracks so he would check back with her in a few days and follow up.

When she saw Janet, one of our interns, Alice revealed she had been feeling depressed for about a year, since she and her best friend had had a falling out, and Alice felt like people took the other girl's side. She had basically just stopped talking to everyone. She felt exhausted all the time and though "I'd never do anything," she said she "wouldn't mind it if God took me off this earth. I mean, I just don't see a big point, you know?"

There was no obvious depression in Alice's family history. Her early developmental landmarks and family relationships sounded relatively normal. But Janet noticed some difficult to characterize emotional reaction she'd experienced while Alice was talking about her parents. They sounded one-dimensional, not that interesting, even though most of what Alice was saying about them was positive. Janet wondered if Alice might have developed an avoidant attachment style in dealing with a mother who hadn't made herself that available.

Until 6 months ago, Alice had played on a select soccer team. Then a boy she liked had started dating another girl Alice used to be friends with and she stopped talking to her. "I guess it was after that I dropped out," Alice said. "I mean, who cares about chasing a ball up and down the field anyway? I couldn't keep my mind on it and the coach yelled at me. It's not like anybody gave a damn when I did it, not even my parents. They go 'Well, whatever you think, dear. As long as you're getting As and Bs you're free to do as you wish.' Yeah, right." Alice felt like she was a loser and everybody was shunning her, and she withdrew into a murky world of resentment and anger. Eventually those feelings turned into a constant sadness, fatigue, feelings of self-loathing, and withdrawal.

"Now I can't get out of it . . . and I don't care anyway."

When Janet met with her supervisor, Betty, later that day, they discussed the appropriateness of antidepressants. "Let's hold off," Betty said. "Let's take awhile and step back and see about the bigger picture. Remember that acronym BASE? It's useful. Let's go through it, starting with the brain." Betty's take was that the brain is built to interact with environmental events and is especially primed for social interactions. "It's the only organ created and maintained by relationships, and what happens in that arena is momentous, especially for kids this age." Betty suggested they look at the *b* in Alice's case from the point of view of these social-biological interactions.

To begin with, Alice was hurt and shaken up by the breakup with her best friend. Her tendency to brood and withdraw gathered steam when she perceived other girls were starting to shun her, and gained more momentum when she lost the attentions of the boy she liked. Through the course of these events, Alice came to rely less on relationships and more on withdrawal as a way of regulating her emotional life. "Understandable? Oh, yes," Betty said. "Good? No. Bad."

As Alice withdrew from activities that had been sources of pleasure and interest, she had fallen into a kind of downward spiral. "Somewhere in here—could be cause, could be effect—her brain got into the act," Betty said. "These setbacks and probably a preexisting tendency to withdraw then hurt the internal balance between her hemispheres. I would bet money that if we could see an imaging study, Alice's right frontal lobe would be hyperactivated and her left frontal lobe would be slacking off." Janet said, "So the more Alice withdraws and ruminates and feels bad, the more those thoughts and feelings become biologically based." "Yup," Betty said, "that guy Hebb again: the more those neurons fire together, the more they wire together. We've got to get her off the emo music!"

The tricky part would be developing attunement with Alice because of her seeming insecure attachment style. Janet knew that they needed more common ground, some basis for forming an emotional bond. She thought that some self-disclosure on her part might serve the purpose. At the next session, Janet shared with Alice an experience she had had being jilted by a boyfriend during high school. "This guy actually was the captain of the football team—really!—and the girl he ditched me for was the prom queen." Alice actually laughed. Although Janet had initially become angry and depressed, after a while she decided that this jock was not going to ruin her entire life. She resolved to fight back by not withdrawing. She'd show him (and herself) that he didn't matter. "In fact, eventually that's exactly what happened. I bounced back to how I was before I even knew the guy." This self-disclosure seemed to increase the attunement between Alice and Janet. Unlike Alice's mother, Janet seemed to have the capacity to feel what she felt like.

When Janet believed she and her client were sharing a solid alliance, she discussed some of her ideas about what they could do to get Alice back to her old self. Alice said there was no way she was going to take drugs. "It would just make me feel too weird, and I don't trust them." She referred Alice to a one-session depression psycho-education class for teens to learn more about depression and the various ways of treating it. The class emphasized CBT. Alice came back to the next session with questions about the method and a willingness to try it out.

At this point, Alice already had completed the first step in the treatment—psychoeducation. The next phase was cognitive restructuring to help her get a clearer idea of how skewed her thinking had become in situations where rejection was even a possibility and to begin to deepen her sense of how her development had left her with some core negative beliefs as part of her legacy. Janet showed Alice a thought record, and they completed one during the session about a recent event at school. The record gave Alice the opportunity to look more closely at how her mind put together these elements:

- The physical setting of the event, the time of day the experience occurred, and who was there
- A factual version of what happened—who said what or did what to whom
- The feelings generated by the factual version, and an estimation of their intensity
- What "automatic thoughts" were playing out just *before* the feeling hit and during the emotional reaction
- Evidence supporting the validity of these thoughts
- Evidence contradicting the cognitive interpretation
- Alternative interpretations based the alternative thought
- A reexamination of the mood after completing the record

Alice's initial reaction was that the thought records looked too much like homework. However, in between sessions with Janet, Alice had dashed into the girls' room and almost physically collided with her old best friend. Neither one had spoken. Alice completed a thought record about the experience and felt better when she got to the "alternative thoughts" column. Together she and Janet started planning the second stage of treatment—behavioral activation. Soon Alice had some successes to report. She had talked with a couple of her old girlfriends, and they actually seemed warm and friendly.

Given that Alice's attachment dynamics left her vulnerable to emotional insult, Janet arranged for regular and longer-term therapy together. The therapy was interrupted by Alice's departure for college, but she wanted to resume during the summer, and this became a routine for a successful intermittent treatment. Janet was able to help Alice find her way to a greater sense of trust and security within close relationships. Three years later, Alice dropped by the office to visit while on a holiday break from college. She was doing well and had made some close friends. She had decided to change her major to psychology. Janet wanted to know whether Alice was thinking about psychology or neuroscience. Alice just smiled. "Well, let's talk about it," she said.

APPENDIX

Primer on the Brain

> The human brain weighs about three pounds. It is one of the most complicated material objects in the known universe. Its connectivity is awe-inspiring: the wrinkled cortical mantle of the brain has about 30 billion nerve cells or neurons and one billion connections. The number of possible active pathways of such a structure far exceeds the number of elementary particles in the known universe.
>
> —Gerald Edelman

THIS OVERVIEW OF the brain is intended for readers who are unfamiliar with or would like to know more about the brain and the neurodynamic processes that are referred to elsewhere in this book. A different version of this material can be found in the companion volume to this book, *Brain-Based Therapy with Adults* (Arden & Linford, 2008).

The brain drives (and is driven by) the history of our species, not to mention our personal histories. As the size of the head of the infants born to our evolutionary ancestors increased over time, it eventually exceeded the capacity of the birth canal to accommodate it. As a compromise between the increasing size of the brain and the architecture of pelvis required for upright bipedal posture, human infants are born in a relatively premature and helpless state. They require an extended period of dependency to survive; and creating and sustaining this arrangement, in turn, demands highly evolved biologically based interpersonal skills in both parents and infants.

In the period of early infantile dependency, the brain begins the enormous project of completing the wiring necessary to produce a fully functional human. As the brain develops and grows in volume through childhood and adolescence, it continues to require more care than the comparable equipment in other species. The emotional intelligence needed to provide this care, and the desire to provide it, are built into humans as a survival mechanism for the brain. The capacity to form mother-infant attachments, an emergent property of the brains of many mammalian species, peaks in humans. Our brains ensure we get the care we need as children and also that we are equipped to give it back when our time comes to be parents. The brain produces psychological phenomena ranging from ecstasy to agony, from moments of euphoria to intractable depression and boredom with everyday life. It endows us with an unparalleled capacity to respond to the environment and be changed by it in turn. As therapists, it behooves us to know as much about the brain's workings as possible; and in this appendix, we provide a sort of basic owner's manual.

NEURONS AND THEIR NEIGHBORHOOD

The nervous system is composed of tens of billions of cells called neurons and many more cells known as *glia*. Although we are only beginning to understand the importance of glial cells, neurons have been studied for more than a century and have revealed many of their secrets. Neurons consist of a cell body (or *soma*) in which are found a nucleus (containing genomic DNA and organelles related to its functioning) and other cytoplasmic cellular subcomponents. Extending from this cell body are two types of *processes Dendrites*, which are numerous small, tentaclelike outgrowths of the soma, that receive input from other neurons and specialized receptors and in turn carry electrochemical impulses into the neuronal cell body, where a sufficient amount of such input may lead to a neuronal discharge, or *action potential. Axons* carry the action impulse away from the cell body in the direction of other neurons or tissues (e.g., glands and muscle).

If any cell can be said to have a social life, it is the neuron (see Figure A.1). Neurons always come in groups; they require the stimulation and interaction of myriad colleagues to survive. In the human brain, the average neuron forms connections with as many as 10,000 other neurons in large, widely distributed networks. Neurons communicate with one another at the microscopic gaps, or *synapses*, between them (see Figure A.2). The synapse is much too small to be seen by the naked eye, which is likely to perceive nerve tissue as a continuous glob of organic mass. The *presynaptic* neuron is the cell on the giving end of a transmission; the *postsynaptic* neuron is the receiving cell.

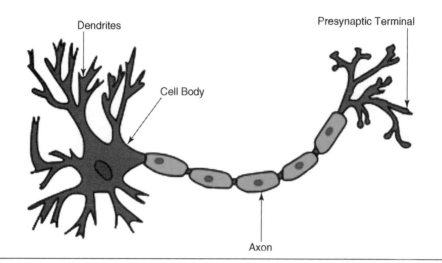

Figure A.1 A Neuron with Cell Body, Axons, and Dendrites *Source:* LifeART image © Wolters Kluwer Health, Inc. Lippincott Williams & Wilkins. All rights reserved.

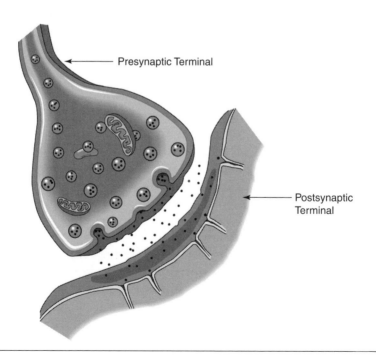

Figure A.2 A Synapse *Source:* LifeART image © Wolters Kluwer Health, Inc. Lippincott Williams & Wilkins. All rights reserved.

As early as the 1800s, some scientists thought that neurons generated tiny amounts of electrical current. Subsequently it was observed that neurons generated this current by exploiting the principle that electrical potentials seek equilibrium—the same principle that powers the chemical batteries inside a flashlight. Neurons function in association with changes in the distribution of positively and negatively charged ions (e.g., sodium, potassium, and chlorine) and other charged particles. Both passive and active chemical processes maintain a slightly skewed balance between negative and positive ions, so that the inside of the cell is electrically negative relative to the outside.

Neuronal membranes contain special proteins capable of controlling access to and egress from the intracellular space and hence the level of electrical potential of the cell. Resting neurons maintain levels of positively charged sodium ions that are low relative to the space between cells (the *extracellular* space) and relatively high levels of positively charged potassium. Negatively charged ions (e.g., chlorine) also are unevenly distributed. This differential puts the neuron's internal environment in an unstable equilibrium relative to the extracellular environment, creating a kind of "edginess," both electrically and chemically, as the natural tendency of chemical systems is to seek equilibrium. The neuron is poised to interact with other neurons and to act as a link in a network of communicating cells.

When incoming stimuli put a neuron sufficiently over its resting threshold, electrical and chemical changes cascade along the axon from the cell body. Axons are efficient conductors of electricity, and the cell's electrical depolarization races along them like fire following a trail of gasoline (only infinitely faster). The nerve impulse rapidly reaches the ends of the axon (the *terminal boutons*), where resulting changes in the electrical potential cause the release of a relatively fixed amount of a chemical neurotransmitter into the synapse. The transmitter substance crosses the synaptic gap (or *cleft*), binding transiently to receptors on the postsynaptic neuron and subsequently changing the electrical potential of the postsynaptic neuron's membrane. These changes may involve either *hyperpolarization* (which inhibits an action potential in the post-synaptic cell) or *depolarization* (which has an excitatory effect). In some cases, substances released from a presynaptic neuron *modulate* the activity of downstream cells rather than producing or inhibiting an action potential. Summing all the presynaptic activity (inhibitory, excitatory, and modulatory) over a very brief window of time, sufficient excitatory input will result in an action potential in the postsynaptic neuron. After the neurotransmitter has carried its message across the cleft, it dissociates from the receptor and is reabsorbed by the presynaptic neuron in a process called *reuptake*. This is how neurons talk with one another.

Neurons ordinarily form synapses with thousands of their colleagues, receiving and sending action potentials. The communication between single pairs of neurons is rarely significant in itself. Many impulses generated by the axon of one cell arrive at the dendrite of the postsynaptic cell without sufficient force to generate an action potential in the receiving cell's dendrites. But the activity of large arrays of neurons—neural networks—is the mechanism by which things get accomplished in the brain. What takes place is a constant background of spontaneous synaptic activity—if we could hear it, it might sound like the noise of a capacity crowd at Fenway Park on opening day. In this case, however, a capacity crowd would mean an attendance in excess of 100 billion. As Grigsby and Stevens (2000) describe it:

> It is as though the brain has a resting "hum" of background chaotic electrical activity, out of which emerges highly organized, synchronized neural activity yielding adaptive response to shifting conditions. (p. 134)

The invisible drama of neuronal communication, reenacted billions of times per second throughout the brain, is the biological foundation of our psychological experience. Estimates vary, but there are probably somewhere in the neighborhood of 100 billion neurons in the brain. The average neuron in the cerebral cortex receives stimulation from between 1,000 and 10,000 other neurons and passes this on to similar numbers of colleagues. A highly connected neuron in the cerebral cortex may have a direct synaptic connection with as many as 20,000 others. The density of synapses is perhaps 800 million to 1 billion per cubic millimeter of cortex (Abeles, 1992). The bottom line is that a cortical neuron receives input from about 100 neurons every millisecond. On average, if 25 additional excitatory inputs are received within a millisecond, a neuron will fire; fewer than this and the depolarization may remain below the threshold for initiating an action potential. After firing, there is a very brief refractory period during which no nerve impulse is possible as the active transport of ions back across the cell membrane is occurring, restoring the "resting" equilibrium. Across the entire central nervous system, the activity of neural networks is dependent on a careful balance between inhibitory and excitatory neuronal behavior. Changes in this balance to conditions that are far from equilibrium may lead the system into various dysfunctional states, with potentially profound psychological consequences, such as epilepsy or stupor.

Cortical neurons spontaneously generate an average of about 5 action potentials per second, and they may discharge up to 100 times per second if receiving strong stimulation. The research of Walter Freeman on the olfactory system (1987, 1992, 1995; Skarda & Freeman, 1987) suggests that a neuron contributes to an overall pattern that conveys meaningful information, whether it is active or inactive at any given time. The plasticity and malleability of this self-organizing system can hardly be overestimated. The brain continually pulls itself up by the bootstraps, becoming more organized and patterned over time. The more often the neural networks that mediate such feats are activated, the more likely they are to be activated in the future, repeatedly producing coherent outputs, but with increasing efficiency. It is impossible to overstate the significance of this simple idea, for it constitutes the basis for such vital psychological functions as memory and for the development of those complex processes often referred to as *psychic structure, ego, habit*, and *character*.

The pioneering Canadian psychologist Donald Hebb fathered the concept, which now bears the name *Hebbian learning*. As he hypothesized:

> [T]he persistence or repetition of a reverberatory activity (or "trace") tends to induce lasting cellular changes that add to its stability. The assumption can be precisely stated as follows: when an axon of cell A is near enough to excite a cell B and repeatedly or persistently takes part in firing it, some growth process or metabolic change takes place in one or both cells such that A's efficiency, as one of the cells firing B, is increased. (1949/1998, p. 62)

The now famous paraphrase of this concept is: neurons that fire together become wired together. *Once the brain (or more specifically, a network of neurons) does something, it is statistically more likely to do it again.* Experience changes the probability of activating a given neural network by increasing or decreasing the strength of the synaptic ties among the individual neurons that comprise the network. This idea of learning as a mechanism that alters the probability that an individual will experience a given perception, emotion, or motivation, or engage in a particular behavior is fundamental to modern neuroscience. This concept is referred to as *synaptic plasticity, neural plasticity*, or *neuroplasticity*.

NEUROCHEMICAL ORCHESTRA

For the last 40 years, biological psychiatry has centered on the one-factor model of "chemical imbalance." We are ready, some would say overdue, for a broadened perspective. LeDoux (2003) has proposed that the one-factor model, which he characterizes in the phrase "No twisted thought without a twisted molecule," ought to be replaced by the concept that synaptic changes underlie mental illness. The old model involved the activity of specific neurotransmitters in response to various medications; in particular, a class of neurotransmitters referred to as monoamines were found to affect cognitive and emotional functioning when potentiated or blocked by these medications.

GABA AND GLUTAMATE

The two main subtypes of neurotransmitter receptors have been described as *the faster and smaller*, and *the slower and more complex*. The faster and smaller (first messengers) are ion channel receptors. They include the glutamate and GABA receptors, and they are faster because they are associated with a rapid change in the ease with which charged ions are able to pass through the cellular membrane.

Until recently, *glutamate* was thought to be important chiefly in the production of *GABA*, the major inhibiting neurotransmitter. Now glutamate is itself recognized as the major excitatory neurotransmitter. Together with GABA, it accounts for much of the neurotransmission in the brain. Although glutamate receptors tend to be located out on the dendrites on the neuron, GABA receptors are typically located closer to or on the neuronal cell body. LeDoux (2003) has described how this balance can tip one way or the other. Each neuron receives glutamate or GABA inputs, and the chance of an action potential depends on the balance between these excitatory or inhibitory influences. This balance is critical because without GABA, inhibitory neurons would fire continuously under the influence of glutamate. Monosodium glutamate (MSG), used in some foods to enhance taste, can increase the amount of glutamate in the body and eventually cause headaches, ringing in the ears, and other symptoms. GABA inhibition can increase as a result of taking a benzodiazepine such as Valium.

Dopamine: Another important neurotransmitter, *dopamine* (DA), is produced in the substantia nigra and other areas in the brain stem. It is associated with the reward system and motor activity. Stimulant street drugs such as cocaine and methamphetamines potentiate (or exacerbate the effectiveness of) dopamine. Mild doses of dopamine energize; overdoses can lead not only to seizures but to psychosis. In fact, the theoretical association between schizophrenia and DA paralleled the development of a wide variety of drugs that blockade the DA receptor sites. Since the initial development of drugs such as chlorpromazine (Thorazine) and haloperidol (Haldol), newer drugs such as clozapine (Clozaril) and risperidone (Risperdal) were developed as researchers gradually learned that there were at least five (if not more) different types of DA receptors in two families, one (D1 and D5) excitatory and the other (D2, D3, and D4) primarily inhibitory or modulatory in its effect.

Treating schizophrenia primarily with these drugs has proved to have its limitations. Type II schizophrenics do not respond well to the drugs. Also, the brain as a self-organizing system responds to the DA blockade by developing new compensatory DA receptor types. Moreover, when patients with schizophrenia are treated with drugs alone, the hospital recidivism rate is poor. By contrast, schizophrenic patients who also participate in psychosocial and vocational rehabilitation programs function better in the community (Arden, 1987).

Dopamine is a neurotransmitter that binds with the slower and more complex G-protein receptors. Upon binding with the transmitter, the shape of the receptor changes slightly, thereby activating an intracellular substance called a G-protein, which in turn leads to the release of a "second messenger" within the neurons. Second messengers help create proteins that *regulate the expression of genes* within the cells and enzymes that aid in the synthesis of neurotransmitters. Because G-proteins produce their effect by influencing gene expression, this process occurs relatively slowly, and its effects wear off slowly—hence G-protein receptors are an example of "the slower and more complex" type of receptor. This is probably one of the reasons antidepressant medications can take as long as 4 weeks to become effective: they work on slow and complex receptor sites and exert their effects by influencing gene expression.

Dopamine is associated with activation and reward. Drugs such as cocaine and methamphetamines stimulate the release or inhibit the reuptake of DA, producing a sense of pleasurable reward. DA also has been associated more generally with motivation. Many dopaminergic systems project to the anterior cingulate and the frontal lobes, specifically the orbitomedial prefrontal cortex (OMPFC). This is probably the basis for DA's links with bonding and attachment behaviors (Insel & Young 2001).

Serotonin: Neurotransmitters are not confined to the brain. As we mentioned in Chapter 9, approximately 95% of the body's serotonin is processed in the digestive tract. And as we just observed with DA, there are several important variations in this transmitter and its receptors. Numerous different serotonin receptors are involved in such processes as starting the flow of digestive enzymes and regulating the peristaltic flow of waste material through the intestines.

Serotonin (5-HT) is produced in the raphe nucleus and operates throughout wide regions of the brain. It has been the focus of much attention in recent years largely because of its role in depression and anxiety. Interest gathered momentum after the Food and Drug Administration approved fluoxetine (Prozac) for the treatment of depression in 1987. Since the introduction of Prozac and other selective serotonin reuptake inhibitors (SSRIs), some types of depression have been thought to be associated with low levels of 5-HT. SSRIs exert their influence through second-messenger cascades. They increase the amount of calcium inside a cell, launching a process that ends with the activation of the genes that manufacture proteins needed in the assembly of new receptors. According to LeDoux (2002):

> A brain on antidepressants can be brought back from a state of isolation from the outside world and encouraged, even forced, to learn. The brain, in other words, is duped into being plastic by these treatments. (p. 281)

Many serotonin fibers terminate in the amygdala, a key element in the brain's emotional systems. Serotonin actually excites the GABA cells and increases the degree to which they inhibit projection neurons. Drugs such as fluoxetine work by increasing the amount of serotonin available in the synapse. In the amygdala, they reduce the activity of the projection neurons, resulting in a down-regulation of activity in this extremely important module. GABA also inhibits the amygdala from firing in response to meaningless stimuli. Similarly, cortisol, one of the major stress hormones, is affected by GABA-glutamate interactions and is secondarily affected by the effects of serotonin on GABA.

Epinephrine and Norepinephrine: Norepinephrine (NE) is produced in the locus coeruleus among other areas of the brain. NE is involved in emergency response and memory. It has been associated with stress and trauma on one hand and defensive responses on the other. High levels of NE have been associated with various fight-or-flight behaviors, including vigilance, defending, or attacking behaviors. NE has also been the target of several different antidepressant medications.

According to Tucker, Luu, and Pribram (1995), a dorsal pathway projects through the cingulate gyrus to the frontal lobes. This pathway relies heavily on noradrenergic activity, and it favors the right hemisphere (RH). The pathway seems to have a motivational bias to sense of self, internal body states, and is spontaneous. In contrast, there is a ventral limbic pathway from the amygdala to the orbitofrontal cortex (OFC). It favors dopaminergic activity and the left hemisphere (LH). It has a motivational bias to details and tight monitoring of behavioral output.

Neuropeptides: Whereas the monoamine neurotransmitters such as DA activate exploratory behavior, neuropeptides such as endorphins, vaso-pressin, and oxytocin mediate intimate behaviors related to fondling, nursing, and caretaking (Panksepp, 1998). Based on research with primates, it appears that when parent and child come together for grooming or play, endorphin levels increase (Keverne, Martens, & Tuite, 1989). Animal studies have shown that maternal behavior is *reduced* by morphine, an exogenous opiate that occupies and blocks endorphin receptor sites (Kalin, Shelton, & Lynn, 1995). There are large numbers of opiate receptors in the central nucleus of the amygdala (Kalin, Shelton, & Snowdon, 1993). This fact, coupled with the correlation of endoge-nous opiates to bonding and nurturance, further supports the hypothe-sis that *maternal nurturance provides neurophysiological relief from anxiety and fear.*

Opiate drug abuse may exploit the neurodynamic pathways of relief from fear and anxiety that are activated in attachment relationships. Interestingly, craving a drug such as cocaine activates the *anterior cingu-late cortex* (ACC), an area of the brain associated with, among other things, bonding and nurturance (Wexler et al., 2001). It may well be that drug abuse provides relief for those individuals deficient in early nur-turance and the subsequent ability to soothe themselves through endog-enous opiates. Similarly, children and adolescents who inflict pain through self-injurious behaviors (e.g., cutting) stimulate the release of endogenous opiates and a linked sense of psychological relief. These same patients are likely to report childhood abuse and neglect. When individuals who inflict self-harm are given naltrexone, a drug that blocks the effects of opiates, their self-injurious behavior decreases (van der Kolk, 1988). This finding supports the theory that self-injurious behavior is a method of providing a sense of being calmed and comforted associated with opiates.

Oxytocin appears to mediate the benefits of positive social interactions and emotions (Uvnäs-Moberg, 1998). Increased physical contact through touch has been shown to increase the level of oxytocin in the blood and increase positive feelings. It activates maternal behavior while decreasing irritability and aggressiveness (Bartels & Zeki, 2004; Insel,

2003). *Vasopressin* is also associated with attachment and pair bonding. Researchers note that it is associated with the maintenance of monogamy in a number of mammalian species (Young, Lim, Gingrich, & Insel, 2001). Both oxytocin and vasopressin have a large number of binding sites on many parts of the amygdala and play a role in inhibiting fear and reducing the production of stress hormones by the hypothalamic-pituitary-adrenal axis (Carter, 2003).

Neurotransmitters, neuromodulators, and hormones are dynamic and, as such, are activated by our experience. Emotional experience mutually interacts with our neurochemistry in complex ways. For example, the testosterone levels of Brazilian soccer fans rose on average 28% following the defeat of their team by Italy in the 1994 World Cup. Interestingly, the levels of Italian soccer fans dropped by almost exactly the same percentage (Bernhardt, et al., 1998).

MODULES AND NETWORKS: BUILDING BLOCKS OF A BRAIN

A great deal happens in melding tens of billions of neurons into a brain capable of reading a book, performing gymnastics, or listening to Beethoven's Fifth Symphony. A single neuron, by itself, is helpless. The only function of these cells is to connect and communicate with other neurons and other specialized cells. A larger view of an individual neuron, and the thousands of colleagues to which it connects, reveals complex networks of neural bundles and neural pathways. Transactions with the ever-changing environment sculpt the raw material of the nervous system across the course of development.

Roughly midway through gestation, a fetus has many more neurons than it will ever need. After birth, and in large part as a result of certain types of experience, those that do not form viable, functional connections with others are "pruned," or weeded out. The technical term for this programmed cellular suicide is *apoptosis*. The most efficient neural networks are those that have the opportunity to communicate and thrive. In addition to this process of neuronal culling, activation enriches and makes neural transmission more efficient. Connections between and within neural networks are forged by use, as new synaptic junctions are formed. After birth, there is a massive establishment of new synaptic connections between neurons. Modifications of receptor density and sensitivity both at the presynaptic (sending) and postsynaptic (receiving) sides enhance efficiency.

The brain is a complex, hierarchical system, composed of widely distributed neural networks containing modular components—many of which are in turn aggregations of still other modular subcomponents, all of which are highly specialized, all of which make different, specific contributions to neural and psychological functioning (Arbib, Érdi, & Szentágothai, 1998; Eccles, 1984; Gazzaniga & LeDoux, 1978). It is tempting (in fact, we find it irresistible) to associate certain areas of the brain with various psychological capacities (e.g., the amygdala as the site of emotional learning, the OFC as the "social brain"). Functional brain imaging, with its fascinating multicolor pictures of the brain, encourages this way of thinking but misses the point about the relationship between structure and function. In fact, the functional architecture of the central nervous system is vastly more complex than these simplifications suggest. It is important that we not become the twenty-first-century version of phrenologists, compiling maps of the brain showing precisely where various psychological "faculties" are located.

The brain is a small but elegant example of the principle that the whole is greater than the sum of the parts. As we are looking at "the parts," or brain modules, in this section we will frequently apply the modifier *neurodynamic* as a means of reminding the reader that each part is highly influenced by the processes and current state of the whole brain. A module exists more as a concept than as a concrete thing. The basic idea is that modules are clusters of cells that exist at different levels of organization. Complex psychological activity typically involves the simultaneous processing of information by numerous modules and the sequential passing along of that information to other nodes in a widely distributed array. Any given module mediates either a specific function or set of functions, or subcomponents of such functions. Although each module operates somewhat independently, each also is bound into the structural-functional organization of the brain. A functional system such as language is mediated not by a single localized brain region (e.g., a phrenologist's "speech area") or even two regions (e.g., Broca's area *and* Wernicke's area) but by a relatively large number of different subcortical and cortical regions throughout the brain. Speech and language involve many different and relatively independent psychological processes (e.g., perception of consonant sounds, production of consonant sounds, understanding of tense, finding words for objects and actions, grammar, gesture, inner speech, and motor control of the tongue—all just for starters). Modules typically are composed of subcomponent modules at several other levels of the brain's hierarchy, and those modules themselves may be subcomponents of higher-level modules.

NEURAL NETWORKS

A *neural network* is an array of neurons that form synapses with one another. Changes in the structure and function of neural networks that are associated with learning involve widely distributed arrays of many neurons. The overall pattern of activity across large groups of neural networks is of primary importance in behavior and in learning. The brain as a whole is organized into dynamic assemblies of such networks distributed throughout different regions. The specific neurons in any given neural network may vary over time, as we learn and adapt to our environment, but the network functions to relatively consistently mediate particular emergent psychological experiences and capacities.

It is important to remember that at the level of neural networks, changes in the strength of connections between neurons (synaptic plasticity) have as their functional outcome an alteration in the probability that the network will respond to a given level and type of input. The behavioral-social-emotional implication of this fact is that, with practice and the repeated activation of neural networks over time, the probability of activation of those networks (and of the experience or behavior that they mediate) changes. This is just another way of saying that the process of learning leads to a change in the *likelihood* that someone will engage in a particular psychological activity (whether perceptual, emotional, cognitive, or motor) in the future. The occurrence of a learned behavior is a *probabilistic* event. The constantly changing status of the internal and external environment (the state) of the organism leaves much room for variation (Globus & Arpai, 1993; Grigsby & Stevens, 2000). Even what seems to be a minor change in a person's state, or in the environment, may produce a very different pattern of neural activity.

Neuronal development, and the formation of networks of neurons, proceeds hand in hand with psychological and physical development. Burgeoning network competence facilitates the development of an infant's capacity to relate to the environment, especially that most salient feature of the external environment: the baby's caregivers. Therapists always have known that good social relationships are essential to healthy development. Today we can demonstrate the difference that loving interaction, or the lack of it, makes in the brains of neglected baby animals and in real-time functional scans of the human brain. The young neuron's sprouting dendrites and axons—the organs of its relatedness, as it were—are stimulated on the macro level by the emotional quality of the relationships with parents and siblings: the smiles and cooing, the frowns and teasing, the pleasure and pain of having one's needs met or frustrated.

The social environment is critical to the development of the brain and its vast networks of neurons. Assuming a temperament that facilitates social interaction and a full complement of cognitive abilities, if we are provided with a healthy nurturing social environment, then that extended development will result in a positive, adaptive, and healthy individual. If, however, during children's extended period of dependency they are exposed to an impoverished, cruel, or traumatic social environment, their brains will be shaped in a way that increases the likelihood of later behavioral and emotional difficulties.

BRIEF TOUR OF THE BRAIN

In attempting to understand how an unhandsome 3-pound lump of gelatinous organic matter produces the beauty, terror, and boredom of human experience, one faces a potentially never-ending task. The brain's unprepossessing appearance is deceptive, masking an awesome complexity. Networks of neurons behave, for the most part, in statistically predictable ways, and seem to perform specific functions in the brain. Yet neurons in almost any network are capable of influencing their colleagues in far-removed regions of the brain. In fact, seemingly trivial events in one area of the brain can produce massive changes in the whole system—and in the blink of an eye. There are no simple, discrete regions in the brain for complex functions, but it is nevertheless possible to make generalizations about specialization.

SUBCORTICAL BRAIN

The *brain stem* sits atop the spinal cord. At the lowest level of the brain stem is the medulla, which helps regulate a number of basic physiologic processes, such as respiration and heart rate. It also carries sensory nerve fibers from the body below to the thalamus and higher centers above and motor neurons from the cortex through the spinal cord to the muscles. At the base of the medulla, fibers to and from the LH cross over to the right side of the spinal cord (and from there to the periphery), and fibers to and from the RH make their way to the left side of the cord.

The *pons* is a structure that bulges toward the anterior (front), positioned between the medulla and the midbrain. In the pons are more centers required for respiration as well as the nuclei for several of the cranial nerves. It relays information to other regions of the brain, having mutual connections with the cerebellum, and plays a role in the regulation of arousal.

Above the pons is the midbrain, which contains a number of important sensory and motor nuclei as well as the substantia nigra, which is closely associated with the basal ganglia. The *thalamus* is a kind of upward extension of the brain stem, split into symmetrical structures in each hemisphere and constituting most of what is referred to as the diencephalon. Its structure and function are quite complex, but in simplified terms, it relays and processes all manner of sensory information, as well as some motor information, between the cortex and subcortical structures. Like the midbrain and pons below it, the thalamus is involved in sleep, wakefulness, and arousal generally. Some strokes affecting the thalamus may cause the Déjerine-Roussy syndrome (a term you may want to use to impress friends, family, or colleagues). Also called thalamic pain syndrome, it involves episodes of severe burning pain.

Here we should also mention the *cerebellum*, which long was thought to be involved solely in motor functioning. Injury to or degeneration of the cerebellum may lead to uncoordination and unsteadiness (*ataxia*), tremor associated with movement (*action tremor*), and abnormalities of muscle tone. Lesions of certain areas of the human cerebellum also affect higher-level cognition, including the so-called executive cognitive functions (usually thought to be confined to the cortex) and the ability to learn by classical conditioning.

The *amygdala* (actually there are two of them, one on either side of the brain), is an almond-shaped structure in the temporal lobe, considered to be part of the *limbic system* (amygdala is the Latin word for "almond"). The amygdala is a complex group of nuclei involved in emotion, learning, memory consolidation, autonomic nervous system regulation, interpretation of facial expression, and other functions. It has gained considerable notoriety as a result of the research of LeDoux, McGaugh, and others, as an important structure in fear conditioning. The amygdala is activated by both positive and negative emotional experience. However, it is activated predominantly by negative/fearful experiences rather than by positive/pleasant experiences. Moreover, it appears that consolidation of certain types of emotional memory (especially those involving lower levels of arousal) may not involve the amygdala at all (Kensinger & Corkin, 2004; LaBar, 2007).

Although it is responsive to both sad and happy faces, the amygdala is especially primed to recognize fear and potential threat (Yang et al., 2002). In fact, amygdala activation decreases when a stimulus is understood as nonthreatening (Whalen, 1998). Davis (1998) found that electrical stimulation of the amygdala (which may induce fear) enhances the startle reflex, whereas lesions of the amygdala can completely block fear-potentiated startle. There are two routes out of the amygdala—a fast one running to the thalamus and a slower one that leads first to the thalamus, then to the cortex, then back to the amygdala. LeDoux (1996) has dubbed the first of these routes the "low road" and the second one the "high road." The low road is quick and imprecise. It is the pathway involved in fear conditioning. In classical conditioning, this occurs when a conditioned stimulus (or CS, the bell in Pavlov's famous experiments) is associated with an unconditioned stimulus (UCS, the dog food). As every psychology undergraduate learns, once a CS ("Ring, ring!") is reliably paired with a UCS ("Chow!"), it is very hard to extinguish the conditioned response (drooling at the sound of a bell).

The high road out of the amygdala is slow and more complex, associated with conscious thinking about the situation at hand and with reality testing. We may say to ourselves, "You know, the last five times that bell rang, I didn't get the chow." The amygdala's low road serves a very adaptive function. If a distant human ancestor saw what he believed to be a hunting female lion and it actually *was* a lion, the amygdala kick-started the appropriate action. False positives—"That wasn't a lion, it was just a bush that looked like one"—are no-harm situations, but false negatives—"Oh my God, the bush is coming after me"—are not. A speedy reaction on the part of the amygdala is more important than the fine-grained distinction between a lion and a bush.

Of course, the downside of the amygdala's speed and sensitivity is that its fast track can frighten us when there is no adaptive reason for it. Moreover, our amygdalas have the capacity to facilitate conditioned responses to internal stimuli, such as perspiration or quickened respiration. By interpreting these internal reactions as threatening on the same level as a charging grizzly bear, the amygdala can set off an escalating, self-reinforcing cycle of stimulation that results in a panic attack. The formation and maintenance of a phobia or flashbacks as part of posttraumatic stress disorder, for example, can occur with little cortical inhibition or participation. Treatment may involve extinguishing this amygdalar response (through exposure) and promoting the slow-track functions of the medial areas of the frontal lobes (through cognitive reframing and psychoeducation).

The amygdala interacts with the medial prefrontal cortex (the part of the prefrontal cortex [PFC] that lies between the hemispheres, in the center of the brain), including the ACC, and the *orbital* prefrontal cortex that lies behind and above the eyes. One role played by the orbitomedial prefrontal cortex is to serve, in conjunction with the amygdala and other regions, as a regulator of emotional processes and our behavioral responses to them. While the amygdala responds to fear, the PFC is involved in controlling the fear and our response to it. The PFC can disrupt amygdala-induced fear responses, and conscious intervention may be required to change or subdue these responses. As we noted, the elimination (extinction) of classically conditioned responses appears to require the participation of the cortex. For better or worse, however, the amygdala is quite capable of ignoring or bypassing top-down inhibition and can go right on stimulating the autonomic nervous system to respond as if the bush indeed were a lion.

The amygdala functions *outside of conscious awareness, but it makes critical contributions to our emotional life, both conscious and nonconscious.* LeDoux (1996) and his colleagues have shown that, thanks to modularity, the amygdala can be conditioned to elicit a fear response without any involvement on the part of the cortex and without ever achieving consciousness. Conditioned fear is mediated by subcortical pathways projecting from the thalamus to the amygdala. This circuit is a robust, nonconscious, subcortical mediator of emotional learning. The amygdala seems, however, to play no significant role in most declarative memory processes. Pavlov's findings regarding the recurrence of "extinguished" conditioned responses, however, are a reminder that the neural pathways of the fear response remain intact even after consciousness has helped suppress them. Investigators from Pavlov on have observed how hard it can be to extinguish conditioned learning.

In contrast to the hippocampus (to be described), the amygdala may become further activated by stress. Chronic stress can modify the system so that we *react* rapidly to danger rather than *thinking* about it. In essence, the connections are stronger going from the amygdala to the cortex than they are going from the cortex to the amygdala. Perhaps because of this, and due to the fact that the neural networks that mediate strong feelings seem to maintain their activity for a relatively long period of time, fearful feelings can affect our conscious thoughts more easily than our thoughts can dampen fear (a factor that prolongs, if it does not outright doom, many cognitive-based anxiety treatments and insight-oriented psychodynamic treatments).

There is a strong reciprocal relationship between the amygdala and cortex. McGaugh (2004), for example, has developed the *memory modulation* hypothesis, which asserts that following an arousing emotional experience, corticosteroid and adrenergic systems are activated by the amygdala, leading to enhanced consolidation of memory by the cortex. Similarly, the PFC appears capable of modulating the release of stress hormones (Diorio, Viau, & Meaney, 1993), but when the amygdala ignores or overrides it, this inhibitory function of the cortex is less efficient, in effect taking the brakes off the amygdala and setting off a reaction pattern that leads to escalating stress hormones and "new learning" that is more resistant to extinction (LeDoux, 1996).

The *hippocampus* (*hippos* being ancient Greek for "horse," appropriate because the hippocampus looks a bit like a seahorse) is another bilateral limbic structure, rather complexly organized, and having more to do with consolidation of declarative memories and navigation than with emotion or emotional learning. The hippocampus links widely dispersed neuronal networks that allow us to remember facts and autobiographical events explicitly, or consciously. There are rich connections between the amygdala and the hippocampus. In some ways these two modules are the "Odd Couple" of the brain, with the amygdala playing the part of the temperamental Felix and the hippocampus that of the more relaxed Oscar. The shared pathways between them allow for the long-term storage and retrieval of emotionally-based memories. There is good evidence that the hippocampus can become impaired because of prolonged stress. Some researchers argue that persons with smaller hippocampi are more vulnerable to posttraumatic stress disorder; others have proposed that it is the neurodynamic experience of stress that leads to hippocampal atrophy (see Bremner, 2006, for a review). Importantly, the hippocampus is the site of new cell growth in the adult brain (*neurogenesis*), a process that appears to be decreased under prolonged stress or depression and that may be facilitated by SSRIs. In contrast, activity in the amygdala is increased by stress, producing a subjective sense of irritability and jumpiness.

In Alzheimer's disease, neurons appear to degenerate in the temporal lobe, and especially in the hippocampus, which lies in the medial temporal lobe, relatively early in the course of the disease. This may be why one of the earliest and most profound symptoms of the disease is forgetfulness. The hippocampus is vital to higher cognitive functions but has little to do with the parts of our experience having to do with emotion. Animal studies show the dominance of the amygdala in early learning. The amygdala is more active than the hippocampus in learning in the brains of rat pups (Rudy & Morledge, 1994; summarized in Grigsby & Stevens, 2000). Rats can learn tasks that require the amygdala but not the hippocampus at a younger age than they learn tasks requiring the hippocampus but not the amygdala. The same appears to be true of children;

[V]ery young children are likely to experience a kind of learning (habit, conditioned responses) that is dissociated from the context. In other words, it may be impossible to recall—at least under ordinary circumstances—the events that led to the acquisition of certain types of behavior. (Grigsby & Stevens, 2000, p. 99)

ANTERIOR CINGULATE CORTEX

The anterior cingulate cortex (ACC) is part of the cingulate gyrus, an area in the medial cortex of the brain. It is situated above the *corpus callosum*, the fiber tract that links the left and right hemispheres of the brain. The cingulate gyrus also has a complex and interesting functional-anatomical organization, and is involved in such important functions as error detection, the sense of agency, social interaction, and determining the focus of our attention (Rudebeck et al., 2006). The ACC acts as a sort of alarm system for physical pain and perhaps also for the threat of rejection, exclusion, or ostracism (Eisenberger & Lieberman, 2004). From an evolutionary point of view, given the social nature of most primates and the fact that our ancestors lived in groups that had to work together for survival, rejection or ostracism could result in death. Certain modules, the ACC among them, became as sensitized to social signaling as to more frank threats in the environment (Eisenberger & Lieberman, 2004). In the modern brain, ACC probably plays a role in social anxiety disorder (Kaiser Permanente, 2008).

The ACC has robust connections to the amygdala, as might be expected. Unlike the amygdala, however, the ACC is involved in both working memory (which holds the contents of consciousness for about the last 30 seconds) and with the functional system associated with the sense of self (Lenartowicz & McIntosh, 2005; Moran et al., 2006). Moreover, connections between the ACC and OFC are thought to be involved in formulating high-road responses and response flexibility. In some cases in which the ACC has been damaged, behavioral changes typical of low-road unmodulated anger and impulsivity have been reported.

CEREBRAL ASYMMETRY

The *cerebral cortex* makes up most of the volume of the brain. It is a 6-layered sheet of neurons covering the surface of the cerebral hemispheres, ranging from 1.5 to 4.5 millimeters in depth. The cortical columns of the RH appear to be organized differently from those in the LH. In the RH, the columns appear to have more horizontal linkages, providing cross-modal representations. This architecture plays a role in the special capacity of the RH to establish a sense of context and its ability to grasp the whole of a situation, compared to the more detail-oriented LH. (One important caveat here is that there are gender differences in hemispheric specialization, with women showing considerably less specialization than do men and more of a tendency to use complex cross-modal processing.)

The 6 layers of the cortex organize for input, output, and bidirectional information flow within the column. The lower levels (5 and 6) take in sensory information to be processed by the higher levels (1 and 2), where it is worked up to what we "perceive." The middle levels (3 and 4) blend both kinds of information (Hawkins & Blakeslee, 2004). More specifically, layer 2 neurons participate in short intercortical connections. Layer 3 neurons participate in longer-range intercortical connections as well as in interhemispheric communication across the corpus callosum. Layer 4 targets nerve fibers from the thalamus (the central switchboard of the brain). Layer 5 is the origin of projections to subcortical structures. Layer 6 neurons project *to* the thalamus (in contrast to layer 4). Very little is known about the connectivity of the neurons in layer 1 (Hawkins & Blakeslee, 2004).

The cortex is folded in a series of *gyri* (the plural of "gyrus," the term for the exposed areas of cortex) and sulci (the plural of "sulcus," the fissures or furrows between the gyri), and this folding increases the surface area of the cortex. The cortex is highly differentiated, with different regions playing varying roles as modular subcomponents of the brain's functional systems. The asymmetrical architecture of the two hemispheres is characteristic of most mammals, and it is visible even in the human fetus. During the course of evolution, the cerebral hemispheres have grown increasingly dissimilar and specialized, especially in males (Gerschwind & Galaburda 1985). The corpus callosum undergoes a growth spurt in early childhood, between the ages of 1 and 4 years. It continues to mature throughout childhood, integrating the two hemispheres so that they function less like autonomous processors and more like large aggregations of nodes in a widely distributed network (Galin, Johnstone, Nakell, & Herron, 1979).

Working with Roger Sperry in landmark research examining patients whose corpus callosum had been severed for the treatment of medically intractable epilepsy, Michael Gazzaniga studied what have come to be known as split-brain patients. He found that, when separated surgically from one another, the hemispheres display markedly different characteristics (Gazzaniga, 1985; Gazzaniga, Bogen, & Sperry, 1962; Gazzaniga & LeDoux, 1978; Gazzaniga, Wilson, & LeDoux, 1977). The right visual field is associated with activation of the posterior LH (the *occipical lobe* in particular), and the left visual field is represented in the posterior RH.

Some researchers have speculated about the meaning of evidence that various more subtle functions and behaviors are controlled predominantly by one hemisphere or the other. Some of this speculation has clinical utility, although the findings are tentative. For example, a reflective gaze to the left may connote the pessimism that several investigators have associated with the RH, while a gaze to the right (activated by the LH) may be more associated with an optimistic perspective (Drake, 1984; Thayer & Cohen, 1985). The RH controls the musculature of the left side of the face, dominating the expression of emotion on that side, and some studies suggest that the left side of the face is more emotionally expressive than the right (Johnsen & Hugdahl, 1991; Sergent, Ohta, & MacDonald, 1992). In addition, people tend to look to the left when recalling autobiographical memories (Wheeler, Stuss, & Tulving, 1997), possibly reflecting activation of right-hemispheric circuits. These data are not conclusive; individual differences abound; and, as mentioned, there are sex differences in hemispheric lateralization and specialization. Nevertheless, they do suggest possibly useful clinical hypotheses to be considered in thinking about patients' nonverbal communications.

The LH has cortical columns that appear to work on their own, permitting a more problem-focused orientation to details. The left side's in-depth and analytic mode depends on facts, while the context-oriented RH looks at the gist of a situation. In general, the RH processes novelty and the LH routine (Goldberg, 2001). This distinction can be illustrated by how the brain processes music. An overgeneralized and now widely disputed belief is that the RH specializes in this task. While musically naive people do process music predominantly with their RH, this is because of the novelty. Trained musicians process music mostly within their LH (Bever & Chiarello, 1974).

Using PET (positron emission tomography) scans to measure blood flow patterns, Alex Martin and colleagues from the National Institute of Mental Health demonstrated that as individuals learn tasks, the information is initially processed by their RH because it is novel. The information is lateralized to the LH when it becomes familiar and routine and this appears to be true for both verbal and nonverbal information (Martin et al., 1997). Novel and obscure faces are processed by the RH; familiar faces are processed mostly by the LH (Henson, Shallice, & Dolan, 2000; Marzi & Berlucchi, 1977).

One's sex plays a significant role in determining the relative contribution of the two hemispheres to different aspects of functioning (Springer & Deutsch, 1998), and these differences begin to appear early in gestation (Trevarthen, 1996). It has been established that, on average, girls develop language earlier than do boys; boys, on average, have greater upper body strength, motor coordination, and visuospatial abilities than do girls (see Kimura, 1999, and Ullman et al., 2008, for reviews). In addition to verbal fluency, females typically test stronger in skills such as grammar, speed of articulation, verbal memory, and verbal fluency; males perform better on tests requiring the duplication of block designs, maze performance, and mental rotation (Hampson, 2008; Kimura, 1999; Maitland, Herlitz, Nyberg, Backman, & Nilsson, 2004).

It is tempting to say that men generally show stronger right-hemispheric abilities in the visuospatial areas and women show stronger language abilities and attention to detail related to the LH, but sex differences in how brain functions (especially language) are lateralized render this an oversimplification of the research data. Moreover, some recent research calls into question findings about supposedly gendered abilities such as mental rotation, where males are thought to have a neurally based advantage. Feng, Spence, and Pratt (2007) found that having both male and female undergraduates practice an action video game for 10 hours reduced the difference between the sexes in performance on the standard test of mental rotation. In general, females demonstrate less lateralization and greater interhemispheric flexibility than do males. Females appear to have more processes that are distributed bilaterally (i.e., processes that either hemisphere can perform or both perform in concert), perhaps in association with a thicker corpus callosum. PET imaging supports greater bilaterality—the neurodynamic equivalent of being ambidextrous—in women than men. In any case, the attempt to assign functions to one or the other hemisphere, whether by gender or not, often fails to take into consideration the fact that the networks mediating most "RH tasks" involve processing nodes in the LH, and the converse also is true. The brain refuses to conform to our tendency to look for simple answers to complex questions. Following the activity in even the simplest neural networks may lead one all over the brain. That having been said, let us briefly indulge ourselves in some tentative generalizations about the right brain and the left brain.

The right cerebral cortex (for the vast majority of right-handers and a large percentage of left-handers) is the so-called nondominant or subordinate hemisphere, because it lacks a capacity for language. This is not to say that the RH is completely devoid of language; there is evidence that it appreciates a good paradox and a well-chosen metaphor. It plays an important role in that aspect of language referred to as *pragmatics*, which includes prosody (poetry), nonverbal behaviors, and perceptions. Although semantic and syntactic language functions generally are found in the LH, the RH seems to be better able to comprehend emotionally laden language, such as swearing (Serlman, 1977). In perceiving emotional meaning in the language of others, in maintaining the sense of a corporeal and emotional self, and in appraising the dangerousness of others, the RH plays a role that is dominant to that of the LH (Devinsky, 2000).

Tightly coupled with the subcortical emotional networks in the "limbic area," the RH is thought by some to be the home of the psychodynamic unconscious (as in "the unconscious," a term you will not hear neuro-scientists using). The RH maintains rich connections with the subcortical areas associated with emotional processes and attachment and is also involved in the endocrine and autonomic nervous system (Wittling & Pfluger, 1990). Accordingly, the RH seems to be more influential in regulating states of body arousal (Damasio, 1994) and also may generate emotion more intensely than the even-keeled LH. Although these are generalizations, and the true situation is obviously more complex, there are indications that the RH may be receptive to the emotional nuances in relationships, to negative affects, and to novelty, and that it mediates withdrawal in social situations. Greater activation of the RH is associated with lower self-esteem in adults (Persinger & Makarec, 1991) and with depression (Nikolaenko, Egorov, & Frieman, 1997).

A growing body of research supports the notion that shifts in the equilibrium of activation of the two hemispheres is associated with expe-riencing a positive (where the shift is RH to LH) or negative (LH to RH) affect. That is, greater activation of the RH is associated with uncomfortable and negative emotions, such as sadness, anxiety, and anger, while activa-tion of the LH is associated with emotions such as contentment and happiness (Davidson, 1992). Several studies have shown an association between affective style and baseline levels of asymmetric activation in the PFC. In general, the more right-PFC activation, the more negative the affect tendency and the greater the left-PFC activation, the more positive the affect tendency (Hugdahl and Davidson, 2003). The capacity to recover from negative emotional states can be regarded as an important aspect of resiliency.

Richard Davidson (2000) has contributed to the landmark research on cerebral asymmetry and mood states. Davidson proposes that those individuals who generally maintain positive moods states and well-being in the face of the adversity are more resilient. They easily bounce back to what can be regarded as their neuropsychological default mode of functioning. Cultivating traits such as optimism, a tendency toward hope, tenacity, positive self-perception, positive outlook on life, and a good sense of humor promote more resiliency in the face of adversity.

These tendencies have been found even in infants. For example, infants who are crying or sad show greater right-frontal electroencephalogram (EEG) activity, while infants displaying what have been called "approach emotions," such as happiness, show more left-frontal EEG activity (Bell & Fox, 1994).

Consistent with the findings that people with right-frontal asymmetry tend to be more negative and withdrawn, Schmidt (1999) found that female undergraduates who rated themselves high in shyness showed right-frontal EEG asymmetry and left-frontal hypoactivation. Their more socially oriented counterparts displayed more left-frontal asymmetry. Right-frontal activation is also associated with more anxiety. In primate studies, anxious states are associated with both elevated levels of stress hormones and with RH activation (Kalin et al., 1998). Raw and intense emotions are represented in the RH (Porges, Doussard-Roosevelt, & Maiti, 1994; Ross, Homan, & Buck, 1994).

The RH's apparent superior emotional sensitivity may be largely a nonconscious appraisal process (Fischer, Shaver, & Carnochan, 1990). The RH seems more adept at reading emotions in the facial expressions of others, irrespective of what they have to say (Ahern et al., 1991). Patients with RH damage are impaired in their ability to read emotional facial expressions and emotional cues in body language (Blonder et al., 1991).

During the first two years of life, the RH develops more rapidly than the LH (Chiron, et al., 1997; Thatcher, Walker, & Giudice, 1987). Schore (1994) has argued that the data support the idea that the LH is mediated by the dorsolateral PFC while the RH is mediated by the OFC (hence, the RH would be more integrated with the limbic system.) This asymmetric development may be associated with the earlier maturation of social-emotional attachment schemata than with the development of other forms of cognition and later verbal behavior. Infants get acquainted with their world on an affective level in the context of a close supportive relationship. Basic patterns of attachment and the processes underlying group identifications are encoded in memory systems lacking access to consciousness. Because critical attachment and identificatory experiences sculpt the brain early in the development of the verbal LH and explicit autobiographical memory, we will always be dealing with a high level of conjecture in reconstructing our patients' early histories.

The LH, viewed from the perspective of a champion of right-brain functioning, would be said to be chatty, loose with the truth, and boringly linear. More neutrally, the LH tends to be directed toward engagement with and interpretation of the world. The LH processes information differently from the RH. It tends to be detail oriented and favors linear, sequential, and time-dependent information. Again, these characteristics seem consistent with the LH's specialization for language.

Gazzaniga (1996) views the LH as having an interpretive function, trying to make sense of what it experiences. The LH specializes in "spin," the generation of narratives that assemble a coherent version of what has happened to us or what is about to occur. If the LH is isolated from the RH, as occurs when the corpus callosum is sectioned, the LH's inter-pretations of RH perceptions are obvious confabulations, explanatory narratives made up on the fly to fit pieces of information but lacking the sense of context and the big picture that the RH has experienced. The research with split-brain patients in general (e.g., Gazzaniga, 1985, 1996; Gazzaniga & LeDoux, 1978) suggests that most of our explanations for what we do have a confabulatory quality—an observation with interest-ing therapeutic implications in terms of the therapist's experience of defensive avoidance and rationalization.

This literature suggests that it may be part of the LH's job to put a positive spin on events. From this perspective, the LH functions like the White House press secretary, issuing authoritative pronouncements that rest on shaky premises, cleaning up the mess after the chief executive's misstatements and mistakes. In a brain that is functioning well, this posi-tive spin may serve an important emotion-regulatory function. Patients who have suffered LH damage that produces markedly decreased activa-tion of the left hemisphere typically become pessimistic and depressed, suggesting the role that the LH plays in balancing the emotional books. The left PFC is active in response to appetitive stimuli that evoke positive affect (Urray et al., 2004).

Spontaneous emotions are thought to be associated with the RH, but socially mediated emotions such as guilt seem to be processed by the LH. When the LH is cut off from communication with the right, it is unable to read and interpret facial expressions. In contrast, the RH readily processes facial expressions and tone of voice (Heller, Etienne, & Miller, 1995; Ross et al., 1994). Conscious coping and problem solving may have become the fiefdom of the LH in part because of its language capacity (Corina, Vaid, & Bellugi, 1992). Some evidence suggests that deaf (as well as hearing) people lateralize the expression and comprehension of signing to the LH (e.g., Neville et al., 1998).

At about 15 months, the left side of the brain undergoes a growth spurt associated with the child's development of expressive and receptive language. By the third year of life, the corpus callosum has matured further, facilitating better integration between the two hemispheres and their respective functions. Children under 3 show the effects of unintegrated hemispheric functioning, and some authors have argued that prior to that age, children are a bit like split-brain subjects (Siegel, 1999)—an interesting analogy that should be taken with a grain of salt. Four-year-olds are better able to process information and use words to describe their inner states and impulses than are younger children, although this reflects the development of language, cognition, self-awareness, and increasingly sophisticated self-representations as well as interhemispheric communication.

Despite the emphasis in this appendix on modules and systems specializing in specific functions, it is perhaps prudent to remind the reader at this point that the brain is an integrated and dynamic system. The adherence to a modular conceptualization of the brain leads to misunderstandings and simplifications of complex problems. It has become part of the language to refer to ourselves and others as "right brained" or "left brained." We agree with Springer and Deutsch (1998), who warned against the dangers of "dichotomania," whereby one overgeneralizes a little scientific information into guiding concepts. The 1980s saw an increase in the focus on the localization of brain function. According to Goldberg (2001), "Gall and his Phrenology enjoyed an odd revival in the name of modularity." He continued:

> In reality the modular theory explains very little, since by lacking the ability to reduce multitudes of specific facts to simplifying general principles, it fails the basic requirement of any scientific theory. Like the belief systems of antiquity, it merely labels its domain by inventing a new notation, it has the seductiveness and illusory appeal of instant explainability—by introducing a new module for every new observation. (pp. 56–57)

FRONTAL LOBES

Dubbed the "executive brain" by Goldberg (2001) and the "executive control system" by his teacher, the great Russian neuropsychologist Alexander Luria, the frontal lobes are a kind of brain within the brain. They direct much of the activity in the rest of the brain and receive the products of the subprocessing of literally billions of other neurons. The prefrontal cortex is a critical node in the neural networks that mediates attention, planning, decision making, inhibition, and initiation of goal-directed behavior. For example, the role of the OFC (the area of the PFC directly behind the eyes) in inhibiting the overreactivity of subcortical structures contributes to its reputation as the heart of the "social brain." The ability to inhibit impulsive emotional reactions to stimulating people makes it possible for us to construct more complex interactions. For countless human generations, the OFC has made it possible for us to enjoy the survival advantages of living in a group of other highly sentient beings. Without the OFC, our behavior with one another would likely be more erratic, emotionally labile, and combative.

The PFC, which makes up a considerable portion of the frontal lobes, is a complex, functionally heterogeneous, and still not entirely understood area of the brain. As recently as the 1960s, Teuber (1964) wrote of the "riddle of the frontal lobes." Once referred to as the "silent cortex," it now is apparent that different areas of the PFC make essential contributions to working memory, emotion regulation, and the executive cognitive functions. Decision making, a higher order cognitive function, is a frontal lobe function. An inability to make decisions is a sign of poor frontal lobe functioning.

The *dorsolateral* prefrontal cortex (DLPFC) is especially important in creating the capacity for working memory. This section of the frontal lobes consists of the top, or *dorsal* surface, and the *lateral*, or side surface of the front of the brain. The location of the dorsal cortex is easier to remember if you recall that a shark's dorsal fin, on its back, sticks out of the water. For the human spinal cord, dorsal refers to the back-facing surface, and for the brain, it essentially refers to the top of the head. Hence, the DLPFC is that area of the prefrontal region on the top and sides of the anterior (forward) frontal lobes. In addition to its involvement in attention and working memory (Rezai, et al., 1993), the DLPFC has been shown to aid in organizing temporal experience (Knight & Grabowecky, 1995). Working memory itself is the short-term memory system (mediated by transient neurochemical changes in the synaptic environment) that allows us to recall and process the flow of information that has entered our awareness. Working memory allows us to keep the spelling of a word we have just looked up in the dictionary in our heads long enough to write it on our word processor. Hence, the contents of working memory are essentially the contents of consciousness. The limited capacity of this memory system is a major reason most processing at any given time occurs nonconsciously. Trying to be aware of just ongoing sensory input, or of the data required to carry out even the most mundane tasks, would overload those circuits involved in conscious awareness.

Previously, we identified the OFC as the part of the frontal lobes that lies directly above and behind the eyes, and the medial PFC as the area between the cerebral hemispheres above the corpus callosum (see Figure A.3). The OFC appears to mediate our ability to choose high-road responses in

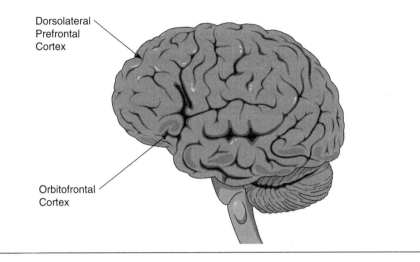

Dorsolateral
Prefrontal
Cortex

Orbitofrontal
Cortex

Figure A.3   Prefrontal Cortex with the OFC and DLPFC Indicated

provocative emotional situations. If the OFC is impaired, it is inhibited in coordinating the activity of such important subregions of the "emotional brain" as the ACC and amygdala. Damage to the OFC results in symptoms that include an inability to inhibit urges, impulses, and emotional expressions. People with OFC damage are impulsive and emotionally uninhibited. They can be reckless drivers on the road. While walking through a store, they may shoplift on impulse and if caught overreact, perhaps even resisting arrest. Interpersonally, they can be rude and sexually inappropriate.

The OFC allows one to be flexible in response to shifting contexts and perspectives (Nobre, Coull, Frith, & Mesulam, 1999) and formulate new responses instead of automatic reflex responses (Freedman et al., 1998). In addition to its other roles, the OFC is involved in regulation of the autonomic nervous system, social perception and theory of mind, moral judgment, self-awareness, and autobiographical memory.

The classic example of what the OFC does for us is the case of Phinias Gage. In a work accident, a steel rod shot through his OFC. With his brain otherwise intact, Gage initially appeared the same but also strangely not himself. He retained his cognitive abilities but seemed to have lost his ability to inhibit impulses. Once an upright man, a supervisor who was widely respected, he became impulsive; and whereas he had been rather emotionally reserved, he became erratic, rude, and generally uninhibited. Gage later did a stint in the circus as a freak and died penniless in San Francisco 20 years later.

The OFC is activated when we make decisions based on emotional information (Teasdale, et al., 1999). Its role in affect regulation is vital. For example, say you are driving to your 6-year-old son's school to pick him up as usual. As other kids come tumbling out of the school and are greeted by their parents, walk off together, or board the school bus, you do not see your son and wonder where he is. After a few more minutes, you start getting the familiar sensations of generalized anxious arousal. Where could he be? Maybe he is talking to his teacher about something. Going into the school, you notice the halls are empty. His classroom is locked; and looking through the little window in the door, you can see no one is in there. *Where is he?* The story you saw on the news last week about a stranger abduction in a nearby community flashes through your mind. Your breathing and heart quicken, and you feel the beginning of panic. Then the thought occurs to you that maybe this is the wrong day. You get out your PDA and sure enough, he is on a field trip and is not due back for a half hour. Your longer-term memory has come into play; the OFC tells your amygdala to stop overreacting and signals the parasympathetic nervous system to put the brakes on the physical symptoms of anxiety.

One way that emotions become conscious is that nonconscious affective responses coming up from subcortical regions get connected to the frontal lobes (LeDoux, 1996). The OFC maintains critical connections to limbic structures and to other cortical areas involved in complex thought. The OFC is therefore very much involved in making plans based on emotion and motivation (Damasio, 1994). It can access explicit memory through its rich connections with the hippocampus. A complex integrating region, the OFC is an essential part of the network involved in assigning emotional valence to events and people. For these reasons, Schore (1994) has proposed it as the principal cortical area involved in emotion regulation. Trauma negatively impacts this cortical-subcortical regulatory process, and invigorating the neural networks in the OFC underlies the psychotherapeutic treatment of patients who have trauma in their histories (as borderline patients, e.g., frequently do).

NEUROPLASTICITY AND NEURODYNAMICS

The production of new neurons is called *neurogenesis*. Although it was once assumed that new nerve growth in the brain was impossible, recent research suggests that there are some important exceptions to this rule. The birth of neurons has been reported in primate and human brains in such critical areas as the hippocampus, (Gould, et al., 1999; Eriksson, et al., 1998). Along the same lines, stem cells—the archetypical cells from which specialized cells evolve—have been found in the olfactory bulb and part of the hippocampus known as the dentate gyrus (Jacobs et al., 2000). Ongoing learning stimulates neurogenesis in the neocortex of adult primates (Gould et al., 1999). The discovery of neurogenesis in the human hippocampus underscores the crucial importance of memory in our species' adaptation to rapidly changing environmental conditions.

Although there is still controversy about how widespread neurogeneis is in the human brain, in many ways the discovery that at least under certain circumstances neurons reproduce (or others cells morph into new neuronal cells), is just one more feature of the brain's neuroplascity. The brain is exquisitely sensitive to environmental change and relentless in reorganizing itself to meet the next challenge. It achieves this environmental sensitivity through individual neurons and cellular networks that can almost instantaneously send large electrochemical waves through the brain.

The neurodynamic capacity for environmentally mediated biological change is one of the signature qualities of the human brain. As a somewhat gruesome illustration, if you were to lose your finger in an accident, the area associated with that finger in the somatosensory cortex would shrink. In contrast, if you were to become an accomplished guitarist, the area related to your principal fret finger would expand. Neuroplasticity is the basis for learning and change over the course of development. As a child develops specific capabilities, the neural nets underlying those capabilities are potentiated. The growth and development of a child's brain follows a process whereby the more primitive areas of the brain mature first. For example, the brain stem and its associated reflexes are online immediately. By some estimates, the prefrontal lobes do not develop fully until the early 20s.

During early development, we are endowed with an overabundance of neurons. Through what Nobel laureate Gerald Edelman (1987, 1989) has dubbed "neural Darwinism," neurons compete to establish connections with other neurons. Initially, neurons are small and underdeveloped. Some grow far-ranging connections through a process called arborization, based on their connectivity with adjacent neurons. Others, through weak connections or lack of use, wither away and die through pruning, or apoptosis. Edelman's evocation of Darwin suggests the concept of the survival of the fittest among these cells. From the beginning of life, the brain is an evolving dynamic system that modifies itself as it interacts with the world, especially the social world it both creates and must adapt to. A corollary to this principle of intense sensitivity to the environment is that it matters to the brain what we do with it. In one study, researchers explored the impact of higher education on vulnerability to dementia. Individuals who by virtue of privileged social circumstances or force of will challenged their brains by going to college were not as impacted by, and seemed to be able to delay, the incidence of dementia compared to individuals who did not pursue formal education into their adult years (Schmand, 1997).

Enriched environments challenge the brain to make the most of its potential. The dendrites that reach out to other neurons to receive information show the effects of exposure to increased environmental stimulation. Dendritic "branching" can be rich and dense (as has been shown to be the case in the parietal lobes of Einstein's brain) or limited to dramatically fewer connections with other neurons. The greater the number of dendritic connections with other neurons, the more complex the information that can be considered and the more readily this information can be creatively reworked. Animal studies have shown that infants raised in enriched (stimulating) environments compared to those raised in impoverished (nonstimulating) ones have more mitochondria activity, more synaptic connections among neurons, more blood capillaries supporting those cells, and increased weight and thickness in the hippocampus (Kempermann et al., 1997, 1998; Kolb & Whishaw, 1998). A variety of other positive environmental effects have been noted, including increases in the level of nerve growth factor in the hippocampus and the visual cortex (Torasdotter et al., 1998), increased activity of glial cells, and increased dendritric length (Kolb & Whishaw, 1998).

Neuroplasticity leans heavily on the concept of "use it or lose it." Use of neurons increases an individual's ability to form new memories and it strengthens the persistence of old ones. Each time the memory is "remembered," the neurodynamic pathways that support it become more robust. If memories are not regularly recalled, old memories (the networks supporting them) tend to fade. Consequently, cramming has few advantages as a way to study for an exam. It is not a good way to learn material because of this principle. Part of "fitness" in Edelman's model of neural Darwinism is actually based on activation, or use.

The process that underlies neuroplasticity is *long-term potentiation* (LTP). LTP describes the changes in synaptic strength occurring after brief bursts of stimulation that enhance future transmissions across the synapse. LTP also occurs when the excitation between cells is prolonged. This prolonged excitation strengthens the synaptic connections and makes them more apt to fire together in the future. LTP is just what it says: its effects are relatively long lasting. The excitatory neurotransmitter glutamate plays a crucial role in LTP. When specialized receptors become available for the binding of glutamate, these receptors detect the match between activity in the pre-synaptic and the postsynaptic neurons, thereby enhancing the efficiency of future transmissions. When these specialized receptors are blocked, experience-based plasticity is disrupted (Kleinschmidt et al., 1987).

Neurotrophins have been identified as another means through which neuroplasticity can occur. Neurotrophins have a tonic effect on the survival rate and growth of neurons. When a neuron fires, a neurotrophic molecule is released from the cell and defuses backward in the presynaptic terminals (Kutz & Shatz, 1996). This promotes new dendritic branching and the sprouting of new synaptic connections in the presynaptic sites that were just active. Neurotrophins also promote synaptic selection by preventing cell death. Only cells that were active can compete for this elixir of neuronal renewal.

Ultimately, psychotherapy is an example of an enriched environment that provides an opportunity for the individuals who participate in it—either as patient or as therapist—to exploit the awesome power of the brain to change itself.

References

Abeles, M. (1991). *Corticonics: Neural circuits of the cerebral cortex.* Cambridge: Cambridge University Press.

Ahern, G. L., Schomer, D. L., Kleefield, J., Blume, H., Rees-Cosgrove, G., Weintraub, S., & Mesulam, M. M. (1991). Right hemisphere advantage for evaluating emotional facial expressions. *Cortex, 27,* 193–202.

Aichorn, A. (1926/1955). *Wayward youth.* New York: Meridian Books.

Ainsworth, M. D. S. (1963). The development of infant-mother interaction among the Ganda. In B. M. Foss (Ed.), *Determinants of infant behavior* (Vol. 2, pp. 67–112). New York: Wiley.

Ainsworth, M. D. S. (1967) *Infancy in Uganda: Infant care and the growth of love.* Baltimore: John Hopkins University Press.

Ainsworth, M. (1969). Object relations, dependency and attachment: A theoretical review of the infant-mother relationship. *Child Development, 40,* 969–1025.

Ainsworth, M. D. S., Blehar, M. C., Waters, E., & Wall, S. (1978). *Patterns of attachment: A psychological study of the strange situation.* Hillsdale, NJ: Erlbaum.

Allman, J. M., Watson, K. K., Tetreault, N. A., & Hakeem, A. Y. (2005). Intuition and autism: A possible role for Von Economo neurons. *Trends in Cognitive Sciences, 9,* 367–373.

Allman, J. M., Hakeem, A., Erwin, J. M., Nimchinsky, E., & Hof, P. (2001). The anterior cingulate cortex: The evolution of an interface between emotion and cognition. *Annals of the New York Academy of Sciences, 935,* 107–117.

Albert, M. S., Jones, K., Savage, C. R., Berkman, L., Seeman, T., Blazer, D., Rowe, J. W. (1995). Predictors of cognitive change in older persons: MacArthur studies of successful aging. *Psychological Aging, 10*(4), 578–589.

Allen, J. G. (2001). *Traumatic relationships and serious mental disorders.* Hoboken, NJ: Wiley.

Allister, L., Lester, B. M., Carr, S., & Liu, J. (2001). The effects of maternal depression on fetal heart rate response to vibroacoustic stimulation. *Developmental Neuropsychology, 20*(3), 639–651.

Allman, J. M. (2001). The anterior cingulate cortex: The evolution of an interface between emotion and cognition. *Annals of the New York Academy of Sciences, 935,* 107–117.

American Academy of Child and Adolescent Psychiatry. (2001). Practice parameters for the assessment and treatment of children and adolescents with suicidal behavior. *Journal of the American Academy of Child and Adolescent Psychiatry*, *40*(Suppl. 4), 24–51.

American Academy of Pediatrics. (2000). Suicide and suicide attempts in adolescents. *Pediatrics, 105*(4), 871–874. American Psychiatric Association. (1980). *Diagnostic and statistical manual of mental disorders* (3rd ed.). Washington, DC: Author.

American Psychiatric Association. *Diagnostic and statistical manual of mental disorders* (3rd ed.). (1980). Washington, DC: Author.

American Psychiatric Association. (1994). *Diagnostic and statistical manual of mental disorders* (4th ed.). Washington, DC: Author.

American Psychiatric Association Task Force on DSM-IV. (2000). *Diagnostic and statistical manual of mental disorders* (4th ed. rev.). Washington, DC: Author.

American Psychological Association. Society of Clinical Psychology. (1995). Training in and dissemination of empirically-validated psychological treatments: Report and recommendations. *The Clinical Psychologist, 48*, 3–27.

American Sleep Disorder Association. (1997). *International classification of sleep disorders: Diagnostic and coding manual.* (Rev. ed.). Rochester, MN: American Sleep Disorder Association.

Anastopoulos, A. D., Rhoads, L. H., & Farley, S. H. (2006). Counseling and training parents. In R. A. Barkley & K. F. Murphy (Eds.). *Attention-deficit hyperactivity disorder: A clinical workbook* (3rd ed.). New York: Guilford Press, 453–479.

Andreason, N. C. (2001). *Brave new brain: Conquering mental illness in the era of the genome.* New York: Oxford University Press.

Angold, A., Costello, E., & Worthman, C. (1998). Puberty and depression: The roles of age, pubertal status and pubertal timing. *Psychological Medicine, 28*, 51–61.

Angold, A., Worthman, C. M., & Costello, E. J. (2003). Puberty and depression. In C. Hayward (Ed.), *Gender differences at puberty.* New York: Cambridge University Press, 137–164.

Arbib, M. A. (2002). Language evolution: The mirror system hypothesis. In M. A. Arbib (Ed.), *The handbook of brain theory and neural networks* (2nd ed., pp. 606–611). Cambridge, MA: MIT Press.

Arbib, M. A., Érdi, P., & Szentágothai, J. (1998). *Neural organization: Structure, function, and dynamics.* Cambridge, MA: MIT Press.

Archer, C., & Burnell, A. (Eds.). (2003). *Trauma, attachment, and family permanence: Fear can stop you loving.* London: Jessica Kingsley.

Arden, J. (1996). *Consciousness, dreams, and self: A transdisciplinary approach.* Madison, CT: International Universities Press/Psychosocial Press.

Arden, J. B. (1987) Psychosocial Vocational Rehabilitation–The Next Step. *Psychosocial Rehabilitation*, Vol. 12, No. 1, 61–64.

Arden, J. (2003). *America's meltdown: Creating the lowest common denominator society.* Westport, CT: Praeger.

Arden, J. & Linford, L. (2009). *Brain-based therapy with adults.* New York: Wiley.

Argyropoulos, S. V., Bell, C. J., & Nutt, D. J. (2001). Brain function in social anxiety disorder. *Psychiatric Clinics of North America, 24*(4), 707–722.

Arnold, P. D., & Richter, M. A. (2001). Is obsessive-compulsive disorder an autoimmune disease? *Canadian Medical Association Journal, 165*(10), 1353–1358.

Aronowitz, B. R., DeCaria, C., Allen, A., Weiss, N., Saunders, A., Marglin, L., et al., (1997) The neuropsychiatry of autism and Asperger's disorders: Review of the literature and case report. *CNS Spectrums, 2*, 43–60.

Arnstein, A. F. T. (1998). Catecholamine modulation of prefrontal cognitive function. *Trends in Cognitive Science, 2*, 436–447.

Ashbury, K., Dunn, J. F., Pike, A., & Plomin, R. (2003). Nonshared environment influences on individual differences in early behavioral development: A monozygyotic twin differences study. *Child Development, 74*(3), 933–943.

Ashman, S. B., Dawson, G., Panagiotgides, H., Yamada, E., & Wilkinson, C. W. (2002). Stress hormone levels of children of depressed mothers. *Development and Psychopathology, 14*, 333–349.

Ayduk, O., Mendoza-Denton, R., Mischel, W., Downey, G., Peake, P., & Rodiguez, M. (2000). Regulating the interpersonal self: Strategic self-regulation for coping with rejection for coping with rejection sensitivity. *Journal of Personality and Social Psychology, 79*, 776–792.

Azuma, H. (1996). Cross-national research on child development: The Hess-Azuma collaboration in retrospect. In D. Schwalb & B. Schwalb (Eds.), *Japanese childrearing: Two generations of scholarship*. New York: Guilford Press.

Baddeley, A. (1994). The remembered self and the enacted self. In V. Neisser & R. Fivush (Eds.), *The remembering self: Construction and accuracy in the self-narrative* (pp. 236–242). Cambridge, UK: Cambridge University Press.

Baird, G., Cox, A., Baron–Cohen, S., Swettenham, J., Wheelwright, S., & Drew, A. (2001). Screening and surveillance for autism and pervasive development disorders. *Archives of Diseases in Childhood, 84*, 468–475.

Balaban, M. T. (1995). Affective influences on startle in five-month-old infants: Reactions to facial expression of emotion. *Child Development, 66*, 28–36.

Baldwin, D. A., & Moses, L. J. (1996). The ontongeny of social information gathering. *Child Development, 67*, 1915–1939.

Barber, B. K. (2002). *Intrusive parenting: How psychological control affects children and adolescents*. Washington, DC: American Psychology Association.

Barinaga, M. (1993). Death gives birth to the nervous system. But how? *Science, 259*, 762–763.

Barkley, R. A. (1997a). *ADHD and the Nature of Self-Control*. New York: Guilford Press.

Barkley, R. A. (1997b). Behavioral inhibition, sustained attention, and executive functions: Constructing a unifying theory of ADHD. *Psychological Bulletin, 121*(1), 65–94.

Barkley, R. A. (2003). Attention-Deficit/Hyperactivity Disorder. In E. J. Marsh & R. A. Barkley (Eds.), *Child psychopathology* (2nd ed., pp. 75–143). New York: Guilford Press.

Barkley, R. A. (2006). *Attention-deficit hyperactivity disorder: A handbook for diagnosis and treatment* (3rd ed.). New York: Guilford Press.

Barlow, D. H., Craske, M. G., Cerny, J. A., & Klosko, J. S. (1989). Behavioral treatment of panic disorder. *Behavior Therapy, 20*, 261–282.

Baron-Cohen, S. (1995). *Mindblindness*. Cambridge, MA: MIT Press.

Baron-Cohen, S. (2000). The cognitive neuroscience of autism: Evolutionary approaches. In M. Gassaniga (Ed.), *The new cognitive neurosciences* (2nd ed.). Cambridge, MA: MIT Press, 1249–1257.

Baron-Cohen, S., Allen, J., & Gillberg, C. (1992). Can autism be detected at 18 months? The needle, the haystack, and the CHAT. *British Journal of Psychiatry*, *161*, 839–843.

Baron-Cohen, S., Ring, H. A., Bullmore, E. T., Wheelright, S., Ashwin, C., & Williams, S. C. R. (2000). The amygdala theory of autism. *Neuroscience and Biobehavioral Reviews*, *24*, 355–364.

Barrett, K. C., & Campos, J. J. (1987). Perspectives on emotional development: II. A functionalist approach to emotions. In J. Osofsky (Ed.), *Handbook of infant development* (2nd ed., pp. 555–578). New York: Wiley.

Barry, R. J., Clarke, A. R., & Johnstone, S. J. (2003). A review of the electrophysiology in attention–deficit disorder/hyperactivity disorder: I. Qualitative and quantitative electroencephlaography. *Clinical Neurophysiology*, *114*, 171–183.

Bartels, A., & Zeki, S. (2004). The neural correlates of maternal and romantic love. *NeuroImage*, *21*, 1155–1166.

Bartsch, K., & Wellman, H. M. (1995). *Children talk about the mind*. New York: Oxford University Press.

Baumeister, R. F., & Muraven, M. (1996). Identity as adoption to social, cultural, and historical context. *Journal of Adolescence*, *19*, 405–416.

Baumrind, D. (1978). Parental disciplinary patterns and social competence in children. *Youth and Society*, *9*, 239–276.

Baumrind, D. (1991). Effective parenting during the early adolescent transition. In P. A. Cowan & M. Hetherington (Eds.), *Family Transitions* (pp. 111–163). Hillsdale, NJ: Lawerence Erlbaum.

Baving, L., Laucht, M., & Schmidt, M. H. (2000). Oppositional children differ from healthy children in frontal brain activation. *Journal of Abnormal Child Psychology*, *28*, 267–275.

Baxter, L. R., Phelps, M. E. Mazziotta, J. C., Schwartz, J. M., Gerner, R. H., Selin, C. E., et al. (1985). Cerebral metabolic rates for glucose metabolism in mood disorders. *Archives of General Psychology*, *42*, 441–447.

Baxter, L. R., Schwartz, J. M., Bergman, K. S., Szuba, M. P., Guze, B. H., Mazziotta, J. C., et al. (1992). Caudate glucose metabolic rate changes with both drug and behavior therapy for obsessive-compulsive disorder. *Archives of General Psychiatry*, *49*, 681–689.

Baxter, L. R., Jr., Schwartz, J. M., Bergman, K. S., Szuba, M. P., Guze, B. H., Mazziotta, J. C., et al. (1992). Caudate glucose metabolic rate changes with both drug and behavior therapy for obsessive-compulsive disorder. *Archives of General Psychiatry*, *49*(9), 681–689.

Baxter, L. R., Jr., Schwartz, J. M., Phelps, M. E., Mazziotta, J. C., Guze, B. H., Selin, C. E., et al. (1989). Reduction of prefrontal cortex glucose metabolism common in three types of depression, *Archives of General Psychiatry*, *46*, 243–250.

Beauchaine, T. P. (2001). Vagal tone, development, and Gray's motivational theory: Toward an integrated model of autonomic nervous system functioning in psychopathology. *Development and Psychopathology*, *13*, 183–214.

Beaulieu, J. M., Zhang, X., Rodriguiz, R. M., et al. (2008). Role of GSK3ß in behavioral abnormalities induced by serotonin deficiency. *Proceedings of the National Academy of Sciences*, *105*(4): 1333–1338.

Beck, A. T. (1976). *Cognitive therapy and emotional disorders*. New York: International Universities Press.

Becking, E., Wilson, M., & Reiser, P. (1999). Therapist Handbook for TOTS: A temperament-based behavioral group therapy for parents and preschoolers. Napa, CA: E.M. Power Publishing.

Beebe, B., & Lachmann, F. M. (1988). Mother-infant mutual influence and precursors of psychic structure. In A. Goldberg (Ed.), *Frontiers in self psychology. Progress in self psychology* (Vol. 3, pp. 3–26). Hillsdale, NJ: Analytic Press.

Beebe, B., & Lachmann, F. M. (1994). Representation and internalization in infancy: Three principles of salience. *Psychoanalytic Psychology*, *11*, 127–165.

Beebe, B., & Lachmann, F. M. (2002). *Infant research and adult treatment*. New York: Analytic Press.

Beidel, D. C., Turner, S. M., & Morris, T. L. (2000). Behavioral treatment of childhood social phobia. *Journal of Consulting and Clinical Psychology*, *68*(6), 1072–1080.

Bell, M. A., & Fox, N. A. (1994). Brain development over the first year of life: Relations between EEG frequency and coherence and cognition and affective behaviours. In G. Dawson & K. Fischer (Eds.), *Human behaviour and the developing brain* (pp. 314–345). New York: Guilford Press.

Benton, D. (1992). Vitamin-mineral supplantation and intelligence of children: A review. *Journal of of Ortho Medicine*, *7*, : 31–38.

Berman, S., Weems, C. F., Silverman, W. K., & Kurtines, W. M. (2000). Predictors of outcome in exposure-based cognitive and behavioural treatment for phobia anxiety disorders in children. *Behavior Therapy*, *31*, 713–731.

Bernfeld, S. (1922). Kinderheim Baumgarten. *Juedischer Verlag* (Berlin).

Bernhardt, P. C., Dabbs, J. M., Jr., Fielden, J. A., & Lutter, C. D. (1998). Testosterone changes during vicarious experience of winning and losing fans at sporting events. *Physiology and Behavior*, *65*(1), 59–62.

Bernieri, F., & Rosenthal, R. (1991). Interpersonal coordination: Behavioral matching and interactional synchrony. In R. Feldman & B. Rimé, *Fundamentals of nonverbal behavior*. New York: Cambridge University Press, 401–431.

Berthoz, S., Armony, J. L., Blair, R. J. R., & Dolan, R. J. (2002). An fMRI study of intentional and unintentional (embarrassing) violations of social norms. *Brain*, *125*, 1696–1708.

Bessette, A. (2004). Obsessive-compulsive disorder. In T. P. Gullotta & G. A. Adams (Eds.), *Handbook of adolescent behavior problems: Evidence-based approaches to prevention and treatment* (pp. 255–283). New York: Springer.

Bever, T. G., & Chiarello, R. J. (1974). Cerebral dominance in musicians and non-musicians. *Science*, *185*(150), 537–539.

Biederman, J. (2004). Impact of comorbidity in adults with attention-deficit/hyperactivity disorder. *Journal of Clinical Psychiatry, 65*(Suppl. 3), 3–7.

Biederman, J. & Faraone, S. V. (2004). The Massachusetts General Hospital studies of gender influences on attention-deficit/hyperactivity disorder in youth and relatives. *Psychiatric Clinics of North America, 27*(2): 225–232.

Birmaher, B., Ryan, N. D., Williamson, D. E., et al. (1996). Childhood and adolescent depression: A review of the past 10 years. Part I. *Journal of the American Academy of Child and Adolescent Psychiatry, 35*(11): 1427–1439.

Black, J. E., Jones, A., Nelson, C. A., & Greenough, W. T. (1998). Neuronal plasticity and the developing mood. In N. E. Alessi, J. T. Coyle, S. I. Harrison, & S. Eth (Eds.), *Handbook of child and adolescent psychiatry* (pp. 31–53). New York: Wiley.

Blonder, L. X., Bowers, D., & Heilman, K. M. (1991). The role of the right hemisphere in emotional communication. *Brain, 114,* 1115–1127.

Blumberg, H. P., Charney, D. S., & Krystal, J. H. (2002). Frontotemporal neural systems in bipolar disorder. *Seminars in Clinical Neuropsychiatry, 7*(4), 243–254.

Bokhorst, C. L., Bakermans-Kranenburg, M. J., Fearon, R. M., Van IJzendoorn, M. H., Fonagy, P., & Schuengel, C. (2003). The importance of shared environment in mother-infant attachment security: A Behavioral Genetic Study. *Child Development, 74,* 1769–1782.

Botvinick, M., Jha, A. P., Bylsma, L. M., Fabian, S. A., Solomon, P. E., & Prkachin, K. M. (2005). Viewing facial expressions of pain engages cortical areas involved in the direct experience of pain. *NeuroImage, 25,* 312–319.

Bowen, M. (1978). *Family therapy in clinical practice.* New York: Jason Aronson

Bowlby, J. (1951). *Maternal care and mental health.* (WHO monograph series No. 2). Geneva: World Health Organization.

Bowlby, J. (1969). *Attachment and loss, Vol. 1: Attachment.* New York: Basic Books.

Bowlby, J. (1973). *Attachment and loss, Vol. 2: Separation.* New York: Basic Books.

Bowlby, J. (1980). *Attachment and loss, Vol. 3: Loss, sadness and depression.* New York: Basic Books.

Bradley, R. G., Binder, E. B., Epstein, M. P., et al. (2008). Influence of child abuse on adult depression: Moderation by the corticotrophin-releasing hormone receptor gene. *Archives of General Psychiatry, 65*(2): 190–200.

Briggs, A. & Macartney, A. (1984). *Toynbee Hall. The first hundred years.* London: Routledge and Kegan Paul.

Bremner, J. D. (2002). Neuroimaging studies in posttraumatic stress disorder. *Current Psychiatry Reports, 4*(4), 254–263.

Bremner, J. D. (2003). Long-term effects of childhood abuse on brain and neurobiology. *Child and Adolescent Psychiatric Clinics of North America, 12,* 271–292.

Bremner, J. D. (2006). Traumatic stress from a multiple-levels-of analysis perspective. In D. Cicchetti & D. Cohen, *Developmental psychopathology, Vol. 2, Developmental neuroscience* (pp. 656–676). Hoboken, NJ: Wiley.

Bremner, J. D., Krystal, J. H., Southwick, S. M., & Charney, D. S. (1995). Functional neuroantonomical correlates of the effects of stress on memory. *Journal of Psychiatry, 156,* 360–366.

Bremner, J. D., Randall, P., Scott, M., Bronen, R., Seibyl, J., Southwick, S. M., et al. (1995). MRI-based measurement of hippocampus volume in patients with combat-related posttraumatic stress disorder. *American Journal of Psychiatry, 152,* 973–981.

Bremner, J. D., Randall, P., Vermetten, E., Staib, L., Bronen, R., Mazure, C. J., et al. (1997). Magnetic resonance imaging–based measurement of hippocampal volume in posttraumatic stress disorder related to childhood physical and sexual abuse—a preliminary report. *Biological Psychiatry, 41,* 23–32.

Bremner, J. D., Vermetten, E., Vythilingam, M., Afzal, N., Schmahl, C., Elzinga, B., et al. (2004). Neural correlates of the classic color and emotional Stroop in women with abuse-related posttraumatic stress disorder. *Biological Psychiatry, 15*(6), 612–620.

Brent, D. A., Holder, D., Birmaher, B., Baugher, M. Roth, C., & Johnson, B. (1997). A clinical psychotherapy trial for adolescent depression comparing cognitive, family, and supportive treatments. *Archives of General Psychiatry, 54,* 877–885.

Brent, D., Kolko, D., Birmaher, B., Baugher, M., Bridge, J., Roth, C., et al. (1998). Predictors of treatment efficacy in a clinical trial of three psychosocial treatments for adolescent depression. *Journal of the American Academy of Child and Adolescent Psychiatry, 37,* 906–914.

Briggs, A. & Macartney, A. (1984). *Toynbee Hall. The first hundred years.* London: Routledge and Kegan Paul.

Briggs, J. (1970). *Never in anger.* Cambridge, MA: Harvard University Press.

Brizendine, L. (2007). *The female brain.* New York: Broadway Books.

Brothers, L. (1996). Brain mechanisms of social cognition. *Journal of Psychopharmacology, 10,* 2–8.

Brothers, L. (1997). *Friday's footprint.* New York: Oxford Press.

Brown, E. S., Rush, A. J., & McEwen, B. S. (1999). Hippocampal remodeling and damage by corticosteroids: Implications for mood disorders. *Neuropsychopharmacology, 21,* 474–484.

Bruder, G. E., Tenke, C. E., Stewart, J. W., Towey, J. P., Leite, P., Voglmaier, M. M., et al. (1995). Brain event related potential to complex tones in depressed patients: Relation to perceptual asymmetry and clinical features. *Psychophysiology, 32,* 373–381.

Burlington, D., & Freud, A. (1943a). *Young children in wartime.* London: George Allen and Unwin.

Burlington, D., & Freud, A. (1943b). *War and children.* London: Medical War Books.

Burns, N. R., Nettelback, T., & Cooper, C. J. (2000). Event-related potential correlates of some human cognitive ability constructs. *Personality and Individual Differences, 29,* 157–168.

Bush, G., Luu, P., & Posner, M. I. (2000). Cognitive and emotional influences in anterior cingulate cortex. *Trends in Cognitive Sciences, 4,* 215–222.

Cadoret, R. J., Yates, W. R., Troughton, E., Woodworth, G., & Stewart, M. A. (1995). Genetic-environmental interaction in the genesis of aggressivity and conduct disorders. *Archives of General Psychiatry, 52,* 916–924.

Calafas, K. J., & Taylor, W. C. (1994). Effects of physical activity on psychological variables in adolescents. *Pediatric Exercise Science, 6*, 406–423.

Cameron, H. A., & McKay, R. (1999). Restoring production of hippocampal neurons in old age. *Nature Neuroscience, 2*, 894–897.

Campbell, F. A., & Ramey, C. T. (1995). Cognitive and school outcomes for high-risk African American students at middle adolescence: Positive effects of early intervention. *American Educational Research Journal, 32*, 743–772.

Carpenter, G. (1974) "Mother's face and the newborn." *New Scientist. 21*: 742–744.

Caron, A. J., Caron, R. F., & MacLean, D. J. (1988). Infant discrimination of naturalistic emotional expressions: The role of the face and voice. *Child Development, 59*, 604–616.

Carr, L., Iacoboni, M., Dubeau, M. C., Mazziotta, J. C., & Lenzi, G. L. (2003). Neural mechanisms of empathy in humans: A relay from neural systems for imitation to limbic areas. *Proceedings of the National Academy of Sciences, USA, 100*, 5497–5502.

Carrion, V. G., Weems, C. F., Ray, R. D., Glaser, B., Hessl, D., & Reiss, A. L. (2002). Diurnal salivary cortisol in pediatric posttraumatic stress disorder. *Biological Psychiatry, 51*, 575–582.

Carskadon, M. A. (1999). *Adolescent sleep patterns: Biological, social, and psychological influences.* New York: Cambridge University Press.

Carter, C. S. (2003). Developmental consequences of oxytocin. *Physiology & Behavior, 79*, 383–397.

Carter, C. S., Braver, T. S., Barch, D. M., Botvinick, M. M., Noll, D. & Cohen, J. D. (1998). Anterior cingulate cortex, error detection, and the online monitoring of performance. *Science, 280*, 747–749.

Carter, C. S., Braver, T. S., Barch, D. M., Botvinick, M. M., Noll, D., & Cohen, J. D. (1998). Anterior cingulate cortex, error detection, and the online monitoring of performance. *Science, 280*, 747–749.

Casanova, M. F., Buxhoeveden, P., Switala, A. E., & Roy, E. (2002). Minicolumnar pathology in autism. *Neurology, 58*, 428–432.

Casey, B. J., Trainor, R., Giedd, J., Vauss, Y., Vaituzis, C. K., Hamburger, S., et al. (1997). The role of the anterior cingulate in automatic and controlled processes: A developmental neuroanatomical study. *Developmental Psychobiology, 30*, 61–69.

Cassidy, J., Parke, R. D., Butkovsky, L., Braungart, J. M. (1992) Family-peer connections: The role of emotional expressiveness within the family and children's understanding of emotions. *Child Development, 63*, 603–618.

Caspi, A., Harrington, H., Milne, B., Amell, J. W., Theodore, R. F., & Moffitt, T. E. (2003). Children's behavioral styles at age 3 are linked to their adult personality traits at age 26. *Journal of Personality, 71*(4), 495–513.

Caspi, A., & Silva, P. A. (1995). Temperamental qualities at age three predict personality traits in young adulthood. *Child Development, 66*, 486–498.

Cassidy, J., Kirsh, S. J., Scolton, K. L., & Parke, R. (1996). Attachment and representations of peer relationships. *Development Psychology, 32*, 892–904.

Cassidy, J., Kirsh, S. J., Scolton, K. L., & Parke, R., (1996). Attachment and representations of peer relationships. *Developmental Psychology, 64*, 1815–1828.

Cassidy, J., Parke, R. D., Butkovsky, L., & Braungart, J. M. (1992). Family-peer connections: The role of emotional expressiveness within the family and children's understanding of emotions. *Child Development, 63*, 603–613.

Castellanos, F. X., Sharp, W. S., Gottesman, R. F., Greenstein, D. K., Giedd, J. N., & Rapport, J. C. (2003). Anatomic brain abnormalities in monozygotic twins discordant for attention deficit hyperactivity disorder. *American Journal of Psychiatry, 160*, 1693–1696.

Chavira, D. A., & Stein, M. B. (2000). Recent developments in child and adolescent social phobia. *Current Psychiatry Reports, 2*, 347–352.

Cherny, S. S., Fulker, D. K., Corley, R. P., Plomin, R., & DeFries, J. C. (1994). Continuity and change in infant shyness from 14 to 20 months. *Behavior Genetics, 24*, 365–379.

Chess, S., & Thomas, A. (1990). The New York Longitudinal Study: The young adult periods. *Canadian Journal of Psychiatry, 35*, 577–561.

Chiron, C., Jambaque, I., Nabbout, R., Lounes, R., Syrota, A., & Dulac, O. (1997). The right brain is dominant in human infants. *Brain, 120*, 1057–1065.

Chisholm, J. S. (1996). Learning respect for everything. In C. P. Huang, M. E. Lamb, & I. E. Siegel (Eds.), *Images of childhood* (pp. 167–183). Mahwah, NJ: Lawarence Erlbaum.

Christoff, K., Ream, J. M., Geddes, L. P. T., & Gabrieli, J. D. E. (2003). Evaluating self-generated information. *Behavioral Neuroscience, 117*, 1161–1168.

Chugani, H. T. (1998). A critical period of brain development: Studies of cerebral glucose utilization with PET. *Preventive Medicine, 27*, 184–188.

Chugani, H. T., Phelps, M. E., & Mazziotta, J. C. (1987) Position emission tomography study of human brain functional development. *Annals of Neurology, 22*, 487–497.

Cicchetti, D., & Curtis, J. (2006). The developing brain and neural plasticity: Implications for normality, psychopathology, and resilience. In D. Cicchetti and D. Cohen (Eds.), *Handbook of developmental psychopathology* (2nd ed., pp. 2–64). Hoboken, NJ: Wiley.

Cicchetti, D., & Rogosch, F. A. (2001a). Diverse patterns of neuroendocrine function. *Development and Psychopathology, 13*, 667–693.

Cicchetti, D., & Rogosch, F. A. (2001b). The impact of child maltreatment and psychopathology upon neuroendocrine functioning. *Development and Psychopathology, 13*, 783–804.

Cicchetti, D., & Tucker, D. (1994). Development and self-regulatory structures of the mind. *Development and Psychopathology, 6*, 531–814.

Clark, C. R., McFarlane, A. C., Morris, P., Weber, D. L., Sonkkilla, C., Shaw, M., et al. (2003). Cerebral function in posttraumatic stress disorder during verbal working memory updating: A positron emission tomography study. *Biological Psychiatry, 53*, 474–481.

Clarke, G. N., Rohde, P., Lewinsohn, P. M., Hyman, H., & Seeley, J. (1999). Cognitive-behavioral treatment of adolescent depression: Efficacy of acute group treatment and booster sessions. *Journal of the American Academy of Child and Adolescent Psychiatry, 38*(3), 272–279.

Cohen, J. A., Berlin, L., & March, J. S. (2000). Treatment of children and adolescents. In E. B. Foa, T. M. Keane, & M. J. Friedman (Eds.), *Effective treatments for PTSD: Practice guidelines from the International Society for Traumatic Stress Studies* (pp. 106–138). New York: Guilford Press.

Cohn, J. K., & Tronick, E. K. (1982). Communication rules and sequential structure of infant behavior during normal and depressed interaction. In E. K. Tronik (Ed.), *Social interchange in infancy.* Baltimore, MD: University.

Collins, W. A., & Laursen, B. (2004). Parenting-adolescent relationship and influences. In R. M. Lerner & L. Steinberg (Eds.), *Handbook of adolescent psychology* (2nd ed., pp. 331–394). Hoboken, NJ: Wiley.

Conners, C. K., Epstein, J. N., March, J. S., Angold, A., Wells, K. C., Klaric, J., et al. (2001). Multimodal treatment of ADHD in the MTA: An alternative outcome analysis. *Journal of the American Academy of Child and Adolescent Psychiatry, 40*, 159–167.

Conteras, J. M., Kerns, K. A., Weiner, B. L., Gentzler, A. L., & Tomich, P. L. (2000). Emotion regulation as a mediator of association between mother-child attachment and peer relationships in middle childhood. *Journal of Family Psychology, 14*, 111–124. (date wrong in text)

Corina, D. P., Vaid, J., & Bellugi, V. (1992). The linguistic basis of left hemisphere specialization. *Science, 255*, 1258–1260.

Corwin, M., Kanitkar, K. N., Schwebach, A., & Muslow, M. (2004) Attention-deficit/hyperactivity disorder. In T. P. Gullotta & G. R. Adams, *Handbook of adolescent behavioral problems: Evidence-based approaches to prevention and treatment* (pp. 159–183). New York: Springer.

Costello, E. J., & Angold, A. (1995). Epidemiology. In J. March (Ed.), *Anxiety disorder in children and adolescents* (pp. 109–124). New York: Guilford Press.

Courchesne, E., Carper, R., & Ashoomoff, N. (2003). Evidence of brain overgrowth in the first year of life in autism. *Journal of the American Medical Association, 290*, 337–344.

Courtin, C. (2000). The impact of sign language on the cognitive development of deaf children: The case of theories of mind. *Cognition, 77*, 25–31.

Courtin, C., & Melot, A.-M. (2005). Metacognitive development of deaf children: Lessons from the appearance-reality and false belief tasks. *Journal of Deaf Studies and Deaf Education, 5*, 266–276.

Cozolino, L. (2002). *The neuroscience of psychotherapy.* New York: Norton.

Cozolino, L. (2006). *The neuroscience of human relationships: Attachment and the developing social brain.* New York: Norton.

Craske, M. G., Meadows, E., & Barlow, D. H. (1994). *Therapist's guide for your mastery of anxiety and panic II and agoraphobia supplement.* New York: Graywind Press.

Creswell, J. D., Baldwin, M. A., Way, M., Eisenberger, N. I., & Lieberman, M. (2007). Neural correlates of dispositional mindfulness during affective labeling. *Psychosomatic Medicine, 69*.

Critchley, H. D., Wiens, S., Rotshtein, P., Öhman, A., & Solan, R. J. (2004). Neural systems supporting interoceptive awareness. *Nature Neuroscience, 7,* 189–195.

Cumberland-Li, A. (2003). The relation of parental emotionality and related dispositional traits to parental expression of emotion and children's social functioning. *Motivation and Emotion, 1,* 27–56.

Curry, J. F. (2001). Specific psychotherapies for childhood and adolescent depression. *Biological Psychiatry, 49,* 1091–1100.

Czeisler, C. A., & Khalsa, S. B. S. (2001). The human circadian timing system and sleep-wake regulation. In M. Kryger, T. Roth, & W. Dement (Eds.), *Principles and practice of sleep medicine* (3rd ed. pp. 353–375). Philadelphia: W. B. Saunders.

Dahl, R. E., Tubnick, L., al-Shabbout, M., & Ryan, N. (1997). Normal maturation of sleep: A longitudinal EEG study in children. *Sleep Research, 26,* 155.

Damasio, A. (1999). *The feeling of what happens: Body and emotion in the making of consciousness.* New York: Harcourt.

Damasio, A. (2003). *Looking for Spinoza's joy, sorrow, and the feeling brain.* New York: Harcourt.

Damasio, A. R. (1994). *Descartes' error.* New York: Putnam and Sons.

Danforth, J. S. (1998). The outcome of parent training using Behavior Management Flow Chart with mothers and their children with oppositional defiant disorder and attention–deficit hyperactivity disorder. *Behavior Modification, 22,* 443–473.

Dantzer, R., Bluthe, R., Gheus, G., Cremona, S., Laye, S., Parnet, P., et al. (1998). Molecular basis of sickness behavior. *New York Academy of Science, 856,* 132–138.

Davidson, F. J., & Fox, N. (1982). Asymmetrical brain activity discriminates between positive versus negative affective stimuli in human infants. *Science, 218,* 1235–1237.

Davidson, R. J. (1992). Emotion and affective style: Hemispheric substrates. *Psychological Science, 3,* 39–43.

Davidson, R. J. (2003). Affective neuroscience and psychophysiology. *Psychophysiology, 40,* 655–665.

Davidson, R. J. (1998). Affective style and affective disorders: Perspectives from affective neuroscience. *Cognition and Emotion, 12,* 307–320.

Davidson, R. J. (2000). Affective style, psychopathology, and resilience: Brain mechanisms and plasticity. *American Psychologist, 55,* 1196–1214.

Davidson, R. J., Jackson, L., & Kalin, N. H. (2000). Emotion, plasticity, context, and regulation. *Psychological Bulletin, 126,* 890–909.

Davidson, R. J., Kabit-Zinn, J., Schumacher, J., Rosenkranz, M., Muller, D., & Santorelli, S. F. (2003). Alterations in brain and immune function produced by mindfulness meditation. *Psychosomatic Medicine, 65*(4), 564–570.

Davidson, R. J., Marshall, J. R., Tomarkken, A. J., & Henriques, J. B. (2000). While a phobic waits: Regional brain electrical and automatic activity in social phobics during anticipation of public speaking. *Biological Psychiatry, 47,* 85–95.

Davis, M. (1998). Are different parts of the extended amygdala involved in fear versus anxiety? *Biological Psychiatry, 44,* 1239–1247.

Davis, K. L., Charney, D., Coyle, J. T., & Nemeroff, C. (2002). *Neuropsychopharmocology: The fifth generation of progress. An official publication of the American College of Neuropsychopharmocology.* New York: Lippincott, Williams, & Wilkins.

Davis, L., & Siegel, L. J. (2000). Posttraumatic stress disorder in children and adolescents: A review and analysis. *Clinical Child and Family Psychology Review,* 3(3), 135–154.

Dawson, M., & Ashman, S. (2000). On the origins of a vulnerability to depression: The influence of early social environment of the development psychobiological systems related to risk for affective disorder. In C. A. Nelson (Ed.), *Minnesota Symposia on Child Psychology: Vol. 31, The effects of adversity on neurobehavioral development* (pp. 245–278). New York: Lawrence Erlbaum.

Dawson, G. (1994). Development of emotional expression and emotion reguation in infancy. In G. Dawson, & K. W. Fischer (Eds.), *Human Behavior and the Developing Brain* (pp. 346–379). New York: Guilford.

Dawson, G., Frey, K., Panagiotides, H., Osterling, J., & Hessel, D. (1997) Infants of depressed mothers exhibit atypical frontal brain activation: A replication and extension of previous findings. *Journal of Child Psychology and Psychiatry, 38,* 179–186.

DeBellis, M. D., Baum, A. S., Birmaher, B., Keshavan, M. S., Eccard, C. H., Boring, A. M., et al. (1999). *A. E. Bennett Research Award—Development traumatology, Biological stress systems. Biological Psychiatry* 15, 1259–1270.

de Decker, A., Hermans, D., Raes, F., & Eelen, P. (2003). Autobiographical memory specificity and trauma in inpatient adolescents. *Journal of Clinical Child and Adolescent Psychology, 32,* 22–31.

Demeyer, M., Shea, P., Hendrie, H., et al. (1981). Plasma trytophan and five other amino acids in depressed and normal subjects. *Archives of General Psychiatry, 38,* 642–645.

DiPietro, J. A. (2004) The role of maternal stress in child development. *Current Directions in Psychological Science, 13,* 71–74.

Derryberry, D., & Reed, M. A. (2002). Anxiety-related attentional biases and their regulation by attentional control. *Journal of Abnormal Psychology, 111,* 225–246.

Derryberry, D., & Tucker, D. (2006). Motivation, Self-regulation, and Self-organization. In D. Cicchetti & D. Cohen (Eds.), *Developmental psychopathology, Vol. 2, Developmental neuroscience* (pp. 502–533). Hoboken, NJ: Wiley.

Devinsky, O. (2000). Right cerebral hemisphere dominance for a sense of corporeal and emotional self. *Epilepsy and Behavior, 1,* 60–73.

DeVries, M. W. (1989). Difficult temperament: A universal and culturally embedded concept. In W. B. Carey & S. McDevitt (Eds.), *Clinical and educational applications of temperament research.* Berwyn, PA: Swets North America.

De Weerth, C. & van Geert, V. (2002). Changing patterns of infant behavior and mother-infant interaction: Intra- and inter-individual variability. *Infant Behavior & Development, 24,* 347–371.

deWolff, M. S., & van IJzendoorn, M. H. (1997). Sensitivity and attachment: A meta-analysis of parental antecedents of infant attachment. *Child Development, 68*, 571–591.

Diamond, G., Reis, B., Diamond, G., Siqueland, L., & Isaas, L. (2002). Attachment-based family therapy for depressed adolescents: A treatment development study. *Journal of the American Academy of Child and Adolescent Psychiatry, 42*, 656–665.

Diorio, D., Viau, V., & Meaney, M. J. (1993). The role of the medial prefrontal cortex (cingulate gyrus) in the regulation of hypothalamic-pituitary-adrenal responses to stress. *Journal of Neuroscience, 13*, 3839–3847.

Dixon, S., Tronick, E., Keeler, C., & Brazelton, T. B. (1981). Mother-infant interaction among the Gusii of Kenya. In T. M. Field, A. M. Sostek, P. Vietze, & P. H. Leiderman (Eds.), *Culture and early interaction.* Hillsdale, NJ: Lawrence Erlbaum.

Donovan, C. L., & Spence, S. H. (2000). Prevention of childhood anxiety disorders. *Clinical Psychology Review, 20*, 509–531.

Draganski, B., Gaser, C., Busch, V., Schuierer, G., Bogdahn, V., & May, A. (2004). Changes in grey matter induce by training. *Nature, 427*, 311–312.

Drake, R. A. (1984). Lateral asymmetry of personal optimism. *Journal of Research in Personality, 18*, 497–507.

Dunbar R. I. (1996). *Grooming, gossip, and the evolution of language.* Cambridge: Harvard University Press.

Dwivedi Y., Rao, J. S., Rizavi, H. S., et al. (2003). Abnormal expression and functional characteristics of cyclic adenosine monophosphate response element binding protein in postmortem brain of suicide subjects. *Archives of General Psychiatry, 60*, 273–282.

Eaton, D.K., Kann, L., Kinchen, S., Ross, J., Hawkins, J., et al. Youth risk behavior surveillance—United States, 2007. (2008). *Morbidity and mortality weekly report.* June 6, 2008, *57*(SS04), 1–131.

Eccles, J. C. (1984). The cerebral neocortex: A theory of its operation. In E. G. Jones & A. Peters (Eds.), *Cerebral cortex: Functional properties of cortical cells* (Vol. 2). New York: Plenum Press.

Edelman, G. M. (1987). *Neural Darwinism: The theory of neuronal group selection.* New York: Basic Books.

Edelman, G. M. (2006). *Second nature: brain science and human knowledge.* New Haven: Yale University Press.

Edelman, G. M. (1989). *The remembered present: A biological theory of consciousness.* New York: Basic Books.

Edelman, G. M. (1993). Neural Darwinism: Selection and reentrant signaling in higher brain function. *Neuron, 10*, 115–125.

Edwards, H. E., & Burnham, W. M. (2001). The impact of corticosteroids of the developing animal. *Pediatric Research, 50*, 433–440.

Egaas, B., Courchesne, E., & Saitoh, O. (1995). Reduced size of corpus callosum in autism. *Archives of Neurology, 52*, 794–801.

Eigsti, I. M., & Cicchetti, D. (2004). The impact of child maltreatment on expressive syntax at 60 months. *Developmental Science, 7*(1), 88–102.

Eisenberg, N., Fabes, R. A., Guthrie, I. K., & Reiser, M. (2000). Dispositional emotionality and regulation: Their role in predicting quality of social functioning. *Journal of Personality and Social Psychology, 72,* 136–157.

Eisenberger, N. I., & Lieberman, M. D. (2004). Why rejection hurts: A common neural alarm system for physical and social pain. *Trends in Cognitive Sciences, 8,* 294–300.

Ekman, P. (1993). Facial expression and emotion. 1992 Award Addresses. *American Psychologist, 48*(4), 384–392.

Ekman, P., & Frieson, W. (1972). Constants across culture in the face and emotion. *Journal of Personaility and Social Psychology, 17,* 124–129.

Elbert, T., Pantev, C., Wienbruch, C., Rockstroh, B., & Taub, E. (1995). Increased cortical representation of the fingers of the left hand in string players. *Science, 270,* 305–307.

Elia, J. (1991). Methylphenidate and dextroamphetamine treatments of hyperactivity: Are there true nonresponders? *Psychiatry Research, 36,* 141.

Ellis, A. (1962). *Reason and emotion in psychotherapy.* Secaucus, NJ: Lyle Stuart.

Ellis, A. (1996) *Reason and emotion in psychotherapy.* Secaucus, NJ: Lyle Stuart.

Ellworth, C. P., Muir, D. W., & Hains, S. M. J. (1993). Social competence and person-object differienciation: An analysis of the still-face effect. *Developmental Psychology, 29,* 63–73.

Emde, R. N., Plomin, R., Robinson, J., Corley, R., DeFries, J., Fulker, D. W., et al. (1992). Temperament, emotion, and cognition at fourteen months: The MacArthur Lognitudinal Twin Study. *Child Development, 63,* 1437–1455.

Erikson, E. (1963). *Childhood and society* (2nd ed.). New York: Norton.

Erickson, P. S., Perfileva, E., Bjork-Erickson, T., Alborn, A. M., Nordborg, C., Peterson, A. A.et al. (1998). Neurogenesis in the adult human hippocampus. *Nature Medicine, 4,* 1313–1317.

Essex, M. J., Klein, J. H., Eunsuk, C., & Kalin, N. H. (2002). Maternal stress beginning in infancy may sensitize children to later stress exposure: Effects on cortisol and behavior. *Biological Psychiatry, 52,* 776–784.

Eysenck, H. (1952). *The structure of human personality.* New York: Wiley.

Farrington, D. P. (1994). Childhood, adolescent, and adult features of violent males. In L. R. Huesman (Ed.), *Aggressive behavior: Current perspectives* (pp. 215–240). New York: Plenum Press.

Fifer, W. & Moon, C. (1995). The effects of fetal experience with sound. In J. P. Lecanuet, W. Fifer, N., Krasnergor, B. W., Smotherman (Eds.) *Fetal development: A psychobiological perspective.* (pp. 351–366). Hillsdale, NJ: Erlbaum.

Field, T. M., Fox, N. A., Pickens, J., & Nawrocki, T. (1995) Right frontal EEG activation in 3-to-6 month old infants of depressed mothers, *Developmental Psychology, 31,* 358–363.

Felitti, V. J., Anda, R. F., Nordenberg, D., & Williamson, D. F. & Marks, J. S. (1998). Relationship of childhood abuse and household dysfunction to many of the leading causes of death in adults. The Adverse Childhood Experiences (ACE) Study. *American Journal of Preventive Medicine, 14*(4): 361–364.

Felton, D. L., Ackerman, K. D., Wiegand, S. J., & Felton, S. Y. (1987). Noradrenergic sympathetic innervation of the spleen: I. Nerve fibers associate with lymphocytes and macrophanges in specific compartments of the splenic white pulp. *Journal of Neuroscience Research, 18,* 28–36.

Feng, J., Spence, I., & Pratt, J. (2007). Playing an action video game reduces gender differences in spatial cognition. *Psychological Science, 18*(10), 850–855.

Feniman, S., Roberts, D., Hsieh, K., Sawyer, D., & Swanson, D. (1992). A critical review of social referencing in infancy. In S. Feinman (Ed.), *Social referencing and social construction of reality in infancy.* New York: Plenum Press.

Ferrell, C. B., Beidel, D. C., & Turner, S. M. (2004). Assessment and treatment of socially phobic children: A cross-cultural comparison. *Journal of Clinical Child and Adolescent Psychology, 33*(2), 260–268.

Field, T. M. (1998). Maternal depression effects on infants and early interventions. *Preventative Medicine, 27,* 200–203.

Field, T. M., Fox, N. A., Pickens, J., & Nawrocki, T. (1995). Right frontal EEG activation in 3-to-6 month old infants of depressed mothers. *Developmental Psychology, 31,* 358–363.

Field, T. M., & Walden, T. A. (1982). Production and perception of facial expressions in infancy and early childhood. In H. W. Reece & L. P. Lippsitt (Eds.), *Advances in child development and behavior* (Vol. 16). New York: Academic Press.

Fifer, W., & Moon, C. (1995). The effects of fetal experience with sound. In J. P. Lecanuet, W. Fifer, N. Krasnergor, & B. W. Smotherman (Eds.), *Fetal development: A psychobiological perspective* (pp. 351–366). Hillsdale, NJ: Lawrence Erlbaum.

Finman, R., Davidson, R. J., Coton, M. B., Straus, A., & Kagan, J. (1998). Psychophysiological correlates of inhibitions to the unfamiliar in children [Abstract]. *Psychophysiology, 26,* 524.

Fischer, K., Shaver, P. R., & Carnochan, P. (1990). How emotions develop and how they organize development. *Cognition and Emotion, 4,* 81–127.

Fisher, L., Ames, E. W., Chisholm, K., & Savoie, L. (1997). Problems reported by parents of Romanian orphans adopted to British Columbia. *International Journal of Behavioral Development, 20,* 67–87.

Fivush, R. (1998). Children's recollections of traumatic and nontraumatic events. *Development and Psychopathology, 10,* 699–716.

Fletcher, P. C., Frith, C. D., Baker, S. C., Shallice, T., Frackowiak, R. S., & Dolan, R. J. (1995) The mind's eye: Precuneus activation in memory-related imagery. *NeuroImage, 2,* 95–200.

Fonagy, P. (2001). *Attachment theory and psychoanalysis.* New York: Other Press.

Fonagy, P., Leigh, T., Steele, M., Steele, H., et al. (1996). The relation of attachment status, psychiatric classification, and response to psychotherapy. *Journal of Consulting and Clinical Psychology, 64,* 22–31.

Fonagy, P., Steele, M., Steele, H., Leigh, T., et al. (1995). Attachment, the reflective self, and borderline states: The predictive specificity of the Adult Attachment

Interview and pathological emotional development. In S. Goldberg, R. Muir, & J. Kerr (Eds.), *Attachment theory: Social, developmental and clinical perspectives* (pp. 233–278). Hillsdale, NJ: Analytic Press.

Fonagy, P., & Target, M. (2006). The mentalization focused approach to self pathology. *Journal of Personality Disorders, 20*(6), 544–576.

Fonagy, P., Target, J., Steele, M., Steele, H., Leigh, T., Levinson, A., *et al.* (1997). Crime and attachment: Morality, disruptive behavior, borderline personality disorder, crime and their relationship to security of attachment. In L. Atkinson & K. J. Zucker (Eds.), *Attachment and psychopathology* (pp. 223–274). New York: Guilford Press.

Ford, D. E., & Kamerow, D. B. (1989). Epidemiological study of sleep disturbances and psychiatric disorders: An opportunity for prevention? *Journal of the American Medical Association, 262,* 1479–1484.

Ford, T., Goodman, R., & Meltzer, H. (2003). The British Child and Adolescent Mental Health Survey 1999: The prevalence of DSM-IV disorders. *Journal of the American Academy of Child and Adolescent Psychiatry, 42,* 2103–1211.

Fox, N. A., Calkins, S. D., & Bell, M. A. (1994). Neural plasticity and development in the first year of life. *Developmental Psychopathology, 6,* 677–696.

Fox, N. A., & Field, T. (1989). Individual differences in preschool entry behavior. *Journal of Applied Development Psychology, 10,* 527–540.

Fox, N. A., Hane, A. A., & Perez-Edgar, K. (2006). Psychophysiological methods for the study of developmental psychopathology. In D. Cicchetti & D. Cohen, *Developmental psychopathology, Vol. 2, Developmental neuroscience* (pp. 381–427). Hoboken, NJ: Wiley.

Fox, N. A., Henderson, H. A., Rubin, K. A, Rubin, K. H., Calkins, S. D., & Schmidt, L. A. (2001). Continuity and discontinuity of behavioral inhibition and exuberance: Psychophysiological and behavioral influences across the first four years of life. *Child Development, 72,* 1–21.

Fox, N. A., Kimmerly, N. L., & Schafer, W. D. (1991). Attachment to mother/ attachment to father: A meta-analysis. *Child Development, 62,* 210–225.

Francis, D., Diorio, J., Liu, D., & Meaney, M. J. (1999). Nongenomic transmission across generations of maternal behavior and stress responses in the rat. *Science, 286,* 1155–1158.

Freeman, J. B., Garcia, A. M., Fucci, C., Karitani, M., Miller, L., & Leonard, H. L. (2003). Family-based treatment of early-onset obsessive-compulsive disorder. *Journal of Child Adolescent Psychopharmocology, 13*(1), 71–80.

Freedman, M., Black, S., Ebert, P., & Binns, M. (1998). Orbitofrontal function, object alternation and preservation. *Cerebral Cortex, 8,* 18–27.

Freeman, W. (1987). Simulation of chaotic EEG patterns with a dynamic model of the olfactory system. *Biological Cybernetics, 56,* 139–150.

Freeman, W. (1995). *Societies of brains: A study in the neuroscience of love and hate.* Hillsdale, NJ: Lawrence Erlbaum.

Freeman, W. J. (1992). Tutorial in neurobiology. *International Journal of Bifurcation and Chaos, 2,* 451–482.

Freud, A. (1946). *The psycho-analytical treatment of children. Technical lectures and essays*. New York: International Universities Press.

Freud, A., & Burlington, D. (1944). *Infants without families*. New York: International Universities Press.

Freud, S. (1888/1990). Aphasie. In M. Solms & M. Saling (Eds.), *A moment of transition: Two neuroscientific articles by Sigmund Freud*. London: Karnac Books.

Freud, S. (1958). Project for a scientific psychology. *New introductory lectures in psychoanalysis*. In J. Strachey (Ed. & Trans.), *The standard edition of the complete psychological works of Sigmund Freud* (Vol. 12, pp. 111–120). London: Hogarth Press. (Original work published 1895.)

Freud, S. (1962). Three essays on the theory of sexuality. J. Strachey (trans.). New York: Basic Books. (Originally published 1905.)

Frith, C. D., & Frith, U. (1999). Interacting minds: A biological basis. *Science, 286,* 1692–1695.

Fuster, J. M. (2000). The prefrontal cortex of the primate: A synopsis. *Psychobiology, 28,* 125–131.

Fuster, J. M. (1997). *The prefrontal cortex*. Philadelphia: Lippincott-Raven Publishers.

Galambos, N. L. (2004). *Gender and gender role development in adolescence*. In R. M. Lerner & L. Steinberg (Eds.), *Handbook of adolescence* (2nd ed., pp. 233–262). Hoboken, NJ: Wiley.

Galin, D., Johnstone, J., Nakell, L., & Herron, J. (1979). Development for the capacity for tactile information transfer between hemispheres in normal children. *Science, 204,* 13301–1331.

Gallese, V. (2001). The "shared manifold" hypothesis: From mirror neurons to empathy. *Journal of Consciousness Studies, 8,* 33–50.

Gallese, V., & Keysers, C. (2001). Mirror neurons: A sensorimotor representation system. *Behavioral and Brain Sciences, 24,* 983–984.

Gallup, G. G. (1997). Absence of self-recognition in a monkey (macaca fasicularis) following prolonged exposure to a mirror. *Developmental Psychobiology, 10*(3), 281–281.

Garmararian, J. A., Lazorick, S., Spitz, A. M. Ballard, T. J., Saltzman, L. E., & Marks, J. S. (1996). Prevalence of domestic violence against pregnant women: A review of the literature. *Journal of the American Medical Association, 275*(24), 1915–1920.

Gaub, M., & Carlson, C. L. (1997). Gender differences in ADHD: A meta-analysis and critical review. *Journal of the American Academy of Child and Adolescent Psychiatry, 36,* 1036–1045.

Gauthier, I., Tarr, M. J., Moylan, J., Skudlarski, P., Gore, J. C., & Anderson, A. W. (2000). The fusiform "face area" is part of a network that processes faces at the individual level. *Journal of Cognitive Neurscience, 12,* 495–504.

Gazzaniga, M. S. (1995). Consciousness and the cerebral hemispheres. In M. S. Gazzaniga (Ed.), *The cognitive neurosciences* (pp. 1391–1400). Cambridge, MA: MIT Press.

Gazzaniga, M. S., Eliassen, J. C., Nisenson, L., Wessinger, C. M., & Baynes, K. B. (1996). Collaboration between the hemispheres of a callosotomy patient: Emergent right hemisphere speech and the left brain interpreter. *Brain, 119*, 1255–1262.

Gazzaniga, M. S. (1985). *The social brain*. New York: Basic Books.

Gazzaniga M. S., Bogen, J. E, & Sperry, R. W. (1962). Some functional effects of sectioning the cerebral commissures in man. *Proceedings of the National Academy of Sciences, 48*, 1765–1769.

Gazzaniga, M. S., & LeDoux, J. E. (1978). *The integrated mind*. New York: Plenum Press.

Gazzaniga, M. S., Wilson D. H., & LeDoux, J. E. (1977). Language, praxis, and the right hemisphere: Clues to some mechanisms of consciousness. *Neurology, 27*, 1144–1147.

Geller, D. A., Biederman, J., Jones, J., Shapiro, S., Schwartz, S., & Park, K. S. (1998). Obsessive-compulsive disorder in children and adolescents: A review. *Harvard Review of Psychiatry, 5*(5), 260–273.

Geller, D. A., Wager, K. D., Emslie, G. L., Murphy, T. K., Gallager, D., Gardiner, C., & Carpenter, D. J. (2002). Efficacy of paroxetine in pediatric OCD: Results of a multi-center study. *Annual Meeting New Research Program and Abstracts* (No. 349). Washington, DC: American Psychological Association.

Gerrard, I., & Anastopoloulos, A. A. (2005, August). The relationship between ADHD and mother-child attachment in early childhood. Paper presented at the annual meeting of the American Psychological Association, Washington, DC.

Gerschwind, N., & Galaburda, A. M. (1985). Cerebral lateralization: Biological mechanisms, associations, and pathology: A hypothesis and program for research. *Archives of Neurology, 42*, 428–459.

Giedd, J. N., Blumenthal, J., Molloy, E., & Castellanos, F. X. (2001). Brain imaging of attention deficit/hyperactivity disorder. *Annals of the New York Academy of Science, 931*, 33–49.

Giedd, J., Shaw, P. Wallace, G., Gogtay, N., & Lenroot, R. (2006). Anatomic brain imaging studies of normal of normal and abnormal brain development in children and adolescence. In D. Cicchetti & D. Cohen (Eds.). *Development psychopathology* (Vol. 2, pp. 127–196). Hoboken, NJ: Wiley.

Gilbertson, M. W., Shenton, M. H., Ciszewski, A., Kasai, K.Lasko, N. B., Orr, S. P., et al. (2002) Smaller hippocampal volume predicts pathologic vulnerability to psychogical trauma. *Nature Neuroscience, 5*(11), 1242–1247.

Glick, S. D., Meibach, R. C., Cox, R. D., & Maayani, S. (1979). Mulitple and inter-related functional asymmetries in rat brain. *Life Science, 4*, 395–400.

Glick, S. D., Ross, D. A., & Hough, L. B. (1982). Lateral asymmetry of neuro-transmitters in human brain. *Brain Research, 234*(1), 53–63.

Globus, G., & Arpai, J. P. (1993). Psychiatry and the new dynamics. *Biological Psychiatry, 35*, 352–364.

Goldberg, E. (2001). *The Executive bain: Frontal lobes and the civilized mind*. New York: Oxford University Press.

Goldberg, J., True, W. R., Eisen, S. A., & Henderson, W. G. (1990). A twin study of the Vietnam War on posttraumatic stress disorder. *Journal of the American Medical Association, 263*, 1227–1232.

Goldman-Rakic, P. S. (1987). Development of cortical circuitry and cognitive function. *Child Development, 58*, 601–622.

Goleman, D. (2004). *Destructive emotions: A scientific dialogue with the Dalai Lama.* New York: Bantam Books.

Goleman, D. (2006). *Social intelligence: The new science of human relationships.* New York: Bantam Books.

Goodman, R., & Stevenson, J. (1989). A twin study of hyperactivity: II. The aetiological role of genes, family relationship, and perinatal adversity. *Journal of Child Psychology and Psychiatry, 30*, 691–709.

Goodwin, R. D., Fergusson, D. M., & Horwood, L. J. (2004). Early anxious/withdrawn behaviors predict later internalizing disorders. *Journal of Child Psychology and Psychiatry, 45*, 874–883.

Goodman, W. K., Price, L. H., Rasmussen, S. A., Mazure, C., Delgado, P., Heninger, G. R., & Charney, D. S. (1989a). The Yale-Brown Obsessive Compulsive Scale (Y-BOCS): Part I. Development, use, and reliability. *Archives of General Psychiatry, 46*(11), 1006–1011.

Goodman, W. K., Price, L. H., Rasmussen, S. A., Mazure, C., Delgado, P.Heninger, G. R., & Charney, D. S. (1989b). The Yale-Brown Obsessive Compulsive Scale (Y-BOCS): Part II. Validity. *Archives of General Psychiatry, 46*(11), 1012–1016.

Goodyer, I. M., Herbert, J., Tamplin, A., & Altham, P. (2000). First-episode major depression in adolescents: Affective, cognitive and endocrine characteristics of risk status and predictors of onset. *British Journal of Psychiatry, 176*, 142–149.

Gould, E., Tanapat, P., Hastings, N. B., & Shors, T. J. (1999). Neurogenesis in adult: A possible role in learning. *Trends in Cognitive Science, 3*, 186–191.

Goren, C. C., Sarty, M., & Wu, P. Y. K. (1975). Visual following and pattern discrimination of face-like stimuli by newborn infants. *Pediatrics, 56*(4), 544–549.

Gottesman, I. I. (1974). Developmental genetics and ontogenetic psychology: Overdue détente and propositions from a matchmaker. In A. Pick (Ed.), *Minnesota symposia on child psychology* (Vol. 8). Minneapolis: University of Minnesota Press.

Gottlieb, G., & Blair, C. (2004). How early experience matters in intellectual development in the case of poverty. *Prevention Science, 5*, 245–252.

Gottman, J., & Katz, L. K. (1996). Parental meta-emotion philosophy and the emotional life of families: The theoretical models and preliminary data. *Journal of Family Psychology, 10*, 243–268.

Gottman, J. M., Katz, L. F., & Hooven, C. (1996). *Meta-emotion: How families communicate emotionally.* Mahwah, NJ: Lawrence Erlbaum.

Gould, E., Reeves, A. J., Graziano, M. S. A., & Gross, C. G. (1999). Neurogenesis in the neocortex of adult primates. *Science, 628*, 548–552.

Gould, E., Reeves, A. J., Graziano, M. S., & Gross, C. G. (1999). Neurogenesis in the neocortex of adult primates. *Science, 286*, 548–552.

Gould, E., & Tanapat, P. (1999). Stress and hippocampal neurgenesis. *Biological Psychiatry, 46*, 1472–1479.

Gould, E., Tanapat, P., McEwen, B. S., Flugge, G., & Fuchs, E. (1998). Proliferation of granule cell precursors in dentate gyrus of adult monkeys is diminished by stress. *Proceedings of National Academy of Science, USA, 95*(6), 3168–3171.

Graber, J. A. (2004). Internalizing problems during adolescence. In R. M. Lerner & L. Steinberg (Eds.), *Handbook of adolescent psychology* (2nd ed., pp. 587–626). Hoboken, NJ: Wiley.

Graczyk, P. A., Connolly, S. D., & Corapci, F. (2005). Anxiety disorders in childhood and adolescents: Theory, treatment, and prevention. In T. G. Gullotta & G. R. Adams (Eds.), *Handbook of adolescent behavioral problems: Evidence-based approaches to prevention and treatment*, pp. 131–159. New York: Springer.

Graeff, F. G., Guimarães, F. S., de Andrade, T. G. C. S., & Deakin, J. F. W. (1996). Role of 5-HT in stress, anxiety, and depression. *Pharmacology Biochemistry and Behavior, 54*(1), 129–141.

Granger, D. A., Granger, G. A., & Granger, S. W. (2006). Immunology and developmental psychopathology. In D. Cicchetti & D. Cohen (Eds.), *Developmental psychopathology Vol. 2, Developmental neuroscience* (pp. 677–709). Hoboken, NJ: Wiley.

Green, B. L., Grace, M., Vary, J. G., Kramer, T., Gleser, G. C., & Leonard, A. (1994). Children of disaster in the second decade: A 17-year follow-up of Buffalo Creek survivors. *Journal of the American Academy of Child and Adolescent Psychiatry, 33*, 71–79.

Greenough, W. T., Black, J. E., & Wallace, C. S. (1987). Experience and brain development. *Child Development, 58*, 539–559.

Gressens, P. (2000). Mechanisms and disturbances of neuronal migration. *Pediatric Research, 48*(6), 725–730.

Grigsby, J., & Stevens, D. (2000). *Neurodynamics of personality*. New York: Guilford Press.

Grossman, K. E., Grossman, K. F., & Warter, V. (1981). German children's behavior toward their mothers at 12 months and their father at 18 months in Ainsworth's Strange Situation. *International Journal of Behavioral Development, 4*, 157–181.

Guerrero, A. P., Hishinuma, E. S., Andrade, N. N., Bell, C. K., Kurahara, D. K., Lee, T. G., Turner, H., Andrus, J., Yuen, N. Y., & Stokes, A. J. (2003). Demographic and clinical characteristics of adolescents in Hawaii with obsessive-compulsive disorder. *Archives of Pediatric and Adolescent Medicine, 15*(7), 665–670.

Gullon, E., & King, N. J. (1997). Three-year follow-up of normal fear in children and adolescents aged 7 to 18 years. *British Journal of Developmental Psychology, 15*, 97–111.

Gundel, H., Lopez-Sala, A., & Ceballos-Baumann, A. O. (2004). Alexithymia correlates with the size of the right anterior cingulate. *Psychosomatic Medicine, 66, 132–140.*

Gunnar, M. R. (1994). Psychoendrocrine studies of temperament and stress in early childhood: Expanding current models. In J. E. Bates & T. D. Wachs (Eds.), *Temperament: Individual differences at the interface of biology and behavior* (pp. 175–198). Washington, DC: American Psychological Association.

Gunnar, M. R., Porter, F. L., Wolf, C. M., Rigatuso, J., & Larson, M. C. (1995). Neonatal stress reactivity: Predictions to later emotional temperament. *Child Development, 66,* 1–13.

Gunnar, M. R., Tout, K., deHaan, M., Pierce, S., & Stansburg, K. (1997). Temperament, social competence, and adrenocortical activity in preschoolers. *Developmental Psychobiology, 31,* 65–85.

Gunnar, M. (2001) Effects of early deprivation. Findings from orphanage-reared infants and children. In C. Nelson & M. Luciana (Eds.) *Handbook of developmental cognitive neuroscience.* (pp. 617–629). Cambridge, MA: MIT Press.

Gunnar, M. R. (1998) Quality of care and buffering of neuroendrocrine stress reactions: Potential effects of the developing brain. *Prevention Medicine, 27,* 208–211.

Gunnar, M. R., & Vazquez, D. (2006). Stress neurobiology and developmental psychopathology. In D. Cicchetti & D. Cohen, *Developmental psychopathology, Vol. 2, Developmental neuroscience* (pp. 533–577). Hoboken, NJ: Wiley.

Gutgesell, H., et al. (1999). Cadiovascular monitoring of children and adolescents receiving psychotropic drugs. *Circulation, 99,* 979.

Halligan, S., Herbert, J., Goodyer, I. M., & Murray, L. (2004). Exposure to postnatal depression predicts elevated cortisol in adolescent offspring. *Biological Psychiatry, 55,* 376–381.

Hallowell, E. M., & Ratey, J. J. (1994). *Driven to distraction: Recognizing and coping with attention deficit disorder from childhood through adulthood.* New York: Pantheon Books.

Hampson, E. (2008). Endocrine contributions to sex differences in visuospatial perception and cognition. In J. B. Becker, K. J. Berkley, N. Geary, E. Hampson, J. P. Herman, & E. A. Young (Eds.), *Sex differences in the brain: From genes to behavior* (pp. 311–325). New York: Oxford University Press.

Hankin, B. L., Abraham, L. Y., Moffit, T. E., Silva, P. A., McGee R., & Angell, K. E. (1998). Development of depression from pre-adolescence to young adulthood: Emerging gender differences in a 10-year longitudinal study. *Journal of Abnormal Psychology, 107,* 128–140.

Hansen, D., Lou, H. C., & Olsen, J. (2000). Serious life events and congenital malformations: A national study with complete follow-up. *Lancet, 356,* 875–880.

Hariri, A. R., Bookheimer, S. Y., & Mazziotta, J. C. (2000). Modulating emotional responses: Effects of a neocortical network on the limbic system. *NeuroReport: For Rapid Communication of Neuroscience Research 11*(1), 43–48.

Hariri, A. R., Goldberg, T. E., Mattay, V. S., et al. (2003). Brain-derived neurotrophic factor val^{66}met polymorphism affects human memory–related hippocampal activity and predicts memory performance. *Journal of Neuroscience, 23*(17), 6690–6694.

Hart, D., Hoffman, V., Edelstein, W., & Keller, M. (1997). The relationship of childhood personality types to adolescent behavior and development. *Developmental Psychology, 33*, 195–205.

Harter, S., Bresnick, S., Bouchey, H. A., & Whitsell, N. R. (1997). The development of multiple role-related selves during adolescence. *Development and Psychopathology, 9*, 835–854.

Harwood, R., Miller, S. A., & Vasta, R. (2008). *Child psychology: Developing in a changing society* (5th ed.) Hoboken, NJ: Wiley.

Hauri, P. J., & Fischer, J. (1986). Persistant psychophysiology (learned) insomnia. *Sleep, 9*, 38–53.

Haviland, J. M., & Lelwica, M. (1987). The induced affect response: 10-week-old infants' response to three emotional expressions. *Developmental Psychology, 23*, 97–104.

Hawkins, J., & Blakeslee, S. (2004). *On intelligence*. New York: Holt.

Hawkins, J. D., Smith, B. H., Hill, K. G., Kosterman, R. F. C., & Abbott, R. D. (2003). Understanding and preventing crime and violence: Findings from the Seattle Social Development Project. In T. P. Thornberry & M. D. Krohn (Eds.), *Taking stock of delinquency: An overview of findings from contemporary longitudinal studies* (pp. 255–312). New York: Kluwer Academic/Plenum Press.

Hayward, C., Killen, J. D., Kraemer, H. C., & Taylor, C. B. (2000). Predictor of panic attacks in adolescents. *Journal of the American Academy of Child and Adolescent Psychiatry, 39*(2), 207–214.

Haznedar, M. M., Buchsbaum, M. S., Wei, T. C., Hof, P. R., Cartwright, C., Bienstock, C. A., et al. (2000). Limbic circuitry in patients with autistm spectrum disorders studied with positron emission tomography and magnetic resonance imaging. *American Journal of Psychiatry, 157*, 1994–2001.

Hebb, D. (1949/1998). *The organization of behavior*. New York: Wiley.

Heim, C., & Nemeroff, C. B. (1999). The impact of early adverse experience on brain systems involved in the pathophysiology of anxiety and affected disorders. *Biological Psychiatry, 46*, 1509–1522.

Heiss, W. D., Kessler, J., Mielke, R.Szelies, B., & Herholtz, K. (1994). Long-term effects of phosphatidylserine, pyritinol, and cognitive training in Alzheimer's disease: A neuropsychological EEG and PET investigation. *Dementia, 5*, 88–98.

Heller, W. (1993). Gender differences in depression: Perspectives from neuropsychology. *Journal of Affective Disorders, 29*, 129–143.

Heller, W., Etienne, M. A., & Miller, G. A. (1995). Patterns of perceptual asymmetry in depression and anxiety: Implications for neuropsychological models of emotion and psychopathology. *Journal of Abnormal Psychology, 104*, 327–333.

Henggler, S. W., Edwards, J. J., Cohen, R., & Summerville, M. B. (1992), Predicting changes in children's popularity: The role of family relations. *Journal of Applied Developmental Psychology, 12*, 205–218.

Henson, R., Shallice, T., & Dolan, R. (2000). Neuroimaging evidence for dissociable forms of repetition primary. *Science, 287*(5456), 1269–1272.

Herschkowitz, N., Kagan, J. & Zilles, K. (1997) Neurobiological basis of behavioral development in the first year. *Neuorpediatrics. 28,* 296–306.

Heuther, G. (1998) Stress and the adaptive self-organization of neuronal connectivity during early childhood. *International Journal of Developmental Neuorscience, 16,* 297–306.

Hickie, I., & Lloyd, A. (1995). Are cytokines associated with neuropsychiatric syndromes in humans? *International Journal of Immunopharmocology, 17,* 677–683.

Hill, J. (2003). Early identification of individuals at risk for antisocial personality disorder. *British Journal of Psychiatry, 182*(Suppl. 144), 11–12.

Hoff, E. (2003). The specificity of environmental influence: Socioeconomic status affects early vocabulary development via maternal speech. *Child Development, 74*(5), 1368–1376.

Horgan, J. (1999). *The undiscovered mind: How the human brain defies replication, medication, and explanation.* New York: Free Press.

Horiuchi, V., Good, J., & Kapos, K. (1996, May 15). He was really a good kid: Did deaths of two students push busjacker over the edge? *Salt Lake Tribune,* pp. A1, A5.

Howe, M. L. (2000). *The fate of early memories: Developmental science and the retention of childhood experiences.* Washington, DC: American Psychological Association.

Howe, M. L., Toth, S. L., & Cicchetti, D. (2006). *Memory and developmental pathology, Vol. 2, Developmental Neuroscience* (pp. 629–655). Hoboken, NJ: Wiley.

Hudson, J. L., Kendall, P. C., Coles, M. E., Robin, J. A., & Webb, A. (2002). The other side of the coin: Using intervention research in child anxiety disorders to inform developmental psychopathology. *Developmental and Psychopathology, 14,* 819–841.

Huff, F., & Growdon, J. (1984). Dietary enhancement of CNS neurotransmitter. *Integrative Psychiatry,* 149–154.

Hugdahl, K., & Davidson, R.J. (Eds.). (2003). *The asymmetrical brain.* Cambridge, MA: MIT Press.

Huttenlocher, P. R. (1990). Morphometric study of human cerebral cortex development. *Neuropsychologia, 28,* 517–527.

Hynd, G. W., Semrud-Clikeman M., Lorys, A. R., Novey, E. S., Eliopulos, D., & Lyytine, H. (1991) Corpus callosum morphology in attention deficit-hyperactivity disorder: Morphometric analysis of MRI. *Journal of Learning Disabilities Research Review, 6*(1), 59–67.

Iacoboni, M. (2003). Understanding intentions through imitations. In S. Johnson (Ed.), *Taking action: Cognitive neuroscience perspectives on intentional acts* (pp. 107–138). Cambridge, MA: MIT Press.

Iacoboni, M. (2005). Understanding others: Imitation, language, empathy. In S. Hurly & N. Chater (Eds.), *Perspectives on imitation: From neuroscience to social science. Vol. I, Mechanisms of imitation and imitation in animals* (pp. 77–100). Cambridge, MA: MIT Press.

Iacoboni, M., & Lenzi, G. L. (2002). Mirror neurons, the insula, and empathy. *Behavioral and Brain Sciences, 25*, 107–138.

Iacoboni, M., Lieberman, M. D., Knowlton, B. J., Molnar-Szakacs, I., Moritz, M., Throop, C. J., et al. (2004). Watching social interactions produces dorsomedial prefrontal and medial parietal fMRI signal increases compared to a resting baseline. *NeuroImage, 21*, 1167–1173.

Insel, T. R. (2003). Is social attachment an addictive disorder? *Physiology & Behavior, 79*, 351–357.

Insel, T. R., & Young, L. J. (2001). The neurobiology of attachment. *Nature Reviews Neuroscience, 2*, 129–136.

Isley, S., O'Neil, R., & Parke, R. D. (1996). The relation of parental affect and control behavior to children's classroom acceptance: A concurrent and predictive analysis. *Early Education and Development, 7*, 7–73.

Izard, C. E., Fantauzzo, C. A., Castle, J. M., Haynes, O. M., Rayias, M. F., & Putnam, P. H. (1995). The ontogeny and significance of infants's facial expressions in the first 9 months of life. *Developmental Psychology, 31*, 997–1013.

Jackson, J. H. (1884/1932). *Selected writings of John Hughlings Jackson*. London: Hodder & Stoughton.

Jacobs, B. L., van Prag, H., & Gage, F. H. (2000). Depression and the birth and death of brain cells. *American Scientist, 88*, 340–345.

Jacobson, L., & Sapolsky, R. (1991). The role of the hippocampus in feedback regulation of the hypothalamic-pituitary-adrenocortical axis. *Endrocrine Reviews, 12*(2), 118–134.

James, W. (1890). *The principles of psychology*. New York: Holt.

Jausovec, N. (2000). Differences in cognitive processes between gifted, intelligent, creative and average individuals while solving complex problems: An EEG study. *Intelligence, 28*, 213–237.

Jausovec, N., & Jausovec, K. (2001). Differences in EEG current density related to intelligence. *Cognitive Brain Research, 12*, 55–60.

Jelicic, L., & Merckkelback, H. (2004). Traumatic stress, brain changes, and memory deficits: A critical note. *Journal of Nervous and Mental Disease, 192*(8), 548–553.

Johnsen, B. H., & Hugdahl, K. (1991). Hemispheric asymmetry in conditioning to facial emotional expressions. *Psychophysiology, 28*, 154–162.

Johnson, M. A. (2004). Hull house. In J. R. Grossman, A. Durkin, & J. L. Reiff (Eds.). *The encyclopedia of Chicago*. Chicago: University of Chicago Press.

Jones, N. A., Field, T., & Davalos, M. (2000). Right frontal EEG asymmetry and lack of empathy in preschool children of depressed mothers. *Child Psychiatry and Human Development, 30*, 189–204.

Jung, C. G. (1971). Psychological types. In W. McGuire (Ed.) *The collected works of C. G. Jung*. Vol. 6. Bollinger Series XX. Princeton, NJ: Princeton University Press.

Kagan, J. (1992). Behavior, biology, and the meanings of temperamental constructs. *Pediatrics, 90*, 510–513.

Kagan, J. (1994). *Galen's prophecy*. New York: Basic Books.

Kagan, J. (1998). *Biology and the child*. In W. Damon (Series Ed.) & N. Eisenberg (Vol. Ed.) *Handbook of child psychology: Vol. 3. Social, emotional, and personality development* (5th ed., pp. 105–176). New York: Wiley.

Kagan, J., Arcus, D., Snidman, N., & Rimm, S. E. (1995). Asymmetry of the forehead temperament and cardiac activity. *Neuropsychology, 9*, 1–5.

Kagan, J., & Herschkowitz, N. (2005). *A young mind into a growing brain*. Mahwah, NJ: Lawrence Erlbaum.

Kagan, J. & Snidman, N. (1991) Temperamental factors in human development. *American Psychologist, 46*, 856–862.

Kagan, J., & Snidman, N. (2004). *The long shadow of temperament*. Cambridge, MA: Harvard University Press.

Kagan, J., Snidman, N., Zentner, M., & Peterson, E. (1999). Infant temperament and anxious symptoms in school age children. *Development and Psychopathology, 11*, 209–224.

Kahn, J. (1995) Adolescent depression: An overview. (Available from the University of Utah Neuropsychiatric Institute, 501 Way, Salt Lake City, Utah, 84108.

Kaiser Permanente Northern California Regional Psychiatry and Chemical Dependency Best Practices, Second Edition Panic Guideline Team. (2001a). *Clinical practice guideline for the treatment of panic disorder in psychiatry* (2nd ed.). Oakland, CA: Kaiser Permanente.

Kaiser Permanente Northern California Regional Psychiatry and Chemical Dependency Best Practices, OCD Guideline Team. (2001b). *Clinical practice guideline for the treatment of obsessive-compulsive disorder in adults and children in psychiatry*. Oakland, CA: Kaiser Permanente.

Kaiser Permanente Northern California Regional Psychiatry and Chemical Dependency Best Practices, Adolescent Depression Best Practices Workgroup. (2003). *Recommendations for the treatment of despression in adolescents*. Oakland, CA: Kaiser Permanente.

Kaiser Permanente Northern California Regional Psychiatry and Chemical Dependency Best Practices, Attention Deficit and Hyperactivity Workgroup. (2004). *Practice recommendations for the diagnosis and treatment of attention deficit hyperactivity disorder*. Oakland, CA: Kaiser Permanente.

Kaiser Permanente Northern California Regional Psychiatry and Chemical Dependency Best Practices, Intimate Partner Abuse Best Practices Workgroup. (2005). *Recommendations for assessing and treating intimate partner abuse*. Oakland, CA: Kaiser Permanente.

Kaiser Permanente Northern California Regional Psychiatry and Chemical Dependency Best Practices, Anxiety Best Practices Workgroup. (2008). *Clinical practice guideline for the treatment of social anxiety disorder*. Oakland, CA: Kaiser Permanente.

Kalafat, J. (2004). Suicide. In T. P. Gullotta & G. R. Adams (Eds.), *Handbook of adolescent behavioral problems: Evidence-based approaches to prevention and treatment* (pp. 231–254). New York: Springer.

Kalin, N. H., Larson, C., Shelton, S. E., & Davidson, R. J. (1998). Asymmetric frontal brain activity, cortisol, and behavior associated with fearful temperament in rhesus monkeys. *Behavioral Neuroscience, 112*, 286–292.

Kalin, N. H., Shelton, S. E., & Lynn, D. E. (1995) Opiate systems in mother and infant primates coordinate intimate contact during reunion. *Psychoneuroendocrinology, 20(7)*, 735–742.

Kalin, N. H., Shelton, S. E., & Snowdon, C. T. (1993). Social factors regulating security and fear in infant rhesus monkeys. *Depression, 1*, 137–142.

Kandel, E. R. (1998). A new intellectual framework for psychiatry. *American Journal of Psychiatry, 155*, 457–469. (Kandel spelled wrong in text)

Kandel, E. R., & Squire, L. (2000). Neuroscience: Breaking down scientific barriers to the study of brain and mind, *Science, 290*, 1113–1120.

Kapp, B. S., Supple, W. F., & Whalen, R. (1994). Effects of electrical stimulation of the amygdaloid central nucleus of neurocortical arousal in the rabbit. *Behavior Neuroscience, 108*, 81–93.

Kashdan, T. B., & Herbert, J. D. (2001). Social anxiety disorder in childhood and adolescence: Current status and future directions. *Clinical Child and Family Psychology Review, 4(1)*, 37–61.

Kaslow, N. J., Adamson, L. B., & Collins, M. H. (2000). A developmental psychopathology perspective on cognitive components of child and adolescent depression. In A. J. Sameroff, M. Lewis, & S. M. Miller (Eds.), *Handbook of developmental psychopathology* (2nd ed., pp. 491–510). New York: Plenum Press.

Katz, F. K., & Woodin, E. (2002). Hostility, hostile development, and conflict engagement in marriages: Effect on child and family functioning. *Child Development, 73*, 636–656.

Katz, L. F., & Gottman, J. M. (1995). Vagal tone protects children from from marital conflict. *Development and Psychopathology, 36*, 569–540.

Kaye, K. (1982). *The mental and social life of babies.* Chicago: University of Chicago Press.

Kazdin, A. E. (1997). Parent management training: Evidence, outcome, and issues. *Journal of Child and Adolescent Psychiatry, 36*, 1349–1356.

Kazdin, A. E., & Weisz, J. R. (1998). Identifying and developing empirically support child and adolescent treatment of antisocial children. *Cognitive Therapy and Research, 21*, 185–207.

Keating, D. P. (2004). Cognitive and brain development. In R. J. Lerner & L. D. Steinberg (Eds.), *Handbook of adolescent psychology* (2nd ed., pp. 45–84). Hoboken, NJ: Wiley.

Kegan, R. (1994). *In over our heads: The mental demands of modern life.* Cambridge, MA: Harvard University Press.

Kemperman, G., Kuhn, H. G., & Gagge, F. H. (1995). More hippocampal neurons in adult mice living in an enriched environment. *Nature, 386(6624)*, 493–495.

Kemperman, G. Kuhn, H. G., & Gage, F. H. (1998) Experience induced neurogenesis in the senescent dentate gyrus. *Journal of Neuroscience. 18*, 3206–3212.

Kemperman, G., Kuhn, H. G., & Gagge, F. H. (2000). Activity-dependent regulation of neuronal plasticity and self-repair. *Progress in Brain Research, 127,* 35–48.

Kendall, P. C., Flannery-Schroeder, E., Panichelli-Mindel, S. M., Southam-Gerow, M., Henin, A., & Warman, M. (1997). Therapy for youths with anxiety disorders: A second randomized clinical trial. *Journal of Consulting and Clinical Psychology, 65*(3), 366–380.

Kendler, K. S., Karkowski, L. M., & Prescott, C. A. (1999). Fears and phobias: Reliability and heritability. *Psychological Medicine, 29*(3), 539–553.

Kendler, K. S., Myers, J., Prescott, C. A., & Neale, M. C. (2001). The genetic epidemiology of irrational fears and phobias in men. *Archives of General Psychiatry, 58*(3), 257–265.

Kensinger, E. A., & Corkin, S. (2004). Two routes to emotional memory: Distinct neural processes for valence and arousal. *Proceedings of the National Academy of Sciences of the USA, 101,* 3310–3315.

Kessler, R. C., Adler, L. A., Barkley, R. Biederman, J., Conners, C. K., Faraone, S. V., et al. (2005). Patterns and predictors of attention-deficit/hyperactivity disorder persistence into adulthood: Result from the national comorbidity survey replication. *Biological Psychiatry, 57*(11), 1442–1451.

Kessler, R. C., Avenevoli, S., & Ries Merikangas, K. (2001). Mood disorders in children and adolescents: An epidemiological perspective. *Biological Psychiatry, 49*(12), 1002–1014.

Kessler, R. C., Berglund, P., Demler, O., et al. (2005). Lifetime prevalence and age-of-onset distributions of DSM-IV disorders in the National Comorbidity Survey Replication. *Archives of General Psychiatry, 62,* 593–602.

Keverne, E. B., Martens, N. D., & Tuite, B. (1989). Beta-endorphin concentrations in cerebrospinal fluid of monkeys are influenced by grooming relationships. *Psychoneuroendocrinology, 18,* 307–321.

Kilts, C. D., Egan, G., Gideon, D. A., Ely, T. D., & Hoffman, J. M. (2003). Dissociable neural pathways are involved in the recognition of emotion in static and dynamic facial expressions. *NeuroImage, 18,* 156–168.

Kimura, D. (1999). *Sex and cognition.* Cambridge, MA: MIT Press.

Kirschbaum, C., & Hellhammer, D. H. (1994). Salivary cortisol in psychoneuroendrocrine research: Recent developments and application. *Psychoneuroendrocrinology, 19,* 313–333.

Klein, M. (1975/1921–1945). *The collected writings of Melanie Klein. Vol. 1, Love, guilt and reparation and other works 1921–1945.* London: Hogarth Press.

Klerman, G. L., Weissman, M. M., Rounsaville, B. J., and Chevron, E. S. (1984). *Interpersonal psychotherapy of depression: A brief focused specific strategy.* New York: Basic Books.

Klerman, G. L., & Weissman, M. M. (1989). Increasing rates of depression. *Journal of the American Medical Association, 261,* 2229–2235.

Kleinschmidt, A., Bess, M. F., & Singer, W. (1987). Blockade of "NMDA" receptors disrupts experience-based plasticity of kitten striate cortex. *Science, 238,* 355–358.

Klimes-Dougan, B., Hastings, P. D., Granger, D. A., Usher, B. A., & Zahn-Waxler, C. (2001). Adrenocortical activity in at-risk and normally developing adolescents: Individual differences in salivary cortisol basal levels, diurnal variation, and responses to social challenges. *Development and Psychopathology, 13*(695), 117–142.

Knight, R. T., & Grabowecky, M. (1995). Escape from linear time: Prefrontal cortex and conscious experience. In M. S. Gazzaniga (Ed.), *The cognitive neurosciences* (pp. 1357–1371). Cambridge, MA: MIT Press.

Kochanska, G. (1994). Beyond cognition: Expanding the search for the early roots of internalisation and conscience. *Developmental Psychology, 30,* 20–22.

Kochanska, G., Murray, K. T., & Harlan, E. T. (2000). Effortful control in early childhood: Continuity and change, antecedents, and implications for social development. *Developmental Psychopathology, 36,* 230–232.

Kolb, B. (1989). Brain development, plasticity, and behavior. *American Psychologist, 44,* 1203–1212.

Kolb, B. (1995). *Brain plasticity and behavior.* Mahwah, NJ: Lawerence Erlbaum.

Kolb, B., Forgie, M., Gibb, R., Gorny, G., & Rowntree, S. (1998). Age, experience, and the changing brain. *Neuroscience and Biobehavioral Reviews, 22,* 143–159.

Kolb, B., & Gibb, R. (2002). Frontal lobe plasticity and behavior. In T. Donald & T. Robert (Eds.), *Principles of frontal lobe function* (pp. 541–556). New York: Oxford University Press.

Kolb, B., & Winshaw, I. Q. (2003). *Fundamentals of human Neuropsychology* (5th Ed.). New York: Freeman.

Kolb, B., & Whishaw, I. O. (1998). Brain plasticity and behavior. *Annual Review of Psychology, 49,* 43–64.

Krawczyk, D. C. (2002). Contributions of the prefrontal cortex to the neural basis of human decision making. *Neuroscience and Biobehavioral Reviews, 26,* 631–664.

Kruczek, T., Salsman, J. R., & Vitanz, S. (2004). Prevention and treatment of post-traumatic stress disorder in adolescents. In T. P. Gullotta & G. R. Adams (Eds.), *Handbook of adolescent behavioral problems: Evidence-based approaches to prevention and treatment* (pp. 331–350). New York: Springer.

Kruesi, M. J. P., Schmidt, M. E., Donnelly, M., Hibbs, E. D., & Hamberburger, S. D. (1989) Urinary free cortisol output and disruptive behavior in children. *Journal of the American Academy of Child and Adolescent Psychiatry, 28,* 441–443.

Kruesi, M. J., Casanova, M. F., Mannhein, G., & Johnson-Bilder, A. (2004). Reduced temporal lobe volume in early onset conduct disorder. *Psychiatry Research, 132,* 1–11.

Kubitz, K. K., Landers, D. M., Petuzzello, S. J., & Han, M. W. (1996). The effects of acute and chronic exercise on sleep. *Sports Medicine, 21*(4), 277–291.

Kuhn, C. M., & Schanberg, S. M. (1998). Responses to maternal separation: Mechanisms and mediators. *International Journal of Developmental Neuroscience, 16,* 261–270.

Kumakira, C., Kodama, K., Shimiza, E., Yamanouchi, N., Okada, S., Noda, et al. (1991). Study of the association between the serotonin transporter gene regulating region polymorphism and personality traits in the Japanese population. *Neuroscience Letters*, *263*, 205–207. (Date wrong in text)

LaBar, K. S. (2007). Beyond fear: Emotional memory mechanisms in the human brain. *Current Directions in Psychological Science*, *16*, 173–177.

Lacasse, J. R., & Leo, J. (2005, November 8). Serotonin and depression: A disconnect between the advertisements and the scientific literature. *PLoS Med.* 2(12): e392. Published online. doi: 10.1371/journal.pmed.0020392.

Lambert, N. M. (1998). Adolescent outcomes of hyperactive children. *American Psychologist*, *43*, 786–799.

Lambert, M. J., & Barley, D. E. (2002). Research summary on the therapeutic relationship and psychotherapy outcome. In J. D. Norcross (Ed.), *Psychotherapy relationships that work: Therapist contributions and responsiveness to patients*. New York: Oxford University Press.

Lane, R. D. (1998). Neural correlates of levels of emotional awareness: Evidence of an interaction between emotion and attention in the anterior cingulate cortex. *Journal of Cognitive Neuroscience*, *10*, 525–535.

Lanius, R. A., Williamson, P. C., Densmore, M., Boksman, K., Neufeld, R. W., Gati, J. S., et al. (2004). The nature of traumatic memories: A 4-T fMRI functional connectivity analysis. *American Journal of Psychiatry*, *161*, 36–44.

Larsen, R. J., Kasimatis, M., & Frey, K. (1992). Facilitating the furrowed brow: An unobtrusive test of the facial feedback hypothesis applied to unpleasant affect. *Cognition and Emotion*, *6*, 321–338.

Last, C., Hansen, C., & Franco, N. (1998). Cognitive-behavioral therapy of school phobia. *Journal of the American Academy of Child and Adolescent Psychiatry*, *37*, 404–411.

Lazar, I., Darlington, R., Murray, H., Royce, J., & Snipper, A. (1982). Lasting effects of early education: A report from the Consortium for Longitudinal Studies. *Monographs of the Society for Research in Child Development*, *47* (Serial No. 195).

LeDoux, J. (1996). *The emotional brain: The mysterious underpinnings of emotional life.* New York: Simon and Schuster.

LeDoux, J. (2002). *The synaptic self: How brains become who we are.* New York: Penguin.

Lee, J. R., Mulsow, M., & Reifman, A. (2003). Long-term correlates of attention deficit hyperactivity disorder: A meta-analysis. *Journal of Family and Consumer Sciences.*

Lenartowicz, A., & McIntosh, A. R. (2005). The role of anterior cingulate cortex in working memory is shaped by functional connectivity. *Journal of Cognitive Neuroscience*, *17*, 1026–1042.

Leonard, H. L., & Swedo, S. E. (2001). Pediatric autoimmune neuropsychiatric disorders associated with streptococcal infection (PANDAS). *International Journal of Neuropsychpharmacology*, *4*(2), 1919–1980.

Leppanen, J., & Hietanen, J. (2003). Affect and face perception. *Emotion*, *3*, 315–326.

Levine, S., (2001) Primary social relationships influence the development of the hypothalamic-pituitary-adrenal axis in the rat. *Physiology and Behavior, 73*, 255–260.

Levitt, J. G., Blanton, R. E., Smalley, S., Thompson, P. M., Gutherie, D., McCracken, J. T., et al. (2003). Cortical sulcal maps in autism. *Cerebral Cortex, 13*, 728–735.

Lewinsohn, P. M., Roberts, R. E., Seeley, J. R.Rohde, P., Gotlib, I. H., & Hops, H. (1994). Adolescent psychopathology: II. Psychosocial risk factors for depression. *Journal of Abnormal Psychology, 103*, 302–315.

Lewinsohn, P. M., Rohde, P., Kleine, D. N., & Seeley, J. R. (1999). Natural course of adolescent major depressive disorder: I. Continuity into young adulthood. *Journal of the American Academy of Child & Adolescent Psychiatry, 38*, 56–63.

Lewis, D. A. (1997). Development of the prefrontal cortex during adolescence: Insights into vulnerable neural circuits in schizophrenia. *Neuropsychopharmocology, 16*, 385–398.

Lewis, M., Alessandri, S. M., & Sullivan, M. W. (1990). Violation of expectancy, loss of control, and anger expression in young infants. *Developmental Psychology, 26*, 745–751.

Lewis, M., & Michaelson, L. (1985). Faces as signs and symbols. In G. Zivin (Ed.), *Development of expressive behavior: Biological-environment interaction.* New York: Plenum.

Lewis, M. D. (1995). Cognition-emotion feedback and the self-organization of developmental paths. *Human Development, 38*, 71–102.

Lieberman, M., & Eisenberger, N. I. (2005). A pain by any other name (rejection, exclusion, ostracism) still hurts the same: The role of dorsal anterior cingulate cortex in social and physical pain. In J. Cacioppo (Ed.), *Social neuroscience: People thinking about people.* Cambridge, MA: MIT Press.

Lilja, A., Hagstdius, S., Risberg, J., Salford, L. G., & Smith, G. L. W. (1992). Frontal lobe dynamics in brain tumor patients: A study of regional cerebral blood flow and after surgery. *Journal of Neuropsychiatry and Neuropsychological Behavioral Neurology, 5*, 294–300.

Linehan, M. (1993). *Cognitive-behavioral treatment of borderline personality disorder.* New York: Guilford Press.

Loehlin, J. C., Neiderhiser, J. M., & Reiss, D. (2005). Genetic and environment components of adolescent adjustment and parental behavior: A multivariate analysis. *Child Development, 76*(5), 1104–1115.

Lougee, L., Perlmutter, S. J., Nicholson, R., Garvey, M. A., & Swedo, S. E. (2000). Psychiatric disorders in first degree relatives of children with pediatric autoimmune neuropsychiatric disorders associated with streptococco infections (PANDAS). *Journal of the American Academy of Child and Adolescent Psychiatry, 39*(9), 1120–1126.

Lonigan, C. J., Philips, B. M., & Ricky, J. A. (2003). Posttraumatic stress disorder in children: Diagnosis, assessment, and associated feature. *Children and Adolescent Psychiatric Clinic of North America, 12*, 171–194.

Lopez, J. F., Akil, H., & Watson, S. J. (1999). Neural circuits mediating stress. *Biological Psychiatry, 46,* 1461–1471.

Luciana, M. (2006). Cognitive neuroscience and the prefrontal cortex: Normative development and vulnerability to psychopathology. In D. Citthetti & D. Cohen (Eds.), *Developmental psychopathology Vol. 2, Developmental Neuroscience* (pp. 292–332). Hoboken, NJ: Wiley.

Lupien, S. J., Ouellet-Morin, I., Hupbach, A., Tu, M. T., Buss, C., Walker, D., Pruessner, J., & McEwen, B. S. (2006). Beyond the stress concept: Allostatic load—A developmental, biological, and cognitive perspective. In D. Cicchetti & D. Cohen (Eds.), *Development psychopathology. Vol. 2, Developmental Neuroscience* (pp. 578–628). Hoboken, NJ: Wiley.

Lynch, M., & Cicchetti, D. (1998). Trauma, mental representation, and the organization of memory for mother-referent material. *Development and Psychopathology, 10,* 235–257.

Maccari, S., Danaudery, M., Morley-Fletcher, S., Zuena, A. R., Cinque, C., & Van Reeth, O. (2003). Prenatal stress and long-term consequences: Implications of glucocorticoids hormones. *Neuroscience and Biobehavioral Reviews, 27,* 119–127.

Madras, B. K., Miller, G. M., & Fischman, A. J. (2002). The dopamine transporter: Relevance to attention deficit hyperactivity disorder (ADHD). *Behavioral Brain Research, 130,* 57–63.

Maguire, E. A., Godian, D. G., Johnsrude, I. S., Good, C. D., Ashburner, R. S., Frakowiak, R. S., & Frith, C. (2000). Navigation-related structural change in the hippocampi of taxi cab drivers. *Proceedings of the National Academy of Sciences, USA, 97*(8), 4398–4403.

Main, M. (1991). Metacognitive knowledge, metacognitive monitoring, and singular (coherent) vs. multiple (incoherent) models of attachment: Findings and directions for future research. In C. M. Parkes, J. Stevenson-Hinde, & P. Marris (Eds.), *Attachment across the life cycle* (pp. 127–159). London: Tavistock/Routledge.

Main, M. (1995). Attachment: Overview, with implications for clinical work. In S. Goldberg, R. Muir, & J. Kerr (Eds.), *Attachment theory: Social developmental and clinical perspectives* (pp. 407–474). New York: Guilford Press.

Main, M., Hesse, E., & Kaplan, N. (1985). Predictability of attachment behavior and representational processes. In K. E. Grossmann, K. Grossmann, & E. Waters (Eds.), *Attachment from infancy to adulthood: Lessons from longitudinal studies* (pp. 245–304). New York: Guilford Press.

Main, M., & Solomon, J. (1990). Discovery of a disorganized/disoriented attachment pattern. In T. B. Brazelton & M. W. Yogman (Eds.). *Affective development in infancy,* pp. 95–124. Norword, NJ: Ablex.

Main, M., & Hesse, E. (1990). Parents' unresolved traumatic experiences are related to infant disorganized status: Is frightened and/or frightening parental behavior the linking mechanism? In M. T. Greenburg, D. Cicchetti, & E. M. Cummings (Eds.), *Attachment in the preschool years: Theory, research, and intervention* (pp. 161–182). Chicago: University of Chicago Press.

Maitland, S. B., Herlitz, A., Nyberg, L., Backman, L., & Nilsson, L. G. (2004). Selective sex differences in declarative memory. *Memory and Cognition, 32,* 1160–1169.

Mangelsdorf, S., Gunnar, M., Vestenbaum, R., Lang, S., & Adresas, D. (1990). Infant proneness to distress temperament, maternal personality and mother-infant attachment. *Child Development, 61,* 820–831.

Manke, B., Saudino, K. J., & Grant, J. D. (2001). Extreme analyses of observed temperament dimensions. In R. N. Emde & J. K. Hewitt (Eds.), *Infancy to early childhood,* 52–72. New York: Oxford University Press.

March, J., & Mulle, K. (1998). *OCD in Children and adolescents: A cognitive-behavioral treatment manual.* New York: Guilford Press.

March, J. S., Franklin, M., Nelson, A., & Foa, E. (2001). Cognitive-behavioral psychotherapy for pediatric obsessive-compulsive disorder. *Journal of Clinical Child Psychology, 30*(1), 8–18.

Markowitsch, H. J.Vanderkerckhove, M. M. P., Lanfermann, H., & Russ, M. O. (2003). Brain circuts for the retrival of sad and happy autobiographic episodes. *Cortex, 39,* 643–665.

Marrocco, R. T., & Davidson, M. C. (1998). Neurochemistry of attention. In R. Parasuranman (Ed.), *The attention brain* (pp. 35–50). Cambridge, MA: MIT Press.

Martin, A., Wiggs, C. L., & Weisberg, J. (1997). Modulation of human medial temporal lobe activity by form, meaning, and experience. *Hippocampus, 7,* 587–593.

Marzi, A., & Berlucchi, G. (1997). Right visual field superiority for accuracy of recognition of famous faces in normals. *Neuropsychologia, 15*(6), 751–756.

Mason, J. W. (1968). A review of psychoendocrine research on the sympathetic-adrenal medullary system. *Psychosomatic Medicine, 30*(Suppl. 5), 631–653.

Masten, A. S., & Reed, M. G. (2002). Resilience in development. In S. R. Synder & S. J. Lopez (Eds.), *The handbook of positive psychology* (pp. 74–88) Oxford, UK: Oxford University Press.

Mathew, S. J., Coplan, J. D., & Gorman, J. M. (2001). Neurobiological mechanisms of social anxiety disorder. *American Journal of Psychiatry, 158*(10), 1558–1567.

Mayberg, H. (2007). *Address to the Kaiser Permanente Medical Center's Annual Psychiatry Conference,* San Francisco, CA.

Mayer, N. K., & Tronick, E. Z. (1985). *Mothers' turn-giving signals and infant turn-taking mother-infant interaction.* In T. M. Field & N. A. Fox (Eds.), *Social perception in infants.* Norwood, NJ: Ablex.

McAdams, D. (1999). Personal narratives and life story. In L. A. Perwin & O. P. John (Eds.), *Handbook of personality: Theory and research* (pp. 478–500). New York: Guilford Press.

McCabe, A., & Peterson, C. (1991). Getting the story: A longitudinal study of parental styles in eliciting narratives and developing narratives and developing narrative skill. In A. McCabe & C. Peterson (Eds.), *Developing narrative structure* (pp. 217–253). Hillsdale, NJ: Lawrence Erlbaum.

McCraty, R., Atkinson, M., Tomasion, D., & Tiller, W. A. (1998). The electricity of touch: Detection and measurement of cardiac energy exchange between people. In K. H. Pribram & J. King (Eds.), *Brain and Values: Is biological science of values possible?* (pp. 359–379). Hillsdale, NJ: Erlbaum.

McDonald, D. G., & Hodgdon, J. A. (1991). *The psychological effects of aerobic fitness training: Research and theory.* New York: Springer-Verlag.

McEwen, B. (1999). Development of the cerebral cortex. XIII: Stress and brain development—II. *Journal of the American Academy of Child and Adolescent Psychiatry, 38,* 101–103.

McEwen, B. S. (1998). Stress, adaptation, and disease: Allostasis and allostatic load. *Annals of the New York Academy of Science, 840,* 33–44.

McEwen, B. S., & Stellar, E. (1993). Stress and the individual—Mechanisms leading to disease. *Archives of Internal Medicine, 153,* 2093–2101.

McEwen, B. S., & Wingfield, J. C. (2003). The concept of allostasis in biology and biomedicine. *Hormones and Behavior, 43,* 2–15.

McFarland, D. (2001). Respiratory markers of conversational interaction. *Journal of Speech, Language, and Hearing Research, 44,* 128–145.

McGaugh, J. L. (2004). The amygdala modulates the consolidation of memories of emotionally arousing experiences. *Annual Review of Neuroscience, 27,* 1–28.

McNaughton, B. L. (1987). Hippocampal synaptic enhancement and information storage. *Trends in Neuroscience, 10,* 408–415.

McNaughton, B. L. (1991). Associative pattern competition in hippocampal circuts: New evidence and new questions. *Brain Research Review, 16,* 202–204.

Meaney, M. J. (2001). Maternal care, gene expression, and the transmission of individual differences in stress reactivity across generations. *Annual Review of Neuroscience, 24,* 1161–1192.

Meaney, M. J., Aitken, D. H., Viau, V., Sharma, S., & Sharrieau, A. (1989) Neonatal handling alters adrenalcortical feedback sensitivity and hippocampus type II glucocorticoid receptor binding in the rat. *Neuroendrocrinology, 50,* 597–604.

Meins, E. (1997). Security of attachment and maternal tutoring strategies: Interaction within the zone of proximal development. *British Journal of Development Psychology, 15,* 129–144.

Mellin, E., & Beamish, P. (2002). Interpersonal theory and adolescents with depression: Clinical update. *Journal of Mental Health Counseling, 24,* 110–125.

Meltzoff, A., & Goopnick, A. (1993). The role of imitation in understanding persons and developing a theory of mind. In S. Baron-Cohen, H. Tager-Flusbert, & D. Cohen (Eds.), *Understanding other minds.* New York: Oxford University Press.

Meltzoff A., & Moore, M. (1977). Imitation of facial and manual gestures by human neonates. *Science, 198,* 75–78.

Meltzoff, P. H. (1995). Understanding the intensions of others: Re-enactment of intended acts by 18-month-old child. *Developmental Psychology, 31,* 838–850.

Mesulam, M. M. (1998). From sensation to cognition. *Brain, 121,* 1013–1052.

Michael, K. D., & Crowley, S. L. (2002). How effective are treatments for child and adolescent depression? A meta-analytic review. *Clinical Psychology Review, 22,* 247–269.

Michelson, D., et al. (2002) Atomoxetine in the treatment of children and adolescent with Attention-Deficit/Hyperactivity Disorder: A randomized, placebo-controlled, dose-response study. *Pediatric electronic abstracts,* e83.

Michelson, D., et al. (2002, November). Once-daily atomoxetine treatment for children and adolescents with attention deficit hyperactivity disorder: A randomized, placebo-controlled study. *American Journal of Psychiatry, 159,* 1896–1901.

Mitchell, S. A., & Black, M. J. (Eds.). (1995). *Freud and beyond: A history of modern psychoanalytic thought.* New York: Basic Books.

Miller, L., Koerner, K., & Kanter, J. (1998). Dialectical behavior therapy. Part II. Clinical application of DBT for patients with multiple problems. *Journal of Practical Psychology.*

Mirescu, C., Peters, J. D., & Gould, E. (2004). Early life experience alters response of adult neurogenesis to stress. *Nature Neuroscience, 7*(8), 841–846.

Mitchell, J. T., & Everly, G. S. Jr. (2000). Critical incident stress management and critical incident stress debriefings: Evolutions, effects, and outcomes. In B. Raphael & J. P. Wilson (Eds.), *Psychological debriefing: Theory practice, and evidence* (pp. 71–90). New York: Cambridge University Press.

Mitchell, S. A., & Black, M. J. (Eds.). (1995). *Freud and beyond: A history of modern psychoanalytic thought.* New York: Basic Books.

Miyake, K., Campos, J., Bradshaw, D., & Kagan, J. (1986). Issues in socioemotional development. In H. Stevenson, H. Azuma, & K. Hakuta (Eds.), *Childhood development and education in Japan.* New York: Freeman.

Miyake, K., Chen, S., & Campos, J. (1985). Infant temperament, mother's mode of interaction, and attachment in Japan. In I. Bretherton & E. Waters (Eds.), Growing points in attachment theory and research. *Monographs of the Society for Research in Child Development, 50* (1/2, Serial No. 209), 276–297.

Monaghan, D., Bridges, R., & Cotman, C. (1989). The excitatory amino acid receptors. *Annual Review of Pharmacology Toxicology, 29,* 365–402.

Monk, C., Sloan, R. P., Myers, M. M., Ellman, L., Werner, E., et al. (2004). Fetal heart rate reactivity differs by women's psychiatric status: An early marker for developmental risk? *Journal of American Academy of Child and Adolescent Psychiatry, 43*(3), 283–290.

Morris, B. J., & Sloutsky, V. (2001). Children's solutions of logical versus empirical problems: What's missing and what develops? *Cognitive Development, 16,* 907–928.

MTA Cooperative Group (1999) A 14-month randomized clinical trial of treatment strategies for Attention Deficit/Hyperactivity Disorder. *Archives of General Psychiatry, 56,* 1073–1086.

Mufson, L., Weissman, N., Moreau, D., & Garfinkel, R., (1997). Efficacy of interpersonal psychotherapy for depressed adolescents. *Archives of General Psychiatry, 56,* 573–579.

Mymberg, J. H. & van Nloppen, B. (1994). Obsessive-compulsive disorder: A concealed diagnosis. *American Family Physician, 49*(5), 1129–1137.

Nachmias, M., Gunnar, M. R., Mangelsdorf, S., Parritz, R. H., & Buss, K. (1996). Behavioral inhibition and stress reactivity: The moderating role of attachment security. *Child Development, 67*, 508–522.

National Academy of Sciences. (2003). *Proceedings of the National Academy of Sciences, 99*(1), 309–314.

Nauert, R. Gene protects from depression after childhood abuse. *PsychCentral.* http://psychcentral.com/news/2008/02/06/gene-protects-from-depression-after-childhood-abuse/1880.html.

Nelson, C. A. (2000). The neurobiological bases of early intervention. In J. Shonkoff & S. Meisels (Eds.), *Handbook of early childhood intervention* (2nd ed., pp. 204–227). New York: Cambridge University Press.

Nelson, E. E., Leibenluft, E., McClure, E. B., & Pine, D. S. (2005). The social re-orientation of adolescence: A neuroscience perspective on the process and its relation to psychopathology. *Psychological Medicine, 35*, 163–174.

Nemeroff, C. B. (1996). The corticotrophin-releasing factor (CRF) hypothesis of depression: New findings and new directions. *Molecular Psychiatry, 1*, 336–342.

Neville, H. J., Bavelier, D., Corina, D., Rauschecker, J., Karni, A., Lalwani, A., et al. (1998). Cerebral organization for language in deaf and hearing subjects: Biological constraints and effects of experience. *Proceedings of the National Academy of Sciences, USA, 95*, 922–929.

Nikolaenko, N. N., Egorov, A. Y., & Frieman, E. A. (1997). Representational activity of the right and left hemispheres of the brain. *Behavioral Neurology, 10*, 49–59.

Nimchinsky, E. A., Gilissen, E., Allman, J. M., Perl, D. P., Erwin, J. M., & Hof, P. R. (1999). A neuronal morphologic type unique to humans and great apes. *Proceedings of the National Academy of Sciences, USA, 96*, 5268–5273.

Nimchinsky, E. A., Vogt, B. A., Morrison, J. H., & Hof, P. R. (1995). Spindle neurons of the human anterior cingulate cortex. *Journal of Comparative Neurology, 355*, 27–37.

Nitschke, J. B., Nelson, E. E., Rusch, B. D., Fox, A. S., Oakes, T. R., & Davidson, R. J. (2003). Orbitofrontal cortex tracks positive mood in mothers viewing pictures of their newborn infants. *NeuroImage, 21*, 583–592.

Nobler, M. S., Sakheim, H. A., Prohovnick, I., Moeller, J. R., Mukherjee, S., Schur, D. B., et al. (1994). Regional blood flow in mood disorders: III. Treatment and clinical response. *Archives of General Psychiatry, 51*(2), 887–897.

Nobre, A. C., Coull, J. T., Frith, C. D., & Mesulam, M. M. (1999). Orbitofrontal cortex is activated during breaches of expectation in tasks of visual attention. *Nature Neuroscience, 2*, 11–12.

Norcross, J. C. (Ed.). (2001). Empirically supported therapy relationships: Summary report of the Division 29 Task Force. *Psychotherapy, 38*(4), 345–356.

Norcross, J. D. (Ed.). (2002). *Psychotherapy relationships that work: Therapist contributions and responsiveness to patients, Chapter 1: Empirically supported relationships, pp. 3–32.* New York: Oxford University Press.

North, T. C., McCullagh, P., & Tran, Z. V. (1990). Effect of exercise on depression. *Exercise and Sport Science Reviews, 18,* 379–415.

Nowicki, S., & Duke, S. (2002). *Will I ever fit in?* New York: Free Press.

Ochs, E., & Schieffelin, B. B. (1984). Language acquisition and socialization: Three developmental stories and their implications. In R. Schweder & R. LeVine (Eds.), *Culture theory: Essays on the mind, self, and emotion.* Cambridge, UK: Cambridge University Press.

Ochsner, K. (2006). How thinking controls feeling: A social cognitive neuroscience approach. In P. Winkleman & E. Harmon-Jones (Eds.), *Social neuroscience.* New York: Oxford University Press.

Ochsner, K., & Gross, J. (2005). The cognitive control of emotion. *Trends in Neuroscience, 9,* 242–249.

Ochsner, K. N., Bunge, S. A., Gross, J. J., & Gabrieli, J. D. E. (2002). Rethinking feelings: An fMRI study of the cognitive regulation of emotion. *Journal of Cognitive Neuroscience, 14,* 1215–1229.

O'Connor, K. P., Aardema, F., Robillard, S., Guay, S., Pélissier, M.-C., Todorov, C., et al. (2006). Cognitive behaviour therapy and medication in the treatment of obsessive-compulsive disorder. *Acta Psychiatrica Scandinavica, 113*(5), 408–419.

O'Connor, P. J., & Youngstedt, M. A. (1995). Influence of exercise on human sleep. *Exercise and Sports Science Review, 23,* 105–134.

O'Connor, T. G., Heron, J., Golding, J., Beveridge, M., & Glover, V. (2002). Maternal antenatal anxiety and children's behavioral/emotional problems at 4 years: Report from the Avon Longitudinal Study of Parents and Children. *British Journal of Psychiatry, 180,* 502–508.

Ogawa, J. R., Sroufe, L. A., Weinfeld, N. S., Carlson, E. A. & Egeland, B. (1997). Development and the fragmented self: Longitudinal study of dissociated symptomatology in a nonclinical sample. *Development and Psychopathology, 9,* 855–880.

Olney, J., Lubruyere, J., Wang, G., Wozniak, D. F., Price, M. T., & Sesma, M. A. (1991). NMDA antagonist neuotoxicity: Mechanism and prevention. *Science, 257,* 1515–1518.

Ollendick, T., & King, N. (1998). Empirically supported treatments for children with phobic and anxiety disorders: Current status. *Journal of Clinical Child Psychology, 27,* 156–167.

Pajer, K., Gardner, W., Rubin, R. T., Perel, J., & Neal, S. (2001). Decreased cortisol levels in adolescent girls with conduct disorder. *Archives of General Psychiatry, 58*(3), 297–302.

Panksepp, J. (1998). *Affective neuroscience: The foundations of human and animal emotions.* New York: Oxford University Press.

Pantev, C., Engelien, A., Candia, V., & Elbert, T. (2001). Representational cortex in musicians: Plastic alterations in response to musical practices. *Annals of the New York Academy of Sciences, 930,* 300–314.

Pantev, C., Oostenveid, R., Engelien, A., Ross, B., Roberts, L. E., & Hoke, M. (1998). Increased auditory cortical representation in musicians. *Nature, 392,* 811–814.

Parent, M. B., West, M., & McGaugh, J. L. (1994). Memory of rats with amygdala regions 30 days after footshock—motivated escape training reflects degree of original training. *Behavioral Neuroscience, 108,* 1080–1087.

Parke, R. D., & Buriel, R. (1998). Socialization in the family: Ethnic and ecological perspective. In W. Damon (Series Ed.), N. Eisenberg (Vol. Ed.), *Handbook of child psychology,* Vol. 3 (pp. 463–552). New York: Wiley.

Pascual-Leone, A. (2001). The brain that plays music and is changed by it. *Annals of the New York Academy of Sciences, 930,* 315–329.

Pascual-Leone, A., & Torres, F. (1993). Plasticity of the sensorimotor cortex representation of the reading finger in Braille readers. *Brain, 116,* 39–52.

Peleaz-Nogueras, M., Field, T., Cigales, M., Gonzalez, A., & Clasky, S. (1994). Infants of depressed mothers show less "depressed" behavior with their nursery teachers. *Infant Mental Health Journal, 15,* 358–367.

Pelham, W., Jr., Wheeler, T., & Chronis, A. (1998). Empirically supported psychosocial treatment for attention deficit hyperactivity disorder. *Journal of Clinical Child Psychology, 27,* 190–205.

Pelphrey, K. A., Sasson, N. J., Reznick, J. S., Paul, G., Goldman, B. D., & Piven, J. (2002). Visual scanning of faces in autism. *Journal of Autism and Developmental Disorders, 32,* 249–261.

Perry, B. D., Pollard, R. A., Blakey, T. I., Baker, W. L., & Vigilante, D. (1995). Childhood trauma, the neurobiology of adaptation and "use dependent" development of the brain; How "states" become "traits." *Infant Mental Health Journal, 16*(4), 271–291.

Persinger, M. A., & Makarec, K. (1991). Greater right hemisphericity is associated with lower self-esteem in adults. *Perceptual and Motor Skills, 73,* 1244–1246.

Phillips, A. (1993) *On kissing, tickling and being bored: Psychoanalytic essays on the unexamined life.* Cambridge, MA: Harvard University Press.

Piaget, J. (1951). *The child's conception of the world.* London: Routledge and Kegan Paul.

Piaget, J. (1952). *The origins of intelligence in children.* New York: International Universities Press.

Piaget, J., & Inhelder, B. (1969). *The psychology of the child.* New York: Basic Books.

Pierce K. and Courchesne, E. (2000) Exploring the neurofunctional organization of face processing in autism [comment]. *Arch. Gen. Psychiatry. 57,* pp. 344–346.

Pike, A., & Plomin, R. (1996). Importance of nonshared environmental factors for childhood and adolescent psychopathology. *Journal of the American Academy of Child and Adolescent Psychiatry, 35,* 560–570.

Pina, A. A., Silverman, W. K., Fuentes, R. M., Kurtines, W. M., & Weems, C. F. (2003). Exposure-based cognitive-behavioral treatment for phobia and anxiety disorders: Treatment effects and maintenance for Hispanic/Latino to European youths. *Journal of the American Academy of Child and Adolescent Psychiatry, 42,* 1179–1187.

Pine, D. S., & Cohen, J. A. (2002). Trauma in children and adolescence: Risk and treatment of psychiatric sequelae. *Biological Psychiatry, 51*, 519–531.

Pollak, S. D. (2001). P3b reflects maltreated children's reactions to facial displays of emotion. *Psychophysiology, 38*, 267–274. (no et al in text)

Pollak, S. D., Cicchetti, D., Hornung, K., & Reed, A. (2000). Recognizing emotional faces: Developmental effects of child abuse and neglect. *Developmental Psychology, 68*, 773–787.

Pollak, S. D., & Sinha, P. (2002). Effects of early experience on children's recognition of facial displays of emotion. *Development Psychology, 38*(5), 784–791.

Pollack, S., & Tolley-Schell, S. (2003). Selective attention to facial emotion in physically abused children. *Journal of Abnormal Psychology, 112*, 323–338.

Porges, S. W., Doussard-Roosevelt, J. A., & Maiti, A. K. (1994). Vagal tone and the physiological regulation of emotion. In N. Fox (Ed.), Biological and behavioral foundations of emotion regulation. *Monographs of the Society for Research in Child Development, 59* (2–3, Serial No. 240), 167–186.

Posner, M. I., & Rothbart, M. K. (1998). Attention, self-regulation, and consciousness. *Philosophical Transactions of the Royal Society of London Biological Sciences, 353*(1377), 1915–1927.

Post, R. M., & Weiss, S. R. B. (1997). Emergent properties of neural systems: How focal molecular neurobiological alterations can affect behavior. *Development and Psychopathology, 9*, 907–929.

Premack, D. G., & Woodruff, G. (1978). Does the chimpanzee have a theory of mind? *Behavioral and Brain Sciences, 1*, 515–526.

Preston, S. D., & de Waal, F. B. M. (2002). Empathy: Its ultimate and proximate bases. *Behavioral and Brain Sciences, 25*, 1–72.

Prochaska, J. O., & Norcross, J. D. (2002). *Systems of psychotherapy: A transtheoiretical analysis* (5th ed.). Pacific Grove, CA: Brooks/Cole.

Puce, A., Allison, T., Gore, J. C., & McCarthy, G. (1995). Face-sensitive regions in human extrastriate cortex studied by functional MRI. *Journal of Neurophysiology, 74*, 1192–1199.

Pynoos, R. S., Steinberg, A. M., & Piacentini, J. C. (1999). A developmental psychopathology model of childhood traumatic stress and intersection with anxiety disorders. *Biological Psychiatry, 46*, 1542–1554.

Pynoos, R. S., Frederick, C., & Nader, K. (1987). Life threat and post-traumatic stress in school-age children. *Archives of General Psychiatry, 44*, 1057–1063.

Pynoos, R. S., Goenjian, A., Tashjian, M., Karakashian, M., Manjikian, R., Manoukian, G., et al. (1993). Post-traumatic stress reactions in children after the 1988 Armenian earthquake. *British Journal of Psychiatry, 163*, 239–247.

Rajkowska, G. (2003). Depression: What we can learn from postmortem studies. *Neuroscientist, 9*(4), 273–284.

Ramey, C. T., Campbell, F. A., Burchinal, M., Skinner, M. L., Gardiner, D. M. & Ramey, S. L. (2000) Persistent effects of early childhood education on high-risk children and their mothers. *Applied Developmental Psychology, 4*, 214.

Ramin, C. J. (2007). *Carved in sand: When attention fails and memory fades in midlife.* New York: HarperCollins.

Ramnani, N., & Miall, R. C. (2004). A system in the human brain for predicting the actions of others. *Nature Neuroscience, 7,* 85–90.

Reiman, E. M., Raichle, M. E., Butler, F. K., Hersocovitch, P., & Robins, E. (1984). A focal brain abnormality in panic disorder, a severe form of anxiety. *Nature, 310,* 683–685.

Reinhertz, H. A., Giaconia, R. M., Lefkowitz, E. S., Pakic, B., & Frost, A. K. (1993). Prevalence of psychiatric disorders in a community of older adolescents. *Journal of the American Academy of Child and Adolescent Psychiatry, 32,* 369–377.

Reiss, D., Neiderhiser, J. M., Hetherington, E. M., & Plomin, R. (2000). *The relationship code: Deciphering genetic and social patterns in adolescent development.* Cambridge, MA: Havard University Press.

Rezai, K., Andreason, N. C., Alliger, R., Cohen, G., Swayze, V., & O'Leary, D. S. (1993). The neuropsychology of the prefrontal cortex. *Archives of Neurology, 50,* 636–642.

Rilling, J. K., Gutman, D. A., Zeh, T. R., Panoni, G., Berns, G. S., & Kilts, C. D. (2002). A neural basis for social cooperation. *Neuron, 35,* 395–405.

Rilling, J. K., & Insel, T. R. (1999). Differential expansion of neural projection systems in primate brain evolution. *NeuroReport, 10,* 1453–1459.

Rizzolatti, G., & Arbib, M. A. (1998). Language within our grasp. *Trends in Neurosciences, 21,* 188–194.

Rizzolatti, G., Fadiga, L., & Gallese, V. (2001). Neurophysiological mechanisms underlying understanding and imitation. *Nature Reviews Neuroscience, 2,* 66–70.

Rizzolatti, G., Fadiga, L., Gallese, V., & Fogassi, C. (1996). Pre-motor cortex and the recognition of motor action. *Cognitive Brain Research, 3*(2), 131–141.

Robert, C., & Bishop, B. (2004). Depression. In T. P. Gullotta & G. A. Adams, *Handbook of behavioral problems: Evidence-based approaches to prevention and treatment* (pp. 200–230). New York: Springer.

Robin, A. L., (2007, October 19). Assessing and treating adolescents with ADHD. Address to the Northern California Psychiatry and CDS ADHD Best Practices Champions, Napa, CA.

Rochat, P. (2002). Various kinds of empathy as revealed by the developing child, not the monkey's brain. *Behavioral and Brain Science, 25,* 45–46.

Roehrs, T. (1993). Alcohol. In M. A. Carskadon, A. Rochtschaffen, G. Richardson, R. Roth, & W. Dement (Eds.), *Principles and practice of sleep medicine* (3rd ed., pp. 414–418). Philadelphia: W. S. Saunders.

Rogosch, F. A., Cicchetti, D., Shields, A., & Toth, S. L. (1995). Parenting dysfunction in child maltreatment. In M. H. Bornstein (Ed.), *Handbook of parenting. Vol. 4, Applied and practical parenting,* pp. 127–159. Mahwah, NJ: Erlbaum.

Roman, T., Szobot, C., Martins, S., Biederman, J., Rohde, L. A., & Hutz, M. H. (2002). Dopamine transporter gene response to methylphenidate in attention-deficit hyperactivity disorder. *Pharmacogenetics, 12,* 497–499.

Rosenberg, I., & Miller, J. (1992). Nutritional factors in physical and cognitive functions of elderly people. *American Journal of Clinical Nutrition*, *55*, 12373–12435.

Ross, E. D., Homan, R. W., & Buck, R. W. (1994). Differential hemispheric lateralization of primary and social emotions: Implications for developing a comprehensive neurology for emotions, repression, and the subconscious. *Neuropsychology and Behavior Neurology*, *7*(1), 1–19.

Rothbart, M. K., & Bates, J. E. (1998). Temperament. In W. Damon (Series Ed.) & N. Eisenberg (Vol. Ed.), *Handbook of child psychology: Vol. 3. Social, emotional, and personality development* (5th ed., pp. 105-176). New York: Wiley.

Rothbart, M. K., & Derryberry, D. (2002). Temperament in child. In C. von Hofsten & L. Bäckmen (Eds.), *Psychology at the turn of the millennium: Vol. 2. Social, developmental, and clinical perspectives* (pp. 17–35). East Sussex, UK: Psychology Press.

Rothbart, M. K., & Posner, M. I. (2006). Temperment, attention, and developmental psychopathology. In D. Cicchetti & D. Cohen (Eds.), *Developmental psychopathology: Vol. 2. Developmental neuroscience* (pp. 465–502). New York: Wiley.

Rubia, K., Overmeyer, S., Taylor, E., Brammer, M., Williams, S. C. R., Simmons, A., et al. (1999). Hypofrontality in attention deficit hyperactivity disorder during higher-order motor control: A study with functional MRI. *American Journal of Psychiatry*, *156*, 891–896.

Rubin, K. H., Bukowski, W., & Parker, J. G. (1998). Peer interactions, relationships, and groups. In W. Damon (Series Ed.) & N. Einsenberg (Vol. Ed.), *Handbook of child psychology: Vol 2: Cognition, Perception, and Language* (pp. 619–700). New York: Wiley.

Rubin, K. H., Burgess, K. B., Kennedy, A. E., & Steward, S. L. (2003). Social withdrawal in childhood. In E. J. Mash & R. A. Barkley (Eds.), *Child psychopathology* (2nd ed., pp. 372–408). New York: Guilford Press.

Rudebeck, P. H., Buckley, M. J., Walton, M. E., & Rushworth, M. F. S. (2006). A role for the macaque anterior cingulate gyrus in social valuation. *Science*, *313*, 1310–1312.

Rutter, M., and the English and Romanian Adoptees (ERA) Study Team. (1998). Developmental catch-up, and deficit, following adoption after severe global early privation. *Journal of Child Psychology and Psychiatry*, *39*(4), 465–476.

Rutter, M., Kreppner, J., & O'Connor, T. (2001). Specificity and heterogeneity in children's responses to profound institutional privation. *British Journal of Psychiatry*, *179*, 97–103.

Saarni, C., Mumme, D., & Campos, J. J. (1998). Emotional development: Action, communication, and understanding. In W. Damon (Series Ed.) & N. Eisenberg (Vol. Ed.), *Handbook of child psychology: Vol. 3. Social, emotional, and personality development* (5th ed., pp. 237–309) New York: Wiley.

Sabbagh, M. A. (2004). Understanding orbital frontal contributions to the theory-of-mind reasoning. Implications for autism. *Brain and Cognition*, *55*, 209–219.

Sadato, N., Pascual-Leone, A., Grafman, J., Ibanez, V., Delber, M. F., Dodd, G., et al. (1996). Activation of the primary visual cortex by Braille reading in blind subjects. *Nature*, *380*, 526–528.

Safran, J. D., & Muran, J. C. (2003). *Negotiating the therapeutic alliance: A relational treatment guide*. New York: Guilford Press.

Salinger, J. D. (1951). *The catcher in the rye*. Boston: Little, Brown.

Sandler, J., & Freud, A. (1985). *The analysis of defense*. New York: International Universities Press.

Sandu, S., Cook, P., & Diamond, M. C. (1985). Rat cortisol estrogen receptors: male-female, right-left. *Experimental Neurology, 92*(1), 186–196.

Sapolsky, R. M. (1997). The importance of a well-groomed child. *Science, 277*, 1620–1621.

Sapolsky, R. M. (1996). Why stress is bad for your brain. *Science, 273*, 749–750.

Sapolsky, R. M. (1998). *Why zebras don't get ulcers: An updated guide to stress, stress-related diseases and coping* (2nd Ed.). New York: W. H. Freeman and Co.

Sapolsky, R. M. (2004). *Why zebras don't get ulcers*. New York: Henry Holt.

Sapolsky, R. M., Romero, L. M., & Munck, A. U. (2000). How do glucorcorticoids influence stress response? Integrating permissive suppressive, stimulatory, and preparative actions. *Endocrine Reviews, 21*, 55–89.

Saxena, S., Brody A. L., Maidment, K. M., Dunkin, J. J., Colgan, M., Alborzian, S., Phelps, M. E., Baxter, L. R., Jr (1999). Localized orbitofrontal and subcortical metabolic changes and predictors of response to paroxetine treatment in obsessive-compulsive disorder. *Neuropsychopharmacology, 21*(6): 683–93.

Saxena, S., Brody, A. L., Maidment, K. M., Smith, E. C., Zohrabi, N., Katz, E., et al. (2004). Cerebral glucose metabolism in obsessive-compulsive hoarding. *American Journal of Psychiatry, 161*(6), 1038–1048.

Scarr, S. (1992). Development and individual differences. *Child Development, 63*, 119.

Scarr, S., (1993) Biological and cultural diversity: The legacy of Darwin for development. *Child Development, 64*, 1333–1353.

Schaie, K. W., & Willis, S. L. (1986). Can decline in adult intellectual functioning be reversed? *Developmental Psychology, 22*(2), 121–128.

Schechter, D. S. (2004). How post-traumatic stress affects mothers' perceptions of their babies: A brief video feedback intervention makes a difference. *Zero to Three, 24*(3), 143–165.

Schiffer, F., Teicher, M. H., & Papanicolaou, A. C. (1995). Evoked potential evidence for right brain activity during the recall of traumatic memories. *Journal of Neuropsychiatry and Clinical Neurosciences, 7*, 169–175.

Schmidt, L. A. (1999). Frontal brain electrical activity in shyness and sociability. *Psychological Science, 10*, 316–321.

Schmidt, L. A., Trainor, L. J., & Santesso, D. L. (2003). Development of frontal electroencephalogram (EEG) and heart rate (ECG) responses to affective musical stimuli during the first twelve months of post natal life. *Brain and Cognition, 52*, 27–32.

Schoenbaum, G., Chiba, A., & Gallagher, M. (2003). Orbitofrontal and basolateral amygdala encode expected outcomes during learning. *Journal of Neurophysiology, 89*, 2823–2838.

Schoenbaum, G., Setlow, B., Nugent, S. L., Saddoris, M. P. A., & Gallagher, M. (2003). Lessons of orbito frontal cortex and basolateral amygdala complex disrupt acquisition of odor-guided discriminations and reversals. *Learning and Memory, 10*, 129–140.

Schore, A. N. (1994). *Affect regulation and the origins of the self: The neurobiology of emotional development*. Hillsdale, NJ: Lawrence Erlbaum.

Schore, A. N. (1997). A century after Freud's Project—Is a rapprochement between psychoanalysis and neurobiology at hand? *Journal of the American Psychoanalytic Association, 45*, 1–34.

Schore, A. N. (2002). Clinical implications of psychoneurobiological model of projective identification. In S. Alhanati (Ed.), *Primitive mental states*, Vol. 2, 1–65. New York: Karnac.

Schore, A. N. (2003). *Affect regulation and the repair of the self*. New York: Norton.

Searlman, A. (1977). A review of right hemisphere linguistic capabilities. *Psychological Bulletin, 84*(3), 503–528. (spelled wrong in text)

Schmand, B., Smit, J. H., Geerlings, M. I., & Lindeboom, J. (1997). The effects of intelligence and education on the development of dementia: A test of the brain reserve hypothesis. *Psychological Medicine, 27*, 1337–1344.

Schwartz, C. E., Wright, C. I., Shin, L. M., et al. (2003). Inhibited and uninhibited infants grown up: Adult amygdalar response to novelty. *Science, 300*, 1952–1953.

Searlman, A. (1977). A review of right hemisphere linguistic capabilities. *Psychological Bulletin, 84*(3), 503–528. (spelled wrong in text).

Seeman, T. E., Glei, D., Goldman, N., Weinstein, M., Singer, B., & Lin, Y. H. (2004). Social relationships and allostatic load in Taiwanese elderly and near elderly. *Social Science and Medicine, 59*(11), 2245–2257.

Seeman, T. E., Lusignolo, T. M., Albert, M., & Berkman, L. (2001). Social relationships, social support, and patterns of cognitive aging in healthy, high-functioning older adults: MacArthur studies of successful aging. *Health Psychology, 20*(4), 243–255.

Segal, L. B., Oster, H., Cohen, M., Caspi, B., Myers, M., & Brown, D. (1995). Smiling and fussing in seven-month-old preterm and full-term Black infants in the still-face situation. *Child Development, 66*, 1829–1843.

Segal, M. (2003). Dendritic spines and long-term plasticity, *Nature, 6*, 277–284.

Segal, Z. V., Williams, J. M. G., & Teasdale, J. D. (2002). *Mindfulness-based cognitive therapy for depression: A new approach to preventing relapse*. New York: Guilford Press.

Sergent, J., Ohta, S., & MacDonald, B. (1992). Functional neuroanatomy of face and object processing. *Brain, 115*, 15–36.

Shaffer, D., Fisher, P., Dulkan, M. K, et al. (1996). The NIMH Diagnostic Interview Schedule for Children version 2.3 (DISC–2.3): Ddescription, acceptability, prevalence rates and performance in the MECA study. *Journal of the American Academy of Child and Adolescent Psychiatry, 35*(7), 865–877.

Sheline, Y. I. (2003). Neuroimaging studies of mood disorder effects on the brain. *Biological Psychiatry, 54*(3), 338–352.

Sheline, Y. I., Sanghavi, M., Mintun, M. A., & Gado, M. H. (1999). Depression duration but not age predicts hippocampal volume loss in medically healthy women with recurrent major depression. *Journal of Neuroscience, 19*, 5034–5043.

Shoda, Y., Mischel, W., & Peake, P. K. (1990). Predicting adolescent cognitive and self-regulatory competencies from preschool delay of gratification: Identifying diagnostic conditions. *Development Psychology, 26*, 978–986.

Shoenthaler, S., Stephen, A., & Doraz, W. (1991). Controlled trail of vitamin-mineral supplementation on intelligence and brain function. *Personal Differences, 12*, 343–350.

Shore, R. (1997). *Rethinking the brain.* New York: Families and Work Institute.

Siegel, D. J. (1999). *Developing mind: Toward a neurobiology of interpersonal experience.* New York: Guilford Press.

Siegel, D. J., & Hartzell, M. (2004). *Parenting from the inside out.* New York: Jeremy P. Tarcher/Penguin.

Siegel, R. E. (1968). *Galen's system of physiology and medicine.* Basel: Kargel.

Silver, L. B. (1999). *Attention-deficit hyperactivity disorder* (2nd ed.). Washington, DC: American Psychiatric Press.

Silverman, W. K., Kurtines, W. M., Ginburg, G. S., Weems, C. F., Rabian, B., & Saraine (1999). Contingency management, self-control, and education support in the treatment of childhood phobic disorders: A randomized clinical trait. *Journal of Consulting and Clinical Psychology, 67*, 995–1003.

Simonian, S. J., Beidel, D. C., Turner, S. M., Berkes, J. L., & Long, J. H. (2001). Recognition of facial affect by children and adolescents diagnosed with social phobia. *Child Psychiatry and Human Development, 32*(2), 137–145.

Singer, B., & Ryff, C. D. (1999). Hierarchies of life histories and associated health risks. *Annals of the New York Academy of Sciences, 896*, 96–116.

Skarda, C. A., & Freeman, W. J. (1987). How brains make chaos in order to make sense of the world. *Behavioral and Brain Sciences, 10*, 161–195.

Smith, B., Waschbusch, D., Willoughby, M., & Evans, S. (2000). The efficacy, safety, and practicality of treatments for adolescents with attention-deficit/hyperactivity disorder (ADHD). *Clinical Child and Family Psychology Review, 3*, 243–267.

Society for Neuroscience (2000). Brain briefings: Astrocytes. http://www.sfn.org/index.cfm?pagename=brainbriefings_astrocytes.

Solms, M., & Saling, M. (1990). *A moment of transition: Two neuroscientific articles by Sigmund Freud.* London: Karnac Books and the Institute for Psycho-Analysis.

Solomon, G. F., & Moos, R. H. (1965). The relationship of personality to the presence of rheumatoid factor in asymptomatic relatives of patients with rheumatoid arthritis. *Psychosomatic Medicine, 27*, 350.

South-Gerow, M. A, Kendall, P. C., & Weersing, V. R. (2001). Examing outcome variability: Correlates of treatment response in a child and adolescent anxiety clinic. *Journal of Child Clinical Psychology, 30*, 422–436.

Spear, L. P. (2000). The adolescent brain and age-related behavioral manifestations. *Neuroscience and Biobehavioral Reviews, 24*, 417–463.

Spence, S. H., Donovan, C., & Brechman-Tousaint, M. (2000). The treatment of childhood social phobia: The effectiveness of a social skills based cognitive-behavioral intervention, without parental involvement. *Journal of Clinical Psychology and Psychiatry, 41*, 731–726.

Spitz, R. A. (1983). *Dialogues from infancy: Selected papers*. R. N. Emde (Ed.). New York: International Universities Press.

Springer, S., & Deutsch, G. (1998). *Left brain, right brain: Perspectives from cognitive neuroscience*. New York: W. H. Freeman

Sroufe, L. A. (1996). *Emotional development: The organization of emotional life in the early years*. New York: Cambridge University Press.

Sroufe, L. A., Egeland, B., Carlson, E. A., & Collins, W. A. (2005). *The development of the person: The Minnesota study of risk and adaptation from birth to adulthood*. New York: Guilford Press.

Stallard, P. (2000). Debriefing adolescents after critical life events. In B. Raphael & J. P Wilson (Eds.), *Psychological debriefing: Theory, practice, and evidence* (pp. 213–224). New York: Cambridge University Press.

Stams, G. J. M., Juffer, F., & Van IJzendoorn, A. H. (2002). Maternal sensitivity, infant attachment, and temperament in early childhood predict adjustment in middle school. *Developmental Psychology, 38*, 806–821.

Stein, P., & Kendall, J. (2003). *Psychological trauma and the developing brain: Neurologically based interventions for troubled children*. Binghamton, NY: Haworth Maltreatment and Trauma Press.

Steinberg, L., Dahl, R., Keating, D., Kupfer, D. J., Masten, A. S., & Pine, D. S. (2006). The study of developmental psychopathology in adolescence: Affective neuroscience with the study of context. In D. Cicchetti & D. Cohen (Eds.), *Developmental psychopathology: Vol. 2. Developmental neuroscience* (pp. 710–741). Hoboken, NJ: Wiley.

Steinberg, L., Lamborn, S. D. Dornbusch, S., & Darling, N. (1992). Impact of parenting practices on adolescent achievement: Authoritative parenting, school involvement, and encouragement to succeed. *Child Development, 63*, 1266–1281.

Sterling, P., & Eyer, J. (1998). Allostasis: A new paradigm to explain arousal pathology. In S. Fischer & J. Reason (Eds.), *Handbook of life stress, cognition and health* (pp. 629–649). New York: Wiley.

Stern, D. N. (1985). *The interpersonal world of the infant: A view from psychoanalysis and developmental psychology*. New York: Basic Books.

Stern, D. N., Sander, L. W., Nahum, J. P., Harrison, A. M., Lyons-Ruth, K., Morgan, A. C., et al. (1998). Non-interpretive mechanisms in psychoanalytic psychotherapy. The "something more" than interpretation. *International Journal of Psychoanlaysis, 79*, 903–921.

Stuss, D. T., Alexander, M. P., Floden, D., Binns, M. A., Levine, B., McIntosh, A. R., et al. (2002). Fractionation and localization of distinct frontal lobe process: Evidence from focal lesion in humans. In D. T. Stuss & R. T. Knight (Eds.), *Principles of frontal lobe function* (pp. 392–407). New York: Oxford University Press.

Sullivan, R. M., & Gratton, A. (2002). Prefrontal cortical regulation of hypo-thalamic-pituitary adrenal function in the rat and implications for psycho-pathology: Side matters. *Psychoneuroendrocrinology, 27*, 99–114.

Susman, E. J., & Rogel, A. (2004). Puberty and psychological development. In R. M. Lerner & L. Steinberg (Eds.), *Handbook of adolescent psychology* (2nd ed., pp. 15–44). Hoboken, NJ: Wiley.

Takahashi, K. (1990). Are the key assumptions of the "Strange Situation" proce-dure universal? A view from Japanese research. *Human Development, 33*, 23–30.

Tangney, J., & Fischer, K. (Eds.). (1995). *Self-conscious emotions: The psychology of shame, guilt, emabarrassment, and pride*. New York: Guilford Press.

Taylor, W. D., Steffens, D. C., MacFall, J. R., McQuiod, D. R., Payne, M. E., Provenzale, J. M., et al. (2003). White matter hyperintensity progression and late-life depression outcomes. *Archives of General Psychiatry, 60*(11), 1090–1096.

Teasdale, J. D., Howard, R. J., Cox, S. G., Ha, Y., Brammer, M. J., Williams, S. C. R., & Checkley, S. A. (1999). Functional MRI study of the cognitive generation of affect. *American Journal of Psychiatry, 156*, 209–215.

Teichner, G., & Golden, C. J. (2000). The relationship of neuropsychological impairment to conduct disorder in adolescence: A conceptual review. *Aggression and Violent Behavior, 5*, 509–528.

Teicher, M. H. (2002). Scars that won't heal: The neurobiology of child abuse. *Scientific American, 286*(3), 68–75.

Teicher, M. H., Andersen, S. L., & Hostetter, J. C. (1995). Evidence for dopamine receptor pruning between adolescence and adulthood in striatum but not nucleus accumbens. *Developmental Brain Research, 89*, 167–172.

Teicher, M. H., Andersen, S. L., Polcari, A., Anderson, C. M., & Navalta, C. P. (2002). Developmental neurobiology of childhood stress and trauma. *Psychiatric Clinics of North America, 25*, 397–426.

Teichner, M. H., Anderson, S. L., Polcari, A., Anderson, C. M., Navalta, C. P., & Kim, D. M. (2003). The neurobiological consequences of early stress and childhood maltreatment. *Neuroscience and Biobehavioral Reviews, 27*, 33–44.

Teicher, M. H., Dumont, N. L., Ito, Y., Vaituzis, C., Geidd, J. N., & Andersen, S. L. (2004). Childhood neglect is associated with reduced corpus callosum area. *Biological Psychiatry, 56*, 80–85.

Teicher, M. H., Glod, C. A., Surrey, J., & Swett, C., Jr. (1993). Early childhood abuse and limbic system ratings in adult psychiatric outpatients. *Journal of Neuro-psychiatry and Clinical Neurosciences, 5*, 301–306.

Teicher, M. H., Ito, Y., Glod, C. A., Andersen, S. L., Dumont, N., & Ackerman, E. (1997). Preliminary evidence for abnormal cortical development in physically and sexually abused children using EEG coherence and MRI. *Annals of the New York Academy of Sciences, 821*, 160–175.

Teuber, H.-L. (1964). The riddle of frontal lobe function in man. In J. M. Warren & K. Akert (Eds.). *The frontal granular cortex and behaviour* (pp. 410–444). New York: McGraw-Hill.

Thatcher, R. W., Walker, R. A., & Giudice, S. (1987). Human cerebral hemispheres develop at different rates and ages. *Science, 236*, 1110–1113.

Thayer, J. F., & Cohen, B. H. (1985). Differential hemispheric lateralization for positive and negative emotion: An electromyographic study. *Biological Psychology, 21*(4), 265–266.

Thomas, A., & Chess, S. (1977). *Temperament and development.* New York: Brunner/Mazel.

Thompson, P. M., Giedd, J. N., Woods, R. P., MacDonald, D., Evans, A. C., & Toga, A. W. (2000). Growth patterns in the developing brain detected by using continuum mechanical tensor maps. *Nature, 404*, 190–193.

Thompson, R. A. (1999). Early attachment and later development. In J. Cassidy & P. R. Shaver (Eds.), *Handbook of attachment: Theory, research, and clinical applications* (pp. 265–286). New York: Guilford Press.

Tillfors, M. (2004). Why do some individuals develop social phobia? A review with emphasis on the neurobiological influences. *Nordic Journal of Psychiatry, 58*(4), 267–276.

Treatment of Adolescents with Depression Study Team. (2004). Fluoxetine, cognitive-behavioral therapy, and their combination for adolescents with depression. *Journal of the American Medical Association, 292*: 807–820.

Treadwell, K. R. H., Flannery-Schroeder, E. C., & Kendell, P. C. (1995). Ethnicity and gender in relative to adaptive functioning, diagnostic status, and treatment outcome in children from an anxiety clinic. *Journal of Anxiety Disorders, 9*, 373–384.

Trevarthen, C. (1993). The self born in intersubjectivity: The psychology of an infant communicating. In U. Neisser (Ed.), *The perceived self: Ecological and interpersonal sources of self-knowledge.* Cambridge: Cambridge University Press.

Trevarthen, C. (1996). Lateral asymmetries in infancy: Implications for the development of the hemispheres. *Neuroscience and Biobehavioral Reviews, 20*, 1–16.

Tronick, E. (1989). Emotion and emotional communication in infants. *American Psychologist, 44*, 112–119.

Tronick, E. Z., & Weinberg, M. K. (1997). Depressed mothers and infants: Failure to form dyadic states of consciousness. In L. Murray, & P. J. Cooper (Eds.), *Postpartum Depression and Child Development* (pp. 54–81). New York: Guilford Press.

Tronick, E. (1989). Emotion and emotional communication in infants. *American Psychologist, 44*, 112–119.

True, W. R., Rice, J., Eisen, S. A., Heath, A. C., Goldberg, J., Lyons, M. J., et al., (1993). A twin study of genetic and environment contributions to liability for posttraumatic stress symptoms. *Archives of General Psychiatry, 50*, 257–264.

Tucker, D., Penland, J., Sanstead, H., et al. (1990). Nutritional status and brain function in aging. *Journal of Clinical Nutrition, 52*, 93–102.

Tucker, D. M., Luu, P., & Pribram, K. H. (1995). Social and emotional self-regulation. In J. Grafman & K. J. Hoyoak,(Eds.), *Structure and functions of the human prefrontal cortex,* (pp. 213–239). New York: New York Academy of Sciences.

Tupler, L. A., Krishnan, K. R., McDonald, W. N., Dombeck, C. B., D'Souza, S., & Steffens, D. C. (2002). Anatomic location and laterality of MRI signal hyper-intensities in late-life depression. *Journal of Psychosomatic Research, 53*(2), 665–676.

Twenge, J. M., & Nolen-Hoeksema, S. (2002). Age, gender, race, socioeconomic status, and birth cohort differences on the Children's Depression Inventory: A meta-analysis. *Journal of Abnormal Psychology, 111,* 578–588.

Ullman, M. T., Miranda, R. A., & Travers, M. L. (2008). Sex differences in the neurocognition of language. In J. B. Becker, K. J. Berkley, N. Geary, E. Hampson, J. P. Herman, & E. A. Young (Eds.), *Sex differences in the brain: From genes to behavior* (pp. 291–309). New York: Oxford University Press.

Underwood, M. K., Coie, J. D., & Herbsman, C. R. (1992). Display rules for anger and aggression in school-age children. *Child Development, 62,* 366–380.

University of Utah Neuropsychiatric Institute. *Adolescent depression: An overview.* Available from author, 501 Chipeta Way, Salt Lake City, UT 84108.

Urry, H. L., Nitschke, J. B., Dolski, I., Jackson, D. C., Dalton, K. M., Mueller, C. J., et al. (2004). Making a life worth living: Neural correlates of well-being. *Psychological Science, 15*(6), 367–372.

Uvnäs-Moberg, K. (1998). Oxytocin may mediate the benefits of positive social interaction and emotions. *Psychoneuroendocrinology, 23,* 819–835.

Vaidya, C. J., Austin G., Kirkorian G., Ridlehuber, H. W., Desmond J. E., Glover, G. H., et al. (1998). Selective effects of methylphenidate in attention deficit hyper-activity disorder: A functional magnetic resonance study. *Proceedings of the National Academy of Science, 95,* 14494–14499.

Van den Boom, D. C. (1994). The influence of temperament and mothering on attachment and sensitive responsiveness among lower-class mothers with irritable infants. *Child Development, 65,* 1457–1477.

van der Kolk, B. A. (1996). The complexity of adaptation to trauma: Self-regulation, stimulation discrimation, and characterlogical development. In B. A.van der Kolk, A. C. Mcfarlane, & L. Weisaeth (Eds.), *Traumatic stress: The effects of overwhelming experience on mind, body, and society* (pp. 182–213). New York: Guilford Press.

van der Kolk, B. A., Perry, J. C. & Herman, J. L. (1991). Childhood origins of self-destructive behavior. *American Journal of Psychiatry, 148,* 1665–1671.

van der Kolk, B. A. (2003). The neurobiology of childhood trauma and abuse. *Child and Adolescent Psychiatric Clinics of North America, 12,* 293–317.

van IJzendoorn, M. H., & Bakerman-Kranenburg, M. J. (1997). Intergenerational transmission of attachment: A move to the contextual level. In L. Atkinson and K. L. Zucker (Eds.), *Attachment and psychopathology* (pp. 135–170). New York: Guilford Press.

Vaughn, B. E., & Bost, K. K. (1999). Attachment and temperament: Redundent, independent, or interacting influences on interpersonal adaptation and per-sonality development? In J. Cassidy & P. R. Shaver (Eds.), *Handbook of attach-ment: Theory, research, and clinical applications,* 198–223. New York: Guilford Press.

Vernadakis, A. (1996). Glia-neuron intercommunications and synaptic plasticity. *Progressive Neurobiology, 49,* 185–214.

Videbech, P., & Ravnkilde, B. (2004). Hippocampal volume and depression: A meta-analysis of MRI studies. *American Journal of Psychiatry, 16*(11), 1957–1966.

Volkow, N. D., Wang, G. J., Fowler, J. S., Gatley, S. J., Logan, J., Ding, Y. S., et al. (1998). Dopamine transporter occupancies in the human brain induced by therapeutic doses of oral methylphenidate. *American Journal of Psychiatry, 155,* 1325–1331.

von Bertalanffy, L. (1968). *General systems theory.* New York: Braziller.

Waas, G. A., & Graczyk, P. A. (2000). Child behaviors leading to peer rejection: A view from the peer group. *Child Study Journal, 29*(4), 291–306.

Walker-Andrews, A. S. (1997). Infants' perception of expressive behaviors: Differenciation of multimodal information. *Psychological Bulletin, 121,* 437–456.

Wallin, D. (2007). *Attachment in psychotherapy.* New York: Guilford Press.

Waslick, B. D., Kandel, R., & Kakouros, A. (2005). Depression in children and adolescents. In D. Shaffer and B. D. Waslik (Eds.), *The many faces of depression in children and adolescents.* Washington, DC: American Psychiatric Association.

Watson, C., & Gametchu, B. (1999). Membrane-initiated steroid actions and the proteins that mediate them. *Proceedings of the Society for Experimental Biology and Medicine, 220,* 9–19.

Weems, C. F., Hayward, C., Killen, J. D. & Taylor, C. B. (2002). A longitudinal investigation of anxiety sensitivity in adolescents. *Journal of Abnormal Psychology, 111,* 471–477.

Weinberg, H. A. (1999). Parent training for attention-deficit hyperactivity disorder: Parent and child outcome. *Journal of Clinical Psychology, 55*(7), 907–913.

Weiner, I. (1998). *Principles of psychotherapy.* New York: Wiley.

Weinfield, N. S., Stroufe, L. A., Egeland, B., & Carlson, E. A. (1999). The nature of individual differences in infant-caregiver attachment. In J. Cassidy & P. R. Shaver (Eds.), *Handbook of attachment: Theory, research, and clinical applications* (pp. 68–88). New York: Guilford Press.

Weissman, M. M., Wolk, S., Goldstein R. B., et al. (1999). Depressed adolescents grown up. *Journal of the American Medical Association, 281,* 1701–1713).

Wellman, H. M., Harris, P. L., Banerjee, M., & Sinclair, A. (1995). Early understandings of emotion: Evidence from natural language. *Cognition and Emotion, 9,* 117–149.

Werner, E. E. (1990). Protective factors and individual resilience. In S. J. Meisels & J. P. Shonkoff (Eds.), *Handbook of early childhood intervention, 2nd ed.* pp. 115–132. New York: Cambridge University Press.

Werner, E. E., & Smith, R. S. (2001). *Journeys from childhood to midlife: Risk, resilience, and recovery.* Ithaca, NY: Cornell University Press.

Wexler, B. (2006). *Brain and culture: Neurobiology, ideology, and social change.* Boston: MIT Press.

Wexler, B. E., Gottschalk, C. H., Fulbright, R. K., Prohovnik, I., Lacadie, C. M., Rounsaville, B. J., et al. (2001). Functional magnetic resonance imaging of cocaine craving. *American Journal of Psychiatry, 158,* 86–95.

Whalen, P. J. (1998). Fear, vigilance, and ambiguity: Initial neuroimaging studies of the human amygdala. *Current Directions in Psychological Science, 7*, 177–188.

Whalen, P. J., Kagan, J., & Cook, R. G. (2004). Human amygdala responsivity to masked fearful eye whites. *Science, 306*, 2061.

Wheeler, R. E., Stuss, D. T., & Tulving, E. (1997). Toward a theory of episodic memory: The frontal lobes and autonoetic consciousness. *Psychological Bulletin, 121*, 331–354.

Winnicott, D. W. (1941/1975a). Primitive emotional development. In *Through paediatrics to psycho-analysis: Collected papers* (pp. 142–160). London: Hogarth Press.

Winnicott, D. W. (1941/1975b). The observation of infants in a set situation. In *Through paediatrics to psycho-analysis: Collected papers* (pp. 52–70). London: Hogarth Press.

Winnicott, D. W. (1953). Transitional objects and transitional phenomena. *International Journal of Psychoanalysis, 34*, 89–97.

Winnicott, D. W. (1965). The theory of the parent-infant relationship. *International Journal of Psycho-Analysis, 41*: 585–595.

Winnicott, D. W., (Ed.) (1965/1990). The maturational processes and the facilitating environment. London: Karnac Books.

Winnicott, D. W., (1967/1971). Mirror role of mother and family in child development. In D. W. Winnicott, *Playing and reality* (pp. 111–118). London: Tavistock.

Winnicott, D. W. (1975). *Holding and interpretation*. New York: Basic Books.

Witelson, S. F., Glezer, I. I., & Kigar, D. L. (1995). Woman have greater density of neurons in the posterior temporal cortex. *Journal of Neuroscience, 15*(5), 3418–3428.

Wittling, W., & Pfluger, M. (1990). Neuroendocrine hemisphere asymmetries: Salivary cortisol secretion during lateralized viewing of emotion-related and neutral films. *Brain and Cognition, 14*, 243–265.

Wolfe, A. E. (2002). Get out of my life, but first could you drive me and Cheryl to the mall?: A parent's guide to the new teenager. New York: Farrar, Straus, and Giroux.

Wolpe, J. (1958). *Psychotherapy by reciprocal inhibition*. Stanford, CA: Stanford University Press.

Wood, J. J., McLeod, B. D., Sigman, M., Hwang, W., & Chu, B. C. (2003). Parenting and childhood anxiety: Theory, empirical, and future directions. *Journal of Child Psychology and Psychiatry, 44*, 134–151.

Wu, J., Kramer, G. L., Kram, M., Steciuk, M., Crawford, I. L., & Petty, F. (1999). Serotonin and learned helplessness: A regional study of 5-HTIA receptors and serotonin transport site in rat brain. *Journal of Psychiatric Research, 33*, 17–22.

Wu, J. C., Buschsbaum, M. S., Hersey, T. G., Hazlett, E., Sciotte, N., & Johnson, J. C. (1991). PET in generalized anxiety disorder. *Biological Psychiatry, 29*, 1181–1199.

Wurtman, R., Hefti, F., & Malamed, E. (1981). Precursor control of neurotransmitter synthesis. *Pharmacology Review, 32*, 315–335.

Yang, T., Menon, V., Eliez, S., Blasey, C., White, C. D., Reid, A. J., et al. (2002). Amygdalar activation associated with positive and negative facial expressions. *NeuroReport, 13*, 1737–1741.

Yehuda, R. (2001). Postraumatic stress disorder. *Journal of Clinical Psychiatry, 62* (Suppl. 17) 23–28.

Yehuda, R., Keefe, R. S. E., Harvey, P. D., Levengood, R. A., Gerber, D. K., Geni, J., et al. (1995). Learning and memory in combat veterans with posttraumatic stress disorder. *American Journal of Psychiatry, 152,* 137–139.

Young, L. J., Lim, M. M., Gingrich, B., & Insel, T. R. (2001). Cellular mechanisms of social attachment. *Hormones and Behavior, 40,* 133–138.

Yule, W. (2001). Post-traumatic disorder in children and adolescents. *International Review of Psychiatry, 13,* 194–200.

Yule, W., Perrin, S., & Smith, P. (1999). Post-traumatic reactions in children and adolescents. In W. Yule (Ed.), *Posttraumatic stress disorders* (pp. 25–50). New York: Wiley.

Zahn-Waxler, C., Cole, P. M., & Baraett, K. C. (1991). *Guilt and empathy: Sex differences and implications for the development of depression.* In J. Garber & K. A. Dodge (Eds.) *Emotional regulation and dysregulation* (pp. 243–272). Cambridge, England: Cambridge University Press.

Zahn-Waxler, C., & Radke-Yarrow, M. (1990). The origins of empathetic concern. *Motivation and Emotion, 14,* 107–130.

Zeisel, S., & Blusztajn, J. (1994). Choline and human nutrition. *Annual Review of Nutrition, 14,* 269–296.

Zuercher-White, E. (1997). *Treating panic disorder and agoraphobia: A step-by-step clinical guide.* Oakland, CA: New Harbinger Publications.

AUTHOR INDEX

SUBJECT INDEX

Page numbers followed by *t* indicate a table and *f* indicate a figure.